AMERICAN LITTLE MAGAZINES OF THE FIN DE SIÈCLE

Art, Protest, and Cultural Transformation

In *American Little Magazines of the Fin de Siècle*, Kirsten MacLeod examines the rise of a new print media form – the little magazine – and its relationship to the transformation of American cultural life at the turn of the twentieth century. Though the little magazine has long been regarded as the preserve of modernist avant-gardes and elite artistic coteries, for whom it served as a form of resistance to mass media, MacLeod's detailed study of its origins paints a different picture. Combining cultural, textual, literary, and media studies criticism, MacLeod demonstrates how the little magazine was deeply connected to the artistic, social, political, and cultural interests of a rising professional-managerial class. She offers a richly contextualized analysis of the little magazine's position in the broader media landscape: namely, its relationship to old and new media, including pre-industrial print forms, newspapers, mass-market magazines, fine press books, and posters. MacLeod's study challenges conventional understandings of the little magazine as a genre and emphasizes the power of "little" media in a mass-market context.

(Studies in Book and Print Culture)

KIRSTEN MACLEOD is a lecturer in English Literature at Newcastle University.

UNIVERSITY OF TORONTO PRESS
Toronto Buffalo London

Toronto Buffalo London
utorontopress.com

Reprinted in paperback 2023

ISBN 978-1-4426-4316-1 (cloth) ISBN 978-1-4426-9557-3 (EPUB)
ISBN 978-1-4875-5643-3 (paper) ISBN 978-1-4426-9556-6 (PDF)

Studies in Book and Print Culture

Publication cataloguing information is available from Library and Archives Canada.

Cover images: alexalenin / iStockphoto; DNY59 / iStockphoto; Rowan Butler / iStockphoto; "The Bookman – April" by James Montgomery Flagg. New York, 1896. Library of Congress, Prints & Photographs Division, LC-DIG-ppmsca-05580.

We wish to acknowledge the land on which the University of Toronto Press operates. This land is the traditional territory of the Wendat, the Anishnaabeg, the Haudenosaunee, the Métis, and the Mississaugas of the Credit First Nation.

This book has been published with the help of a grant from the Federation for the Humanities and Social Sciences, through the Awards to Scholarly Publications Program, using funds provided by the Social Sciences and Humanities Research Council of Canada.

University of Toronto Press acknowledges the financial support of the Government of Canada, the Canada Council for the Arts, and the Ontario Arts Council, an agency of the Government of Ontario, for its publishing activities.

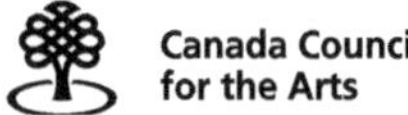

Contents

Illustrations

Colour Plates *(found following page 242)*

Acknowledgments

This book originated as one topic within a larger project about manifestations of decadent literary culture in America 1890–1950, undertaken in 2003 just as the ink was drying on my PhD diploma. I had discovered Frederick W. Faxon's 1903 bibliography of "ephemeral bibelots" and had looked at some of the better-known titles, including *The Chap-Book* and *M'lle New York*. Itching to get at the hundreds of other publications included in Faxon, I was convinced that these magazines would yield untold, and as yet untapped, riches of decadent and modernist literature and art. Ultimately, I did not get what I expected. Yes, there is decadence, of a kind, for those that care to find it, but as I combed my way through the archive, title after title, issue after issue, page after page, these magazines told a different tale of America at the onset of the twentieth century. And this is the story I tell here.

Over the thirteen years that I have been working on this project, I have become indebted to many for their guidance, support, interest, and patience. A test run of this book was the subject of an MLIS dissertation undertaken post-PhD at the University of Alberta. Margaret Mackey, my supervisor, challenged me in all the right ways, and Alvin Schrader and Joan Greer offered welcome encouragement. My research on these magazines has also been realized as an exhibition at the Grolier Club in 2013. The work for this project and the new contacts I made helped significantly in reshaping and rethinking the early draft manuscript. I have benefitted greatly from the knowledge and collections of Mark Samuels Lasner, Philip Bishop, Jean-François Vilain, and David Lowden. I am indebted greatly, too, to many colleagues and fellow researchers. Mary Chapman, who helped me to become part of Ann Ardis and Patrick Collier's symposium "Transatlantic

Print Culture" at University of Delaware, where my eyes were first opened to the wider field of periodical studies. Paul Hjartarson, Faye Hammill, and Hannah McGregor played a similar role, involving me in a symposium on Magazines and/as Media at the University of Alberta that was instrumental in consolidating my theoretical approach for the book. At these and other events and encounters with scholars of periodical studies, transatlantic print culture, the fin de siècle, and modernism, I have been enthused and inspired by Laurel Brake, Margaret Diane Stetz, David Earle, Adam McKible, Patrick Collier, Giles Bergel, Barbara Green, Mary Chapman, Ann Ardis, Faye Hammill, Maria Di Cenzo, Hannah McGregor, Matt Huculak, Dean Irvine, Will Straw, Vincent Sherry, Johanna Drucker, Ellen Gruber Garvey, David Weir, Kate Hext, Alex Murray, Robert Scholes, and, not least, Brad Evans, who shares my particular passion for what Faxon calls "this somewhat useless, but very interesting class of periodicals." In the publishing realm, I must acknowledge the University of Toronto Press. I am grateful for the support and patience of Leslie Howsam, editor of the Studies in Book and Print Culture Series and Siobhan McMenemy, acquisitions editor of the Scholarly Publishing Division at UTP when this book was contracted. In the latter stages of shepherding this manuscript through the press, I owe thanks to Mark Thompson, current acquisitions editor; Barb Porter, associate managing editor; and Michel Pharand, who copyedited the manuscript. I must acknowledge, too, my gratitude for the sound wisdom and advice of the three anonymous readers who read the manuscript at various stages. It is a much better book thanks to their input.

I am grateful to the following institutions, whose significant collections of these little magazines I have made use of: The Harry Ransom Center, University of Texas at Austin; the Sterling Library and the Beinecke at Yale; the New York Public Library; the Huntington Library; Princeton University Library; UCLA library; the Center for Southwest Research, University of New Mexico; University of Illinois at Urbana-Champaign; Columbia University Library; and University of Wisconsin-Madison.

This project has been supported by a Social Sciences and Humanities Research Council of Canada Grant and a Harry Ransom Research Fellowship. Newcastle University, meanwhile, provided research leave to enable me to complete the book.

Earlier versions of sections of chapter 2 and the afterword have appeared in "The Fine Art of Cheap Print: Turn-of-the-Century American Little Magazines," *Transatlantic Print Culture 1880–1940: Emerging*

Media, Emerging Modernisms, ed. Ann Ardis and Patrick Collier (Houndmills, UK: Palgrave, 2008), 182–98; "American Little Magazines of the 1890s and the Rise of the Professional-Managerial Class," *English Studies in Canada* 41.1 (2015), 41–68; and *American Little Magazines of the 1890s: A Revolution in Print* (Sunderland: Bibelot Press, 2013). Grateful acknowledgment is given to the publishers for permission to use this material in the present work.

Last, but not least, I want to thank those close friends and family whose support, if less clearly visible in this scholarly endeavour than that of colleagues mentioned above, has been equally important. These are the people who have reminded me over the past thirteen years that sometimes there is, indeed, life outside the bubble of fin-de-siècle American little magazines (yes, really!). Thank you to the members of the clans Macleod, Chalmers, and Kelly, with whom I have enjoyed diverting trips and visits. Thanks to dear friends Ella Dzelzainis and Jane Gerard, two of the most formidably intelligent women of my acquaintance. And thanks to those I can never give enough thanks to: my mother, Hilary, who, like so many of the little magazinists I have studied, is multi-talented, able to do anything she sets her mind to; my father, Alec, a fervent iconoclast and brilliant wit after the manner of the best little magazinists; and my husband, Gary, whose incisive mind and unflagging support I value beyond words.

AMERICAN LITTLE MAGAZINES OF THE FIN DE SIÈCLE

Art, Protest, and Cultural Transformation

Introduction
Reviving the American Little Magazines of the 1890s

The day of the freak magazines seems to have arrived. A perfect flood of publications, strange in form, weird as to illustration and quaint of type, is pouring out and almost engulfing the familiar and more sober monthly literature to which we have been accustomed. We can hardly afford to call it a flood either. That almost seems too dignified. An outbreak, an eruption, an epidemic would indicate it better.

– Sewell Ford, "The Freak Magazine,"
Waterloo Daily Courier (IA), 2 April 1896, 4

This remarkable literary revolution that broke out in the winter of 1895–6 is now in 1898 about played out – moribund … these pamphlets promoting independence in thought and expression are rapidly disappearing or dwindling into ludicrous fatuity, as a consequence of the lack of public encouragement … But a brief review of the whole "epoch" may be interesting to collectors of curious literature.

– Walter Blackburn Harte, "A Little Revolt in American Literature,"
Philosopher 3, no. 3 (March 1898): 103

In 1898 the race had almost died off, but early in 1900 signs of a revival were manifest and though no longer sought by collectors as curiosities, many new chap-books were started, most of them short-lived. Hardly any one now collects these publications, and unless the names, and the dates of their births and deaths are somewhere recorded, no future collector will ever be able to obtain accurate information concerning this large, somewhat useless, but very interesting class of periodicals.

– Frederick Winthrop Faxon, *"Ephemeral Bibelots": A Bibliography of the Modern Chap-books and Their Imitators*, 5

Until you get different SPECIFIC interests (and angles of incidence) into ONE vortex, focus, you have no kulch, no civn/ nowt by [*sic*] Hubbards and Monahans running one man mags.

– Ezra Pound to William Watt, 11 March 1957, in Ezra Pound, *Ezra Pound's Letters to William Watt*, n.pag.

These comments document the rapid rise, fall, and obsolescence of a prolific, yet ephemeral, print phenomenon of the fin de siècle. The first American little magazines emerged in the mid-1890s, concurrent with the rise of their popular counterparts, mass-market magazines. Reaching a peak in 1896, they floundered in 1898, rallied in 1900, and appeared to sputter out over the next few years. In this brief period, however, hundreds of such periodicals sprang into being, conveying the impression, one expressed hyperbolically by Ford and Harte, of a "flood," an "outbreak," an "eruption," an "epidemic" – a "revolution" even! By Faxon's estimate, close to 300 titles came into being between 1894 and 1903 ("Bibliography of Ephemeral Bibelots," "Ephemeral Bibelots," and *"Ephemeral Bibelots"*). Elbert Hubbard, meanwhile, a leading figure in the movement, claimed that as many as 1100 titles emerged between 1895 and 1896 alone ("Joseph Addison" 78). By the time of the next, and more famous, rise of the little magazine in the 1910s and 1920s, however, this extraordinary print phenomenon would be largely forgotten. Modernists were either ignorant about or, like Pound, dismissive of, these precursors. By the 1950s, two of the movement's key figures – Hubbard and Michael Monahan – would serve for Pound in his advice to a young poet, William Watt, as exemplars of how not to run a little magazine. Pound, at least, knew of the existence of these magazines, which, otherwise, had suffered the fate anticipated by Faxon in 1903.

Harte's and Faxon's accounts of these magazines as "interesting" but "useless" "curiosities," appealing merely to "collectors of curious literature" and curiouser print phenomena, do these publications no favours in terms of promoting them for posterity. And these men were among the most strident proponents of the genre! It is not surprising, then, that by the 1930s and 1940s, as new bibliographies of the genre were issued, these earlier publications were mostly ignored. David Moss's 1932 bibliography of 376 titles includes only thirty-eight little magazines that were published up to and including 1903, twenty of which are found in Faxon, eighteen additions of Moss's own. Frederick Hoffman, Charles Allen, and Carolyn Ulrich's subsequent, and more substantial, history and bibliography of the genre documents over six hundred titles, only four of which are pre-1905 titles, three of these from Faxon.[1] This influential genre-defining work, then, effectively erased these magazines from cultural memory, accounting for the subsequent scholarly neglect of this earlier moment in the history of the little magazine.

The importance of American little magazines of the 1890s as a field of scholarly study and an area of collecting has been underestimated.[2] Certainly, they need to be understood as something more than humble precursors to their modernist counterparts. Indebted to Faxon's "attempt at a bibliography" for its mapping of the field, ever interested in the "curious" in literature, and approaching the subject with the twin sensibility of scholar and collector, I document, in this book, the cultural importance of this forgotten print phenomenon of the 1890s. The study is based on an extensive examination of single issues, partial runs, and full runs of over 60 per cent of 334 titles identified in an updated bibliography of American little magazines of the 1890s that has been compiled for this volume (see Appendix).[3] My key claims in the book address the importance of these publications in both the media and social landscape. First, the little magazine was a new print media genre produced largely by and for an emerging professional-managerial class that played a role, alongside emerging mass-market magazines, in transformations to American cultural life at the turn of the century. It was a vehicle of expression and a source of cultural capital for an emerging intellectual and professional middle-class elite. Second, the little magazine was a part of major developments in print media and the growth of new media in this period, contributing to the transformation of the broader media landscape. Third, the little magazine of this period contributed significantly to the emergence of new intimate and personal editorial styles that would come to characterize the early twentieth century press. Fourth, little magazines were a notable venue for literary and artistic experimentation and for the dissemination of reformist, progressive, fringe, and alternative beliefs, ideals, and values that would come to shape twentieth-century American cultural life. In short, these little magazines were a big deal.

Historical Contexts: The American Little Magazine of the 1890s as New Media Genre

The little magazine phenomenon in America began in earnest with the publication of *The Chap-Book* in May 1894 by two Harvard undergraduates, one month after the issuing of the first number of its more renowned British counterpart, *The Yellow Book*. *The Chap-Book*, however, was not without precedent in America. Intellectual and artistic coteries in the Harvard-based Boston/Cambridge area had spawned two earlier productions in *The Mahogany Tree* and *The Knight Errant*. *The Chap-Book*, though, would set the standard for a new, modern type of magazine, artistically printed and engaging with the latest trends in literature and the visual arts. Its success drew attention to what was otherwise a coterie-restricted medium, generating a few hundred imitators within the first wave of the little magazine movement, which flourished from 1895 to 1897. One of these imitators was *The Philistine*, issued from East Aurora, New York. While exhibiting the same interest in odd formats, quaint type, and queer literature that characterized the aesthetic revolt of *The Chap-Book* and its ilk, *The Philistine*, subtitled "a periodical of protest," soon distinguished itself as a magazine oriented towards social and political, as opposed to literary and artistic, revolt. In this guise, *The Philistine* led a second wave of the movement that peaked in 1901. Though the little magazine did not literally die out in 1903 when Faxon attempted to preserve its memory for posterity, its status as a notable and noted cultural phenomenon would not be equaled until the rise of the twentieth-century modernist little magazine. It is for this reason that the scope of this study is limited to little magazines that made their first appearance before 1904, a period in which these magazines constituted a *new* and identifiable *movement*.

The little magazine was a new print media genre at a time of considerable innovative and entrepreneurial activity in periodical and book publishing and in the context of emerging media forms. The novelty and strangeness of these publications is attested to by the manner in which they were discussed. For clarity, I identify them as little magazines throughout, though this was just one, and not even the most dominant, of a plethora of terms ascribed to them. These included ephemerals, bibelots, ephemeral bibelots, chap-books, decadents, dinkeys, pamphlets, leaflets, booklet magazines, fin-de-siècle periodicals, greenery-yallery periodicals, periodical bantlings, freak journals, freak magazines, freakazines, fad magazines, fadazines, fadlets, journalettes, magazettes, magazinelets, mushroom magazines, toy magazines, small magazines, diminutive magazines, miniature magazines, brownie magazines, magazines of protest, magazines of individual opinion, etc. This multiplicity of terms attests to the sense, in the period, that what was being witnessed was the birth of a new genre – one that would not be established definitively as the "little magazine" until sometime after the modernist period.[4] While consensus over terminology may have been lacking, these terms are highly suggestive of what constituted what I call "little magazineness" – i.e., the quintessential characteristics of the genre. They were small. They were short-lived. They were precious and collectible. They were artistic – associated especially with the decadent and aesthetic movements. They were rebellious. They were radical. They were youthful. They were playful. They were prolific. They were idiosyncratic. They were unique.

While *The Chap-Book* originated in an Eastern locale strongly associated with the American elite – notably Boston Brahmin culture – *The Philistine*'s East Aurora, New York roots are indicative of the scope and breadth of the movement. Far from being the preserve of established cultural centres of a gentry elite, little magazines flourished across the country. Alongside little magazines of Boston, Philadelphia, New York, Chicago, and San Francisco, then, existed those of Wausau, Wisconsin; Muskegon, Michigan; Boone, Iowa; Morgantown, West Virginia, and other such locales. This publication context was a significant aspect, as Jonathan Freedman has argued, of the American "culture boom" of the 1890s (113). The top tier of these magazines, publications such as *The Chap-Book*, he suggests, enabled the wide circulation of European avant-garde literature and art as well as the work of talented American imitators (124). At the same time, less prestigious but, nevertheless, interesting magazines, tending towards "the eccentric, the outré, and the ephemeral," imported international and national figures to America's smaller cities and towns, and provided publication opportunities for aspiring locals who lacked connections to major centres and venues (Freedman 124). On one level, then, these magazines, like their modernist successors, were central to the expression and development of the literary, artistic, and socio-political ideals and values of writers, artists, and intellectuals. On another, they served this purpose for a broader group that encompassed amateurs and the culturally aspiring middle classes, the most significant element of which was the emerging professional-managerial class.[5] They were an alternative venue for the expression of ideas: alternative in the sense of counter-cultural or anti-establishment; alternative also, however, in a more mundane sense – representing, quite simply, another choice of venue, one easier to access and that accrued greater cultural capital.

Scholarly Contexts: The American Little Magazine of the 1890s as Forgotten Media Genre

The particularities of the American little magazine of the 1890s – notably its democratic character and its highly personalized nature – have rendered it largely irrelevant to trends in modernist studies. Hoffman, Allen, and Ulrich's criteria as outlined in their history and bibliography of the little magazine have set the tone for studies of the genre. They helpfully identify experimentalism, anti-commercialism, and an investment in supporting new and unknown writers as key qualities of the little magazine, while acknowledging the need for flexibility in applying such criteria (2–6). They also invoke what they admit is a more subjective criterion – namely that "in the authors' estimation," a little magazine ought "to have had some importance in the history of modern literature or have published some work of merit" (vii). This criterion most certainly informs their cursory dismissal of almost all the fin-de-siècle little magazines documented by Faxon, of which they were certainly aware.[6] Of these, they say, "Most of our nineteenth century [advance guard] periodicals were not very inspiring … [and] the first decade of the twentieth century seemed as barren as any decade of the nineteenth" (7). Ultimately, these fin-de-siècle magazines are "not very inspiring" for Hoffman, Allen, and Ulrich because they do not fit into the triumphalist narrative of the modernist avant-garde's "battle for a mature literature" that was emerging in scholarship of this period and that their work helped to perpetuate (Hoffman, Allen, and Ulrich 1). The American little magazines of the 1890s could not figure in this history because they published few writers who would go on to achieve canonical status. Hoffman, Allen, and Ulrich's canon- and literary-oriented study has had repercussions for understanding the history of little magazines. On the one hand, it neglects a prolific earlier manifestation of the little magazine movement – the subject treated in this book. On the other, it almost certainly overlooks a significant body of twentieth-century modernist-era magazines that failed to meet their authors' subjective criteria – a subject beyond the scope of this book to tackle, but one worthy of pursuit in future scholarship.

While Hoffman, Allen and Ulrich have long set the tone for little magazine research, recent turns in scholarship across the humanities have rendered the American little magazines of the 1890s ripe for recuperation. The digital turn, for example, including developments in digital humanities and new media studies, has had an impact on modernist magazine scholarship. In practical terms, the emergence of databases and online collections and archives has made more magazines accessible to researchers.[7] In theoretical terms, the field of new media studies has provided a new frame of reference and a critical vocabulary for modernist scholars working on "old" media.[8] In addition, materialist, book history, and interdisciplinary turns have been central to the study of periodicals as undertaken by literary scholars, expanding the range of approaches taken.[9] There is an increased interest in the cultural work that magazines perform as well as in how materiality and publishing and reception contexts create meaning and value. The field of modernist studies has also been galvanized by research that considers the dialectical relationship between elite and popular culture. This relationship, as Robert Scholes and Mark Morrisson maintain, is central to modernism as it emerged in the 1890s and to the mass-market and little magazines that were an important cultural product of the period (Scholes 217; Morrisson 4–5). With respect to scholarship on little magazines, there has been a significant rethinking around defining the little magazine, with a trend towards a more fluid understanding of the genre, which has resulted in the recuperation of neglected or forgotten publications.[10] Together, these developments across various fields of scholarship have informed the rise of new research and new resources on modernist magazines that have increased the breadth and the scope of the field.

Within this context, American little magazines of the 1890s have received some significant, if not extensive, treatment. Of this scholarship, most is narrowly focused, concerned with a small handful of better-known titles.[11] The focus here tends to be on publications that might be considered "proto-modernist," i.e., those that are most easily accommodated to literary approaches and/or to existing narratives about the little magazine as a modernist genre. The best of this work has sought to theorize about the specific nature of the aesthetic effects and experience of these little magazines; to arrive at a better understanding of the genre as a whole by expanding the purview beyond a select few; to complicate our understanding of the relationship between high and popular culture; to draw attention to the social and cultural import of these publications; and to reconsider the relationship of these 1890s little magazines to their modernist successors.

Methodological Challenges and Approaches: Defining the American Little Magazines of the 1890s

This book builds on and extends this work, taking up a number of the claims made in this scholarship, testing them out in a wider social, cultural, literary, and media context, and across a broader and more representative range of titles. It draws on the scholarship and methodologies of cultural studies, new media studies, book history, literary studies, and the history of visual art and graphic design to construct a historicized understanding of the little magazine as it existed in a particular moment. In so doing, it confronts certain methodological challenges. The first of these challenges is a definitional one: how to account for the lack of fit between the American little magazine of the 1890s and the genre as it has been defined by Hoffman, Allen, and Ulrich and subsequent modernist scholars. The second is a challenge posed by periodicals more generally: how to read them – in the sense of critically managing and processing the vast archive of disparate content housed in a body of hundreds of magazines and millions of pages.

In terms of defining the little magazine as it manifested itself in America during this period, I resist the dominant modernist paradigm that traditionally structures approaches to the genre. Rather than seeking to fit these magazines within parameters that privilege particular kinds of modernist manifestations of the genre, I adopt, instead, a historicist view, asking, "what would the little magazine look like if we took the American 1890s model to be paradigmatic, using Faxon's account of the field as a basis for a definition?" It is true that Faxon's bibliographies are not without their problems. Certainly, if seen through a modernist lens, many of the titles he includes seem out of place. He includes some story magazines, for example, as well as hobby magazines, general monthly type magazines, and those that seem popular or mainstream in style. At the same time, there are internal inconsistencies among his bibliographies – titles in the 1897 bibliography, for example, are omitted from the 1903 version without explanation, and there are slight differences in titles between his 1903 versions. In his brief introductions, he expresses uncertainty, noting that some of his inclusions differ from the artistically produced "chap-book" class that he considers most authentic but for their "strange" titles and ephemerality (*"Ephemeral Bibelots"* 4). One might also point to notable exclusions, some university-associated little magazines as well as some political- and spiritual-oriented publications associated with the genre as it emerged in this period. Overall, then, Faxon's bibliographies *seem* to pose more problems than provide solutions for arriving at a historicized understanding of the little magazine as it manifested itself in the American 1890s.

Faxon's inconsistencies, however, seem far less problematic if we understand them as documenting a genre *in the making* in the context of major transformations to the media and social landscapes. Along with the rise of new technologies and new media, existing forms of media were undergoing a period of growth and expansion, none more so than the magazine. There was significant innovation and entrepreneurship in the magazine field that resulted in the production of thousands of new publications and new types of publications, of which the top-selling mass-market magazines represent a small proportion. That the boundaries between new types of magazines might be blurry is understandable given their massive proliferation in this period. What Geoffrey B. Pingree and Lisa Gitelman argue about new media, for example, applies equally to new *forms* of existing media, such as the little magazine of the 1890s:

> There is a moment, before the material meanings and conceptual modes of new media have become fixed, when such media are not accepted as natural, when their own meanings are in flux. At such a moment, we might say that new media briefly acknowledge and question the mythic character and the ritualized conventions of existing media, while they are themselves defined within a perceptual and semiotic economy that they then help to transform. (xii)

The 1890s witnessed an explosion of print, and little magazines, as I demonstrate, were influenced by and influenced other print media forms. Aspects of the character and format of little magazines were quickly adopted and adapted, resulting, as James Doyle argues, in "straightforward imitations of the *Chap-Book*," more "elaborately designed" arts and crafts book-art inspired productions, parodies, as well as "blatantly commercial productions put out by mass-circulation publishers in an attempt to maintain their dominance of the magazine industry" (86). In retrospect, some magazines documented by Faxon might well be classed differently as, indeed, Frank Luther Mott would in his *History of American Magazines*.[12] At the time of their emergence, however, the various forms of "ephemeral bibelots" that Faxon documented made sense to him as a specific body of magazines. He was not the only one who regarded them in this way. The coverage of, and discourse around, these publications in the periodical press, especially newspapers of the day and little magazines themselves, suggest that an understanding of the genre in its early manifestation must look to how it was constituted in this particular historical moment, before more fixed meanings would begin to coalesce. At the same time, of course, it is important to acknowledge that the subsequent history of the development of print media might alter the way we think about some of these publications. In hindsight, for example, we can see that the story magazines that Faxon tentatively includes and that Sewell Ford also discusses as an aspect of the "freak magazine" movement (4), are precursors to the all-fiction and pulp magazines of the twentieth century and might certainly be included in a history of that genre. By virtue of their reception in the period, however, they are also undoubtedly part of the early history of little magazines, and I treat them in this light.

As a print phenomenon, the American little magazines of the 1890s differ from their modernist counterparts in terms of both audience and contributors. Modernist little magazines, generally speaking, addressed a small, select audience, primarily of artists and intellectuals, and Hoffman, Allen and Ulrich conceptualize them as a literary phenomenon insofar as they published "80% of our most important post-1912 critics, novelists, poets and storytellers" (1). The American little magazines of the 1890s, by contrast, had a wider audience in view and they are far better understood and accounted for as a cultural, rather than strictly literary, phenomenon. While some little magazine producers and contributors were indeed part of a young and emerging literary and artistic avant-garde, more were from the broader field of the intellectual and professional-managerial class. If the 1890s publications cannot lay claim to as impressive a roster of contributors as modernist little magazines in literary historical terms, their value lies elsewhere. A large number of their makers and contributors, as I demonstrate, were part of the key movements driving the social and cultural transformations of the Progressive Era.

This study, then, embraces a rather capacious and, in some respects, counterintuitive definition of the little magazine, acknowledging a spectrum that ranges from elitist coterie publications to more blatantly commercial ones; accepting that a lack of generic specificity is normal in a period of media transformation; and positing the little magazine as more middle-class than avant-garde. The book confronts, too, an equally capacious archive that poses particular challenges across its 334 titles and millions of pages of content. This material is largely uncharted and unknown territory. These magazines constitute what Margaret Cohen calls "unconceptualized texts," an "archive of forgotten literature"(59), a body of material that, by her account, requires a particular approach to make sense of it.[13] Though Cohen's theorization is developed for her study of novels, the approach is suitable across a range of types of "forgotten" texts and has proved useful for thinking about little magazines. The vast majority of little magazine content is by obscure figures and is quotidian, banal, ephemeral. Some, for example, takes the shape of unfamiliar genres and subgenres, once dominant, that have fallen out of use. Furthermore, its meanings and terms of reference, particular to the historical moment and intelligible to readers of that period, are often opaque to the twenty-first century reader. Even in the rare cases when familiar writers, texts, or genres are encountered, the context in which they appear often defamiliarizes them. The "coherence and significance" of forgotten texts, as Cohen argues, "changes, sometimes radically, once they are reframed within a horizon of aesthetic expectation that has been erased" (62). Such texts are generally unsuited to the kinds of critical and aesthetic frameworks scholars tend to deploy in literary and cultural studies and require, instead, a form of "distant reading" to make sense of them (Cohen 58, 59).[14]

Among Cohen's strategies for engaging with "unconceptualized texts" and deriving meaning from them, those most applicable to an analysis of the American little magazines of the 1890s are "reading for patterns," "just enough reading" (59), and the "representative example" (61). Her concept of "reading for patterns" acknowledges the necessity of seeking to identify the patterns, themes, and motifs that recur – ones that would have been "intuitively recognizable" to those reading the texts in their historical moment (59). "Just enough reading," in turn, acknowledges that limits must be set in engaging with vast archives. The point at which to stop is once a coherent pattern emerges. In the case of this study, for example, there came a point at which the key genres and subgenres of the field were established, where the unfamiliar became familiar, where newly examined titles confirmed, rather than added significant new dimensions to, the findings and analysis. In more precise terms, "just enough reading" for this project constituted an examination of single issues, partial runs, and full runs of 60 per cent of the titles included in the updated bibliography of the Appendix. In reporting on such a vast body of material that will be unknown to the majority of readers, meanwhile, the importance of selection is paramount and involves careful thinking about what constitutes enough evidence to make a convincing claim about this forgotten literature. Given the unfeasibility of an exhaustive and comprehensive account of a vast archive, my approach in this study, after Cohen, relies on the notion of "representative examples," texts or case studies in which "the features under discussion emerge with particular force" (61).

Given the obscurity and unfamiliarity of these publications, I provide here a preliminary outline of the dominant "patterns" in this body of material that I have established in conceptualizing the field: the key genres of little magazines and their dominant features. Though the definition of the little magazine of this period is quite broad, it is possible to propose some general principles of categorization. This study identifies three main types: aesthetic little magazines, periodicals of protest, and hybrid magazines. A few, which do not quite fit these, are accorded the status of miscellaneous in the updated bibliography. Aesthetic little magazines, which dominate in the first wave of the movement, are those devoted wholly or predominantly to literary and/or artistic subject matter. This class includes magazines featuring a mix of fiction, poetry, critical essays and commentary and, in some cases, art. Exemplary of this type is *The Chap-Book* and its many imitators. Here, we are likely to find publications most like modernist little magazines of the next generation. In addition, as a subset of this category, are magazines of a more specialist nature in their literary and artistic interests. Among this group are fiction-focused progenitors of pulp magazines such as *The Black Cat*, *The Gray Goose*, *The White Owl*, *The White Rabbit*, *The White Elephant*, *Smart Set*, *Nickell Magazine*, *The Pocket Magazine*, etc. Another notable subset of the aesthetic little magazine is a body of publications centred on the graphic arts, belletristic, bibliophilic and book-collecting interests that includes the following titles: *The Bibelot*, *Noon*, *Personal Impressions*, *Modern Art*, *The Poster*, and *Poster Lore*. Decorative arts and arts and crafts focused magazines also fall within the aesthetic little magazine category, and include forerunners to home and lifestyle magazines of today, such as *The Craftsman*, *Forms and Fantasies*, *Handicraft*, and *The House Beautiful*. The last of these titles, founded originally by Herbert Stone of *Chap-Book* fame, is still in existence. Finally, the category of aesthetic magazines encompasses publications that exploited the popularity of the genre or parodied the movement by adopting an identifiable little magazine aesthetic, including ones considered "fads" by Faxon.

The second significant category is the periodical of protest, a publication wholly or predominantly concerned with political topics, social commentary, and/or alternative lifestyles and movements. While these magazines often contained literary content of some kind, it was usually in the service of a social or political agenda. These publications dominated the second wave of the little magazine movement. If, in aesthetic little magazines, we see the origins of modernist little magazines and all-story pulps, protest magazines, in their most typical form, are progenitors of another prominent genre of the twentieth century, the "journal of opinion." Casey Blake defines this genre, the origins of which he traces to the late nineteenth century, as "a forum where intellectuals can discover one another, explore unconventional political and cultural positions, and work to expand the boundaries of contemporary public debate" (355).[15] The periodicals of protest of the 1890s operated in exactly this way. Most characteristically they did so as journals of opinion led by single figures, creating what Hoffman, Allen, and Ulrich have called the "one-man magazine": a publication overseen by a charismatic figure that takes the form of "a continuous editorial on a great variety of subjects, supplemented by quotations from the great and the 'near great' and by a few original contributions" (245–6). Exemplary of this type is *The Philistine* and its host of imitators. Within the broader category of the periodical of protest, I include magazines advocating particular social, political, health, or spiritual movements and lifestyles. The cause is usually the focal point of these magazines, though there may be a charismatic figure associated with them. Examples include the reform-oriented periodical *The New Time*; socialist periodicals such as *The Comrade* and *The Socialist Spirit*; New Thought publications such as *The Essene* and *The Higher Law*; and magazines dedicated to physical culture and other health fads, including *The New Race* and *What to Eat*.

The third major category of little magazine of this period is the hybrid magazine, a form that combined elements of the aesthetic magazine and periodical of protest. These were magazines committed equally to artistic and literary development and to social and/or political causes. Where aesthetic little magazines invariably eschewed direct engagement with topical social issues, hybrid little magazines are often conducted by a charismatic figurehead who is outspoken on social and political issues. Such periodicals differ, however, from periodicals of protest, insofar as they are less prone to exploiting literary content in the service of social or political ends, seeing these as separate realms. At the same time, though generally reformist, progressive, or socialist in their political views, they comment more generally on topical subject matter rather than stand explicitly for specific social or political causes or parties. Exemplars of this type are *The Papyrus* and *The Philosopher*, magazines in which significant literary content sat alongside topical social and/or political discussion.

Having established the main types, it is now possible to consider the patterns that emerge in theorizing the key factors that constitute "little magazineness." The American little magazines of the 1890s at the heart of this study are characterized by one or more of the qualities outlined below, which are elaborated more fully through the course of the book. Clearly, those magazines that embody more of these characteristics are the most "genuine," or, to use a less loaded term, most "typical" of the genre as it manifested itself in this period. In practice, these magazines are the most privileged in my analysis, though I do draw on titles with fewer aspects of "little magazineness" to provide a flavour of these types. These titles might be considered members of the wider family or neighbours and, as Cohen articulates, can be important in articulating a coherent pattern (60). In these instances, I generally focus on the "little magazine" qualities of these publications, rather then dwell on the features that link them with other magazine genres. Such is the case, for example, when I treat as little magazines some of the reformist and socialist publications that have been considered in the context of the American radical press of the period, publications such as *The Socialist Spirit*, *The Comrade*, and others.

In brief, the three key features of the American little magazines of the 1890s are as follows:

1. Aesthetic Appearance: "Yes, you can judge a book by its cover" – i.e., a magazine by its appearance. In the case of these publications, format and appearance, I argue, are key signifiers of "little magazineness," as many of the terms applied to the genre of the day indicate (e.g., bibelot, decadent, greenery-yallery, diminutive, etc.). As Faxon says, little magazines are "easily distinguishable by their appearance" (*"Ephemeral Bibelots"* 3), which included odd shapes and sizes, innovative fonts, distinctive paper, arts and crafts or art nouveau stylistic features, and a chap-book or pamphlet format. These are some of the ways publications asserted their "little magazineness." At the same time, titles also perform this work – especially titles suggestive of quirkiness or ephemerality. Most, though not necessarily all, of the little magazines of this period are self-consciously aesthetic in appearance in a manner that aims to distinguish them from the mainstream.

2. Little Magazine Discourse: "**It's not what you say, it's the way that you say it**." Much of the little magazine content of this period is neither experimental nor avant-garde in the way we have come to expect from the genre. In many respects, the "littleness" of the 1890s magazines derives from discursive practices through which their founders, editors, and contributors situate these publications as media of personal expression. A certain bravado, pluckiness, and irreverence led these publications to be described as "freak" periodicals. Questions to consider in assessing the "little magazineness" of a periodical on the basis of its rhetorical style are: Does it take a flippant approach to periodicity, readership, advertising, or other aspects that define mainstream magazines? What is the tone of the editorial voice? Does it represent itself as oppositional, controversial, strongly opinionated? Does it attack mainstream periodicals? Does it position itself, or is it positioned by others, within the community of little magazines, through friendly or adversarial commentary? Most little magazines have a characteristically bold and highly individualized style of self-representation in appearance and/or tone.

3. Content. It's (not) what's inside that counts. This aspect of "little magazineness" is placed controversially at the end of the list, though the order of this list is not meant to be hierarchical. Content has been a focus of much of the scholarship on modernist little magazines, where it is considered an important criterion. For the purposes of this study, it is merely one factor among others. The little magazines of this period, as I have said, included fairly traditional content. At the same time, mainstream magazines at this time often included more attention to high and avant-garde culture than might be expected. Content alone cannot be said to determine definitively the "little magazineness" of a publication. Generally, it depends on another factor too – appearance or discourse. In terms of content, little magazines are curiously positioned within a nexus of high, popular, radical, and alternative social, cultural, literary, and artistic trends. In literature and the arts, there is a strong interest in European avant-garde movements – especially arts and crafts, aestheticism, decadence, symbolism, art nouveau – though more popular forms may also be represented. In this domain, little magazines largely mediated between culture and commerce, promoting the new, the modern, and the avant-garde in literature and art, but also the conventional, traditional, and popular. In terms of social and political content, these little magazines reflected some of the elitist and reformist ideals of the residual genteel culture of the Gilded Age, while embracing emerging populist and democratic (and sometimes reactionary and corporatist) principles that were emerging in the Progressive Era.

American Little Magazines of the 1890s: The Big Picture

In his consideration of the little magazine as a global form, Eric Bulson makes a large claim for the genre and notes its adaptability to particular historical and social conditions:

> The little magazine ... doesn't just make history. It *is* history. Which is to say, it is a medium shaped by the material conditions of its time and place, including everything from print technologies and prudish censors to postal rates and paper costs. It takes on different shapes and actively responds to the particular audience, literary tradition, and print culture out of which it emerges. When it comes to the little magazine, one size does not fit all ... [T]he sheer variety of structural differences in little magazines indicates just how malleable the form could be ... (268)

The aim of this book is to consider how the American little magazine of the 1890s both makes and is history. It does so by considering, in detail, the material conditions of time and place that produced this genre and the uses to which it was put, addressing the who, what, when, where, why, and how of the movement. Who made, contributed to, and read these magazines? How were they made? Where were they made? Why were they made? When where they made – and why at this particular time especially? What conditions made it possible for them to be made? What was in these magazines? How did these magazines figure in relation to other print media of the period? Why did they die out? What is their historical importance and legacy? This book addresses these questions.

The first section, "Social, Media, and Little Magazine Contexts," consists of three chapters that take a broad view of the field, situating these publications in their social and print cultural milieus. Chapter 1 establishes the social context for the emergence of little magazines, documenting the transformation of American cultural life from the Genteel Age to the Progressive Era. It argues that these magazines and their makers and contributors – referred to throughout as "little magazinists" – reflect the literary, artistic, social, and cultural interests and values of the middle-class, particularly the professional-managerial faction, and the shift from a culture of character to a culture of personality. The chapter makes extensive use of cultural histories of the period to establish a macro-context through which it reads a series of representative figures and trends within the little magazine movement. The analysis draws on biographical and autobiographical material, local history and archival material, and contemporary newspaper and magazine coverage.

Chapter 2 turns to the print culture and media context for the emergence of little magazines. Informed by new media studies concepts of "remediation" and "mediamorphosis" as outlined by David Bolter, Jay Grusin, and by Roger Fidler, and grounded in a book history-oriented understanding of print culture, it examines closely the interrelationship between the little magazines of the 1890s and existing and emerging forms of print media. It documents the little magazine's links to notable print revolutions of the period: the fine press movement, the poster movement, and the rise of the mass-market magazine. It argues that, in appropriating and adapting elements of these other forms of print media, the little magazine manufactured a distinctive identity, one that asserted a highly individualized personality, was situated complexly between high and popular print, and was in keeping with the genre's roots in professional-managerial class culture and its appeal to a class seeking to assert and display its cultural distinction.

While the first two chapters provide a narrative of the little magazine from a social and broad media perspective, chapter 3 considers the evolution of the genre in its own context, documenting the most representative and influential little magazines and their innovations and contributions.

The second section turns from the contextual focus of the first to an in-depth consideration of the content of little magazines. Each of the six chapters treats a specific type of content characteristically found in little magazines: fiction, poetry, art, literary essays and commentary, social and political essays and commentary, and sayings (aphorisms, quotations, proverbs, etc.). The sheer scope of content across the hundreds of little magazines presents a challenge in terms of analysis. In particular, each of these genres poses specific problems for identifying representative examples and has required different methodologies to draw these out. In some instances, I have relied on a sampling method, basing my analysis on content across a fixed body of issues of little magazines. In other cases, analysis is based on specific figures or magazines that best speak to the characteristic features of the type of content under discussion. In general terms, these chapters attend to the privileging of short forms in these magazines, a preference in keeping with their own "little" format and status. At the same time, the chapters situate the magazines' engagements with various genres in relation to the broader literary, media, and cultural context. They attend to the aesthetic and cultural politics of genre and form, and consider distinctions in treatment across the range of publications. Running throughout this section is a concern with how little magazine content is positioned in relation to high or avant-garde culture and the popular, between tradition and fin-de-siècle modernity, and, to some extent, between European and American culture. Chapter 4, which deals with fiction, for example, focuses on the development of the short story in the little magazine. I argue that while, to a large extent, the little magazine took up the same popular genres and themes as mass-market magazines, there was greater scope for more progressive, controversial, and radical treatments of these topics. In poetry, meanwhile, as chapter 5 shows, little magazines of the period were largely resistant to emerging modernist poetic sensibilities, in striking contrast to their counterparts of the later period. The chapter explores the degree to which these little magazines instead privileged experimentation with fixed forms, as well as topical political poetry. Perhaps the most modernist aspect of the little magazines of the 1890s was their engagement with developments in visual art, the subject of chapter 6, which focuses on the key artistic trends and innovations through a consideration of art in *The Chap-Book*, *Bradley His Book*, and *M'lle New York*.

Chapters 7 and 8 turn to non-fiction prose, with chapter 7 devoted to literary and belletristic essays and commentary and chapter 8 to social and political editorials and discussion. The chapters detail the main topics of discussion and debate, while focusing on how little magazines contributed to the development of new, more personal styles of the essay and editorial in the context of broader transformations to the field, as a culture of character gave way to a culture of personality. A final, and appropriately short, chapter considers the role of the shortest of short literary forms in little magazines: the saying, by way of aphorism, epigram, proverb, and quotation. Often regarded simply as filler for magazines and newspapers, sayings performed significant cultural work in little magazines, serving as a shorthand medium for the expression of artistic, literary, social, and political ideals of a magazine's makers and its intended readership.

A concluding section in the way of an afterword reflects on the aftermath and legacy of the little magazines of the 1890s. While this legacy is invisible if considering these magazines through the lens of modernist literary studies, it is substantial when considered from a broader cultural perspective. The little magazines bore fruit in the twentieth century in diffuse and unanticipated ways, linked to important transformations in the culture and media of the era.

Finally, an updated bibliography of little magazines amalgamates the three Faxon bibliographies and contributes additional titles. Like Faxon, I do not claim this bibliography to be exhaustive. It is, however, indicative of the key forms of little magazine in the period and will serve as a necessary resource for anyone wishing to pursue further research in this field.

Ultimately, the big picture approach of this book means that it is about more than just little magazines. Certainly, it will be of most use to those with an interest in the little magazines of the 1890s and little magazines more generally. Use of it, in whole or parts, can be made, however, by a range of other scholars and researchers, whether professional or amateur. There is material in the book to appeal to those interested in literary studies and history; in the history of graphic design and the visual arts; in the American arts and crafts movement; in the history of printing, publishing, the small press and amateur press movements; in the history of mass-market magazines, media, and journalism; in American studies; in local history; and in the social, cultural, and political history and movements of the period. Little they may have been, but these magazines, as this book insists, are implicated in a big way in American cultural life of the period and beyond.

PART 1

Social, Media, and Little Magazine Contexts

CHAPTER 1

The Social and Cultural Formation of the Little Magazinist

Art is not a thing; it is a way.

– Elbert Hubbard, "Thomas Arnold," *Little Journeys* 23, no. 2 (August 1908): 29

The Late-nineteenth Century American Cultural Landscape

The creators of, contributors to, and readers of the American little magazines that emerged in the 1890s were largely born and would come of age in the post-Civil War period that witnessed the rise of America's power as a nation and the growth in size and influence of the middle class. They originated in or were aspirants to this class, and were socially and culturally formed by its ideologies and values. Comprised earlier in the century of small businessmen, farmers, entrepreneurs, artisans, and independent professionals (sometimes called the "old middle class"), the middle class underwent a shift between 1870 and 1910. Indeed, this period is notable for the emergence in cultural discourse of the term "middle class," as particular kinds of people began to coalesce as a recognized class (Rebecca Edwards 72). Of particular note in this development was the rise of a professional-managerial class.[1] This class faction included doctors, lawyers, teachers, medical men, engineers, architects, corporate managers, and government workers, for example. This transformation affected the realm of cultural production also, which saw the rise of an increasingly professionalized cadre of journalists, writers, editors, advertising men and women, commercial artists, and other cultural workers in literary, artistic, and intellectual domains. As defined by John and Barbara Ehrenreich, the professional-managerial class is distinct from the "old middle class" or "petty bourgeoisie" of independent, self-employed professionals and business owners (17). Its members, rather, are "mental workers *who do not own the means of production* and whose major function in the social division of labor may be described broadly as the *reproduction of capitalist culture and capitalist class relations*" (Ehrenreich and Ehrenreich 12; emphasis added). It was this class, with its "high material expectations and cultural aspirations," that drove the shift from the genteel Gilded Age to the Progressive Era, shaping the nation's social and cultural values (Smith and Dawson 5). It was these men and women, too, along with some members of the petty bourgeoisie – independent professionals, small business owners, and artisans – who served, largely, as the producers of and audience for the little magazines that emerged in the 1890s.

It is important to emphasize that the little magazines of the 1890s were not simply a product of, and largely for, a small literary and artistic intellectual elite. They addressed a far wider array of cultural, social, and political alternative and fringe interests than are typically associated with the genre. Certainly they were, in most instances, niche publications with low circulations in comparison with the mass-market magazines of the period that, as Richard Ohmann has shown, were addressed to, and helped to shape, a professional-managerial class readership (*Selling Culture*). Nevertheless, these little magazines undoubtedly addressed this same class, if but a fraction of it, and were rooted in the broader middle-class context that witnessed the growth of the professional classes and the rise of a professional-managerial ethos that would drive the shift from genteel middle-class to progressive values and ideals. The little magazines of this period served as a means of self-expression and of cultural distinction, in the sense theorized by Pierre Bourdieu, for their producers and contributors, and of self-culture and cultural distinction for their largely professional middle-class readership. Little magazinists and their readers were those among this class possessed of a keen sense of individuality and distinction, both men and women. They included writers, artists, journalists, printers, publishers, and other print media workers and cultural producers, of course, but also those from existing, developing, and emerging professional and managerial occupations: schoolteachers, professors and college teachers, lawyers, doctors, architects, professional orators, clergymen, engineers, land valuation experts, bankers, librarians, advertising agents, etc. Though claims about historical readerships are often speculative, the fact that so many of these little magazinists were, or would become part of, the professional class is telling. Evidence of this readership is also suggested by the advertising, such as it is, that appears in little magazines, and in commentary in the magazines in some cases. Life member lists for Elbert Hubbard's *Philistine*, for example, include Supreme Court justices, senators, congressmen, politicians, doctors, preachers, lawyers, artists, actors, writers, journalists, publishers, and booksellers (advertisement, *Philistine* 18, no. 3).[2] Michael Monahan, editor of *The Papyrus*, meanwhile, complained early on in the run of his magazine that his readership consisted largely of women ("Side Talks," *Papyrus* 1, no. 2, 1), an insight that tallies with a broader perception that educated, sophisticated, and artistic women enjoyed these magazines. As his magazine continued, however, Monahan seems to have attracted a readership akin to Hubbard's, as evidenced in the membership list for his Society of Papyrites.[3] Finally, readership can also be gauged from bookplates and marks of ownership in the copies of the magazines held at various institutional locations, evidence which supports my contention. Overall, it is reasonable to assume that there was a considerable male and female readership for these magazines.

While little magazinists and their readers can be understood to have been predominantly middle-class and Caucasian, there are instances of the medium being engaged with by Native American and African-American communities. Ora V. Eddleman (1880–1968), for example, was a Cherokee woman who edited a little magazine called *Twin Territories*, directed at a mixed audience, featuring the literary work of Native Americans and reaching a circulation of 8,000.[4] In Canada, black lawyer and author Abraham Walker established *Neith* in 1903 to address racial equality in a magazine aimed at a mixed audience (Irvine 606). A similar undertaking was made by Albion Tourgée (1838–1905) in America, who, though white, was a noted advocate for racial equality. He actively sought black contributors and readers for his hybrid magazine, *The Basis*, though seems to have struggled to do so (Chesnutt).[5] Elbert Hubbard's *Philistine* may have been more successful in this respect, apparently attracting a core of African-American readers, including activist Booker T. Washington, friend to Hubbard and founder of the Tuskegee Institute in Alabama, a school established by and for African Americans that was inspired by arts and crafts ideals (Bieze

29). Little magazines, then, could function for a range of aspirational communities, though it is safe to say that their core producers and intended audience were predominantly America's culturally aspiring white middle classes.

Little magazines are an important document of the ideals and anxieties of an emerging professional-managerial class consciousness, one caught between the cultural values of the Gilded Age's genteel middle class and those of an increasingly consumerist and capitalist society. The dominant ethos of this class, broadly speaking, through the Gilded Age and the Progressive Era, was based on self-improvement and social reform (Thomas Schlereth 243–70; Bledstein 26–45, 104–20). Central to these interests was an investment in culture, which, for the middle classes of this era, denoted "cultivation and refinement," "aesthetic sensibility," "higher learning," and the "sacralization of art and culture" (Trachtenberg 220–1). Alan Trachtenberg argues that for America's middle classes, culture offered a powerful antidote to the threatening forces represented by the lavish and conspicuous consumption of the nation's wealthy plutocrats and the squalor of the masses. It "offer[ed]" he writes, "a middle ground, and insofar as it was based on education, it offered a democratizing influence, accessible to all those willing to raise themselves to the status of American" (143). At the same time, "culture" assuaged middle-class guilt about complicity in sustaining an exploitative economic system of industrial capitalism: "As culture came to seem the repository of elevating thoughts and cleansing emotions, it seemed all the more as if the rough world of masculine enterprise had called into being its redemptive opposite" (145). An investment in this notion of culture became even more necessary for the emerging professional-managerial class, which was more complicit than the old middle class in sustaining the capitalist economy. This class, the Ehrenreichs argue, recognized that its "self-interest was bound up in reforming capitalism" and that its role was "to mediate the basic class conflict of capitalist society" (19). Culture or "art," as Hubbard insisted, as a "way of life" ("Thomas Arnold" 29), was important to this task. It represented solace from the marketplace and, in making culture available, in a variety of ways, to anyone interested in acquiring it, the middle classes played a role in bettering the nation through reformist and philanthropic activities. This view of culture extended beyond America's middle classes to inform those among the nation's working classes who aspired to improve their social position in a democratic country. It also extended upwards to the nation's plutocrats who, while exploiting their workers on the one hand, deployed their wealth in philanthropic enterprises on the other, founding a variety of cultural institutions, including schools, libraries, museums, and so on. Of course, culture, in this sense, was not without its insidious aspects. It served as a powerful agent of social control for the middle and philanthropic wealthy classes (Trachtenberg 147).[6]

The middle-class zeal to acquire culture exhibited itself in a number of ways at the end of the nineteenth century, notably through the proliferation of educational and cultural institutions. In this period, high school education became a virtual prerequisite for entry into white-collar, professional jobs that were predicated on mental, rather than manual, skills (Thomas Schlereth 248). At the same time, while the number of Americans who entered higher education was still relatively small, it was on the rise, serving an increasing portion of the population whose livelihood would depend upon expertise (Rebecca Edwards 116). By 1870, America had more colleges, medical schools, and law schools than all of Europe (Thomas Schlereth, 249; Bledstein 33). Americans also, however, educated themselves in other ways. The principle of self-culture that emphasized individualism and self-development originated in the Unitarian ideals of William Ellery Channing in the 1830s, but became more secularised as the century progressed. Intellectual development and aesthetic appreciation were increasingly valued, as many Americans turned to art and culture for consolations hitherto sought in religion (Sicherman 287). One key way in which Americans sought to develop their minds was through self-education. The Chautauqua movement, founded in 1874, provided this opportunity for hundreds of thousands of adult Americans through hometown study circles and summer camps. The aim of its Literary and Scientific Circles, for example, was "to promote habits of reading and study in nature, art, science, and in secular and sacred literature, in connection with the routine of daily life (especially among those whose educational advantages have been limited) so as to secure to them the college student's general outlook upon the world and life" (Vincent 75). Other means of self-education were provided by the many libraries, museums, and artistic, literary, and cultural societies and institutes founded in this period, organizations with a mandate to diffuse knowledge, taste, and refinement to the broad public. The Chautauqua schools and the rise of public institutions of culture in this era are indicative of the democratic and reformist principles that underwrote the zeal for culture.

Middle-class Americans who invested in self-improvement and reform also found outlets for their interests through religion and spirituality, which served as a means of coping with the stresses and conflicts of an increasingly commercial and industrialized society. The period was notable for a rise in the number of church-going Americans and for the emergence of new forms of religious expression and belief. While Protestantism in its various forms prevailed, the landscape was being transformed by an influx of immigrants with their own religions. It was, as Rebecca Edwards contends, "an era of immense creativity in American spiritual life" when "faiths were ... being molded and modernized in America" (173). Reformist impulses were at the heart of the social gospel and Christian socialist movements, both of which were concerned with social inequality, justice, poverty, and labour issues. Other popular new movements, meanwhile, such as the pantheistically oriented Theosophy, Christian Science, and New Thought, were challenging conventional Christianity. Unlike outward-facing, socially conscious, and reformist Christian movements, these were more personal forms of religious experience, suited to the increasing emphasis on individualism and self-development in the period.[7] Elements of these movements exerted a cultural influence beyond their immediate adherents. Theosophy, for example, with its borrowings from Judaism and Asian religions, did much to popularize Kabbalah, Hinduism, and Buddhism. Christian Science and New Thought, meanwhile, with their self-help-oriented philosophies concerning the connection between mind power, healing, and self-realisation, were broadly influential for members of a class whose value lay in their mental powers.

Indeed, Warren I. Susman has identified the New Thought movement as it manifested itself in the 1890s as central to the shift from the "culture of character" that dominated the middle-class ethos of much of the nineteenth century to the "culture of personality" that came to the fore in the first decade of the twentieth century. Susman contrasts the "culture of character," which conceptualizes the self as private, moral, and serious, to a "culture of personality" that idealizes a public, charismatic, idiosyncratic, and self-expressing individual (273–4, 276). An early popularizer of conceptions of personality was Walt Whitman, who made frequent use of the term. His poem "To a Pupil" (1860), for example, insists that successful reform, an ideal of middle-class culture, depends upon personality and the charismatic individual:

Is reform needed? Is it through you?
The greater the reform needed, the greater the Personality you need
to accomplish it.

You! Do you not see how it would serve to have eyes, blood, complexion,
clean and sweet?
Do you not see how it would serve to have such a body and soul that
when you enter the crowd an atmosphere of desire and command enters with you, and everyone is impressed with your Personality.

Oh the magnet! the flesh over and over!
Go, dear friend, if need be give up all else, and commence to-day to inure
yourself to pluck, reality, self esteem, definiteness, elevatedness,
Rest not till you rivet and publish yourself of your own Personality.[8] (302)

Whitman's conception of personality was influential. It registered notably with New Thought leaders whom Susman identifies as transitional figures that initially "attempted to combine the qualities of the works on character with a religious and even mystical stress on a spiritual vision of the self; they insisted not only on a higher moral order but also on the fulfillment of self by a striving to become one with a higher self" (276). Gradually, however, as the culture of personality emerged as dominant, subjection to a higher moral order in the sense of duty, honour, or integrity carried less weight than duty to one's self (Susman 280). In the period in which little magazinists were coming of age, both models were in play, a still dominant "culture of character," strongly aligned with genteel values and ideals, and an emerging "culture of personality," that would come to characterize the Progressive Era, its professional-managerial class, and the little magazines themselves.

Reform, self-improvement, self-development, and self-help were also at the centre of a seemingly infinite array of alternative and fringe movements that emerged in Gilded-Age and Progressive-Era America and were tied to the growth of the professional middle classes. Ruth Clifford Engs has dubbed this era the "second clean living movement" and documents the interests in physical culture, alternative therapies, food and diet trends, the promotion of free love and birth control, eugenics, etc., that characterized it. Reformist and self-improving agendas were also part of the era's political and socio-political movements – populism, socialism, Christian socialism, and anarchism. Though these movements were of most relevance to the working classes, their leadership was often dominated, as the Ehrenreichs argue, by members of a professional-managerial class who understood their role as reforming capitalism and healing class conflict (24, 19). Experimental modes of living practiced in back-to-the-land projects such as the cooperative movement and the arts and crafts and utopian colonies that sprung up in the period were also a means through which ideals of reform and self-development were realised.[9] These colonies were largely populated by professionals and others of the middle class seeking an escape from industrialist and capitalist life. Often these movements and causes overlapped or were sympathetic to each other. Politics and religion, for example, informed the social gospel movement and Christian socialism. At the same time, concepts of personal magnetism and mind cure that were central to New Thought and Theosophy also pervaded a number of the health and diet clean living fads.

The double drive for culture and reform that characterized the middle-class ethos of this era is nowhere better exhibited than in the widely popular arts and crafts and aesthetic movements, which combined an aesthetic and social mission.[10] It is worth devoting attention to these movements, as they were important to American middle-class life in the latter part of the nineteenth century and were a significant context for little magazine production and consumption. Though originating in Britain through the ideas of John Ruskin, William Morris, Walter Pater, and others, they had a profound influence in America, a nation that, as Alex Zwerdling and Lawrence Levine have argued, was still largely dominated, in cultural terms, by its former colonial master (Zwerdling 15; Levine 144–5). Arts and crafts and aestheticism represented a reaction against industrialization, the degradation of architecture, and mass-produced goods. Their proponents promoted the creation of beautiful objects for everyday use and extolled the craftsman and the dignity of labour. This ideology was appealing to a nation characterized by a strong work ethic and founded on the notion of democracy. Americans took to these cultural movements with zeal, joining societies and clubs, reading arts and crafts-oriented periodicals and books, attending exhibitions, taking courses, founding and joining arts and crafts communities, and going to the lectures of prominent figures associated with the movement, such as Oscar Wilde, who toured America in 1882, and Walter Crane, who visited in 1891 (Wendy Kaplan, “Spreading” 298).

Americans were not simply consumers of arts and crafts and aestheticism. They were also prodigious producers, with an ability to appropriate and adapt European trends for the conditions of American life. These movements manifested themselves in American architecture, furniture design, literature, painting, the decorative arts, graphic design, and even everyday living. Arts and crafts and aestheticism were, after, all, promoting not only a particular aesthetic, but also a way of life – the life beautiful. In America, these movements, as Eileen Boris suggests, attracted diverse figures: "traditionalists" and "primitivists," whose response to capitalism manifested itself in a yearning for pre-industrial society, such as architect and little magazinist Ralph Adams Cram, who advocated a return to the medieval guild system; "modernists," such as Oscar Lovell Triggs and Frank Lloyd Wright, proponents of the "new industrialism" that sought to adapt craft ideals to a modern capitalist context; "socialists" who promoted the craft ideal as a way to improve the lives of people and workers, including Ellen Gates Starr and Jane Addams, leaders of the American Settlement House movement; and "promoters" and "popularizers," including Elbert Hubbard and Gustav Stickley, also little magazinists, who exploited the craft ideal for commercial ends as producers of furniture, domestic goods, and decorative arts ("Dreams of Brotherhood" 208).

Overall, these movements were even more popular in America than in Britain. Indeed, for Boris the history of arts and crafts in America is the history of the American middle class itself. It "encapsulat[es]," she writes, "[the middle class's] fear and hatred of class conflict, its own loss and redefinition of autonomy and independence, its creating of rebels within its own midst. The idealistic, optimistic spirit of the crafts movement reflects the class that turned to arts and crafts as a solution and escape from the industrial world it did so much to forge" ("Dreams of Brotherhood" 208). The success of arts and crafts and aestheticism in America is attributable to their ability to harmonize the contradictory aspects of middle-class culture. For the middle and professional classes, with their cultural and material interests, these art movements served a number of functions. Freedman, for example, has said that aestheticism "provided a means for the newly rising professional and managerial elites to challenge the cultural hegemony of the established gentry elite," while enabling an artistic, literary, and intellectual cadre to "experience and express their ... sense of alienation" (112). Certainly aestheticism and other art movements played a role in the larger battle for cultural authority in middle-class culture of the era. For an emerging professional-managerial class, knowledge of cultural domains "privileged by the gentry" gave it power and status as this class increasingly sought to assert its own cultural authority (Freedman 113).

At the same time, these movements functioned to harmonize culture and commerce in accord with middle-class and professional ideals. Ultimately, as Wendy Kaplan argues, America's producers and consumers of arts and crafts were less ambivalent than their British counterparts about the relationship between art and industry, seeing "no contradiction between championing both the handcrafted and the improvement of the mass-produced" ("Spreading" 306). The situation with aestheticism was similar, as Freedman and Michèle Mendelssohn have demonstrated. Already existing in Britain as what Freedman has described as an "expression in aesthetic and cultural terms of the ethos of consumption" (59), aestheticism manifested this quality with even greater force in capitalist America, informing an "aestheticized consumerism" that emerged as early as the 1880s and that presented aestheticism in a "popular, smilingly consumerist form" (Freedman 109; Mendelssohn 13). The same was true even for the darker manifestation of aestheticism represented in the decadent movement, which, in Europe, was so strongly based on a rejection of the bourgeoisie and of commercial culture. The "capitalist commercial context" of America meant that decadence, as David Weir says, was far more implicated with commercial culture than in Europe (xvi). As a consequence, the reach and influence of arts and crafts, aestheticism, and even decadence, were broader in America than in Britain, supporting at one and the same time the middle class's cultural and material interests. These movements strongly informed the literature, art, and print culture of the American 1890s, notably in the areas of printing and book design, little magazines, and the rise of the art poster for advertising.

For the American middle and professional classes of this period, print was central to the expression and development of their cultural aims, ideals, and aspirations. The late nineteenth century witnessed an explosion of print, and the written word, according to Burton J. Bledstein, became the favoured medium of exchange in American life: "Every serious activity found a literary expression, including a distinct vocabulary that sympathetic persons could share" – everything from "cycling, gardening, physical health, mental hygiene, cooking, and fashion to spiritualism, art, unions, professions, etc." (65). Literacy rates were on the rise in this period and Americans increasingly expressed and bettered themselves through reading and writing. The number of books published tripled alongside the expansion of consumer and collector markets. Practical books, including etiquette books, "house pattern books," and "how-to" books were popular forms of reading matter (Lehmann-Haupt et al. 197–8). These types of books and the broader culture of self-help oriented health and spiritual trends in American life catered especially to the middle classes as the professional-managerial ethos began to dominate. This ethos, one based on anxieties about class reproduction, held that one's inner life must be "continuously shaped, updated, and revised by … ever mounting numbers of experts: experts in childraising, family living, sexual fulfillment, self-realization, etc., etc." (Ehrenreich and Ehrenreich 30). Reading was part of one's ongoing education, self-development, and self-improvement.

Periodicals were most crucial to the development of this identity. The circulation of newspapers increased sevenfold between 1870 and 1900 (Emery and Emery 198), while the magazine-purchasing public grew by ten times between 1890 and 1895 (Tassin 340). Magazines, like books, appealed to an array of middle-class cultural and professional interests. "Every interest," writes Mott, "had its own journal or journals – all the ideologies and movements, all the arts, all the schools of philosophy and education, all the sciences, all the trades and industries, all the professions and callings, all organizations of importance, all hobbies and recreations" (*History* 10). Magazines catered to a middle class, "eager for entertainment and culture as well as material comfort and status," to an emerging professional-managerial class faction seeking "guidance in articulating material, artistic, and intellectual markers of status," and to the growing immigrant population eager to develop its literacy (Sedgwick 417; Smith and Dawson 7). Characterized in the period by a journalist for the *Chicago Graphic* as "a school of literature, … science, art, and politics," magazines were a means of self-culture and education (qtd. in Mott, *History* 12). At the same time, they were "a key component," Eric Lupfer insists, "of group identity" for the middle classes (249), enabling the consolidation of cultural values and ideals that would shape them.

Americans were not only avid consumers of print, they also actively sought ways to express themselves through print. Book collecting, scrapbooking, and amateur printing, for example, were popular pastimes. As with many cultural pursuits in America, book collecting became a democratized pastime, extending down from wealthy robber barons such as Henry Huntington and J.P. Morgan to an increasingly educated and professionalized middle class that valorized the printed word and for whom the ownership of beautiful books was a means of cultural distinction. This pastime reached a height in the 1890s, identified by Robert Alan Shaddy as the "Golden Age" of book collecting. Printing, meanwhile, emerged as a popular middle-class hobby for youth with the introduction of a cheap novelty press in the 1860s. Widely advertised in juvenile magazines, the novelty press was a prized acquisition for young persons, and the establishment of the National Amateur Press Association in 1876 was a testament to the appeal of amateur printing and of the desire to create networks to exchange publications.[11] In its aims and ideals, amateur journalism reflects perfectly middle-class and professional-managerial class interests of the period. Participants in the movement, for example, described it as "a means of mutual intellectual culture" and a tool for "self-improvement" (Spencer 3). In addition, it was a way to "cultivate a taste for pure and wholesome literature," to give one a "practical knowledge of the world," and "to teach one to think and act for [one's] self" (Spencer 3). In a similar vein, scrapbooking, a form of making one's own book from ephemeral print culture, especially magazines and newspapers, was linked to the interest in self-culture and self-expression.[12] In the 1880s, E.W. Gurley, for example, endorsed scrapbooking as a means of "promoting family harmony and solving the problems of both idleness and unfocused reading" (qtd. in Tucker et al., Introduction 9).

Beyond these more private forms of engagement with print, many middle-class Americans participated in public ways, as amateur writers of books and of content for magazines and newspapers. The Zborays, for example, document the importance of this form of authorship for the antebellum literary marketplace (*Literary Dollars*). Later in the period, the passing of the International Copyright Act in 1891 and the massive expansion of the newspaper and periodical press in the mid-1890s were important in professionalizing authorship and journalism, making these fields more attractive career pursuits for the middle classes. At the same time, in a period in which, as the Zborays note, "institutional certifications were still in their infancy," print "was one of the only ways" professionals could "assert … expertise" (*Literary Dollars* 199). Though the number of persons declaring authorship as an occupation decreased between 1890 and 1900, the number of journalists (including editors), by contrast, rose markedly from 21,849 to 30,038 (US Census Office xxiv). In this period, authorship and journalism were respectable fields for middle-class men and women, whether in an amateur or professional context, and the growth of the magazine industry brought about a new category of writer – the magazinist: one who writes first and foremost, possibly only, for magazines, and who may earn a good living without achieving literary fame (Mott, *History* 37). William Dean Howells described the emergence of this new breed of writer in 1893: "the prosperity of the magazines has given a whole class existence which, as a class, was wholly unknown among us before the [Civil] war. It is not only the famous or fully recognized authors who live in this way, but the much larger number of clever people … who may never make themselves a public but who do well a kind of acceptable work" ("Man of Letters" 432). While the Zborays contend that a postbellum industrialized and commercialized field transformed the nature of amateur engagement with print (*Literary Dollars* xiv), it clearly did not put an end to it. The little magazine emerged as a venue in which amateurs, aspirants, and professional writers and artists could, and did, express themselves.

Little Magazinists in the Late-nineteenth-century American Cultural Landscape

> Paper is now so cheap and the type-setting machine has so reduced the cost of some kinds of printing that any young man, or group of young men, who cannot get their writings printed in the magazines or newspapers can easily start a magazine of their own. It is desirable to have it printed on rough paper, with deckled edges, but that is not essential. The essential thing, beyond a plentiful provision of the capital I, is to abuse the editors and writers whose copy is printed and read.
>
> – "The Little Magazines," *The Times* Philadelphia, 7 (1896)

This social and cultural context set the stage for the men and women who would create, contribute to, and consume little magazines. In these publications and other cultural pursuits, little magazinists would adapt and challenge the genteel values that they had inherited in the development of an emerging professional-managerial ethos. Many were born to the culturally aspiring "old middle-class," genteel and artistic – if not always prosperous – families, or wealthy ones with Northern European roots. Often they lived in homes where literature, music, and the arts were cultivated, where "culture," in Trachtenberg's sense, was avidly sought out. A handful of key figures can stand as largely representative of the backgrounds of thousands of little magazinists.[13] Percival Pollard (1869–1911), little magazine editor and prolific contributor, was born to a British grain-merchant father and a German opera singer mother, emigrating to America in the 1880s when his father became a successful realtor (Dunsmore). Michael Monahan (1865–1933), founder of *Papyrus*, was also foreign-born, an Irishman and son of teachers who came to America in 1870 ("Monahan, Michael"). Ernest Crosby (1856–1907), Ralph Adams Cram (1863–1942), and Vance Thompson (1863–1925), all founders of, and contributors to, little magazines, were sons of clergymen (Applegate; Cram; Shand-Tucci, *Boston Bohemia* and *Ralph Adams Cram*; "Thompson, [Charles] Vance"). Cram's father was a radical Unitarian and Transcendentalist, an abolitionist who had refused to serve in the Civil War, his mother part of the New England country elite. Crosby's parents, meanwhile, were politically conservative wealthy New Yorkers. He would develop political leanings opposite to those of his father, involving himself in reform and socialism at the turn of the century. Elbert Hubbard (1856–1915), founder of *The Philistine*, was the son of an eccentric and free-thinking doctor.[14] Gelett Burgess (1866–1951), founder of *The Lark* and other little magazines, was the son of a well-to-do painting contractor and his "genteel Unitarian" wife (Gale). James Huneker (1857–1921), co-editor of *M'lle New York*, was the son of a prosperous Philadelphia house painter, decorator and collector of prints, and an intellectual mother, a "second Madame de Staël," as she was described (Schwab 2; Huneker). Huneker's family's social network included actors, musicians, and writers, notably Edgar Allan Poe and Edwin Booth. Bliss Carman (1861–1929), short-term editor of *The Chap-Book* and contributor to many little magazines, was the son of a barrister and came from Canadian of United Empire Loyalist stock with connections to the ancestors of Ralph Waldo Emerson (Muriel Miller). Thomas Mosher (1852–1923), founder of *The Bibelot*, was the son of a sea captain and ship owner (Strouse). Ingalls Kimball (1874–1933), founder of *The Chap-Book*, was the son of a business entrepreneur (Kramer; Wendy Schlereth).

While female little magazinists will be mentioned in other contexts, it is worth highlighting some aspects of their backgrounds. Though only a handful of little magazines were published and/or edited by women, there were many female contributors to these magazines. Like their male counterparts, they were often raised in cultivated homes and provided with a genteel education, a number of them described as socialites, society women, or club women in newspapers of the day. Notable ones include Carolyn Wells (1862–1942), the daughter of a wealthy realtor, who was one of the most prolific female little magazinists (Wells, *Rest of My Life*); Louise Imogen Guiney (1861–1920), daughter of a prominent lawyer, and herself a notable "mother figure" in the Harvard-based little magazine set (Fairbanks); Mary Learned (1873–1960), daughter of an Omaha mayor, prominent real estate businessman, and lawyer and, as editor of *The Pebble* with Louise McPherson, one of a handful of female little magazine founders and editors ("Mrs. Myron D. Learned"); and Myrtle Reed (1874–1911), prolific little magazinist whose father was a preacher and founder of the first Midwestern literary magazine and whose mother was a theological scholar and author (Clegg).

A number of female little magazinists were "modern," seeking or engaged in careers, and/or practicing bohemian lifestyles as single, married, or divorced women. Guiney and Wells, for example, were librarians for a time. More usually, though, these women were pursuing literary, journalistic, or artistic careers, often on a freelance basis. Emma Carleton (1850–1924) and Zoe Anderson Norris (1860–1914), for example, who contributed to little and mainstream magazines, are typical of Mott's magazinist, earning a livelihood, often a precarious one, through magazine work ("Emma Carleton"; "Zoe A. Norris"). Norris would be at the centre of New York bohemian life in the early twentieth century and would establish her own little magazine, *The East Side*, much later, in 1909. Norris's contemporary, Elia W. Peattie (1862–1935) was the first "girl" reporter on *The Chicago Tribune*, writing for a wide range of publications that included mainstream and little magazines ("Biography of Elia Wilkinson Peattie"; Peattie). Among female little magazine founders and editors, Dorothy Maddox (dates unknown), a woman's page columnist for *The Philadelphia Inquirer*, established her own little magazine, *The Dorothy Maddox Magazette*, a scarlet-covered magazine – "Red outside and read all through" – "written by a woman for women, but men will read it" ("Magazines" 6). Page Waller Sampson (1863–1935) and Marion Thornton Egbert (1874–?) created a stir with *The Bachelor Book*, a witty and sophisticated magazine directed at bachelors and promoting bachelorhood. The magazine was issued from their studio in the famed Auditorium Building in Chicago, where they also hosted a salon known as "sinner's corner" for "pucca bohemians" who came to drink tea and cocktails ("Egbert Divorce Case").

A number of little magazinists had family connections to the periodical, publishing, or printing industries that were growing rapidly in this period. Herbert Stone (1871–1915), founder of *The Chap-Book*, was the son of a newspaper owner (Kramer; Wendy Schlereth), while George Gough Booth (1864–1949), founder of the *Cranbrook Papers*, was the son of a man who made numerous attempts to found newspapers, son-in-law of the founder of *The Detroit News*, and a newspaperman in his own right (Arthur Pound). Claude F. Bragdon (1866–1946), prolific little magazinist contributor, and Bruce Porter (1865–1953), founder of *The Lark*, were sons of newspaper editors (Bragdon, *Secret Springs*; "Bruce Porter" [Designer])." Others, including Horace Traubel (1858–1919), founder of *The Conservator*, Will Bradley (1868–1962), founder of *Bradley His Book*, and Elia W. Peattie, had printer fathers (Karsner; Koch, *Will H. Bradley*; "Biography of Elia Wilkinson Peattie"). Traubel was the son of an immigrant German-Jewish printer, engraver, and lithographer, who inherited his father's trade and was a journalist before becoming a freelance writer. Bradley, too, had a printer father who had aspired to be an artist and had high hopes for his son. Though printing was a wage-earning trade rather than a middle-class profession, printers were highly literate and skilled workers, often characterized as "intellectuals of the working class" or "labor aristocrats" (Laurie 77). Some youths with printer fathers exploited the resources available to them to produce their own publications. At least one little magazine, addressed to young people, emerged from this context. *The Hoppergrass*, of Ashland and, later, Richmond, Virginia, was written and published by the Bryce children, boys and girls, aged thirteen, eleven, ten, and seven when the publication began. Their father was a surgeon, consultant, and specialist in electro-therapeutics, an alternative medical practice of the day, as well as the printer, publisher, and editor of various medical journals. The young Bryces issued their magazine from his jobbing shop.[15]

If family connections inspired youth to take an interest in this endeavour so, too, of course, did the availability of hobby presses and the rise of the amateur press movement. Many of those involved with little magazines in the 1890s took up amateur printing in various forms as youths. John J. Corell (1873–1954) and Robert T. Sloss (1872–1920), founders of *John-a-Dreams* and the Corell Press (W.J.K. 415), each owned an amateur press as boys, while California printer Charles Murdock (1841–1928), who printed *The Lark*, noted in his memoirs that, as a young boy, he looked upon printing "as the first rung on the ladder of journalism" (78). At the age of six, Carolyn Wells wrote and bound a book that included a frontispiece with tissue paper leaf (Wells, *Rest of My Life* 31). Bruce Rogers (1870–1957), whose designs appeared in little magazines and who would become a famous typographer of the twentieth century, lamented the fact that, as a boy, he had not had access to a hobby press (Bruce Rogers xliii–xliv). He made do though, designing a hand-lettered edition of a poem by popular poet William Cullen Bryant that included imitation etchings and plate marks created by a kitchen iron (Zarobila). Wells's and Rogers's endeavours indicate the allure of printing and bookmaking for youth of the period.

This fascination held true even when printing was work. Such, certainly, was the view of Bradley and Tim Thrift. Bradley's youthful enthusiasm for printing led him to purchase a hobby press with money he earned as a delivery boy, but soon, due to his father's death, he was apprenticed into the trade as a printer's devil (Bradley, *Will Bradley* 92). Timothy Burr Thrift (1883–1947), founder of *The Lucky Dog*, also devilled and used the facilities at his workplace after hours to produce early issues of his magazine (Marjorie Wilson). Like Bradley, Thomas Wood Stevens (1880–1942), founder of *Blue Sky*, owned a hobby press before taking up a job, on the death of his parents, in the printing and engraving section of the advertising department at the Santa Fe Railway Company. While employed in this capacity, he also edited, printed, and published *Blue Sky*, and operated a small press that issued books as well (Melvin R. White 280–1).

If the hobby press allowed youth to print at home, the amateur press movement established networks for sharing enthusiasms and exchanging publications. Opportunities for amateur printing and publishing, for example, existed in high schools through school newspapers and magazines. These were distributed, as Rebecca Edwards notes, to other schools, creating "lively networks of gossip and debate" (116). One such example, which shows a connection between amateur high school publications and little magazines is Oakland High School's *Aegis*. In 1901, Irving Morrow (1884–1952) and Colman Schwartz (1884–1920) were involved with this magazine when it published a story by Jack London, who had attended the school in 1895, and was, by this time, establishing himself as a writer. In addition to working on the school magazine, Morrow and Schwartz were involved in the production of a little magazine, *The Muse*, which would feature the first appearance of a story by London, as well as work by other prominent California writers.[16] Beyond schools, amateur publishing was also promoted by groups such as the National Amateur Press Association, which had local and national networks. Like high school students and teachers who might be involved in school publications before going on to little magazine work, amateurs might also follow this route, a trajectory that would see them move from amateurism and an exchange-based model to the semi-professional and semi-commercial realm of little magazine publication with subscription and/or newsstand distribution. In some cases, the next step might be into the world of professional mainstream or trade publishing and magazine work.

The cultural pursuits of the little magazinists coming of age in the 1880s and 1890s were fostered into adulthood by the nation's growing higher education system. Some little magazinists were among the privileged few who attended college or university, which was 4 per cent by 1900 (Bledstein 278). Indeed, *The Critic*'s charge that "any youth just out of college, or any freshman just in college may have his own organ," shows the perceived connection between college education and the production of little magazines ("Fad Periodicals" 12). Though the formal study of English Literature in American universities was just being established in the late nineteenth century, literary culture was extremely important to campus life at least until the twentieth century when, as Gerald Graff notes, it would be superseded by fraternity, sorority, and athletic culture (44). Campuses had literary societies, debating clubs, literary magazines, and there were opportunities to attend readings and lectures. Campuses were also the sites of production for little magazines, as in the case of *Morningside*, issued from Columbia University, and *The Lotus*, which, in its early period, was an undergraduate intercollegiate magazine in Kansas City, Missouri. Other campuses served as a breeding ground for producers of, and contributors to, little magazines. *The Kiote* of Lincoln, Nebraska, for example, described as "a fad or freak magazine ... dedicated to the prairie yelper," was edited and published by students and faculty at the University of Nebraska ("Journalistic Notes" 518; "Additional Locals"). Clinton Scollard (1860–1932), who is considered in detail in chapter 5, was an English professor at Hamilton College and the leading magazine poet of his age (Mott, *History* 120). Katharine Lee Bates (1859–1929), meanwhile, most famous as the writer of the words for "America the Beautiful," was an Oxford-educated professor at Wellesley who regularly contributed to periodicals, including little magazines ("Katharine Lee Bates").

The most significant educational establishment to serve as a breeding ground for little magazines and magazinists, however, was undoubtedly

Harvard. It is no coincidence that this ferment occurred at Harvard, where Charles Eliot, President from 1869 to 1909, radically secularized and modernized the curriculum, establishing what would now be considered a liberal arts program (Rebecca Edwards 120). Cambridge and Boston were home to a strong bibliophilic network and there were numerous literary and artistic societies, including the Pewter Mug Associates, the Visionists, and the Procrastinatorium.[17] More formal organizations included the Boston Arts and Crafts Society (founded by Charles Eliot Norton in 1897) and the Club of Odd Volumes (Boston, founded 1888). The area also had its representative fine books publisher in Copeland and Day, founded by Harvard graduates of the 1880s, who were the North American publishers of *The Yellow Book* and other titles issued by London's Bodley Head, famed for its association with decadent and New Woman fiction. Harvard also had a number of influential professors on its staff. Eliot's cousin, Charles Eliot Norton (1827–1908), for example, was professor of fine arts at Harvard and "the chief precursor of Arts and Crafts ideology" in America (Lears 66). Similarly, George Santayana (1863–1952), professor of philosophy, revolted against American puritanism to espouse an Epicurean ethos. Both professors conceived of themselves as alienated from mainstream American culture (Graff 83–4), and influenced the intellectual, aesthetic, and spiritual ideals of undergraduates who would go on to play a formative role in the professional and cultural development of the nation. At the same time, their students were being drawn to new, more hedonistic manifestations of the aesthetic and philosophical doctrines of their mentors – in particular, the decadent and symbolist movements.

The atmosphere in and around Harvard, then, was accommodating to the aesthetic interests of young men who came together with shared literary, artistic, and bibliophilic interests. Ralph Adams Cram, for example, noted: "there was the underlying conviction that it was a great world – that romance and poetry and beauty were coming back to a drab century, and that in some way I was to find my place amongst the bearers of glad tidings. The time-honoured organ of such an evangel always has been, I suppose always will be, some sort of magazine" (54). Though Cram's family was not wealthy enough to send him to college, he came into the orbit of the charmed Harvard circle and was involved in the creation of a number of early little magazines, including *The Mahogany Tree*, *The Knight Errant*, and, most notably, *The Chap-Book*. This atmosphere may also have played a role in the emergence of other little magazines of a range of types created by students and alumni, including *The Shadow*, which was issued out of Cambridge and whose editorial board consisted of a number of Harvard students; *The Higher Law*, a New Thought-oriented publication founded by Horatio W. Dresser (1866–1954); *The Magpie*, an aesthetic little magazine founded by Kenneth Brown (1868–?); *Pickwick*, an aesthetic little magazine edited by Arthur N. Hosking (1874–1970); the bibliophilic publication *Book Culture*, edited by Nathan Haskell Dole (1852–1935); *The Lincoln House Review*, a magazine devoted to the settlement house movement, edited by William Anthony Clark (1868–?); and *Medical Tractates*, a medical-focused "faggot of facts and fancies picked up and tied together by Leon Noel," the pen name of alumnus Charles Everett Warren (1858–1916).[18]

Examples of other educational institutions and the little magazinists they fostered include the following: MIT, where Elisha Brown Bird (1867–1943), who contributed art to numerous little magazines, and Gelett Burgess, founder of the San Francisco-based *Lark*, were educated ("Notes on the Artists" 184; Gale); the Art Institute of Chicago (founded 1879), which issued its own little magazine, *Brush and Pencil*, from 1897 and whose staff and students contributed to Chicago-based little magazines such as *The Rubric* and *Four-O'Clock* (Fleming); the Frank Holme School of Illustration in Chicago (1895–1903), where, for example, *Blue Sky* contributors Frederick Goudy (1865–1947) taught and William A. Dwiggins (1880–1956) was a student (Paul Shaw 29); the Art Students League of New York (founded 1875), whose students and staff produced a little magazine, *The Limner*, in 1895; the Pennsylvania Academy of the Fine Arts (founded 1805), where John Sloan (1871–1951), contributor to *The Chap-Book*, *Moods*, and *The Echo*, received training (Sloan); The Mark Hopkins Institute of San Francisco (founded 1893), where Florence Lundborg (1871–1949), illustrator and poster designer for *The Lark*, was instructed ("Notes on the Artists" 189); the American Art Association in Paris, whose little magazine, *Quartier Latin*, featured art, fiction, essays, and advertisements by its members. These examples are by no means exhaustive, but provide a sense of the relationship between established and emerging educational institutions and little magazines. Students and instructors at these and many other such institutions all across the country contributed significantly to the movement.

If they did not have the privilege of an education through a university, college, or technical institute, little magazinists were often products of the zeal for self-culture. Good examples of this form of self-education among little magazinists include Thomas Bird Mosher, Elbert Hubbard, and Carolyn Wells. Mosher, founder of *The Bibelot*, left formal schooling at age twelve. Thereafter, his education was confined to reading all he could get his hands on in his voyages with his sea captain father. His love of books brought him into the world of bookselling, and eventually he became a printer and publisher at the age of thirty-nine. Like Mosher, Hubbard was self-educated, a successful product of the popular Chautauqua movement, serving as president of the East Aurora branch in 1890 and graduating in 1894 (MBS [Marjorie B. Searle] 45) after an unsuccessful stint at Harvard, which he found stifling and elitist. His printing, publishing, and arts and crafts community, the Roycrofters, established in 1896, would produce one of the most successful little magazines of the era, *The Philistine*. Another prolific contributor to little magazines, Carolyn Wells, had the opportunity and was expected to go on to college. She, however, regarded it as "waste motion ... to the nth power," and opted instead to pursue education independently, seeking out tutors and friends to teach her things she wanted to learn (Wells, *Rest of My Life* 36).

Yet another important feature that characterized the cultural formation of the little magazinist was a connection with formal and informal literary, artistic, and bibliophilic societies and salons in cities and towns that grew up across the country in this period. The kinds of societies that served Harvard students and the intellectual elite in Cambridge and Boston existed across the country. Chicago and New York were especially rich in such organizations. The book and little magazine publishers, Stone and Kimball, for example, after moving headquarters from Cambridge to Chicago, organized "chap-book" teas for artists and writers (Fleming 800). There was also the "Little Room," a salon in the studio of artist Ralph Clarkson in Chicago's Fine Arts Building and the "Saints and Sinners" bibliophilic group that met in the Rare Book Room (known as the Amen corner) of McClurg's bookstore where little magazinists Thomas Wood Stevens and Will Bradley met publishers, journalists, writers, and artists including Nixon Waterman, Irving Way, and Herbert Stone (Melvin R. White 281; Koch, *Will H. Bradley* 34). Chicago also had an Arts and Crafts Society (established 1897) and the Industrial Art League (established 1899). In a more amateur vein, the Cypher Club, which endorsed "Bohemia in its highest and truest sense," met weekly in the 1890s and had its own publication (W.D. 1). New York's societies and salons included formal clubs such as the Grolier Club (founded 1884), devoted to the book arts, and the Pleiades Club (founded 1894), which promoted the appreciation of the allied arts, as well as informal gatherings at bookshops, newspaper and magazine offices, and restaurants. Many New York bohemian journalists, editors, and authors, for example, congregated at Maria's spaghetti house or various French restaurants (Mount 67–8). Other notable clubs beyond the major literary and publishing centres of Boston, Chicago, and New York included the Portfolio Club of Indianapolis (founded 1890) (Hyman 107), the Bohemian Club (San Francisco, founded 1872), and the more informal and frolicsome Camp Ha Ha, founded by the coterie that established *The Lark* (San Francisco, 1890s) (Hart, Introduction vi). These organizations were by no means confined to larger cities. In Wausau, Wisconsin, for example, Helen and Philip Van Vechten and William Ellis organized a group known as "the Philosophers," which consisted of journalists, a federal judge, a state senator, and several lawyers, and formed the network upon which the editor drew for his little magazine, *The Philosopher* (Wallin). In Nebraska, there was the Art Workers' Society of Omaha, open to anyone with an interest in art (Clarke G. Powell). Little magazinists joined and/or established these cliques of would-be writers, artists, publishers, printers, and typographers. These were the networks out of which many forms of literary and artistic production of the era would emerge, including little magazines.

It is important to highlight, however, that this type of cultural exchange existed not only for those with shared interests in literary, artistic, and bibliophilic matters. Publications, specifically those of the protest variety, also grew out of and/or fostered networks in other realms of cultural life relevant to the interests of the professional-managerial class. Particularly notable is the interest of little magazinists in spiritual, health-related, and political movements, which sometimes served as the focus of little magazines. Though magazines dealing with such topics, even from unconventional or esoteric perspectives, existed in other formats, the little magazine was an appealing medium, especially after the success of *The Chap-Book* and *The Philistine*. Proponents of various causes exploited aspects of "little magazineness" – its format, which was cheap to produce, and/or its characteristic offbeat rhetorical style or subject matter, a function of the emerging culture of personality. At the same time, the inclusion of literary and/or artistic content added appeal. With respect to socialist and Christian socialist periodicals of this type, for example, Howard H. Quint points to their founders' interests in producing publications characterized by "good socialist propaganda and literary excellence," something one "could show with pride to … non-socialist friends" ("*Social Crusader*" 46). The little magazine was an efficient medium to popularize, if not in a mass-market sense, the variety of social and political movements and trends that resonated with a professional-managerial readership.

The middle-class interest in self-help therapies, physical culture, New Thought, eugenics, sexuality, temperance, and pure food and drugs that characterized the "second clean living movement," was reflected in a range of protest and hybrid magazines that were more general in nature. They were also, however, subject to more focused attention in a body of medical and health-oriented little magazines that emerged. These magazines were usually produced by doctors, "author-physicians," as one medical journal of the day called them (Review of *The Isle of Content* 685), or by those with vested personal or political interests in medical and health movements. They included Ralcy Halsted Bell's *Moody's Magazine of Medicine*, "a medico-surgical literary journal"; George F. Butler's *Doctor's Magazine and How to Live*; J.H. Tilden's *Stuffed Club for Everybody*; Paul Pierce's *What to Eat*; and David Reeder's *New Race*. Bell's magazine's "littleness" consisted in its inclusion of literature and art characteristic of the genre – curious Whitmanesque poetry and poster-style nude art – as well as its "revolt" against conventional medical journalistic practice. Critics thought that in its attempt to appeal to a mixed audience of professionals and laypersons, it threatened the "dignity of the profession" by putting before a "prurient" and "prying" public, subjects suited only for discussion within the medical community ("Book Reviews" 502; "Editorial" 523). While Bell's magazine, it is true, targeted a mixed audience, its medical content was written in highly technical language; so, though this content was available to a general readership, it was not pitched at it, as was such content in other little magazines that sought more explicitly to popularize medical knowledge. Butler's, Tilden's, Pierce's, and Reeder's magazines, for example, were of this kind, focusing on personal hygiene, sanitation, physical culture, and dietetics through a self-help-oriented lens, content that appeared alongside fiction, poetry, and, in some cases, art.

The context for George F. Butler's *Doctor's Magazine and How to Live*, for example, was his work as medical superintendent at Alma Springs Sanitarium in Michigan, one of a number of high-class spas that catered to an upper middle-class and wealthy clientele, the most famous of which was Kellogg's Battle Creek Sanitarium. Signalling its self-help ethos with its "how to" title, it was directed at an educated audience, some of whom had likely visited the sanitarium. In addition to an interest in self-help, author-physicians like Butler, and to an even greater extent, Tilden, were concerned with educating their readership about medical "quackery," "fakes and shams," both within and without the professional medical world. These aims, for example, were identified as a feature of Butler's work in an endorsement for his magazine in *Medical Era* ("How to Live" 232, 233). Tilden, meanwhile, an early proponent of naturopathy, offered practical health advice to his readers and engaged in a broad-minded spirit with a range of alternative medical therapies and practices, with comment, for example, on the healing philosophies of New Thought and Christian Science. Butler and Tilden's magazines indicate the increasingly complex role of the medical professional in a capitalist, consumer-oriented marketplace. The expertise of figures like Butler and Tilden was required to help the middle classes to navigate the array of competing consumer products and therapies available.

While Tilden was outspoken and opinionated in his views, other little magazinists gave voice to competing practices in their publications. Paul Pierce's *What to Eat*, a Minneapolis-based little magazine that exploited the faddish poster style in its design and was aimed at an upper middle-class readership, aimed for wide appeal. It addressed readers in the highly personalized first-hand account style increasingly characteristic of mass-market and little magazine rhetoric. "No school or practice will be slighted," he announced in the first issue, professedly in an aim to let readers judge for themselves (18). Its first number, for example, featured a first-hand account of the "Salisbury Treatment," a beef and hot water based diet for the cure of dyspepsia, which was seen as the root of larger chronic diseases (Gilbert Pierce 21–2). Quackery finds its place in this issue in a feature on Ralstonism (Jungen), a cultish health movement of the era with racist and eugenicist undertones. It catered to middle-class anxieties about modernity with the premise, "no person is really wholly and perfectly well" because of "strife in daily business" and "the rush and irritability of the times" (Jungen 7). Its adherents, reportedly 800,000 in number, included doctors, lawyers, judges, Supreme Court justices, merchants, clergymen, and bankers (Jungen 7). Led by the charismatic Webster Edgerly (who also went by the names Edmund Shaftesbury and Dr. Ralston) and a clear manifestation of the emerging culture of personality, Ralstonism was informed by principles of self-help and self-development, stressing the connection between mental power and physical well-being in striving towards the development of personal magnetism.[19] Though *What to Eat*, as Andrew P. Haley has argued, was catholic and largely non-partisan in its coverage, overall its tendency was to promote simple eating after the model of Theodore Roosevelt's endorsement of the "simple life" (130, 132). Increasingly, however, it would come to promote Pierce's reformist advocacy for legislation for a Pure Food and Drug Act.

Ralstonism found a stronger proponent in David H. Reeder, an instructor at a Ralston health club ("Ralston Health Followers," 9), who edited a movement-based publication out of Kansas City called *The New Race*. Its topics went beyond the food and diet focus of *What to Eat* to explore the farther shores of Ralstonism, covering hygiene, dietetics, exercise, posture, punctuation, and personal magnetism. It also included fiction, poetry, and features on art, much in the style of a general monthly. Its first issue in December 1896 contained a feature on Ralstonism by its founder, hints on physical culture for businessmen, articles on cereal foods and digestion, and a woman's department. Reeder, who was not a real doctor and who, in 1916, was exposed as a quack (American Medical Association), followed Ralston in much, inventing a health product called Renew-U Food; establishing a Home Health Club through which he issued a series of mail-order books; and selling patent medicines, a practice that went against the largely anti-drug emphasis of these health movements (Daniels 332–3).

Esoteric, metaphysical, and spiritual movements and trends that appealed to the professional classes were also a significant feature of periodicals of protest and engendered a subset of specialist publications. These movements were often concerned with physical and mental health and well-being as well as self-help and self-realisation. Little magazines were one of a number of print venues, especially magazines, that promoted New Thought, for example, which, as Eva S. Moskowitz has argued, was largely "a movement of the printed word," rather than one of personal contact, for many of its followers (18). New Thought little magazinists include Horatio W. Dresser, editor of *Higher Law*, and Grace Mann Brown and James Arthur Edgerton, editors of *The Essene*. Dresser was the son of a prominent early New Thought leader, friend to philosopher and psychologist William James, and author of the best-selling New Thought text, *The Power of Silence: An Interpretation of Life in Its Relation to Health and Happiness* (1895). As a creedless and fragmented movement, New Thought manifested itself in different forms in this period. Dresser, for example, was associated with the rational and practical side of the movement. *Higher Law*'s deliberate avoidance of "special" or "doctrinal" interests was intended to distance the magazine from sectarian or school-based aspects of the movement and to promote New Thought principles in relation to everyday life ([Dresser] 63; front matter). The issue for March 1902, for example, attempts to explain the relationship between science and New Thought and provides an account, aimed at teachers, of what a New Thought-oriented teaching practice would be ("What Is Science?"; Newell). *The Essene*, by contrast, was of the sectarian type opposed by Dresser and was edited by Brown, one of a number of female proponents of New Thought, and Edgerton, a poet of the New Thought and populism. The magazine brings together the psychological, philosophical, and metaphysical aspects of the rationalist arm of the movement with a strong Christian emphasis and a hint of socialism, characteristic of other branches of New Thought. It idealizes the ancient Essenes, identifies Christ as one of their number, and defines their key values as anti-commercialism, liberty, democracy, moral and physical cleanliness, spirituality, and faith in healing, principles resonant in many of the New Thought-inspired movements of the day ("The Essenes"). In addition, the magazine promotes Edgerton's socialistic interest in the Church of the Living Christ, a religious and political sect promoting a "democracy of worship" (i.e, having no paid or professional priests) and a "cooperative commonwealth" as the "logical outcome of Christ's teachings" ("Church of the Living Christ" 33, 34).

While New Thought and its many offshoots had, and would continue to develop, widespread appeal, there were even more esoteric movements that found expression in, and sought to extend their reach through, little magazines. The popularity of these fringe movements and of figures like Madame Blavatsky and Mary Baker Eddy among America's middle, professional, and wealthy classes served as an inspiration for aspiring charismatic spiritual leaders. Little magazines represented an inexpensive means for them to establish networks. Such was the case for Naphthali Herz Imber, for example, a Galacia-born Jewish Hebrew poet who came to America in 1891, aspiring to become the Kabbalah equivalent of Blavatsky. Imber published pamphlets and articles, offered classes and lectures, and issued a short-lived little magazine, *Uriel*. In seeking to "establish a new cult" in the West (Wall 17), he understood the importance of the charismatic personality for attracting adherents and tried to harness this power. Imber identified himself as the "chosen" one to expound the teachings of the Kabbalah, carefully positioning himself in relation to Blavatsky (Wall 17). Writing under the name Herzel in *Uriel*, Imber celebrates her as a powerful woman and "pointer," but criticizes her failure to illuminate the "truth" and her poor understanding of the Kabbalah (Herzel 57). Imber himself was hardly an expert. As Boaz Huss has argued, Imber "combin[ed] his first-hand knowledge of some Jewish kabbalistic texts with Western esoteric perceptions of the Kabbalah" (409). In an age of invented religions and spiritual philosophies, however, lack of expertise did not matter. In his aim to become a spiritual leader, Imber was cobbling together something he thought might appeal. Had he been successful (which he was not), any first-hand knowledge, however slight, would have enabled him to distinguish himself enough from Western adoptions of kabbalistic teachings to make him novel, while his borrowings of Western esoteric interpretations would have made his philosophy accessible to prospective followers seeking something at once new and familiar in their spiritual quest.[20]

Another eccentric European who sought to attract a following for his quasi-spiritual movement and exploited the little magazine to this end was Orlof N. Orlow, a "European philanthropist," head of the Orlow Institute and Society of Human Endeavour in San Francisco, and editor/publisher of *Atmos* ("Influence" 387).[21] In *Atmos*, Orlow brought together a range of fin-de-siècle trends popular with the upwardly mobile and wealthy audience he sought to attract, including New Thought, Theosophy, arts and crafts, communitarian living, and physical culture. Orlow's philosophy sought to "understand Life through the rational knowledge of natural Laws" and "to recognize a divine principle in man and in all creation" (front matter). Topics covered in the magazine and in institute talks included self-help, evolution, success, truth, natural remedies for disease, theories of colour in relation to mental and spiritual well-being, breathing, vibration, nerve theory, etc. Orlow's New Thought propensities were allied with an arts and crafts and communitarian ethos. His United Crafts and Arts Corporation, the name of which was strikingly similar to Gustav Stickley's United Crafts, emulated his more famous counterpart in selling handcrafted furniture and goods, while his magazine promoted the services of an artist, a gold and silversmith, a curio collector, and a wood carver ("Economics" 30–1). At the same time, he aspired to, though never achieved, the establishment of "schools, homes, settlements, and communities" founded on his principles in the manner of more successful counterparts like Elbert Hubbard (front matter).

Spiritual and arts and crafts philosophies were also often part of the politicized agenda of many little magazinists whose publications engaged robustly with reform, populism, socialism, anarchism, and Christian socialism in the Progressive Era. These magazines included *The Social Crusader*, *The Socialist Spirit*, *The Comrade*, *Ariel*, *New Occasions*, *The New Time*, *The Vanguard*, *The Challenge*, *Wilshire's*, and *The Whim*. Content included political commentary and literary content also, as many reformist and progressive little magazinists were missionary aesthetes who believed that literature and the arts could play an important role in social and political change. Little magazines were just a small part of a much wider range of activities on behalf of reform that these editors and contributors engaged in. These little magazinists were part of a large interconnected network of mostly middle-class and wealthy reformers. These socialistic movements, according to the Ehrenreichs, were the sites of some of the strongest professional-managerial class anti-capitalist ideology of the period (24). In terms of Christian social reform, for example, Peter J. Frederick claims there were at least one hundred such groups and he places reformer Ernest Crosby and popular poet Edwin Markham at the centre of efforts to coordinate these activities (187). Frederick's work does not discuss the role of little magazines in these efforts, though both Crosby and Markham were prolific in this domain. Crosby contributed across a range of little magazines and was editor of *The Whim*, a hybrid magazine that combined political commentary with literary content, while Markham's poetry and prose were widely published in these magazines. Other notable reformers who were involved with these publications included Eugene Debs (1855–1926), union leader, socialist political leader, and one-time presidential candidate; John Spargo (1876–1966), lecturer and editor of *The Comrade*, a socialist little magazine modelled after the values of Morrisian arts and crafts; George Herron (1862–1925), clergyman, college professor, and a leading figure in the social gospel movement that combined socialist and Christian principles; Leonard Abbott (1878–1953), radical, anarchist, free speech advocate, and editorial board member of *The Comrade* and *The Socialist Spirit*; F.H. Wentworth (1866–1954), editor of *The Social Crusader*, a Christian socialist publication, and its successor, *The Socialist Spirit*, which adopted a more secular approach; George

Littlefield (1863–?), Unitarian Minister and socialist, editor of the little magazine *Ariel*; Charles Kerr (1860–1944), radical editor/publisher of books and little magazines, including *New Occasions* and *The New Time*; Frederick Upham Adams (1859–1921), inventor, engineer, and editor of *New Occasions*; B.O. Flower (1858–1918), populist, reformer, and editor of *The New Time*; Gaylord Wilshire (1861–1927), millionaire socialist and real estate developer, editor of *The Challenge* and *Wilshire's*; and J.M.A. Spence, clergyman and editor of *The Vanguard*, a little magazine that, as it declared in its first number, promoted "rational religion," "scientific socialism," "practical psychology … [or] the New Thought," as well as physical health (qtd. in Cady 84). Spence's magazine, which also included literary content, demonstrates the degree to which broadly progressive interests in spirituality, politics, art, culture, and health and well-being often naturally overlapped in these periodicals. These figures, and many others connected with the various reformist, populist, and socialist causes, contributed across the range of these political-oriented magazines and other types of little magazines also.[22] Collectively, they represented the variety of ideological and political beliefs that characterized the many strains of socialistic thought of the period: from those that promoted collectivism and cooperation, to those that endorsed individualism and personal freedom; from those that were religious or spiritual in nature, to those that were atheistic.

Other important cultural contexts for the production of little magazines were the communitarian and cooperative colonies that arose in this period in relation to social, religious, and artistic movements and that comprised largely a professional middle-class and artisan class trying to escape the pressures of urban capitalist life. A number of these communities became sites of production for little magazines that promoted their aims, ideals, values, tastes, and lifestyles to a broader public. The most notable of these communities, in terms of a relationship to the little magazine movement, were arts and crafts colonies that also often produced and sold handicrafts, such as Rose Valley, Pennsylvania (founded 1901) and New Clairvaux, Massachusetts (founded 1902).[23] Horace Traubel, Whitman acolyte and admirer of Ruskin, founded Rose Valley with Will Price and Hawley McClanahan. Its participants included radical intellectuals, professionals, professors, and students. Its publication, *The Artsman*, promoted the arts and crafts ideology of subsistence production and cottage industry. In a similar project, Unitarian minister Edward Pearson Pressey (1869–1934) established New Clairvaux, from where he published *Country Time and Tide*, a magazine that endorsed reform and idealized a self-sufficient lifestyle and arts and crafts.

More famously, and on a larger scale than Rose Valley or New Clairvaux, Elbert Hubbard established the Roycroft Campus in East Aurora, New York. Unlike his more idealistic counterparts, Hubbard took a business-minded approach to his community, a factor that played a role in its success and longevity. The Roycroft campus was what Freeman Champney has called "quasi-communal" (64), and Hubbard, by some accounts, was more a "benevolent capitalis[t]" than the egalitarian socialist he claimed to be (Boris, *Art and Labor* 147). Hubbard owned the land but provided excellent working conditions for the Roycrofters, while bringing a communitarian feel to the enterprise through the provision of common meals, meetings, sports, studies, and a library (Champney 80). While the Roycrofters produced a range of books and goods, the magazines – *Little Journeys*, *The Philistine*, and *The Fra* – were key to the widespread proliferation of arts and crafts ideals, social reform, and radical social and political ideas in America in this period. Regardless of whether he was liked or hated, Hubbard could not be ignored and was, therefore, a continual reference point for those undertaking similar enterprises in communitarian living, arts and crafts colonies, and fine press book and magazine publication. Indeed, Roycroft attracted many aspiring littérateurs and little magazinists, who visited or joined for varying lengths of time. Among them were Walter Blackburn Harte, editor of *The Fly Leaf* and *The Lotus*, who was involved in an unsuccessful attempt to establish a partnership with Hubbard in the running of *The Philistine*; Michael Monahan, editor of *Papyrus*; Bliss Carman, poet and one-time editor of *The Chap-Book*; Richard Hovey, poet and contributor to *The Chap-Book*; Tudor Jenks, lawyer and prominent writer of books for children and general readers who contributed to numerous little magazines, including *Bradley His Book*, *Chips*, and *The New Bohemian*; and Frank B. Rae, a private pressman who was also associated with *The Blue Sky* and *The Bachelor Book* (Champney 67).

The little magazine, then, served an important function in promoting the interests of a vast array of literary, artistic, social, and political causes and movements that were central to the middle and professional classes of the period. Though circulations of little magazines were small in comparison with mass-market magazines and were rooted in quite personal or localized contexts, they did, indeed, consolidate and extend networks. The little magazine served as a print equivalent of the artistic, social, and political societies, clubs and organizations that many belonged to. It expanded their horizons, however, beyond the local, enabling readers to imagine themselves as part of a virtual community of like-minded souls in a national context. Little magazines explicitly sought to reinforce this virtual sense of community. Subscribers were often conceptualized as members of a club or society. One did not have to be physically present in East Aurora to be part of Hubbard's Roycroft Community, for example. From 1897 on, Hubbard advertised lifetime memberships to the "American Academy of Immortals" (see, for example, advertisement, *Philistine* 14, no. 1), which, for ten dollars, included a ninety-nine year subscription to *The Philistine* plus available back issues; a subscription to *Little Journeys*; other select Roycroft publications; attendance at the annual dinner; and "Success, Health and Love Vibrations sent daily by the Pastor [i.e., Hubbard] or Ali Baba." Hubbard's formula was imitated by other little magazinists. One-time Roycrofter, Michael Monahan, editor of *Papyrus*, established the Society of Papyrites along similar lines from 1905 on. Other little magazinists offered membership as a token gesture to all subscribers, as in the instance of doctor little magazinist George F. Butler's "How to Live" club (*Doctor's Magazine*, advertisement). Harold Llewellyn Swisher, meanwhile, following Hubbard's quirky style, labelled himself Chief and dubbed subscribers to his Morgantown, West Virginia based magazine "members of the Ghourki Tribe." In *Soundview*, a publication out of Olalla, Washington, L.E. Rader, a journalist and one-time populist member of the state legislature, and Frank T. Reid, lawyer and former judge, conceptualized their readers as "Evergreens," "men-not-afraid-of-an-idea (and women), whose prime object in life is to learn to think and think to learn, with a view to securing the greatest amount of truth, enjoying the greatest amount of happiness and doing the greatest good to the greatest number, for the greatest length of time possible" (Rader and Reid 1). These memberships represented virtual versions of the social and cultural clubs in which so many middle-class professionals took part in real life.

The transformations to middle-class culture effected by the rise of the professional-managerial class furnished the conditions for the emergence of the little magazine at the end of the nineteenth century. Key factors in its rise were the zeal for culture, self-culture, reform, self-development; self-expression, personality, and individuality; the reverence for print; the existence of many different kinds of societies, groups, and networks for the exchange of literary, artistic, and cultural interests;

and the availability of resources to express oneself through the written word. Created largely by and for members of, or aspirants to, the emerging professional-managerial class, little magazines represented a resistance to older genteel culture, expressing the values and ideals of a new cultural elite. While this chapter has focused on the little magazine's links to emerging and alternative forms of culture, the following one will consider how it was established as an alternative and distinctive print form by considering its position in a media context. Together, these factors combined to create a medium that Nancy Glazener has argued represented "an alternative kind of cultural capital" for its makers and readers (237).

CHAPTER 2

Print Revolutions and the Making of the Little Magazine

The craze for "fad magazines," ("fadazines," we called them) was at its high noon. It was in that miraculous year of our Lord, 1896, and whoever could get possession of a printing press in the United States was helping to burden the news-stands with monthly rubbish, filled with cheap satire and sententious pretension. Art was running amuck through Posterdom, Literature was staggering blindfold, in a drunken spree, and every dog was having his day in journalism.

– Gelett Burgess, *Bayside Bohemia* 25 (1954)

While the socio-cultural transformations of the era instilled in those of an emerging professional class the will to express themselves in print, a way to do so was provided with rapid developments of new media and technologies and the expansion of existing forms. The term "revolution" is one much, and controversially, used in relation to the history of media and communications.[1] It is frequently invoked, for example, in relation to the newly industrialized, mechanized, and democratized nineteenth- and early twentieth-century mass media landscape, which is said to have given rise to a quick succession of media revolutions. In the realm of print media alone, for example, scholars have identified a "magazine revolution," a "revolution in fine printing," and a "poster revolution."[2] The little magazine, as I shall outline, was connected to all these revolutions and, if we accept little magazinist Walter Blackburn Harte's view, it was a "literary revolution" in its own right also ("Little Revolt" 103).

What precisely does it mean to speak of print revolutions in the context of fin-de-siècle American culture? While certainly the technologies and new media were transformational, this study follows the approach of Adrian Johns and others who are interested in the "cultural history of print" as opposed to the "history of print culture" – emphasizing the uses to which print technologies and media were put by producers and consumers in galvanizing social and cultural change. As I have suggested in the previous chapter, print media in this period was central to the development and transformation of America's middle class, notably the rise of a young professional-managerial class that exploited a discourse of revolution and reform to distinguish itself from the previous generation and to promote its values and ideals as the dominant middle-class ethos. Central to this ethos were a commitment to self-culture and self-improvement, economic and social reform, and a cautious optimism about the positive role that a consumption- and commodity-oriented culture might play in realizing these ideals.

Scholarship on the revolutionary nature of the explosion of print media in this period has largely focused on mass-market magazines and their relationship to the development of middle-class consumer identity. Ohmann, for example, says of these magazines:

> They ... constituted a figurative yet very real cultural space homologous to the literal spaces that came more and more to define the [professional-managerial class's] understanding of itself and the world. Magazines circulated nationally to people with common values and interests; they entered similar homes everywhere, and were part of what made those homes similar. And of course magazines helped shape the values and interests of [professional-managerial class] people, including an interest in the brand named commodities advertised there. (*Selling Culture* 128)

These conditions also, however, enabled the emergence of another new kind of periodical, identified by Burgess as the "fad" magazine, "fadazine" (*Bayside Bohemia* 25) or, what is called in this book, the little magazine. The little magazine served a purpose similar to that of its mass-market counterpart for the professional class that was at the centre of these developments in media and of the transformations to middle-class identity. There were key differences between these kinds of publications, however. First, if mass-market magazines "shaped" the values and interests of professionals, little magazines enabled this class to take an active role as shapers themselves of their culture. They provided a means of self-expression for aspiring media professionals and for amateur writers and artists whose "professional" expertise may have lain elsewhere. Second, while mass-market magazines emphasized the "common" nature of the values and interests of their audiences, little magazines framed these as unique and distinctive in ways that were important for both makers and readers, especially in the context of the rise of the culture of personality. For makers, the little magazine was a highly individualized and, sometimes, personal form, important to a class that valued self-expression through the printed word. Indeed, the little magazine might be regarded as a natural outgrowth of the ethos and practices of scrapbooking and amateur journalism. This new print media landscape turned what had been private, amateur, and narrowly networked forms of personal media, reflective of a culture of character, into a public, semi-professional or professional mode in keeping with the evolving culture of personality. For readers, the little magazine was, as Glazener has suggested, an "alternative kind of cultural capital" (237), one that appealed both to their interests in self-culture and/or self-realization and to their desire for cultural distinction. If mass-market magazines enabled the mobilization of a professional-managerial class identity, little magazines gave voice to the interests of this class in individualism, personality, and self-realization and they did so in a more personalized and aesthetically distinctive nature than their mainstream counterparts.

The little magazine may have been a new and alternative form, but it did not emerge in a vacuum. In addition to its place within the broader magazine revolution, it was connected to two other print revolutions alluded to by Burgess: the revolution in fine printing and the poster revolution. This chapter provides an overview of the production contexts of little magazines with a focus on their positioning within these three print revolutions and their relationship to existing and emerging print media associated with these movements. It also considers how, through an engagement with other media forms, the little magazine developed a distinctive identity as a periodical genre characterized by particular features that constituted "little magazineness." Underlying the analysis are concepts from new media studies and textual scholarship. Dave Bolter and Jay Grusin's theories of remediation and Roger Fidler's related concept of mediamorphosis, for example, are helpful for considering the fluid relationship between print media forms. For Bolter and Grusin, there is no such thing as a new medium: "a medium," they argue "is that which remediates. It is that which appropriates the techniques, forms, and social significance of other media and attempts to rival or refashion them" (65). Roger Fidler, meanwhile, has coined the term "mediamorphosis" to describe a

> way of thinking about the technological evolution of communication media. Instead of studying each form separately, it encourages us to examine all forms as members of an interdependent system, and to note the similarities and relationships that exist among past, present, and emerging forms. By studying the communication system as a whole, we will see that new media do not arise spontaneously and independently. (23)

The emphasis that Bolter, Grusin, and Fidler place on the rivalrous, competitive, and interdependent aspects of relationships between media is fruitful for a consideration of how American little magazines of the 1890s derived cultural meaning and value. Through a remediation of other forms, the little magazine was established as a distinctive vehicle of communication in an ever-expanding media context. Bolter, Grusin, and Fidler acknowledge, too, however, the importance of other forces in shaping media – social, political, technical, material, economic, and so on – and the analysis in this chapter attends to these as and where necessary.

In foregrounding the little magazine's rootedness in the socio-cultural transformations in American middle-class life, however, this consideration of the media context attends with particular interest to social forces that Lisa Gitelman argues are often underemphasized in new media scholarship. She criticizes Bolter and Grusin, for example, for downplaying human agency, writing about media as though they are "intentional agents," who "purposefully refashion each other and do 'cultural work'" (9). This kind of critique was also launched, earlier in the history of media studies, against Marshall McLuhan's abstract formulation of media, notably by Raymond Williams, who insisted on understanding media as material social practice. My analysis highlights the importance of human agents and their socio-cultural context in the construction of meaning around media, while also considering materiality in another important sense as articulated in recent textual scholarship and book history. Jerome McGann's (*Textual Condition*) and George Bornstein's conceptions of "bibliographic" and "contextual" codes are central to understanding how the material embodiment and conditions surrounding the production and reception of texts generate meaning. This theory has been influential in recent magazine scholarship, which has developed a discipline-specific version of these key concepts in the notion of "periodical codes" (Brooker and Thacker, "General Introduction" 5–9). These codes include elements such as design, typeface, layout, format, binding, price, size, production and distribution contexts, illustration, etc. Implicit to the argument throughout this book is an insistence on the importance of bibliographic, contextual, and periodical codes in the media discussed, with a particular emphasis on how meaning is generated through a strategic and self-conscious exploitation of materiality on the part of little magazinists, but also, more generally, through production and reception contexts and associations with other print forms. Materiality, as explored in relation to little magazines, includes not only the form, or look, of the magazine, but also the "voice" that it projects through paratextual linguistic codes that play a role in making a first impression – notably, titles, subtitles, and mottoes.[3] The processes of mediamorphosis in which little magazinists were engaged as they remediated other forms of print to establish a characteristic look and voice for the little magazine, this chapter argues, informed, and were informed by, changing social and cultural dynamics. This engagement reveals as much about the position of little magazines within a changing media landscape as it does about the role of print culture in the social transformations of the period, namely the emergence of a professional-managerial class ethos in the age of progressivism and of a medium for the personal expression of that ethos.

The Magazine Beautiful and the Revolution in Fine Printing

Wherever we look today … a perfect race in the production of the best possible type and the most beautiful appearance of books has begun, which happily extends from the costliest to the cheapest. That it has extended to the latter, I consider … most promising … and important … Improve the taste and the understanding of the beautiful in the masses, and you create the groundwork for future improvement in every direction.

– Carl Edelheim, "The Kelmscott Press," *Modern Art* 4, no. 2, 39 (1896)

[The] judgement [of those interested in the revival of printing as a fine art] was a body of opinion by no means to be ignored. It carried no weight, to be sure, with the rank and file of the printing trade. It was in a sense a camp in opposition. It was, nevertheless, exerting a vigorous influence upon printing, the effect of which was already to be seen in the books of certain publishing firms and in the product of several commercial presses. It was recruited from outside the craft, from the ranks of students of design, from architects, artists and amateurs of printing.

– William A. Dwiggins, "D.B. Updike and the Merrymount Press," *Fleuron* 3, 2 (1924)

Though little magazines were periodical publications, their most important relationship, in many respects, was to books and book culture. Indeed, a number of these publications were direct products of what Susan Otis Thompson has called the "revolution in fine printing." This association of little magazines with fine press books and publications garnered significant cultural prestige for the genre. Inspired by the "revival" of fine printing in Britain led by William Morris, the "revolution" in fine printing was part of the larger zeal for arts and crafts in America. It was a "revolution" in America, rather than a "revival," because, as Susan Otis Thompson explains, in a nation where printing had been largely driven by utilitarian aims, there was no tradition to revive (1). The revolution manifested itself in a nationwide emergence of small presses and publishing houses dedicated to the production of beautiful books, usually reprints of classic nineteenth-century works, as well as those of the Pre-Raphaelite or aesthetic tradition. Though small in scale, these presses had, as Dwiggins points out, a significant influence on the commercial end of the printing and publishing industry, transforming the productions of jobbing presses and larger trade publishers (2). The small presses that were part of this movement must be distinguished from "private presses" in the strict sense of the term – i.e., non-commercial presses run by private individuals. They were invariably commercial enterprises to one extent or another, operated, however, on what John Carter has described as a "private press principle": "The fundamental principle of private press printing [is] that whether or not the press has to pay its way, the printer is more interested in making a good book than a fat profit. He prints what he likes, how he likes" (5). Like little magazines, then, these small presses were, as Edelheim and Dwiggins suggest, a product of the democratizing and reformist ideals of a late nineteenth-century professional ethos that sought to harmonize culture and commerce. Edelheim argues for the book beautiful, even in cheap form, as a force for moral, cultural, and social betterment for the masses. Dwiggins's comments, meanwhile, characterize the transformation of the printing trade in oppositional terms, as a change that comes about through rebellion from without – from the ranks of a younger, professionalized cadre whose efforts serve both art and commerce. These presses often produced publications in a variety of formats and at different price points to suit collectors of varying incomes.

If the emphasis in the revolution in fine printing was initially on books and achieving the ideal of what Thomas Cobden-Sanderson, a key exponent of the British revival of fine printing, called the "book beautiful" (William S. Peterson 281), magazines soon became a focus. That small presses and publishers should become interested in magazines is not surprising. There was already a precedent for this connection in the mainstream industry where major firms such as Harper and Scribner also published magazines. Magazines could perform an important function for small presses, enabling them to promote and feature content from their list. At the same time, the magazine format represented a perfect vehicle for experimentation with design. The revolution in fine printing would be instrumental in establishing a key feature of "little magazineness": an aesthetic appearance rooted in fine press and antiquarian print culture. Through its link with the revolution in fine printing and its remediation of the fine press book, the little magazine became a "magazine beautiful," accruing the status of a collectible print object at an affordable price for a class seeking to assert its distinction.

Those little magazinists who either operated in this realm or idealized the private press principle often explicitly asserted a relationship between their publications and fine book culture. They appropriated terms from this realm in titles, subtitles, and mottoes, for example. Many eschewed the term magazine, referring instead to their publications as books or booklets, as in *Bradley His Book*, *The Bachelor Book*, *The Black Book*, and *The Cornhill Booklet*. In addition, they employed terms from book design and/or manuscript and early print culture appealing to a bibliophilic sensibility, with titles such as *The Rubric*, *The Red Letter*, *The Fly Leaf*, *The Scroll*, *The Papyrus*, *The Goose-Quill*, *The Lotus*, *The Manuscript*, and *The Chap-Book*. This relationship between the little magazine and the book beautiful was further consolidated through the remediation of fine press book design and format. Notable features of the book beautiful in this period, as Susan Otis Thompson explains, were derived not only from Morris's arts and crafts style, but also from the aesthetic movement and art nouveau, sometimes in combination (10–15). These included handmade paper; plentiful white space; wide margins; deckle edges; uncut pages;

old-fashioned typefaces, especially Caslon, Jenson, and Gothic; rubrication and illuminated lettering; chiaroscuro effects; fleurons and other decorative ornaments, sparingly used; woodcuts and wood engravings; art nouveau style decoration and illustration; and a small chap-book or pamphlet size (see Figures 2.1–2.2).

This book aesthetic was adopted by little magazines of all types, whether produced by small presses or not. In the more commercial-minded spirit of the broader arts and crafts movement in America, little magazinists were not averse to exploiting new technologies to achieve the look of pre-industrial print objects. The magazine format, as has been said, allowed for experimentation, and little magazinists sought to rival each other in the production of ever more distinctive publications. Paper, for example, represented an important means of achieving distinction. Most little magazinists used machine-produced imitation laid paper. Stone and Kimball had one specially designed with a watermark of the publisher's imprint for *The Chap-Book* and their other publications (Kramer 209). Some little magazinists, however, especially those associated with small presses, preferred handmade paper. *Bibelot* publisher and editor, Thomas Mosher, for example, used handmade paper and was critical of Stone and Kimball, writing to Edmund Clarence Stedman in 1895, "I far prefer [my paper] to any machine made, wood-pulp imitation of a genuine deckle-edge hand made rag paper such as they use! Nor do I like their [*sic*] color of it, or the finish" (qtd. in Susan Otis Thompson 191). For his part, *The Chap-Book* editor was cattily critical of Mosher: "Mr. Mosher might to advantage use a better quality of paper" ("Notes," *Chap-Book* 2, no. 11, 446).[4] The fetish for novelty in paper could go to extremes. *The Ghourki*, for example, was printed on butcher paper, *The Lark* on bamboo paper (see Figure 2.3), and *Le Petit Journal des Refusées* on wallpaper (see colour plate 1). *Bradley His Book* and *Moods*, for their part, experimented with specially designed coated papers. Overall, arts and crafts, aesthetic, and art nouveau design elements borrowed from the fine press book helped little magazines transcend their ephemeral and lowly status as periodicals by aligning them with collectible print culture. As individual issues, little magazines resembled antiquarian forms of the chapbooks, booklets, and pamphlets that were much sought after by collectors (see colour plate 2). At the same time, attractive and fanciful publishers' bindings and casings meant that, when bound, the little magazine was equally collectible, taking on a decorative fine press book form (see, for example,

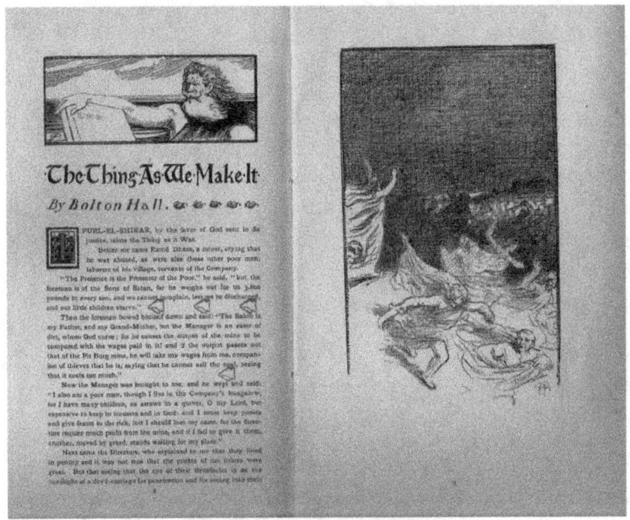

The Thing As We Make It

By Bolton Hall.

VOL. III THE CHAP-BOOK NO. II.

A BALLAD OF AN ARTIST'S WIFE

IN vain the war-worn nations sought
A means of peace; and folk in vain
By vote and party tumult thought
To re-establish Saturn's reign.

Yet still the gracious stars above
Gave audience to ancient rhymes;
For men and women fell in love
As deeply as in happier times.

"Sweet wife, this heavy-hearted age
Is nought to us; we two shall look
To Art, and fill a perfect page
In Life's ill-written Doomsday Book."

He wrought in colour; blood and brain
Gave fire and might; and beauty grew
And flowered with every magic stain
His passion on the canvas threw.

Figures 2.1–2.2 The fine press book aesthetic as adapted to little magazines. 2.1 Pages from *The Rubric*, October 1901, with design features inspired by the revolution in fine printing, including rubrication, decorated initial lettering, fine paper, and artistic typography. 2.2 Page from *The Chap-Book*, 15 October 1895, with decorative borders by Frank Hazenplug in arts and crafts style with rubricated initial letter and decorative features. Both items in possession of author.

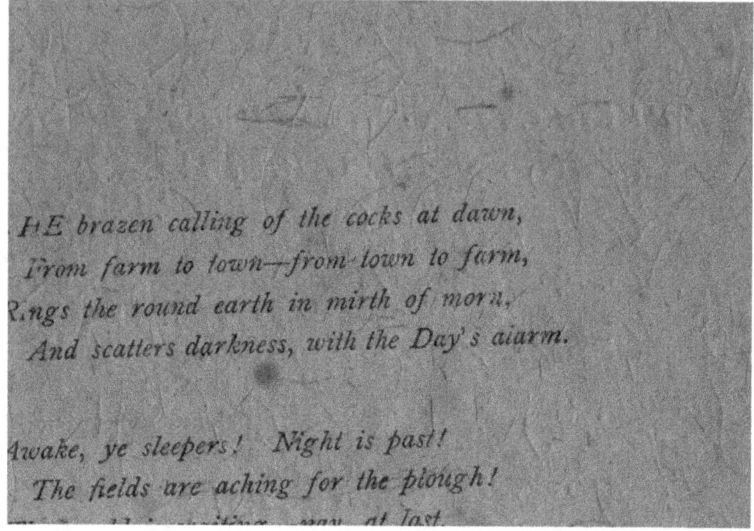

HE brazen calling of the cocks at dawn,
From farm to town—from town to farm,
Rings the round earth in mirth of morn,
And scatters darkness, with the Day's alarm.

Awake, ye sleepers! Night is past!
The fields are aching for the plough!

Figure 2.3 Bamboo paper used for *The Lark*, the graininess of which led to smashed type on the page. In possession of author.

Figure 3.5 and colour plate 11). Though this was a period in which even mainstream magazines were bound and collected by their readers, little magazines were far more attractive as artistic objects.

The most significant print media forms for the little magazine in relation to the fine press movement were undoubtedly the chap-book and the pamphlet. The term chap-book was adopted as a title by the most influential little magazine of the movement, used as a subtitle by *The Kit Bag*, and was often applied to the genre as a whole in this period. Many little magazines took a chap-book format, being small in both size and number of pages. This served to distinguish them physically from their mainstream magazine counterparts, but little magazinists also sought to appropriate the social and cultural significance of the chap-book in their remediation of the form. This significance, as Giles Bergel notes, was ambiguous in the period: on the one hand, the chapbook was a popular and populist form of cheap print of the hand press era; on the other, in the context of the 1890s, it was a term known to few beyond the rarified world of book collecting in which antiquarian chapbooks were highly prized (158). This ambiguity, however, is consonant with the contradictory ideals not only of little magazines but also of the professional-managerial ethos of the era, which were at once culturally elitist and populist.

If some little magazinists sought high cultural prestige and/or populist credentials through their remediation of the chap-book, others invoked the pamphlet for what they identified as its revolutionary significance. Walter Blackburn Harte, for example, aligned his periodical, *The Fly Leaf*, with this spirit, using the term pamphlet in his subtitles. Dubbing it variously as a "pamphlet periodical of the new" (covers for December 1895–February 1896) and a "pamphlet of the Century-end" (covers for March and April 1896), Harte saw his magazine, and the 1890s little magazine movement more generally, as part of a tradition of pamphlet literature as social protest. In an impassioned defence of the movement, he described the "pamphlet" as an historically radical form of print and a model for 1890s little magazines, "a form that has served the purposes of genius and freedom of thought and belief, when every door of court and church and school was barred with bars of gold and power to all non-conformists" ("Bubble and Squeak," *Lotus* 3, no. 2, 59). Given the role of the pamphlet during the American Revolution, when Tom Paine's *Common Sense* had been central to the promotion of independence and republicanism, the pamphlet form was particularly resonant in America, registering the kind of socially progressive and radical spirit that defined the little magazine and the ethos of its makers. This spirit was invoked particularly by periodicals of protest with their socially progressive and reformist aims.

The remediated chap-book and pamphlet formats of many of the little magazines of the period quickly came to serve as a defining feature of the genre, signifying "little magazineness." On the one hand, the features of, and associations with, fine book culture distinguished the little magazine from commercial, industrial, mass-produced, and aesthetically undistinguished counterparts such as *Harper's* (see Figures 2.4–2.5). On the other, the chap-book format, in particular, differentiated it from its European counterparts. American little magazines, it is true, had much in common with their European counterparts, including *The Yellow Book*, *Savoy*, *The Century Guild Hobby Horse*, *La Plume*, *Le Mercure de France*, and *La Revue Blanche*. They shared an interest in aesthetic, decadent, and symbolist literature, art, and the graphic arts. In format, however, the American publications were distinctive for their strong association with the chap-book and pamphlet as against European little magazines that generally adopted a quarto, tabloid, or book format. Overall, the situating of little magazines of the 1890s in

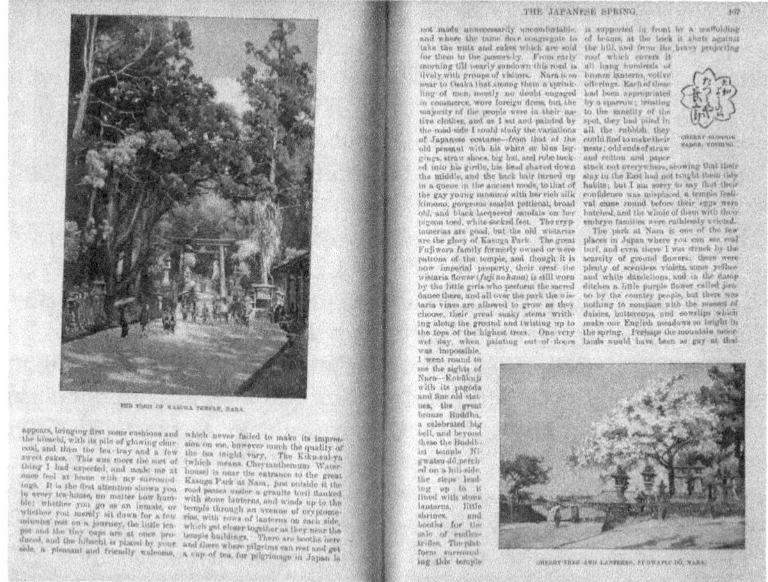

Figures 2.4–2.5 *Harper's*, June 1894, with generic monthly cover (2.4) and interior layout (2.5). In possession of author.

relation to book and book collecting culture distinguished them in the realm of mainstream and avant-garde transatlantic print culture, making them attractive to an emerging intellectual and professional-managerial middle class seeking distinction through an alternative form of cultural capital.

The influence of the fine press book aesthetic on little magazines was a clear consequence of their rootedness in the industry. Small presses and related enterprises were key sites of production for little magazines, and it is important to consider this socio-cultural context in more detail in order to understand the mutually beneficial nature of the mediamorphic relationship between the fine press and little magazine movement. The most successful and well-known titles emerged directly from this context and had an influence on how the genre, as a whole, was received. These magazines were the products of small presses or, alternatively, of "literary publishers," Susan Otis Thompson's term for "amateur bookmen" who engaged in trade publishing, but with a dedicated interest in the production of aesthetically pleasing books (38). A notable example of a small-press produced little magazine is *The Philistine*, issued from Hubbard's arts and crafts Roycroft community, the heart of which was its printing and publishing business. Lesser-known presses that produced little magazines and are noteworthy for attractive productions are the Philosopher Press of Wausau, Wisconsin (see Figure 2.6), and the Blue Sky Press of Chicago, both of which issued eponymously titled little magazines alongside a sizable list of attractively designed books.[5]

An extreme example of the small press issuer of a little magazine, one that exhibits the ideals of the private press in a purist sense, is George Gough Booth's Cranbrook Press. Booth was a newspaperman and his press was, effectively, an expensive hobby. His print shop, designed after the manner of Plantin and Gutenberg, was situated in the attic of his Detroit newspaper office (see Figure 2.7). From it, he produced *The Cranbrook Papers*, a highly elaborate publication printed on a Franklin hand press on handmade paper, using stocks of old-style types – Jenson and Satanick – and featuring hand illumination of letters and decorations (Susan Otis Thompson 200–2; Cave 160–1; Arthur Pound 251–8). *The Cranbrook Papers* was, however, exceptional within the field, its elaborate and expensive production not in keeping with the more entrepreneurial and democratic spirit of the movement.

Significant literary publishers of the day, meanwhile, whose publications included magazines and books, were Thomas Mosher, who

Figure 2.6 The print shop of the Philosopher Press (Wausau, Wisconsin), with Helen Bruneau Van Vechten, one of the most successful female fine press printers of the day, noted for her technical innovation of perfectly registering print on both sides of deckle-edged paper. The print shop is decorated with magazine poster art. Courtesy of Marathon County Historical Society, Wausau, WI.

issued *The Bibelot*, and Stone and Kimball, of *Chap-Book* fame. These publishers were inspired by the latest developments in the revolution in fine printing, but hired this work out to others. Together, these small presses and literary publishers participated in the transformations to book design celebrated by Dwiggins. All came from outside the industry, bringing an amateur interest in printing or other knowledges – including training in architecture, art, and design – to the field. Indeed, some came to the work with no apprentice experience in a print shop. At the same time, these figures played a major role in

Figure 2.7 Cranbrook Press Room, June 1906. Unidentified photographer. Center for Creative Studies records, 1906–82. Courtesy of Archives of American Art, Smithsonian Institution.

elevating printing from its working-class associations as a trade for "labor-aristocrats" to a professional and more artistic status. The printers, in particular, distinguished their work from the "rank and file of the printing trade," as Dwiggins called it, by claiming specialized knowledge of printing *as an art* to publish luxury, collectible print objects (2).[6] Their status was further enhanced by their ownership of small businesses and by their additional role as publishers (a gentlemanly pursuit). Print media here is, in Raymond Williams's sense, social practice. The transformation to the medium of the book and fine press print is a consequence of new skills, techniques, codes, and conventions being brought to the trade, resulting in its embourgeoisement.

In their publications, these presses and publishers catered to a book collecting market and to those interested in self-culture through reading. They cultivated an appreciation for the physical format of print material as well as its content, seeking to put "beautiful" publications of "literary distinction … within reach of those who appreciate beauty but cannot possess it at exorbitant prices" (Blumenthal 42). Literary distinction, in this context, meant the reprinting of classic nineteenth-century works as well as those that were part of the Pre-Raphaelite or aesthetic tradition. Small press favourites of the period included *The Rubáiyát of Omar Khayyám* (see, for example, colour plate 3), a work popularized through the translations of Edward FitzGerald,[7] as well as the works of writers including Robert Browning and Elizabeth Barrett Browning, Algernon Charles Swinburne, Alfred Tennyson, John Keats, William Morris, Dante Gabriel Rossetti, George Meredith, Walter Pater, Ralph Waldo Emerson, and others. Some presses might also issue works by contemporary writers. Regional presses, for example, published works by local writers, while larger firms, such as Stone and Kimball, published high-profile figures associated with symbolism and decadence, including Oscar Wilde, Maurice Maeterlinck, and Paul Verlaine. The little magazines issued by these presses complemented their publishing lists, featuring work by, about, or related to, the authors of their book publications.

Literary publishers who did not do their own printing, such as Mosher and Stone and Kimball, were able to produce beautifully designed publications because the influence of the revolution in fine printing extended beyond small presses to other kinds of printers. It was this pervasive influence across the general industry that accounts for the prolific nature of the little magazine in this period in America in comparison with smaller European manifestations of the movement. Thus, while small presses produced some of the most distinctive little magazines and their aesthetic defined the genre, many of these publications were actually issued from general printers and jobbing shops that existed in cities and towns across the nation. These shops occupied the more commercial end of the field. They had more kinds of printing equipment, old and new, and were the most versatile of printers. As Michael Winship argues, jobbing printers were less susceptible than newspaper or book printers to the incursions of new machines, which, because more specialized, were often far less versatile than the old (47). Thus, even print shops with the most up-to-date equipment might use older equipment if, for example, quality rather than quantity was preferred. For those who could not afford to establish an arts and crafts small press, general printers or jobbing shops were a means to publication. At the same time, a number of jobbing shop proprietors issued little magazines alongside broader profit-making ventures: for-hire publications of autobiographical material; memoirs; family history; genealogies; literary works; and various kinds of printing for universities, libraries, churches, and businesses (Lehmann-Haupt et al. 267). Howard Llewellyn Swisher's Acme Publishing Company, for example, was a Morgantown, West Virginia jobbing print shop and bindery worth $50,000 that employed between twenty-five and fifty people and issued his little magazine, *The Ghourki*, alongside more general printing work ([Swisher], "Harangues," *Ghourki* 2, no. 11, 2; Chief's Print Shop, advertisement).

As Susan Otis Thompson notes, little magazines were, in fact, instrumental to the growth of jobbing shops in the 1890s that catered specifically to interests in artistic printing (205). The little magazine phenomenon, then, played a role in extending fine press principles to commercial realms of print and to those of the professional and middle classes who might use the services of jobbing presses that offered printing of pictorial art of various kinds, including books, artistic advertising, posters, broadsides, bookplates, and vanity publications (205). Examples of this type of press include the Corell Press of New York and the Jenson Press of Philadelphia. The Corell Press, which published the little magazine *John-a-Dreams*, notable as a venue for the early work of Booth Tarkington, was established by two self-taught amateur printing enthusiasts whose mission was to provide "a better class of commercial printing and advertising work" (W.J.K. 416). The Jenson Press, meanwhile, which issued *Moods*, was less commercially oriented than Corell. It advertised itself as "Makers of Unique

Volumes," able to design, print, and publish private editions or works out of print and offering design services for illustrations, cover pages, bookplates, prospectuses, posters, bookmarks, etc. (Jenson Press, "To Authors, Publishers, and Bibliophiles").

Little magazines were also important for developments in amateur printing, though they themselves might be regarded as an outgrowth of this earlier form. Both were vehicles of self-expression, the little magazine representing a more professionalized and artistic form than the amateur journal. Strangely, Susan Otis Thompson discounts the amateur press in her otherwise thorough account of the revolution in fine printing on the basis that, as opposed to "'artistic' private presses," it is "more concerned with content than form" (5). Amateur press historian Sean Donnelly, however, has documented the influence of the fine press movement on amateur journals of the 1890s and early 1900s, noting that dozens of them reflect the aesthetic ideals of the revolution in fine printing (9).[8] A notable example is "the rubricated old cloister edition" of *The Torpedo* (6, no. 3) for February 1907 (see colour plate 4), produced by Frank Austin Kendall (d. 1913) and done after the style of medieval illuminated manuscripts. Kendall's magazine, which he struggled to issue with any kind of regularity, required 40,000 impressions to produce two hundred copies, as each colour required a separate impression ("Short Stories" 6).[9] In addition, of course, to being inspired by the fine press movement more generally, amateur publications were also notably influenced by the little magazines that emerged in this period. The transformations to amateur journals are indicative of the interrelationship between forms of media in mediamorphosis. While little magazines developed from amateur journals, these in turn adapted elements of little magazines. While it would be misleading to categorize all amateur and school publications, which have their own specific histories and contexts, as little magazines, it is important to identify those which self-consciously position themselves in this realm. The amateur publications relevant for the history of little magazines of this period are those that self-identify as such through references, in their pages, to little magazines; those which move beyond an exchange system to subscription and/or newsstand distribution; and those that register the influence of the little magazine movement in their aesthetic appearance. Timothy Burr Thrift's (1883–1947) *Lucky Dog* is a good example. Thrift, a National Amateur Press Association member, began his publication as an amateur journal for exchange, eventually developing it into a subscription and newsstand magazine with a circulation of 5,000 copies (Marjorie Wilson). It has the chap-book format and aesthetic appearance of the little magazine and references other little magazines in its content. Like *Lucky Dog*, *The Clique* of Maywood, Illinois, was a product of National Amateur Press Association members who aspired to circulate their self-printed and published magazine nationally and internationally (front matter [2]). Its format, poster aesthetic, and literary content are highly characteristic of *The Chap-Book* and other aesthetic little magazines (see colour plate 5).

The widespread existence of general and specialist jobbing shops that printed little magazines meant that aspiring little magazinists did not literally need to "get possession of a printing press," as Burgess said, to issue publications (*Bayside Bohemia* 25). Affordable printing services were available to those who wanted to see themselves in print in an attractive format but had no particular interest in printing. The revolution in fine printing that asserted itself across all aspects of the trade enabled the rise of the amateur or self-publisher as an important figure in the little magazine movement. While Susan Otis Thompson characterizes literary publishers such as Stone and Kimball as amateurs in the sense of "amateur bookmen" (38), amateur publishing manifested itself in the movement in two other contexts. First, the little magazine was exploited as a medium by amateur publishers in the sense of "organization[s] whose primary purpose is other than publishing," such as art galleries, museums, schools, sporting clubs, genealogical or historical societies, etc. (Mackenzie 21). While it is true that artistic, social, and political organizations issued periodicals earlier in the era, the 1890s little magazine vogue drew broader attention to some of these publications, notably those that reflected the kind of progressive, reformist, or idiosyncratic subject matter that was associated with the little magazine. Examples of these kinds of institutional amateur publications that appear in Faxon include *The Lincoln House Review*, an organ of the settlement house movement, and *The American Cooperative News*, one of the few print resources for what was a fairly scattered movement in America at this time. The "little magazineness" of these publications, which can be classed as "periodicals of protest," lies primarily in their interest in progressivism and socialism and their inclusion of relevant types of literary content.

A much more characteristic instance of amateur or self-publishing within the movement, however, was the individual, rather than organization, whose primary purpose (or means of living) is not publishing

– i.e., whose publishing enterprise is a hobby or amateur pursuit, possibly linked to one's professional life. Germane here are the doctor little magazinists discussed in chapter 1. Another notable example is William S. Lord, owner of a large dry goods store in Evanston, Illinois, and publisher, in conjunction with Plymouth Press, of *Noon*, a belletristic magazine after the manner of Mosher's *Bibelot*, and two little magazine parodies, *The Book Booster* and *The Bilioustine*. Other kinds of amateurs in the little magazine world were those with no previous publishing experience, but who had aspirations to professional literary or artistic careers. Not having to focus on the labour of printing meant that these little magazinists could devote themselves to developing the quality of the content of their magazines and to building circulations. There are a number of highly impressive little magazines emerging from the ranks of amateurs that sit well alongside top publications like *The Chap-Book* and those of the small presses. The high-school based *Little Chap*, later *Chapters*, for example, modelled after *The Chap-Book*, is comparable, aesthetically, to its more professional counterpart and does not stand out as particularly "amateurish" in comparison with many of the other little magazines in the field. An even more striking example, however, is *The Muse*, a magazine issued by teenagers from the thriving Jewish community in Oakland, California. *The Muse* is impressive for the quality of its production and content. The product of well-heeled young persons, *The Muse* was conceptualized as a magazine "to foster a true appreciation of Art and Letters, and to bring together in a pleasing form, choice bits from both, for the delectation of its readers" (Shirk, "Musings" 27). At the same time, however, the ambitious editorial team (which included an editor, managing editor, two associate editors, and two art editors) attracted a larger amount of advertising than was usual for a little magazine – between eight and twelve pages – and the magazine circulated nationally, offered by subscription or through newsstands across the country. Though printed by a local jobbing printer advertised in its pages as doing "legal work," "brief work," "commercial work," and "society printing" (Baker Printing Co.), *The Muse* is strongly characterized by the bibliophilic interest in typography, design, illustration, and layout that marked so many little magazines of the period, including tipped in, hand-coloured prints, which may have been printed elsewhere by the contributors. The ambitions of the founders of *The Muse* speak at once to the high cultural and commercial spirit that broadly characterized the little magazine and related arts and crafts movement in America.

Ultimately, the revolution in fine printing was instrumental in the development of the American little magazine of the 1890s. First, as a form of print media, the little magazine was indebted to the aesthetics associated with fine press publishing in this period, which accrued for it a high degree of cultural capital. It derived signature features of "little magazineness" from this realm, notably its chap-book and pamphlet formats and its typographic and design features. Second, in practical terms, the small presses that emerged served as some of the most important sites of production for little magazines. Third, the widespread influence of the fine press principle led to the emergence of other notable sites of production for little magazines in the way of amateur journalism, general printing, and jobbing presses. Finally, the consequence of this proliferation of fine press principles was the rise of amateur or self-publishers who constituted a significant proportion of little magazinists. In broader cultural terms, as one aspect of the revolution in fine printing, the little magazine was part of a movement that was transforming printing from craft to art through an influx of professionalized experts in other domains. At the same time, it played a role in providing a means of self-culture and distinction for an emerging professionalized and culturally aspiring middle class.

Art *and* Advertisement: Little Magazines and the Poster Revolution

> The people who still scoff at posters and poster collecting ... should bear in mind ... that the great periods of art were those in which it allied itself most intimately with the daily life of the people, and that in this craze for posters, "the poor man's picture art gallery" as they are called, is seen almost the first sign of a renaissance in which the spirit of the century, which is so largely a commercial one, will find an utterance in beauty instead of ugliness.
>
> – Claude F. Bragdon, qtd. in Singleton, "In this Dusk," *Poster Lore* 1, no. 1, 24 (1896)

If little magazines derived cultural capital from their remediation of old forms of print media and their connections to the revolution in fine printing, they also benefitted from an association with new art forms. In particular, the little magazine was associated with the artistic advertising poster, a medium that also owed its rise to new printing technologies. Also sometimes conceived as a revolution, the transatlantic poster movement was contemporaneous with, and connected to, the revolution in fine printing, the magazine revolution, and the rise of the little magazine.[10] As Bragdon's remarks suggest, the poster, like the fine press book, was seen as a force for the democratization of culture, reflecting, again, the ethos of a class that was seeking to align its cultural aspirations with its materialistic interests.

The poster that emerged in this period was a graphic manifestation of many of the same artistic and literary movements that fuelled the revolution in fine printing.[11] It drew inspiration from arts and crafts, aestheticism, art nouveau, French rococo, Celtic medieval art, Byzantine art, and Japanese prints and woodblocks (Margolin 15). The movement originated in France where, through the latter part of the nineteenth century, artists such as Jules Chéret sought to improve commercial design and pictorial advertising. In America, the movement was slower to take hold because posters were regarded merely as an advertising tool by most lithographers, who sought photographic fidelity rather than artistry in their work (Margolin 9, 23). By the 1890s, however, the movement in Europe had grown considerably and Americans began to take notice of Chéret, Eugène Grasset, Georges Meunier, Aubrey Beardsley, Théophile Alexandre Steinlen, Henri de Toulouse-Lautrec, Alphonse Mucha, and others whose advertising posters were highly regarded as works of art (see colour plate 6 and Figure 2.8). Soon, America developed its own school of poster artists, who designed for and contributed artistic content to mainstream and little magazines. Notable figures included Edward Penfield, J.C. Leyendecker, Frank Leyendecker, Will Bradley, Will Carqueville, Frank Hazenplug, Maxfield Parrish, Louis Rhead, and Ethel Reed (see Figures 6.5 and 6.6, and colour plates 7, 9, 13, 14, and 18). At the same time, the printing of posters became specialized and an increasing number of printers began to focus on lithography (Margolin 21). American poster artists generally offered tamer representations of subjects than their European counterparts, either out of a sense of what was acceptable to the American public or based on their own tastes. Rhead, for example, found Chéret's work "invariably commonplace and often lewd" (qtd. in [Clemens]). The "poster girls" depicted by American artists sat somewhere between the iconic and idealized American Gibson girl (see Figure 2.9) and the racier ladies of Chéret and other European poster artists (see colour plate 6).

In their marriage of art and commerce, posters were understandably popular in a nation characterized, on the one hand, by a drive to acquire culture and cultural capital and, on the other, a materialistic

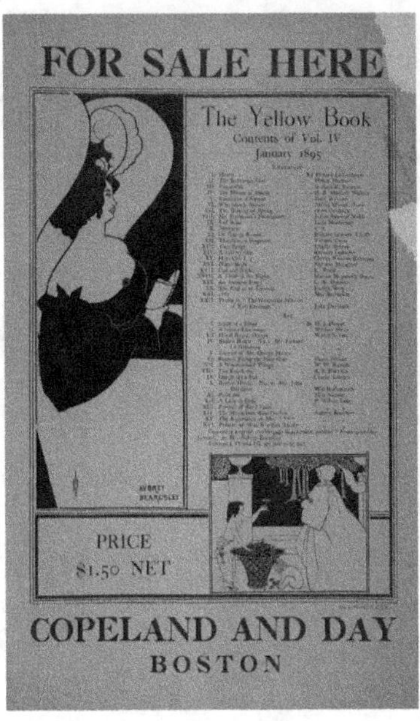

Figure 2.8 American advertising poster for *The Yellow Book* and its American publisher, Copeland and Day. Aubrey Beardsley. "*The Yellow Book*," 1895. Art & Architecture Collection, Miriam and Ira D. Wallach Division of Art, Prints and Photographs, New York Public Library, Astor, Lenox and Tilden Foundations.

and commercial spirit. Like the books produced in the context of the revolution in fine printing, posters were collected by those of a class eager to assert its cultural distinction and modern taste. Coinciding with the rise of an American school of poster artists was a collecting frenzy that rivaled the medium's popularity in Europe (Neil Harris, "American Poster" 13). Poster mania exhibited itself in a variety of ways. Magazines featured articles on posters and poster art; periodicals and books devoted to posters and poster collecting emerged; poster exhibitions were held; poster design contests were sponsored by magazines and organizations; parties with people dressed as their favourite poster personality were a popular fad; the bold colours used in this medium influenced women's fashion; and poems, songs, stories, and plays on poster themes abounded (Neil Harris, "American Poster" 16, 17; Margolin 21).

Figure 2.9 The Gibson girl. Charles Dana Gibson. "Eleanor." Postcard. Detroit Publishing Co., 1901. In possession of author.

The poster movement, however, was not without controversy. As in the printing trade, there was a tension between the artisanal practices of the old school of bill posters and lithographers and young upstarts with an interest in turning craft into art. As Michèle Bogart claims, traditional designers and lithographers "resented" the "introduction of new, costlier processes and standards" that art posters required and "were … put off by the air of snobbery surrounding" the medium (85). Critics claimed they were bad advertising *and* bad art. Charles Austin Bates, for example, an advertising agent of the day, felt that the privileging of image over word in the art poster was detrimental to its effect as an advertising vehicle:

> A poster will be a poster when it ceases to be simply an artistic freak, and becomes a businesslike production … An advertisement that does

> not tell facts about the article advertised isn't an advertisement. It isn't even a good sign. I don't care if it's the work of Chéret or Grasset. It may be ever so artistic, but it doesn't advertise to the masses. It doesn't even advertise to the classes, save to the few who are interested in the collection fad. (115–16)

An editorial in *Billboard Advertising* in 1895, meanwhile, attacked, in equal terms, the art poster's claims to high artistic status: "The [art poster's] further encroachment upon the domain of legitimate art should be promptly and effectually terminated. It is no longer original, no longer effective, no longer anything but utterly wearisome and monotonous" (qtd. in Bogart 87).

For the cultural industry, however, book and magazine publishers in particular, the art poster seemed an ideal vehicle to appeal to the "sophisticated tastes and aspirations" of a new, emerging professional-managerial class (Bogart 82). Consequently, publishers "promoted posters as a new art, as collectibles, and as a means to beautify cities" (Bogart 82). The association of publishing with the art poster began in 1889 when Harper's commissioned Grasset to produce a cover and a poster for a holiday issue of their magazine. Over the next few years, Grasset, and soon Rhead, produced posters for mainstream magazines (Johnson 172). The practice emerged with particular force in 1893 when Penfield was commissioned to design monthly posters for *Harper's*. His posters were so popular that often more were printed than copies of the magazine itself (Johnson 172).

The little magazine and poster movements peaked at the same time, were mutually beneficial, and equally short-lived. Little magazine publishers engaged aspiring artists and illustrators to design posters. Posters served, quite literally, as advertisements for these publications, but little magazinists also benefitted financially from posters. Many aesthetic little magazines generated income by selling specially designed posters, costing from twenty-five cents to a dollar, a price substantially more than the magazine itself. For Stone and Kimball, the selling of posters became a significant source of income (Kramer 36–7). Little magazines, for their part, functioned, in some degree, as an advertisement for posters. They were said, for example, to have "made a fad of artistic posters" in their promotion of the movement (Pollard, "In Eighteen Ninety-Five" 172). Notably, what was referred to at the time as the "poster style" – later to be called art nouveau (Sloan) – was, alongside the arts and crafts style, a key signifier of "little magazineness." In this sense, the poster movement bore an even more intimate relationship with little magazines than it did with mainstream magazines.

Little magazines exploited the poster not only as advertisement, but also for content. They contained art and illustration in the poster style and often offered free posters as an enticement to subscribers. At the same time, the poster became a prominent theme in essays on the movement and its figures, and was widely taken up as a topic in the fiction and poetry of magazines. Two little magazines specifically devoted to posters were produced – *The Poster* and *Poster Lore*. Another magazine, *The Echo*, out of Chicago, and later New York, featured beautiful poster covers, in colour, and reported on and reprinted works from illustrated magazines in Europe and America. By far the most significant aspect of the mediamorphic relationship between the little magazine and the poster was the remediation of poster art as covers for little magazines. Little magazines were innovators in the now standard industry practice of issuing changing monthly illustrated covers (Finlay 48). Pioneered by Will Bradley in his design of twelve poster-style covers for the trade journal the *Inland Printer* (Thomson, *Origins* 42), the practice soon spread to little magazines, whose creators recognized that the visual appeal of poster-style covers would make their publications stand out on the newsstands and in the bookstores where they were sold. This practice blurred the distinctions between the two media. Little magazines looked like posters and vice versa (see colour plates 8 and 9). Which medium was art? Which was advertisement? Both media, ultimately, were positioned between high and popular culture, art and commerce, promoting the democratization of culture through affordable and collectible print objects.

At the height of the popularity of these movements, posters and little magazines became linked in the public mind, driving the fad and the zeal for collecting of both. The use of the poster as advertisement for books and magazines, however, soon lost favour. Nancy Finlay has argued that the collectible status of posters as art undermined their ability to function as advertising (51–2). Posters stole the thunder of the products they advertised. In 1901, *The New York Tribune* reported the demise of the poster as an advertising medium for magazines, declaring that many people "did not think of buying the magazine advertised; they only wanted the poster" (qtd. in Finlay 51). Posters sold posters, not magazines. Increasingly, Finlay argues, publishers exploited poster effects for their books and magazines, hiring illustrators to create poster-like covers and designs (50–3), so that, in effect, they became their own advertisements. These publishers may well have taken their cue from the little magazines that had paved the way in their appropriation of the poster-style aesthetic for their publications.

As with their relationship to the revolution in fine printing, little magazines derived a key feature of "little magazineness" from their link to the poster movement. Again, this was in the way of aesthetic appearance and graphic design. The cultural value that little magazines accrued from this connection, however, was different. Where many of the publications most strongly associated with the fine press movement were belletristic in tendency, tied to a genteel tradition of self-culture, refined taste, and private cultural pursuits, those aligned with the poster movement were more of the moment. In contrast with the fine press movement, the aesthetic of which was largely defined by the past, the poster signified the modern, the brash, the risqué, and was associated with public spectacle and display (Iskin 259). If fine press publishing renounced or sought to efface signs of the commercial and industrial, posters self-consciously "bridged the separation between art and commerce," as one commentator of the era said ([Bowles]). Little magazines that exploited the poster aesthetic, then, were more consciously appealing to the interests of a class optimistic about the relationship between culture and commerce and increasingly invested in a public-facing culture of personality over a more private culture of character.

Little Magazines in a Big Market: The Magazine Revolution

> There is no reason on earth why wit and wisdom and fancy are not as good in a small and handy pamphlet as in a bulky literary sandwich magazine – of 136 pages of dubiously varied matter and 1,000 pages of "ads."
>
> – Walter Blackburn Harte, "Bubble and Squeak," *Lotus* 2, no. 8, 298 (1896)

From its association with the chap-book and pamphlet formats and the aesthetics of the fine press movement, the little magazine accrued symbolic capital as a high cultural and socially rebellious print medium. Its link to the artistic poster, meanwhile, was symbolic of spectacle, display, and the culture of personality. Ultimately, however, the little magazine was neither book nor poster, but was a magazine, circulating alongside countless others on the newsstands in a period that witnessed an explosion of periodical print. Whatever its origins or the ideals of its creators, it became, on the newsstand, part of an increasingly commercialized and industrialized context brought about by what Mott and other magazine scholars have dubbed the "magazine revolution" (Mott, "Magazine Revolution"; Ohmann, *Selling Culture*; Schneirov). Little magazines bore a complex relationship to this revolution and to popular periodical print, namely the emerging mass-market magazine, existing genteel magazines, and, to some extent, the newspaper. They were at once a part of, and a reaction against, popular magazines, situated between interests in the *art* that linked them to the fine printing and poster movements and the *commerce* that drove the periodical press.

The little magazines of the 1890s were a small part of a much larger expansion of the field brought about by an increasing demand for print; developments in printing technology, such as the introduction of the rotary press, the linotype machine, and the halftone photoengraving process; advances in distribution, including the growth of railway lines, cheaper postal rates, and the spread of newsstands; the lowering of magazine prices enabled by the development of national advertising; increased literacy rates; and, most significantly, the establishment of a new economic basis for production – advertising.[12] The turn to an advertising-based rather than subscription-based revenue model enabled enterprising magazine publishers, such as pioneer Frank Munsey, to offer a high-quality general monthly magazine at the inexpensive price of ten cents where, traditionally, such magazines cost twenty-five to thirty-five cents. Revolutionary in industry terms, the ten-cent magazine was also represented as a cultural revolt. As Munsey put it, the "smash[ing] down" of the price of the general magazine "to a popular figure" was also a "smash[ing] down of conventionality in magazine-making" (434). This conventionality characterized the traditional genteel magazines of the era, notably *Scribner's*, *Harper's*, *Century*, and *The Atlantic Monthly*. Upstarts such as *Munsey's*, *Cosmopolitan*, and *McClure's* challenged the perceived stodginess of these periodicals, Munsey said, with "a new type of magazine, a magazine of human interest, a magazine giving the people what they wanted ... instead of giving them ... what they ... thought the people should have" (434).

Lured by the promise of financial reward, many players entered the field. The number of magazines soared, as did circulations. In 1885, there were only about 3,300 magazines in the United States, but between that year and 1890, 1,000 new ones emerged. In the twenty-year period between 1885 and 1905, 11,000 magazines were issued. Of these, 7,500 were newly created. At any given time in the 1890s there might be between 4,400 and 5,500 titles available. If sales of 100,000 had seemed large in the 1880s, by 1895 circulations of half a million were being achieved by leading periodicals, reaching a million just after the turn of the century. While there was much to be gained financially in magazines, they required an investment of money and time to make them successful. At least half, in this period, were not. Between 1885 and 1905, about one in every two magazines issued was discontinued or merged.

Though the advent of national advertising represented unprecedented opportunities for profit, successful magazines were expensive to produce, factoring in the costs of content, production, and distribution. Frank H. Scott of the *New York Tribune* estimated that an issue of a popular monthly mainstream magazine cost $10,000 for contributions alone (qtd. in Mott, *History* 15). Editors of major magazines commanded between $100 and $200 per week, amounting to $5,000 to $10,000 a year (Sedgwick 414). "Star" authors could earn significant sums for magazine work in this period – over $10,000 for a serial in some cases (Sedgwick 419). The situation was even better for star illustrators who were generally paid twice as much as writers (Sedgwick 408). For the majority of writers, however, such work was less remunerative. Quality publications paid up to $10 a page or ¾¢ per word, popular mass-markets paid half as much, and some magazines paid as low as ½¢ per word (Mott, *History* 39). Poetry garnered a somewhat better pay rate – 25¢ a line might be expected (Mott, *History* 40). While a hard-working magazinist, one willing to publish in newspapers also, might earn between $750 and $1000, the equivalent of the salary of a clerical worker or federal employee, most earned closer to a working-class than a professional wage (Sedgwick 422, 424). Meanwhile, just as "star" illustrators could earn more than "star" authors, so too could their workaday counterparts. A young illustrator might expect to make $5 to $8 dollars a week, while more established artists might earn $25 a week (Beegan 140).

Printing and distribution costs represented further expenses. In terms of printing, improvements in technology such as the development of the rotary press, stereotype engraving, and photoengraving, brought costs down and made larger print runs and design innovations possible. Rotary presses, employed by many of the mass-circulation periodicals, resulted in a production time ten times faster than flatbed presses. Major periodicals often ran their own printing plants, updated with the latest technologies. Large print shops such as these used mass-production techniques – assembly lines, conveyer systems, and timed production scheduling – producing as many as 25,000 copies per day (Waller-Zuckerman 724). Distribution was similarly oriented to mass production, monopolized by the American News Company and its agencies across the country, which took a chunk representing half the price of the magazine from revenue derived from newsstand sales (Waller-Zuckerman 745–6; Mott, *History* 18–19). Under this system, subscription sales were obviously preferred and magazines conventionally passed on savings to subscribers, charging $1.00 per year for a ten-cent magazine. For big magazines, which were lavish in appearance and substantial in amount of content, subscription and newsstand sales promised little, if any, profit. Beginning in this period, advertising far surpassed sales as a revenue generator. Major magazines charged between $150 and $250 per page for advertising and, though these magazines did not have the 1000 pages of ads hyperbolically claimed by Harte, they routinely had over 100 (Mott, *History* 21).

The magazine revolution, however, involved more than just the few top sellers, whose contexts have been described. It was an expansion, overall, of the industry and marketplace. To focus solely on top sellers distorts the larger picture, which involved thousands of magazines below these few in a highly risky and volatile industry. What might the context look like if considered from the point of view of the average, rather than the exceptional, magazine of the period or, more to the point, the little magazine that is the focus of this study? Theodore Peterson, for example, has calculated that the average sale of a single magazine issue in 1900 was 18,571 (54), a number far below the circulations of top mainstream magazines, and well above the majority of little magazines. *Most* magazines, in other words, achieved moderate circulation rates at the turn of the century. Little magazines, of course, were part of the overall magazine boom, though a small one, representing, at a safe estimate, certainly less than 5 per cent of available publications at any given time from the 1890s to the early 1900s. They were also among the most ephemeral, most of them expiring within two years. In terms of circulation, little magazines averaged runs of 3,000 to 10,000, most in the 3,000–5,000 range, and certainly some of them seem to have been sustainable on these terms.[13] A few achieved sales beyond this. *The Philistine*, for example, exceeded 100,000 at its height. While, in general, little magazine circulations fall well below Peterson's average for a general monthly, if put in the context of a close relation, the literary magazine, they are not insignificant. The circulation of *The Bookman* in 1897, for example, exceeded 12,500

(*American Newspaper Directory* 1142), *The Literary World* was about 2,500, and *The Critic* about 5,500 (*N.W. Ayer and Sons American Newspaper Annual* 340, 563).

Little magazines were complexly situated in relation to transformations to the magazine field and to their mainstream counterparts in practical and ideological terms. The field included a range of types, some quite ambitious in commercial terms, and it is difficult to indicate what the average little magazine of the period might cost to produce. This problem is exacerbated by the lack of data more generally about costs of production for these magazines, though there are some suggestive bits of evidence. Certainly, the costs of production were far less than the $10,000 (before printing) of a top-end general monthly. Hubbard's claim, however, that "every man with ... ten dollars capital" might issue a little magazine seems a bit of an exaggeration, except, perhaps, for those at the amateur end of the scale ("Joseph Addison" 78). More believable is Stone's claim in the *Chicago Daily News* that an issue of *The Chap-Book* cost over $500 to produce, the bulk of the expense due to payments for contributors (qtd. in Bergel 171). A Memorandum of Agreement between Mosher and his printer Smith and Sale concerning *The Bibelot*, by contrast, indicates that his magazine, of a similar size and number of pages to *The Chap-Book*, cost $65 for a monthly print run of 5,000 copies, but Mosher supplied his own paper and silk for stitching, which would have represented an additional cost (Memorandum). Content, mostly in the way of reprint material not protected by copyright, represented a notable saving for Mosher. Falling somewhere between these two publications was *The Lark*, the first number of which, by Burgess's account, cost $100 for a publication of sixteen pages, highly illustrated with wood-cuts, and issued in a run of 3,000 copies (Wells, "What a Lark").[14]

Even without more detailed information, there is plenty to be said about how the economics of the production of little magazines differed from their mainstream counterparts. Certainly, in comparison with the mainstream industry, payment for contributions was negligible. If it was difficult to earn a living solely through mainstream magazine work, it was even more challenging to do so through little magazines. As might be expected, contributors to little magazines were at the bottom end of the pay scale. Solicitations for contributions to little magazines that appeared in the trade magazine, *The Editor*, were frequently apologetic about low rates. Walter Blackburn Harte, for example, solicited contributors for his magazine in *The Editor*, saying, "while our checks will not always be large, we will always have a complete understanding with the contributors before using their work" ("Notes of Periodicals" 18). Harte, who did much of the writing for the magazine himself, was eventually able to offer remuneration to contributors based on advertising revenue (Doyle 93, 95). Similarly, the editor of *The Red Letter* reported to *The Editor*, "rates of payment ... are not high as yet and they depend entirely upon merit, not length ... Editorial management is frank and reliable" (Poole 245). These comments concerning editorial reliability point to problems authors had in securing payment. Many of these magazines were fly-by-night operations or on the verge of financial crisis. Even *The Chap-Book*, one of the most successful little magazines, had complaints made against it regarding terms and payment (Wendy Schlereth 11–12). If some magazines offered no money or were remiss in their payments, others may have charged the author, an unscrupulous practice that prevailed across the industry and that was a subject of frequent commentary in *The Editor*. This practice accounts for Howard Llewellyn Swisher's quip in the front matter of *The Ghourki*: "We pay for no contributions and charge nothing for printing those we accept." Indeed, nonpayment seems to have been fairly standard. The editor of *John-a-Dreams* was reported in *The Editor* as having said, "the labor and expense necessary to ... give a hearing to worthy work" makes it impossible to offer payment for accepted manuscripts for at least a few years ("American Fraternity of Writers" 87). Little magazines relied largely on the dreams of aspiring writers and artists or on generosity. Will Bradley was lucky enough to scoop noted writer Richard Harding Davis, who offered a free contribution for the first issue of *Bradley His Book* (Bradley, *Will Bradley* 60). Other magazines, especially those issued by small presses, relied on a coterie, as did *The Lark* and *Blue Sky*. For little magazines that were cash-strapped but more ambitious and commercial-oriented, such as *The Lotus* and *The Raven*, contests served as a means of attracting contributors without having to pay for all content (back matter, *Lotus*; "Prizes for Stories" 4).

Little magazine editors fared hardly better, though if they were editor-publishers they might scrape a profit. Successful little magazines, such as *The Chap-Book*, may have offered a reasonable wage. Stone and Kimball, after all, secured popular poet Bliss Carman as editor, if only for a short time. Walter Blackburn Harte, however, made only $8 a week as editor of *The Lotus* (Doyle 107). Gelett Burgess reportedly made over twice as much as that for editing *The Lark* – $75 per month by the second year of the magazine's publication (Harlan 28). These salaries, nevertheless, stand in sharp contrast with the $100 to $200 per week paid to editors of major magazines. Harte's yearly editorial salary, on these terms, was less than that of a manufacturing labourer (Sedgwick 415). Meanwhile, *The Ghourki* was undoubtedly wholly a labour of love for its editor, Howard Llewellyn Swisher, who worked full time running a print shop. He called it a "recreation," a diversion," and cited his full-time job as the reason for the irregular frequency of the publication ("Harangues" *Ghourki* 1, no. 5, 162).

It was printing and distribution that accounted for the major costs for most little magazines, which is unsurprising given the emphasis many placed on their appearance. The printing of little magazines, as has been discussed, occurred in a range of contexts including amateur home printing outfits, small presses, general and specialist jobbing shops, and general printers – all of these, of course, on a much smaller scale than top-end magazines. Whatever context they were printed in, there was generally an effort to distinguish the publications in aesthetic terms and there was experimentation in production with old technology and new. Some were not averse to exploiting newer technologies in the service of achieving a hand-produced look. *Chips*, for example, sought to deliver "the best in literature, typography, and art," experimenting with running flat bed presses at a low speed to "obtain the best results in printing" for a print run of 10,000 copies ("*Chips* for 1896"). Another enterprising commercial-oriented production, *Four O'Clock*, also experimented with machine production. Its unique feature was the inclusion of tipped-in illustrations. The labour of doing this by hand, however, was too much for a magazine whose aim was to reach a circulation of 100,000. Its producers therefore, devised "a mechanical device for attaching … illustrations" ("Announcement," *Four O'Clock*). The cases of *Chips* and *Four O'Clock* exemplify how little magazines of this period often mediated between fine press and commercial/entrepreneurial ideals of the age.

As was the case for mainstream magazines, distribution of little magazines came at a considerable cost. They were, after all, subject to the same conditions as their mass-market counterparts, with half the newsstand price going to agent and newsdealer. Some little magazinists sought to avoid these costs by dealing directly with the trade. Thomas Mosher's *Bibelot*, W.E. Price's *Book-Lover*, and Gelett Burgess's *Lark*, for example, were issued in this manner. Michael Monahan, meanwhile, issued *The Papyrus* by subscription only after an unsatisfactory experience with the American News Company: "I have had a six-months' Whirl with the benevolent assimilators of the News Trust, and while there may have been Gaiety, there surely was no Profit in it – for me" (untitled announcement, 10). These cases, however, were unusual. Most little magazinists paid the costs of having their publications circulated on the newsstands.

This situation was far more problematic for little magazines than for mainstream ones. Unlike their popular counterparts, little magazinists were generally unwilling or unable to exploit advertising as a revenue generator. In the former case, some were keen to distinguish themselves from the increasingly commercial mass-market magazine; in the latter, while some may have been willing to exploit advertising, the little magazine, with its small circulation, was not an appealing medium for advertisers. These contexts, along with the ideals and ambitions of little magazinists, informed the advertising that appeared in them. Primarily, these magazines promoted the socio-cultural realm out of which they emerged, featuring ads for publishers, small presses, booksellers, artistic printers, and other little magazines. Such ads were often non-remunerative, based on exchange for services or payment in kind. When little magazines ventured beyond this kind of advertising, the products advertised were those appealing to the young, emerging professional classes, products such as bicycles, tobacco, typewriters, and pianos. Bicycles, for example, controversial in the period, were associated with modernity, speed, and progressivism with respect to women's freedom.[15] Bicycle ads appeared in *The Chap-Book*, *Bradley His Book*, and *The Clack Book*, among others. Quaker Oats breakfast cereal, the first packaged advertised food product, was another product promoted in little magazines such as *The Clack Book* and *Four O'Clock*, as well as mainstream ones.[16] Quaker Oats employed poster-style advertising as it faced competition from an increasing number of breakfast cereals introduced in the 1890s in the context of the clean living movement (see colour plate 10). Generally, little magazinists professed discrimination in their exploitation of advertising. *Chips*, for example, declared "[t]wo pages only of each issue are devoted to advertising of the better class. The publishers reserve the right to reject advertisements not meeting with their approval" (front matter). Will Bradley, meanwhile, undertook the design of the advertising in his magazine so it would meet his artistic standards ("At the End of the Book").

Advertising rates varied across publications and were usually stated as "available on request," but invariably fell well below the $150 or more per page charged by large mainstream magazines. *The Thistle*, a modest little magazine with a likely circulation of a few thousand, charged $18 a page for advertising and had about eight pages an issue ("*Thistle* Advertiser" iv); *Chips*, with a stated circulation of 10,000, charged $30 a page and had about three pages of advertising (back matter); and *Alkahest*, aspiring to a rather unlikely circulation of 50,000 – "to be distributed in all parts of the civilized world" – charged $20 a page, with about three pages per issue (front matter, *Alkahest* 1, no. 2).[17] Of the more famous little magazines, *The Chap-Book* charged two dollars an inch (Bergel 165), while *Bradley His Book* charged more. At $50 a page, Bradley's advertising was still, however, less expensive than that of mainstream magazines and he designed the ads himself (back matter, *Bradley His Book*). *Bradley His Book* had a high proportion of advertising, though its artistic poster style meant that it blended well with the other artistic and literary content. Hubbard's advertising fees, meanwhile, approached those of mass-market magazines, but only once *The Philistine* entered the big league, with a circulation of 110,000, when he began to charge $100 a page (back matter, *Philistine*).

Ultimately, in a context in which half of magazines failed, little magazines were no riskier than larger publications – and they stood to lose less. It was not impossible for the founders of little magazines to make modest earnings, though this was not necessarily the aim, except at the more ambitious and commercial end of the scale. They played, however, an important role in the larger field of magazines. Most obviously, as Burgess insisted, they "open[ed] to younger writers opportunities to be heard before they had obtained recognition from the autocratic editors" of major magazines (Burgess and Porter). They were important, also, to existing writers, magazinists, and printing and publishing establishments. Though these publications circulated, for the most part, in the competitive, commercial, and professional world of magazines, they were often a byproduct of other work, possibly subsidized by that work. That work might be a small press or job printing enterprise or a publishing concern. It might, equally, be a sideline of or alternative venue for journalists or editors from the mainstream media, or, indeed, authors. In this sense, the value of the little magazine was more symbolic than economic. If it represented an alternative kind of cultural capital for readers, it might also do so for editors and contributors. Famously, Henry James, for example, who regularly published in the mainstream press, contributed to the most influential British and American little magazines – *The Yellow Book* and *The Chap-Book*. Though he complained about poor payment (Diebel; Wendy Schlereth 11–12; Bergel 167–8), these magazines accrued prestige for him, establishing his authority as "the master" with the younger generation of writers. Bliss Carman also recognized the possible prestige of the little magazine when he turned down a stable and lucrative position on the staff of the popular mass-market magazine *Cosmopolitan* to become the editor of *The Chap-Book* (Muriel Miller 119, 121). In this venue he could promote his interests and those of his literary and artistic circle. There were many others, less famous now, but notable in their day, who used the little magazine to establish a similar kind of prestige in the context of broader careers in mainstream newspapers and magazines. These included James Huneker, co-editor of the influential little magazine *M'lle New York*, who was involved with dozens of newspapers and mainstream magazines of the day; Walter Blackburn Harte, who worked for general monthly magazines such as the *New England Magazine* and *Arena* before becoming the key proponent of the little magazine movement; Douglas Malloch, who worked for the *Muskegon Daily Chronicle*, edited a lumber trade journal, and was known as "the lumberman's poet," published *In Many Keys*, "a little magazine made up entirely of" his own writing; Louis N. Megargee, a popular newspaperman and writer, whose *Seen and Heard* (aka *Seen and Heard by Megargee*) continued to be issued after his death; and Erasmus Wilson, Pittsburgh's most popular columnist, whose little magazine was called the *Quiet Observer*. Just as the little magazine enabled literary artists to benefit from the cultural cachet the medium afforded, journalists could use it to advantage also.

In most senses, then, little magazines as print media commodities differed mainly in degree rather than kind from their popular mainstream counterparts. Little magazinists, whose social conditioning gave them cultural and material aspirations, a zeal for self-expression through the printed word, and an optimism about the democratization of culture through commercial means, were well-served by the magazine revolution, which expanded the industry at all levels and resulted in considerable experimentation. At the same time, the magazine revolution created the conditions for the emergence of little magazines in an ideological sense. In practical terms, these publications might easily be perceived as lesser than their high-circulation, big-budget, big-name mainstream counterparts. Little magazinists, however, took advantage of the transformations that the rise of the mass-market magazine and increasing commercialization brought to the field to enhance their cultural prestige.

Most significant here was the ambivalent reaction to the phenomenal rise of the magazine in this period. Many in America and Britain thought highly of the American magazine and the quality of its illustration. The *Chicago Graphic*, for example, accorded the American magazine the status of "a school of literature" (Tebbel 120). Others, however, were troubled by the commodification of literature and art that mass-market magazines brought about. Earnest literary types such as Francis Browne, editor of the important literary periodical *The Dial*, for example, deplored the state of American magazines and newspapers, complaining about an increase in mediocre and conservative content and a privileging of pictures over text ([Browne] 204). Meanwhile, genteel general monthlies, which continued to sell for twenty-five to thirty-five cents, rankled at the competition. The editors of these magazines styled themselves as "steward[s] or custodian[s] of a revered cultural heritage" (Schneirov 46). Driven by the zeal for culture and reform that characterized the era, they believed that "the appreciation of good art would serve to improve middle-class tastes and help … readers to transcend the mundane world of commerce and consumption" (Schneirov 39). With the rise of the mass-market magazine, the learned and cultivated qualities of the genteel magazine, with its long review articles, were on the wane, giving way to a lively journalistic style, short and snappy articles, gossip, timely content, plentiful illustration including half-tone photographs, short stories, and abundant advertising that characterized the new popular magazines. Eventually, the genteel monthlies began to transform, pressured to compete with their increasingly popular and cheaper counterparts. This change created the opportunity for another kind of magazine – the little magazine – to take the cultural high ground.

Little magazinists positioned themselves and their publications in relation to their genteel and mass-market mainstream counterparts in strategic ways, emphasizing their cultural superiority and/or their modernity and up-to-dateness. Some little magazinists rejected the old-fashioned manner of the genteel magazines, but retained similar reformist and elitist ideals. Walter Blackburn Harte, for example, had an earnest desire, like genteel editors, to improve the taste of American readers. His aim was to "create a more catholic taste," and to bring about a "modern era" in American culture ([Harte], "Bubble and Squeak," *Lotus* 3, no. 2, 60). The achievement of this aim for Harte, however, involved a brash rejection of the stuffy ways of the genteel generation – "an intellectual revolt," as he stated, "against the tyrannical, intolerant Smugocracy in Letters" ("Bubble and Squeak," *Lotus* 3, no. 2, 60). At the same time, little magazinists were critical of the new cheap, mass-market upstarts that were, in the words of *The Chap-Book* editor, "merely picture books" appealing to the "superficiality of our public" (Notes," *Chap-Book* 5, no. 1, 47, 48). Situated between genteel and modern values, little magazinists aspired to serve as arbiters of taste for modern and progressive new middle classes, while employing discourses and strategies associated with mass-market media and the emerging culture of personality.

Stemming from Hoffmann, Allen, and Ulrich's pioneering work, most scholarship on little magazines has emphasized the aesthetically and socially radical nature of their content with respect to mainstream publications. Indeed, the apparent lack of avant-gardist radicalism in American little magazines of the 1890s has been largely responsible for their critical neglect. In broad terms, little magazines of this period featured content quite similar to both their genteel and mass-market mainstream counterparts and, at the same time, followed the trend towards brevity and a lively journalistic style. Many engaged with timely literary and artistic culture, featuring popular genres of fiction and poetry, such as local colour writing and historical romance. At the same time, American mainstream magazines were not without merit in terms of the inclusion of weighty cultural content. Many demonstrated interests in the same kind of fin-de-siècle European literature promoted by aesthetic little magazines. Wilde's *Picture of Dorian Gray*, for example, appeared in *Lippincott's Monthly Magazine* in 1890, while *Harper's* featured writing by Britain's decadent avant-garde, including Arthur Symons's essay "The Decadent Movement in Literature" and Walter Pater's story "Apollo in Picardy" in 1893. As for non-literary content, mainstream magazines also covered fringe social, political, and religious trends and movements and were the sites of radical and reformist journalism, focusing on many of the same figures and topics as those taken up in the periodical of protest style of little magazine. The Spanish-American War, the Standard Oil controversy, the Pullman Strike, and the anti-trust movement were covered across popular and alternative media in a manner akin to today's segmenting of the American news market across conventional networks and liberal and conservative outlets such as MSNBC and FOX news. The boundaries between little magazines and the mainstream press, then, were actually quite porous.

"Little Magazineness": Identity and Distinction in the Periodical Field

There will be more to say about the specific nature of little magazine content in the chapters in section 2. Considered in more detail here are features that signified "little magazineness" in this period and served to distinguish these periodicals from their mainstream counterparts. Ultimately, if the little magazine, as Glazener has it, represented "an alternative kind of cultural capital" (237), this status was as much a consequence of its manner of mediating its content – its "dress," or material form, and its "voice," or rhetorical style – as it was the content itself. By this, I mean to say that much of the cultural meaning of little magazines lay in their presentational features – namely a format derived from small press and poster culture and a rhetorical style linked to the emerging popular press. Dress and voice were central to the little magazine's remediation of, and strategic relationship to, periodical print of the era. Together, these features constituted an aesthetics of resistance and cultural distinction that were key to the identity of little magazines, guiding their readers' approach to content within.

That little magazines might be understood as remediating content from popular periodicals can be evidenced by a few examples. There is a relationship, for example, between little magazine content and the literary and miscellaneous pages of newspapers of the day. These pages featured some combination of poetry, aphorisms, anecdotes, human-interest stories, reports on cultural events, book reviews, editorial columns, correspondence, and historical narratives. *The Brooklyn Daily Eagle* for 18 August 1895 furnishes an example. Notable are its coverage of the little magazine phenomenon in "Some Fads and Fadists" [*sic*], including an image of the poster-style cover of the little magazine *Moods*; reviews of recent fiction of a type popular also in little magazines – short stories of Ambrose Bierce, who is deemed a "new Poe," and a "decadent" novel by Richard Marsh; poetry; and crudely executed images of poster-style girls (see Figure 2.10). This kind of material, and the amount of it, is in keeping with aesthetic little magazine content, which might be regarded as a reformatting of the newspaper's miscellaneous page. Where the newspaper presented

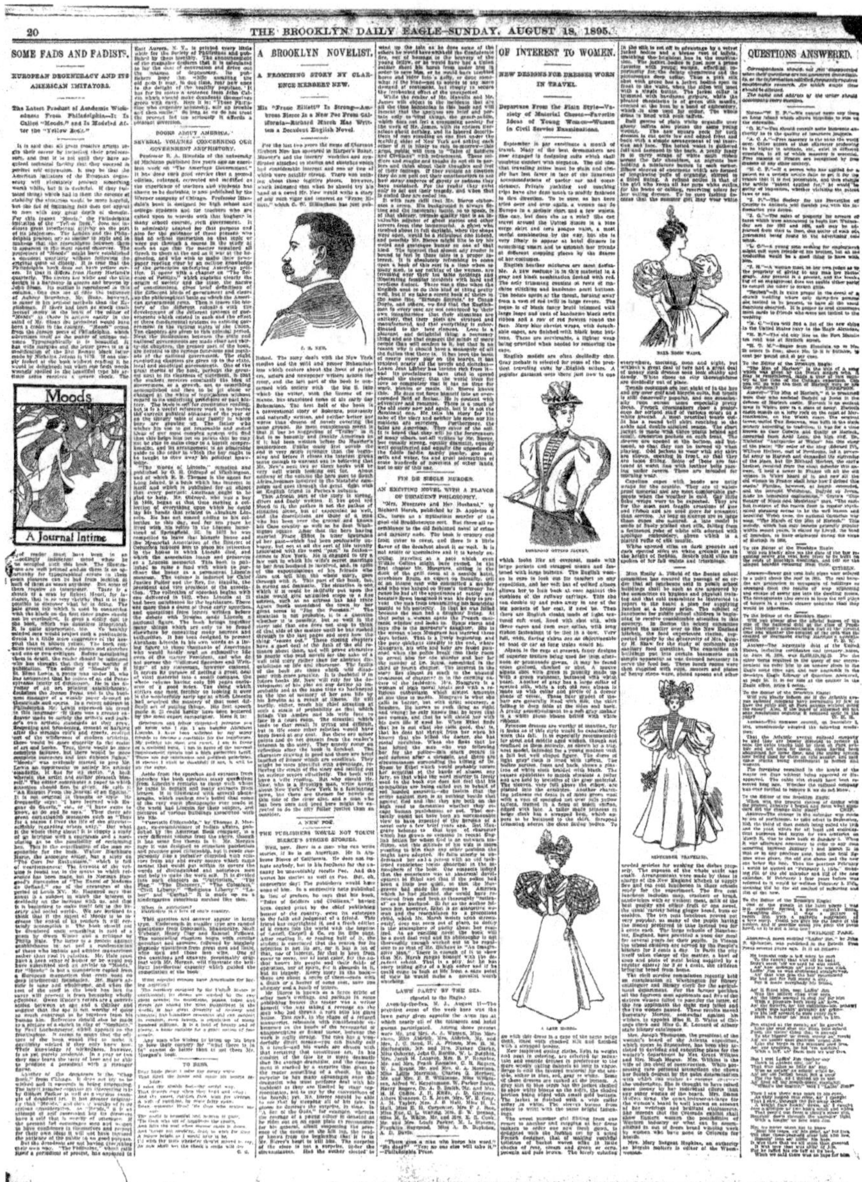

20 THE BROOKLYN DAILY EAGLE—SUNDAY, AUGUST 18, 1895.

SOME FADS AND FADISTS.

EUROPEAN DEGENERACY AND ITS AMERICAN IMITATORS.

A BROOKLYN NOVELIST.

OF INTEREST TO WOMEN.

QUESTIONS ANSWERED.

Figure 2.10 Miscellaneous page of *The Brooklyn Daily Eagle*, 18 August 1895. Courtesy of Newspapers.com.

Figure 2.11 Page from *Chicago Daily Tribune*, 30 April 1901, featuring Bert Leston Taylor's *Bilioustine* (outlined), a parody of *The Philistine*. Courtesy of Newspapers.com.

this material on one page across several densely packed columns of print, the little magazine presented it more attractively, across a number of pages, with generous spacing and margins.

While this example shows how similar content might appear in both media, there are examples of the *same* content appearing across media, where remediation has implications for meaning. A striking instance of how form transforms meaning in the move from newspaper to little magazine is Bert Leston Taylor's parody of the little magazine *The Philistine*, which first appeared in instalments in his *Chicago Tribune* "Line O'Type or Two" column and subsequently in little magazine format. While in its newspaper context the piece clamours for attention with other content on the page (see Figure 2.11), in little magazine format it comes into its own. The parody is able to function visually as well as verbally in its imitation of the little magazine aesthetic (see Figure 2.12).

The chap-book and pamphlet formats derived from fine press publications enabled content to be more focused and distinctive than in other periodical forms, whether that was the miscellaneous and densely

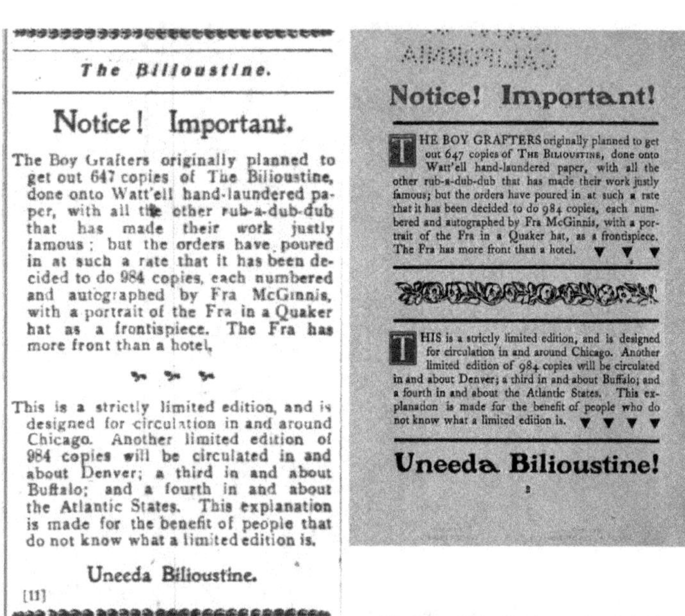

The Bilioustine.

Notice! Important.

The Boy Grafters originally planned to get out 647 copies of The Bilioustine, done onto Watt'ell hand-laundered paper, with all the other rub-a-dub-dub that has made their work justly famous; but the orders have poured in at such a rate that it has been decided to do 984 copies, each numbered and autographed by Fra McGinnis, with a portrait of the Fra in a Quaker hat as a frontispiece. The Fra has more front than a hotel.

This is a strictly limited edition, and is designed for circulation in and around Chicago. Another limited edition of 984 copies will be circulated in and about Denver; a third in and about Buffalo; and a fourth in and about the Atlantic States. This explanation is made for the benefit of people that do not know what a limited edition is.

Uneeda Bilioustine.

[11]

Notice! Important!

THE BOY GRAFTERS originally planned to get out 647 copies of The Bilioustine, done onto Watt'ell hand-laundered paper, with all the other rub-a-dub-dub that has made their work justly famous; but the orders have poured in at such a rate that it has been decided to do 984 copies, each numbered and autographed by Fra McGinnis, with a portrait of the Fra in a Quaker hat, as a frontispiece. The Fra has more front than a hotel.

THIS is a strictly limited edition, and is designed for circulation in and around Chicago. Another limited edition of 984 copies will be circulated in and about Denver; a third in and about Buffalo; and a fourth in and about the Atlantic States. This explanation is made for the benefit of people who do not know what a limited edition is.

Uneeda Bilioustine!

2

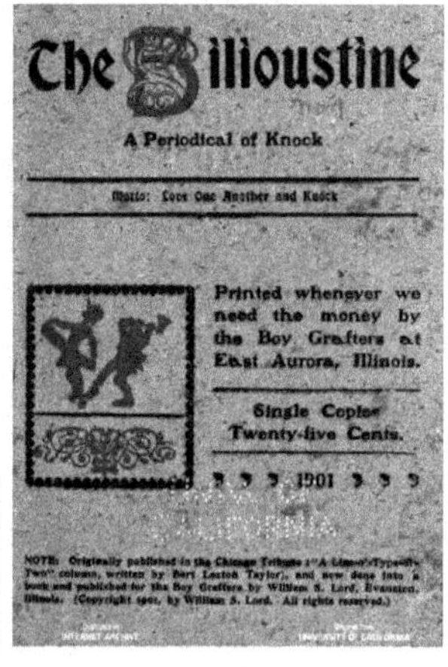

The Bilioustine

A Periodical of Knock

Motto: Love One Another and Knock

Printed whenever we need the money by the Boy Grafters at East Aurora, Illinois.

Single Copies Twenty-five Cents.

1901

NOTE: Originally published in the Chicago Tribune ("A Line-o'-Type-or-Two" column, written by Bert Leston Taylor), and now done into a book and published for the Boy Grafters by William S. Lord, Evanston, Illinois. (Copyright 1901, by William S. Lord. All rights reserved.)

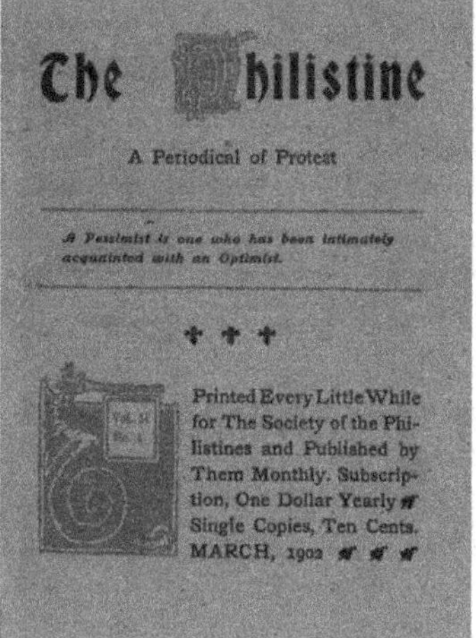

The Philistine

A Periodical of Protest

A Pessimist is one who has been intimately acquainted with an Optimist.

Printed Every Little While for The Society of the Philistines and Published by Them Monthly. Subscription, One Dollar Yearly. Single Copies, Ten Cents. MARCH, 1902

Figure 2.12 Section from the *Tribune* parody alongside the "little magazine" version of this content (above). *Bilioustine* alongside *The Philistine*, its parodied little magazine original (below). *Tribune* parody courtesy of newspapers.com; *Bilioustine* courtesy of HathiTrust; *Philistine* in possession of author.

packed newspaper page as in the examples above, or what Harte called the "bulky literary sandwich magazine" ("Bubble and Squeak," *Lotus* 2, no. 8, 298). This type of magazine contained well over a hundred pages of content, including one or more serials and/or short stories; biographical, historical, and travel features; essays on literature and the arts; literary or art notes; poetry; an editor's section; comics; and abundant illustration throughout. Celebrity gossip and features, as well as topical political and social commentary, were a notable feature of the emerging mass-market magazines. Thus, even when mainstream magazines did attend to high culture in their pages, this matter was cheapened and diluted by its placement alongside vulgar and sensational human-interest stories, gossip, timely journalistic material, features on celebrities and personalities, and its framing within as much as one hundred pages of advertising.

The little magazine, by contrast, represented a more selective publication and this selectivity was strategic and symbolic. Ranging usually from between sixteen and sixty-four pages, with little or no advertising, the content of little magazines was more limited and focused. History, biography, and travel nonfiction pieces, so prominent in mainstream magazines, were rare, except in little magazines at the more commercial end of the spectrum. Fiction and poetry were predominant, while music, dramatic pieces, and art were also occasionally included. Non-fiction was generally geared towards literary and artistic criticism and commentary or reviews. A typical issue of an aesthetic little magazine might include a couple of short stories, a few poems, an essay or two, literary notes and reviews, and an editorial commentary section. Illustrations, if included, were often minimal, though important to the overall design and aesthetic of the magazine. Advertising usually occupied no more than a couple of pages. Periodicals of protest, meanwhile, featured a similar amount of content that was focused, however, on topical issues of the day and editorial commentary, with some including literary content, fiction or, more often, poetry. Overall, the more focused nature of the little magazine meant that the high cultural content of aesthetic periodicals and the socially radical content of periodicals of protest were more concentrated than in mainstream publications. The value of such packaging in terms of promoting particular artistic and political agendas was notable. In the case of aesthetic little magazines, for example, it gave the sense of there being a significant literary and artistic movement in America, a perception enhanced by the more exclusive focus on such content in contrast to the more general nature of mainstream monthlies. This presentation was significant, too, for periodicals of protest in relation to newspaper editorial journalism. In newspapers, the editorial voice, even if radical, was competing with an array of other types of content. In the little magazine, however, this voice took centre stage, registering more pointedly as protest literature.

Walter Blackburn Harte's suggestion that "wit, wisdom, and fancy" might come across more coherently in "a small and handy pamphlet" ("Bubble and Squeak," *Lotus* 2, no. 8, 298) was expressed by other little magazinists. In a paean to what he called "the booklet magazine," William Ellis of *The Philosopher* claimed, "the day is gone when there is hope in large things" ("Book Corner" 154). Similarly, William McIntosh, co-founder with Hubbard and Harry Taber of *The Philistine*, insisted on the superiority of the little magazine to the newspaper precisely on the basis of its size: "[The little magazine] is born of the surfeit of the big newspaper. Readers seek it out – stawed [*sic*] with too much for their money. And it is a hopeful sign for individuality in literature that a clean cut idea is valued over time more than the quantity of words on paper ... Tonnage has had its day in the literature of America" (132). McIntosh values not only the littleness of the overall format but also the littleness of its individual components, praising brevity and clarity of expression over verbose eloquence. This privileging of short forms was, as Gerry Beegan argues, a trend of the 1890s: "the distinctive cultural form was the fragment. From the short story, the aphorism, and journalistic causerie, to the essay, the snapshot, or the pen-and-ink sketch, the brevity of these forms seemed appropriate for a period of rapid social upheaval and constant change" (138). These short forms, then, were regarded both as aesthetically superior, valued by the artistic and cultural élite, and relevant to the experience of modernity. Readers may not have got as much for their ten cents in the little magazine, but what they got, it was implied, was of high quality, mediated through a personalized perspective that assured its "individuality."

The remediation of mainstream media style content had significant repercussions for its cultural value and that of the little magazine also. The little magazine presented advantages over the "big newspaper" and the "literary sandwich magazine." The framing and packaging of content made it distinctive and drew focused attention to the personalities of its creators. The idiosyncratic look of the little magazine, as compared with the impersonal and uniform appearance of full newspaper pages, or with the bulky standardized format of general monthlies, powerfully conveys that a different kind of reading experience and connection to content will be had. Key, then, to the alternative cultural status of the little magazine in this period, was a format that signalled not so much a radical difference in content but, rather, selectivity, an 1890s version of today's notion of "curated content."

Early newspaper historian Algernon Tassin makes much of the importance of the look of the little magazine along with a second distinguishing feature of "little magazineness" – its voice: "the cult magazine ... was a personal utterance. The cult magazines were all slender things, merely embodied voices like that pocket prima-donna who was once heralded as 'Little but Oh My!'" (356). The little magazine, then, exuded personality, and Tassin and Sidney Kramer credit it as a major innovator in bringing the "personal note" into journalism (Tassin 357–8; Kramer 29–30). Establishing this voice was crucial in a medium that sought to emphasize personality and individuality. In the first issue of *The Magpie*, Kenneth Brown articulates his concern about getting this aspect just right:

> I hesitated some time between the editorial We of ordinary periodicals and the omniscient I of other miniature magazines. I inclined rather to the plural and was going to call this department MIKRO-KOSMOS. But friends came and said, "Now don't try to spring any long words on us: you know you don't know what that means." And they said other things which convinced me that little i and "Little Things" were more appropriate to the humble opinion my friends had of me. (14)

Brown's difficulty was not his alone. It faced all little magazinists. In constructing an editorial identity, little magazinists, as Brown's comments indicate, were self-conscious about their position in a broader field that encompassed not only other "miniature magazines," but "ordinary periodicals" also. Certainly they wanted to distance themselves from a stuffy, genteel "royal we" style associated with traditional magazines. They were by no means unanimous, however, in their understanding of what might constitute a little magazine "I/i." Against an omniscient little magazine "I" that is, as Brown implies, more "know-it-all" than "all-knowing," he and some others would posit the more modest, whimsical self of the "i." In either case, the editorial identity of little magazinists was carefully fashioned with a view to expressing individuality.

This issue was of concern more broadly across the industry also. Kramer, for example, argues that the substitution of "intimacy" for "impersonality" in establishing a "personal note" was a feature of new mass-market publications also (29–30), while Ned Stuckey-French and Matthew Schneirov have asserted the importance of "intimacy" to the older genteel magazines. Stuckey-French, for example, demonstrates how the genteel editor was represented as an avuncular type of gentleman chatting by the fireside (15–19), while Schneirov stresses the "congenial," if at times "patronizing," manner in which these editors related to readers as "friends" (41, 42). This mode of address worked for some time but, by the 1880s, seemed increasingly old-fashioned and was beginning to lose relevance in the context of social change. As Ohmann argues, these magazines were coming to be seen as "stodgy, bland, and impersonal, almost as if their editors wanted to repel readers – aside from the few who already belonged to the club – rather than attract them" (*Selling Culture* 33). This state of affairs undoubtedly accounts for Brown's representation of ordinary periodicals as being voiced by the magisterial "We." It became necessary, then, to reconceptualize a relationship to readers, to develop a personal and intimate one in a modern register, and this is what new mass-market and little magazines did. For Edward Bok, for example, editor of the hugely successful mass-market *Ladies Home Journal*, a successful engagement with readers required personality: "America love[s] a personality" and the task of the editor is to "project his personality through the printed page" as "a real human being who could talk and not merely write on paper" (163). Bok's invocation of the term "personality" is apt, evidence of the shift from a "culture of character" to a "culture of personality" identified by Susman that would be realized more fully in the twentieth century (273–7). The values upheld by genteel editors were those associated with character – honour, integrity, manners, morality – and the manner in which they addressed readers assumed these shared ideals. Bok's call for personalities demonstrates the shift in understandings of self-expression and self-realization that came with the culture of personality. Little magazinists, it might be argued, took to a further extreme the mass-market media's interest in individuality and personality in relation to dress and voice, foregrounding, above all, idiosyncratic personae characterized by highly individualistic self-expression. In aesthetic terms, they took a fine press format to remediate as high art what may have been fairly standard content. In rhetorical terms, meanwhile, little magazinists employed a popular press discourse to deliver what was framed as a high cultural product in a manner that distinguished their publications from their stodgier, genteel counterparts who were seeking to claim the cultural high ground in the periodical field.

Thus little magazinists' conceptions of editorial identity were situated complexly, mediating, as was often the case, between the elitist cultural values of their genteel predecessors and the progressive, democratic, and personality-driven ideals of mass-market media. They strove to create the kind of intimacy that might be understood as elitist and cliquish, but did so by exploiting, to an extreme, new and popular conceptions of personality. Tassin is right, however, to identify the difference in effect that this personal note has when embodied in the distinctive format of the little magazine: a publication small in size, small in circulation, aesthetically distinctive, and with relatively little advertising. Together, these features meant that, whatever it adapted from the new popular discourse of mass-market print, it looked and sounded distinctive. The editorial identity established by little magazines, one that espoused individuality and idiosyncrasy, was a key part of their challenge to the cultural authority of their mainstream contemporaries. At the same time, for periodicals of protest, the emphasis on personal opinion, independent expression, and muckraking contributed to the emergence of new journalistic styles of writing. The characteristic "voice" of little magazines projected personality and individuality, which were fast becoming cultural ideals for emerging professional classes. Little magazinists may have been akin to their mass-market counterparts in their exploitation of the personal note, but their use of it was more pointed and extreme in the service of cultural distinction and social revolt.

Notions of the personal, the intimate, and individuality were central to the construction of editorial identity and personality in the little magazines. The medium itself was understood by Burgess to be a means of "personal expression" (*Bayside Bohemia* 19), and the terms "personal" and "intimate" were part of the discourse around these publications. The little magazine *Personal Impressions*, for example, a literary and bibliophilic journal, exploited this notion in its title, but also in styling itself a "record of current literature *enlivened by the touch of the personal*" (front matter 1; emphasis added). Individuality, meanwhile, was foregrounded in Michael Monahan's *Papyrus* through its subtitle – a "magazine of individuality" – and also in William Ellis's account of periodicals of protest as "magazines of individual opinion"

("The Book Corner" 154). Intimacy was also marked out as a desirable feature of the little magazine. *The Blue Sky* was praised by *The Philosopher* as being "sprightly, piquant, and intimate" (Ellis, "In the Smoking Room," *Philosopher* 6, no. 4, 127), while *The Lark* was declared by *The Chap-Book* to be "intimate in its charm" ("Notes," *Chap-Book* 3, no. 3, 112), so intimate, in fact, that *The Clack Book* declared, "one feels sometimes as if one were eavesdropping and hearing a lot of charming nonsense not intended for publication at all" ("Clacks," *Clack Book* 1, no. 3, 82).

The voice of little magazines established itself, of course, in editorial commentary, but is also apparent in paratextual features. Interestingly, in this respect, one commentator of the period remarked that the cover of one of the little magazines was "quite loud enough to be heard" ("Fad Periodicals" 12). In addition to covers, titles, subtitles, and mottoes functioned as a form of shorthand in broadcasting the distinctive identity of these magazines, especially as a form of alternative media. In a fast-paced modern context, potential readers could gauge their flavour in an instant. As Brown's comments suggest, little magazinists exploited a range of rhetorical modes to achieve distinction. In a cultivated mode, they might deploy a rhetoric that registered subtle opposition to the mainstream, especially mass-market magazines. The association with bibliophilic culture and the employment of terms associated with books and manuscripts for titles discussed previously, for example, is an important instance of how little magazines voiced cultural distinction in an elitist and genteel register. This resistance was, often, however, expressed less subtly, voiced in titles that deliberately positioned little magazines in opposition to convention, as in *The Ishmaelite*, *The Philistine*, *The Freak*, *The Knocker*, and *The Kansas Knocker*. These titles, with their invocation of outsider identities, stood out in a media landscape where mainstream magazines so often employed name brands (*McClure's*, *Munsey's*, *Scribner's*, *Harper's*), invoked the public sphere (*The Arena*, *Forum*), or aligned themselves with culturally elite concepts (*Cosmopolitan*, or, more obliquely, *The Atlantic Monthly* for its Boston Brahmin associations). At the same time, of course, such titles also registered the rebellious nature of social and political movements that appealed to the emerging professional-managerial class and were transforming the cultural landscape. Titles such as *The Knocker* and *The Kansas Knocker*, in their employment of a new colloquialism of the period, meaning "to disparage, find fault with, criticize captiously" (*OED* s.v. "knock"), demonstrate how little magazines, like their mass-market counterparts, exploited contemporary popular discourse. Other examples of such usage occur in the exploitation of terms such as "new," modern," and "young" in titles, subtitles, and mottoes. Overall, the new personal style of mass-market and little magazines was one that was forthright and provocative, deliberately opposing a stodginess associated with genteel periodicals.

The little magazine version of this rhetoric, however, manifested itself in a different way than in the popular press. First, it was a more pervasive aspect of the little magazine genre. As with content, it was concentrated, rather than diluted. Second, its rhetoric of resistance and revolt was often underpinned by a playful, irreverent spirit that stood as the keynote of the personality of the little magazine. This irreverence was often directed at the magazine industry. Little magazines were, indeed, Ishmaelites and philistines in the realm of print, just as they addressed those who identified with a spirit of progressivism, protest, and resistance. Little magazinists represented their publications as scofflaws in the realm of print culture, revolting against the conventions, regulations, and expectations governing magazine publication. These expectations were shaped socially but also legislatively. The 1878 postal legislation mandated that in order for a publication to be eligible for second class mail rates, it must: be issued at regular, stated intervals; be sent from a known office of publication; be made of printed paper without substantial binding as with books; and be published with the intention of disseminating "information of a public character, or devoted to literature, the sciences, arts or some special industry" for a legitimate list of subscribers (Casper 186). While little magazinists usually kept within the realm of these laws to ensure distribution, they voiced resistance to these expectations and conventions in various ways. They were casual, for example, about publication schedules, proudly so. *The Ghourki*, for example, was "published from time to time" (front matter); *The Hatchet*, "at odd spells"; *Home Craft*, "every new moon or thereabouts"; and *Lucifer's Lantern*, "whenever the spirit moves" (Faxon, "Ephemeral Bibelots" 92, 106). Many other examples of this casualness towards periodicity might be given. In some respects, this defiance was part of the pose of little magazinists' rebellion against the mainstream. Often, however, they did have difficulty keeping up a regular schedule, as, for example, remarked upon by the editor of *John-a-Dreams*:

> The subscription price of this magazine is One Dollar, which entitles the subscriber to twelve numbers. Just when these numbers will be published is hard to definitely foretell, but since I have called the attention of Mr. Dreams to the statement of Assistant Postmaster-General Ker, that "when a publication changes its periodicity, it loses its continuity," he sees with me, the importance of making it as nearly a monthly as possible. (*John-a-Dreams*, "*John-a-Dreams*, His Ad")

Little magazinists were also irreverent about the informational nature of their content, another postal legislation requirement. Titles such as *The Whim*, *Whims*, *The Fad*, and *The Lark* fly in the face of the legislation's implication that periodicals have some use value. So, too, do subtitles: *The Philosopher*, for example, touted itself as "thoughtful but not too thoughtful"; *Powder Magazine* offered "a little off the top for those who are up to snuff"; *The Wet Dog* declared itself "a paper for those with money to burn"; and *Pot-Pourri* represented itself as "an illustrated vagary of paper and ink conducted by a freak" (Faxon, "Ephemeral Bibelots," 107, 125, 126).

This paratextual discourse serves as a taste of the rhetorical voices that were more fully developed in editorials that "projected personality," in Bok's sense, onto the page. These editorials also served to establish the nature of the relationship to readers. Hints as to the nature of that personality are often conveyed in titles of the editorial sections, as in the case of Brown's "Little Things," suggestive of modesty and humility. His cultivation of an unassuming stance is paralleled by Thomas Wood Stevens's "Stray Clouds" editorial column in *Blue Sky*, a title that also suggests a whimsicality identified with little magazines. Page Waller Sampson and Marion Thornton Egbert's "Jingo! What's This?" in *The Bachelor Book* and Walter Blackburn Harte's "Bubble and Squeak" in *The Fly Leaf* and *The Lotus* also reflect this trend. The notion of the gentlemanly chat by the fire, though losing favour in this period, still has potency as a symbol of cultivated appreciation in the context of the rise of mass-market print. It is an image invoked especially in little magazines issued by small presses, as in William Ellis's "Smoking Room" column in *The Philosopher*, and *John-a-Dreams*'s "By the Fireside." Mary Learned and Louise McPherson of *the Pebble*, meanwhile, opt for "The Sanctum," evoking a sacralized notion of art that carries over from traditional genteel culture into the new cultural elitism of the Progressive Era. Others foregrounded the intimate nature of the communication in ways that registered the older genteel notion of the chat, but that reinforced the more egalitarian relationship between editor and reader being promoted by new magazines. The editor of *Whims*, for example, invokes the reader with the title "Entre Nous," as does Tim Thrift of *The Lucky Dog* in his "Heart Communion Talks." Elbert Hubbard's "Heart to Heart Talks With Philistines by the Pastor to His Flock," meanwhile, combines a custodian sensibility in its implication of a pastoral relationship with a sense of egalitarianism in its invocation of an intimate form of communication. The more modern, aggressive spirit of the new journalism with its sensationalistic and muckraking tone is also at play in titles of these editorial sections, notably in *The Clack Book*'s "Clacks," *The Ghourki*'s "Harangues to the Ghourki by the Chief of the Tribe," and *The Bauble*'s "Condemned Contemporaries" and "Among the Fools." These examples provide a sense of the range of personae deployed within Brown's conception of the "omniscient I" and "little i" of the little magazine editorials and the ways in which they were situated among and between existing and emerging trends.

Within these editorial sections, little magazinists ranged freely in their discussions across literary and artistic topics, in the case of aesthetic magazines and hybrids, and across social, political, and cultural issues, in the case of periodicals of protest and hybrids. This content was rarely presented in a traditional way – i.e., as a lengthy discourse on a single topic. Rather, in keeping with the interest in short forms, it tended to be digressive and bitty, including multiple short opinion pieces; anecdotes; rants and raves about particular issues; manifestoes; commendations and critiques of the popular press and other little magazines; epigrams; jokes and satire; gossip; and personal anecdotes and narratives about the trials and tribulations of the magazine itself. Whether it was because these sections were inexpensive to supply or because they were popular among the readership, they became a prominent feature, occupying, in some cases, a third or more of the content. The personalized forms of critical commentary that appeared in these editorial sections in the way of opinions on literary, artistic, social, and political matters were important in defining the tastes and values of the little magazinists and the emerging professional-managerial audience they addressed, and these will be discussed in more detail in chapters 7 and 8. Addressed here, is the aspect of this content that functions most to individualize the little magazine as a personal and intimate medium: that is, self-referential and self-reflective commentary as an aspect of "little magazineness." This commentary, characteristic of little magazine rhetoric, served to construct a vivid picture of the social and discursive world of these publications and their makers, one depicted as at odds with the mainstream press, and one that was itself divided into different factions and camps. In a precarious field where the average life expectancy was often little more than a year or two, editorial commentary was a source for the latest news – births, deaths, and milestones – in the little magazine world, providing a useful navigation tool for readers who were being introduced to what was, in effect, new periodical terrain.

The editorials also bear witness to the jockeying for power and position within the field – petty disputes, allegiances and alliances, and so on. In its first issue, *Quartier Latin*, for example, a little magazine created by American art students in Paris, appeals to its "sister" magazines back home, striving to be associated with *The Chap-Book*, *The Lotus*, *The Philistine*, *The Bibelot*, and *The Lark* ("Announcement," *Quartier Latin* 2). *The Clack Book*, for its part, was a magazine careful to distance itself from controversial decadence, employing the kind of language used to condemn such literature against *The Optimist* of Detroit, which it deems "the most revolting gutter filth under the name of literature," "the unadulterated, unperfumed stench of the sewer" ("Clacks," *Clack Book* 1, no. 4, 123). It accords value in the field of little magazines to publications with an aesthetic or arts and crafts bent, such as *Bradley His Book*, "the most esthetic piece of printing one can find among the Magazines in Miniature" ("Clacks," *Clack Book* 2, nos. 2–3, 112). *The Bauble*, a publication that existed almost solely to parody stereotypical little magazine tropes, skewers all equally in a uncompromisingly mean-spirited, though humorous, way:

> [*The Shadow*] should now emulate the example of the fabled groundhog. Its editors have emerged into the light of periodicals, they have cast a shadow that is certainly enough to frighten anyone not steeled against such Gorgon's heads, and they should immediately retire into the oblivion whence they came filled with a proper disgust of their own reflections …
>
> *Whims* is the latest addition to the list of superfluous publications of the red-letter order. At first it seems to be a cross between *M'lle New York* and *The Philistine*, combining the very suggestive verse of the former with the maudlin romance of the latter. The only really humorous conceit I have been able to discover about this magazinette is the statement that it is issued from the American Tract Society Building. ("Condemned Contemporaries" 53–4)[18]

The *Bauble* asserts authority, then, not by invoking strategic alliances as *Quartier Latin* does, nor by demonstrating discrimination like *The Clack Book*. Rather, its claim to authority lies in its cynical misanthropic stance towards the entire field, a field which it nonetheless participates in and profits from. Certainly, notices about, and brief commentary on, other magazines were a regular source of editorial content in the press in this period. The little magazines, however, "enliven" this content, to borrow the motto of *Personal Expression*, with "the touch of the personal," in a chatty manner that invites readers to engage in this world, develop their own likes and dislikes, identify their tastes with particular periodicals, and cultivate the modern aesthetic and socio-political sensibility and discourse that these publications model.

A number of editors took this notion of developing a personal and intimate discourse further through personal anecdotes about themselves and their coteries, documenting the problems of starting and sustaining a magazine and reporting on their day-to-day activities. This was particularly the case for periodicals associated with small presses. Notable among these were *The Philistine*, which provided glimpses of the Roycroft community as well as Hubbard's personal experiences; *Papyrus*, in which Monahan discussed his home and town life and his struggles to produce his own magazine; *The Erudite*, with Albert Lane's evocations of Concord life; *John-a-Dreams*, which fictionalizes this world through the use of pseudonymous identities for some of the coterie; and *Blue Sky* and *The Philosopher*, notable for the manner in which they capture the culture of the small press environment that sustained these magazines.

An extract from Thomas Wood Stevens's opening editorial manifesto in *Blue Sky* serves as an example of this content and its discursive style. The transcription follows Stevens's inclusion of the pilcrow, the kind of typographic idiosyncracy employed frequently in little magazines:

> It would, perhaps, be well to explain *The Blue Sky* by a Stray Cloud, so I am doing it. You may skip it if you like. It is not at all necessary. ¶ Now we are printing this booklet simply because we have nothing better to do. We couldn't have anything better, for we like to do this. Also some folks we knew said they would subscribe. (Some of them did.) ¶ We have no theories, to amount to anything. Mr. Ellis, who runs *The Philosopher*, up on the old Wisconse, says that no one ever made money by publishing a booklet. We don't care. We went into it to lose a few superfluous

> millions. ¶ Mr. Ellis started a school of philosophy up there, and a very delightful school it is. That was all right – for him. We shall not found any schools of any kind. There are too many of 'em now. ¶ We are not going to decide any of the burning questions of the day. We shall not bother ourselves with anything so very, very solemn. We do not know everything. ¶ Printers who set up long dry things about Problems and Relations and such stuff all day, become pessimists, and drink beer out of a pail, and all that. Now we don't like beer, so in order to prevent such catastrophes to our cheerful mental temperament, we shall print things that keep us feeling like a week in the country. And that's all about it. ("Stray Clouds," *Blue Sky* 1, no. 1, 29–30)

Notable in this editorial stance are the assertion of a distinctively idiosyncratic personality and an abnegation of responsibilities associated with genteel editorship. The *Blue Sky* coterie seeks to please itself, making no claims to reformist impulses. This attitude is common enough among little magazinists though, as the editorial comment indicates in its reference to the more serious aims of "Mr. Ellis," not all took this lighthearted approach. This style of informal jokey banter continues throughout the nearly three-year run of the magazine as the world of the Skytes, as they called themselves, is recounted in columns conducted by the editor and the printer. Though Stevens speaks for the Skytes as a whole in this introductory piece, he more often invokes the "small i" in discussing the mundane world of the Skytes. The goings-on of the print shop are recounted with tales of the editor and printer, the B.M. (business manager), Alfred G. Langworthy, and the Art Editors (first Frank B. Rae, an exile from the Roycroft community and, later, Harry Everett Townsend). There are also anecdotes about their extended coterie within the little magazine world, documenting friendly relations with editors of *The Philosopher*, *The Bachelor Book*, and *The Pebble*, and this attention is often reciprocated.[19] These anecdotes are contrasted with jibes and digs at magazines of which they do not approve – *The Philistine*, *The Goose-Quill*, and *The Stiletto*, for example.

The editorials of *Blue Sky* and comparable sections in other little magazines show, in extreme form, how these publications substituted intimacy for the perceived impersonality of genteel magazines. The intimate discourse differs significantly from the fireside chat model of an earlier genteel culture, providing readers with highly individualized personalities that the new mass-market context seemed to demand, while keeping it esoteric enough to be distinct from the popular press. The little magazine, then, adapted and appropriated from the two editorial models – providing access to an exclusive artistic realm, but in an accessible and individualized manner. This was a glimpse of artistic bohemia at a time when, as Joanna Levin has documented, bohemianism was a source of fascination for middle-class Americans. At the same time, this content posed a challenge through its often-obscure references and allusions. Little magazines did certainly contain in-jokes. In the case of *Blue Sky*, for example, it is unlikely that anyone outside the immediate network would know that Michael Kinmarck – about whom Stevens tells a story in the first "Stray Clouds" and whose work is published in the magazine – is Stevens himself. Other examples include Hubbard's discussions of the Roycrofters, particularly his stories about Ali Baba, his folksy handyman and a source of humour.

The highly personalized and cliquish nature of this discourse and content suggests that little magazinists themselves constituted a significant proportion of the readership of little magazines. This is evident in the high degree of cross-referencing, cross-promotion, and crossover contributors within these magazines. Indeed, this network effect was central to establishing very quickly the little magazine as a distinctive field within a broader periodical realm. This cliquishness, however, did not necessarily limit its audience. Rather, it may well have generated curiosity in readers seeking a challenge or those interested in the personal, idiosyncratic, and offbeat form that the little magazine represented. Whether the worlds invoked were more or less familiar seems hardly to have been the point. Obscurity was not necessarily a deterrent. The informal tone and the gossipy nature of the editorial discourse put readers in the position of eavesdropper, much in the manner that *The Clack Book* attributed to *The Lark*, fostering a kind of cultish sensibility. If readers are at first confused, persistence and a following up of cross-references soon puts them in the know, enabling them to become masters of an alternative and counter-cultural universe. Beegan, drawing on Peter Bailey, identifies this phenomenon as "knowingness" – "the shared, up-to-date knowledge of a broad range of ephemeral, contemporary material" – that he sees as a source of comfort in the context of the "swiftly changing present" that characterizes modernity and urban life (22, 26). As he argues, "the readers of the [late-nineteenth-century] press experienced a good deal of pleasure in assembling and using fragmentary information in order to feel that they knew what was happening at that moment" (26). While "knowingness," as Beegan articulates it, is exploited in the mass-market press also, the little magazines offer a distinctive and more highly personalized variation on it. The elusive nature of little magazines – as bodies of esoteric knowledge and as ephemeral media that might not last from one month to the next – provided a more extreme challenge and was key to their frisson, inspiring a desire in readers to collect them and to try to make sense of the endless self- and cross-references.[20] Indeed, the challenge and charm of these magazines, as Brad Evans argues, lay in the way they created a "gossamer thread of allusion and open-ended citation that depended not on a popular audience, but one sensitive enough to the rapidly changing modern art scene to be able to take it all in" ("Ephemeral Bibelots" 136). Evans goes on to compare the way little magazines operated with viral phenomenon on the web today: "Aesthetic effect in this circle was generated by a public of readers and art producers that not only delighted in witty or ironic variations on themes that had appeared elsewhere first, but that was faddishly devoted to reproducing and multiplying the links – and posting the hits – between them" ("Ephemeral Bibelots" 137).[21] Though Evans's focus is on aesthetic little magazines, his observation is equally applicable to the periodical of protest style of little magazine, where there is an expectation that the reader be up on the changing social and political scene and aware of mainstream and alternative media perspectives, much in the way that, today, news junkies survey the perspectives of mainstream, conservative, liberal, and alternative media on topical issues. Indeed, these magazines did not expect exclusive allegiance. They depended on readers informed as much about the mainstream media as the world of little magazines and address those same readers, though in a more culturally distinctive form and format.

Through its appropriations and adaptations of the techniques, forms, and social significance of fine press print, the art poster, and the mainstream magazine and newspaper, the little magazine established a distinctive identity as a print media commodity. This identity was one in keeping with the ethos of its creators and of the professional-managerial class of which they were a part. Alongside the mass-market magazine that Ohmann has claimed was central to the consolidation of professional-managerial class identity, little magazines also reveal much about the changing values that gave rise to a new kind of middle class. Evident in its engagements with other forms of print media is a reflection of this class's interest in harmonizing the conflicting claims of culture and commerce, of the traditional and the new, of the elite and the populist, and of an identity politics of character versus one of personality.

CHAPTER 3

The Big Little Magazines and the Evolution of the Genre

The long smouldering passion of revolt at conservatism in English art and literature … resulted in a bilious explosion, *The Yellow Book* … The seed fell, as British seed usually does, on America; it grew, and began to flourish … Strangely fashioned periodicals, preaching fantastic doctrines, uttering weird thoughts, began to appear like mushrooms after a shower.

– Percival Pollard, "In Eighteen Ninety-Five," *Echo* 1, no. 8, 172–3 (1895)

Turning from the broad social and media contexts, this chapter considers the evolution of the genre within the little magazine field itself, focusing on the most influential publications and their innovations that served to define and establish the genre: *The Knight Errant* (1892–3), an important American precursor; *The Chap-Book* (1894–8), the instigator of the first wave of the movement and a model for the aesthetic little magazine; *The Bibelot* (1895–1914), one of the longest running of 1890s little magazines; *The Philistine* (1895–1915), also longest running and a model for the periodical of protest; and Gelett Burgess's *Lark* (1895–7), *Phyllida, or the Milkmaid* (1897), *Le Petit Journal des Refusées* (1896), and *L'Enfant Terrible* (1898), magazines inspirational for their spirit of irreverence and play.

Embryonic Stirrings: *The Knight Errant* and the British Influence

What we aimed to do was to take the English *Hobby Horse* and … go it one better.

– Ralph Adams Cram, *My Life in Architecture*, 54 (1936)

With its exploitation of the familiar trope of the belated nature of America's literary development vis-à-vis Britain, Pollard's account of the emergence of the little magazine makes good copy, but it is not wholly accurate. Undeniably, *The Yellow Book* influenced the growth of the movement beginning in 1895. The phenomenon he describes, however, was actually a more public manifestation of coterie activities in Boston and Cambridge in 1892 and 1893 that resulted in the publication of two little magazines, *The Mahogany Tree* (1892) and *The Knight Errant*. These publications were the product of the thriving community of Harvard students, professors, and other Boston and Cambridge professionals and intellectuals who established groups and societies to socialize and share their artistic, social, and cultural views. This community included many who would go on to contribute to the little magazine movement, the revolution in fine printing, and the development of the graphic arts as writers, artists, designers, and publishers: Bliss Carman, Louise Imogen Guiney, Richard Hovey, Herbert Stone, Ingalls Kimball, Herbert Copeland, Fred Holland Day, and Herbert Small. It also included two architects, Ralph Adams Cram and Bertram Grosvenor Goodhue, who were active in the little magazine and arts and crafts movements of the period. *The Mahogany Tree* and *The Knight Errant* were vehicles for the expression of this community's interests in arts and crafts, aestheticism, decadence, and the book arts. As a weekly literary magazine based on the contributions of non-professionals, *The Mahogany Tree* was an ambitious project that expired after six months, undoubtedly as a result of the difficulty of getting material together in a timely fashion. It may also have been that, as Patricia J. Fanning suggests, interest turned to a new publication, one that represented a "*physical* manifestation of the philosophical ideals of [this group], ones only talked about in the weekly journal" (*Through an Uncommon Lens* 33; emphasis added).

This publication was *The Knight Errant*, a quarterly rather than a weekly, which, though less ambitious in terms of frequency, was, by design standards, more challenging than the conventional-looking *Mahogany Tree*. Its precedent, as Cram indicated, was *The Century Guild Hobby Horse* (1884–93), an organ of the arts and crafts movement in Britain founded by Arthur Mackmurdo, an architect, who, like William Morris, was interested in book design and printing. *The Hobby Horse* was fashioned according to these interests, printed on handmade paper, featuring woodblock illustrations, and designed with attention to typeface, spacing, leading, margins, and so on. The founders of *The*

Knight Errant sought to rival their British counterpart, as Cram indicated, with a periodical that would "be not only an expression of the most advanced thought of the time ... but as well, a model of perfect typography and the printer's art" (54).[1] *The Knight Errant* was, indeed, an elaborately produced publication: a thirty-two-page, large, quarto-size volume on handmade linen book paper with generous margins. Goodhue designed the cover (see Figure 3.1); Fred Holland Day, who would soon establish the literary publishing house of Copeland and Day, was responsible for pagination and layout; and Francis Watts Lee printed it in a run of only five hundred copies. More strikingly, paper, typeface, initials, and tailpieces were all specially designed for the magazine. Day's and Lee's interest in photography is reflected in the inclusion, in the first issue, of a photogravure of a painting by Renaissance artist Bernardino Luini. In contrast with the newly developed cheap half-tone reproduction process for photographs, photogravure resulted in extremely high quality reproductions and was an important medium for those, like Day, Lee, and, more famously, Alfred Stieglitz, who wished to establish photography as an art. The magazine's high aesthetic quality was matched by its content, which, in addition to the lesser-known figures of the coterie, included contributions from luminaries of the arts and crafts movement. The first issue, for example, included an account of cultural conditions of American life by Charles Eliot Norton, Harvard professor of Art and American proponent of arts and crafts ("A Portion"). Walter Crane, meanwhile, a major British exponent of the movement, responded to Norton in the second number with his views on the European situation ("Of Aesthetic Pessimism"). Topics covered in the magazine included Paul Verlaine, William Morris's bookmaking, Japanese art, attacks on mainstream literary journalism, and other issues of relevance to the magazine's high cultural interests in Pre-Raphaelitism, arts and crafts, aestheticism, and decadence. Containing no advertising, this expensive production, as Cram noted, was made possible only through the generosity of "a group of guarantors, the list reading like a 'blue book' of the New England Intelligentsia" (88).

In form and content, *The Knight Errant* exemplified private press ideals and those of the literary and artistic movements that it valorized: it was a labour of love, created without thought of profit, in a fierce spirit of anti-commercialism. As a going concern fostered by an idealism about the socially transformative power of the arts, however, it was a failure in a number of respects. First, and quite practically,

Figure 3.1 *The Knight Errant*, 1892, an early American little magazine, modeled after the British arts and crafts magazine *The Century Guild Hobby Horse*. Part of the title is rubricated (The Knight Errant), as are the city and date of publication. Courtesy of JSTOR.

its ideals of labour-intensive design and production, while suitable for books, were difficult to sustain with the regularity that periodical publication necessitates. Though intended as a quarterly, *The Knight Errant* was issued erratically, its four numbers appearing over a period of two years, rather than one. Second, and more importantly, its limited circulation and expensive price ($3.00 a year) militated against its "quest." This "quest," as its editors called it in their opening manifesto, was to fight for the causes of beauty, idealism, and imagination against materialism, realism, and commercialism, and to play a role in the cultivation of taste in America that contributor Charles Eliot Norton believed was so vital (The Editors, "The Quest" 1–2). The editors addressed these issues in their final number, which appeared in October 1894, more than a year and a half late. It was certainly in violation, then, of postal regulations mandating that publications qualifying as second-class matter be issued at regular, stated intervals. Humorously discounting expectations of regular and timely publication in a manner that, as has been indicated, would become characteristic of little magazines, they declared: “if you hold that a periodical should be issued periodically, marry, you are no true aesthetic editor, nor do you wot of the weird ways of elect authors, printers, and paper-makers” (The Editors, “By Way of Epilogue”). In addition, while acknowledging that much that they had “hoped to change remain[ed] amazingly intact,” they staked their success on their influence on bookmaking and printing (The Editors, “By Way of Epilogue”).

It is curious that they should make no claim for their role in fostering the rise of artistic periodicals. This omission is particularly striking given that the last pages of this issue discuss magazines, including the newly established *Yellow Book* and *Chap-Book*, that “quest in fellowship” with *The Knight Errant* and “herald” the coming of more such publications (G.E.B. and B.G.G. 126, 128). The privileging of book over magazine in *The Knight Errant*, however, is telling. The producers of *The Knight Errant* were not interested in the magazine form per se, nor in competing within the broader magazine market. Rather, for the creators of *The Knight Errant*, the magazine was primarily a vehicle for consideration of the book and the book arts. In the American context, this style of little magazine would be rare, the only other notable example being George Gough Booth’s elaborately designed *Cranbrook Papers*. This attitude, however, was already beginning to change and, in a very short time, little magazinists would recognize the specific advantages of the magazine proper as a fruitful medium for cultivating an appreciation of the beautiful beyond the limits of a narrow coterie. While *The Knight Errant*, then, serves as an important precursor to the American little magazines of the 1890s, it is not exemplary or revolutionary in the way that its successor, *The Chap-Book*, would be.

The Seed Planted: Stone and Kimball and *The Chap-Book*

The success of *The Chap-Book* incited a little riot of Decadence and there was a craze for odd sizes and shapes, freak illustrations, wide margins, uncut pages, Jenson types, scurrilous abuse and petty jealousies, impossible prose and doggerel rhyme.

– Gelett Burgess, in Burgess and Porter, “Memoir,” *Epi-Lark* 25 (1897)

On 15 May 1894, Harvard undergraduates Herbert Stone and Ingalls Kimball launched *The Chap-Book*, a semi-monthly magazine, which would run for one hundred issues, ceasing publication in July 1898. The magazine was initially issued from Cambridge, with its heavily Boston Brahmin–based culture. By the end of 1894, however, Stone and Kimball relocated the enterprise to Chicago, a move symbolic of the change they would bring to the genre of the little magazine. Chicago was, after all, at once a commercial, industrial city and an increasingly important cultural centre, especially after the 1893 World's Fair. *The Chap-Book* would become associated with the rise of the city as a literary and artistic centre and Chicago would serve as home to a score of little magazines, including *Blue Sky*, *The Bachelor Book*, *The Echo, Four O'Clock*, *The Goose-Quill*, *The Rubric*, *House Beautiful*, and others.[2] Chicago was an ideal location for the development of a new kind of little magazine that would, as Bartholomew Brinkman contends, "enact … a dialectic of the old and the new, the ephemeral and the permanent, the elite and the popular" (195). In this respect, *The Chap-Book*'s form of cultural engagement is very much in keeping with the emerging professional-managerial ethos that was seeking to harmonize culture and commerce and the traditional and the modern.

The magazine would involve many of Stone and Kimball's friends and acquaintances from Harvard and the larger Boston bohemian intellectual community of which they were a part. A number of those involved with *The Mahogany Tree* and *The Knight Errant* would contribute also to *The Chap-Book*, notably poet and critic Bliss Carman, who would serve, for a short time, as the magazine's editor. *The Chap-Book*, however, would be far more influential than its earlier counterparts in establishing the little magazine as a distinctive genre in this period. And, while Pollard gives warranted credit to *The Yellow Book* for kick-starting the little magazine movement in America, this British publication was more of an inspiration in terms of literary and artistic styles than a model for a magazine. It was *The Chap-Book*, which followed the launch of its British counterpart by only a month, that established the distinctive miniature format the little magazine would take in America in the 1890s, a form that would ultimately be far more prolific here than in Britain or the rest of Europe (see colour plate 2). *The Chap-Book* did indeed "incite a riot of Decadence," as Burgess claimed (Burgess and Porter), innovating, popularizing, and revolutionizing a form that would be imitated widely in the first wave of the movement (1895–7). At the same time, it established, in particular, a model for the aesthetic little magazine.

The Chap-Book's decadence was not that of *The Knight Errant*. If its predecessor's decadence, as the *Chap-Book* editor claimed, was "delightful in its opposition to commercialism," the new upstart was market savvy ("Notes," *Chap-Book* 1, no. 7, 174). Where *The Knight Errant* represented a crystallization, in aesthetic form and content, of the artistic interests of *The Mahogany Tree*, *The Chap-Book* turned the magazine as aesthetic object into an aesthetic commodity. It was in this respect that *The Chap-Book* was the offspring of the British *Yellow Book*, whose publisher, John Lane, understood how to market the aesthetic and decadent avant-garde beyond a narrow coterie.[3] Indeed, *The Yellow Book* is an example of what Freedman has characterized as the "commodification of the critique of commodification" (63), taking aestheticism and decadence, movements that opposed commercialism and the bourgeoisie, and marketing them to the middle classes. The contradictions inherent in this project were less apparent in a more democratic and commercial America, where, as has been suggested, these movements existed in more popularized forms. In this context, publications like *The Mahogany Tree* and *The Knight Errant*, while conforming to the received understanding of the little magazine as established by Hoffman, Allen, and Ulrich, are revealed, actually, to be anomalies in the context of the American little magazines of the period. *The Yellow Book*, too, is exceptional with respect to its American counterparts, even if its commercial nature is acknowledged. If we see the American little magazines of this period as situated within an Anglo-American fin-de-siècle context that Freedman characterizes as "an advanced consumer society [able] to transform criticisms of that society into objects of consumption themselves" (60), nowhere was society more advanced in this respect than America; and nowhere was the little magazine bigger, as a phenomenon, in this period, than in America, thanks, largely, to Stone and Kimball.

Before discussing their innovations to the little magazine format, it is important to recognize the relationship of *The Chap-Book* to Stone and Kimball's larger publishing enterprise. Given the bibliophilic and bookmaking interests of their social and intellectual set, it should not be surprising that it was books that served as Stone and Kimball's entry into the publishing world. Their circle included a number of "literary publishers" invested in the book beautiful, including Copeland

and Day, who, in addition to publishing new American writers, were the American issuers of *The Hobby Horse*, *The Yellow Book*, and the book publications of John Lane's Bodley Head, which showcased decadent and New Woman writers. Before *The Chap-Book* was launched, Stone and Kimball had already published a range of notable contemporary American and British writers, including Kenneth Grahame, Hamlin Garland, Joaquin Miller, Eugene Field, Maurice Thompson, George Santayana, and Bliss Carman. For Stone and Kimball, the magazine, as first conceived, was a means to an end in relation to their book publishing, "an advertisement and prospectus" as Stone described it to his family, for their list (qtd. in Bergel 157). In magazine form, they could circulate this material free through the post as second-class matter, saving considerable expense. It appears, then, that *The Chap-Book* was, at first, a sideline to the more serious business of publishing books of distinction for a middle-class audience. The quick success of *The Chap-Book*, however, revealed that, unlike publications such as *The Mahogany Tree* and *Knight Errant*, a little magazine might be sustained as a going concern in a broader publishing enterprise based on fine press principles. As such, Stone and Kimball served as a model for similar small press and publishing enterprises of the era that issued both books and little magazines.

The Chap-Book's skillful mediation between culture and commerce made it ideally suited to an emerging professional middle-class readership. Stone and Kimball turned an elite coterie form into an affordable aesthetic commodity. In terms of the magazine, the most striking evidence of Stone and Kimball's efforts to popularize the form are denoted by price and circulation, aspects in which *The Chap-Book* differed from *The Hobby Horse*, *Mahogany Tree*, *Knight Errant*, and *Yellow Book*. For example, while four issues, or a year's subscription to the *Knight Errant*, cost $3.00, the twenty-four yearly issues of *The Chap-Book* cost $1.00, later $2.00, when its price would rise from five to ten cents. *The Hobby Horse* and the *Yellow Book* were comparably expensive, both priced at $6.00 for a year's subscription in America. Differences in circulation methods and numbers, too, are significant for thinking about Stone and Kimball's innovations to the little magazine. Both *The Chap-Book* and *The Yellow Book* eschewed the largely subscription-based models of other little magazines of the day, instead using a combination of subscription and newsstand sales. These magazines' willingness to engage with commercial methods of distribution meant that their circulation targets were higher than their coterie counterparts. Where *The Hobby Horse*, *Mahogany Tree*, and *Knight Errant* were issued in five hundred copies, *The Yellow Book* and *Chap-Book* circulated in the thousands. The Bodley Head, for example, issued 7,000 copies of the first two numbers of the *Yellow Book*, reducing the number to 5,000 from October 1894 (James G. Nelson 108). *The Chap-Book*, meanwhile, was more successful, reaching a peak of 16,500 (Kramer 208). The *Chap-Book*, then, was revolutionary in terms of its offering of a choice aesthetic print object at a price that placed it on a par with the new ten-cent monthly mass-market magazines, a precedent that would be taken up widely by its successors. Similarly, its impressive circulation, while not often matched by subsequent little magazines, was an aspiration. Overall, a number of these American little magazines did as well as, or better than, *The Yellow Book*. *The Chap-Book* demonstrated that there was a market, and a reasonably significant one, too, for a coterie-style fine press publication.

What precisely did *The Chap-Book* offer its readership for their five or ten cents? Here, *The Chap-Book* also set a high standard for its imitators. Stone's wealthy newspaper magnate father not only financed the project, he also had transatlantic connections in the literary world. Thus, while *The Chap-Book* did much to help aspiring and emerging American artists and writers, it also attracted an impressive roster of European figures, including Henry James, H.G. Wells, Max Beerbohm, Aubrey Beardsley, John Davidson, William Butler Yeats, Hamlin Garland, Israel Zangwill, Paul Verlaine, Anatole France, Thomas Hardy, Stephen Crane, Stéphane Mallarmé, and Kenneth Grahame. While such a prestigious list was not equaled by other little magazines, it is reflective of the variety and genres of literature and art that would become staples of these publications. What is notable about this list, and the contents of *The Chap-Book* more broadly, is the range of styles of writing that extend its reach beyond the narrower limits of earlier British and American aesthetic periodicals. Though arts and crafts, aestheticism, and decadence are represented, more popular forms of realist writing are also featured in *The Chap-Book*, and the old was not fetishized at the expense of the new. *The Chap-Book* was as engaged with fine press ideals that valorized the past as it was with the new – modern art forms such as the poster movement, for example. Like *The Yellow Book*, *The Chap-Book* had a reputation as decadent, even while playing it safe in its balancing of conventional and avant-garde content.[4] While some of its successors were more daring, the general tendency towards balance between high and popular modes that *The Chap-Book* represents is characteristic of little magazine content broadly speaking, as discussed in more depth in some of the chapters in section 2.

In terms of formal innovations to the little magazine genre, *The Chap-Book*'s most important contribution was format, which was signalled by its title. Against the large quarto size of *The Knight Errant* and the bulky hardback format of *The Yellow Book*, *The Chap-Book* adopted the small dimensions of the historic form it took its name from, measuring 7.5 x 4.5 inches for most of its run. This format, as I have suggested, would come to denote "little magazineness," a feature that highlighted the ambiguous cultural status of the genre as at once elitist and populist. *The Chap-Book* educated its readership about the form, including, for example, a feature on chap-books by historian John Ashton, and by printing examples of chap-book woodcuts. Though the chap-book represented an historically cheap format, its appearance was in keeping with private press ideals that looked to the preindustrial hand press era, favouring old style fonts, woodcut or woodblock illustrations, handmade paper, uncut pages, wide margins, and rubrication. Instead, however, of recreating the laborious and time-consuming methods that had been employed in the expensive, low-circulation *Knight Errant*, Stone and Kimball found ways to economise in order to enable production in numbers of 10,000 or more to sell at a cost of five and, later, ten cents, while still maintaining an attractive publication. It was unnecessary, for example, to create new typefaces or use handmade paper. Old-style fonts were increasingly available as a consequence of the interest in fine printing, and imitation handmade and laid paper were popular with little magazinists. Printing methods varied through the run of the magazine. At one point, Stone and Kimball employed two separate presses, one to do typesetting and another to do presswork (Kramer 209). This distinction between the artistic and mechanical sides of printing was one that was emerging in this period with the revolution in fine printing and the rise of graphic arts as a distinctive professional field (Thomson, *Origins* 11). Frederick Goudy, who would become one of the most prolific typeface designers of the twentieth-century, was responsible for the typesetting at his small print shop, the Camelot Press, when *The Chap-Book* was produced in this manner, and it is significant that he found this to be a transformative moment in his career. The work for Stone and Kimball, he said, gave him a "new conception of art and literature [and of typography on] a higher plane than mere commercialism" (31). This view is important because it attests to the role of *The Chap-Book*, and little magazines more generally, in transforming book and magazine production for the twentieth century and in bringing fine press ideals to a wider audience.

The difficulty of maintaining the balance between high cultural and commercial aims soon became apparent with the sudden success of the magazine and the host of competitors that emerged to challenge *The Chap-Book*'s domination of the field of the high-class but inexpensive magazine. The magazine began to rely more on advertising, a course that its predecessor, *The Knight Errant*, had dismissed as a means of survival (The Editors, "By Way of an Epilogue"). The more commercial *Yellow Book*, by contrast, though no stranger to exploiting techniques of advertising, did not contain advertisements, other than for publishers' lists, and this may well have been a factor in its demise. *The Chap-Book* initially followed this practice but, within a few months, it featured advertising for railway companies, soap, perfume, pianos, hats, bicycles, medicines, beer, and other products, lessening its credibility as an artistic production.[5] An additional strain came from competitors – the so-called riot of Decadence that Burgess claimed *The Chap-Book* generated (Burgess and Porter). At the height of the first wave of little magazines in 1895 and 1896, there were close to a hundred such publications on offer. There was constant pressure to innovate and outdo one's competitors in the production of ever-queerer formats, illustrations, and content. *The Chap-Book* was generally disparaging towards its imitators, nowhere more so than in December 1896 when it announced its intention to abandon its signature format: "[*The Chap-Book*] has long ceased to desire any comparison with the numerous obvious imitations of it, the so-called miniature magazines. These papers … had indeed destroyed any charm which the small size originally had" ("Announcements" xxi).

The 15 January 1897 issue marked the publisher's intention to establish the magazine as a "sane and entertaining … journal of the first rank," styled after literary reviews such as *The Athenaeum* and *The Academy* ("Announcements" xxi). In addition to abandoning its chap-book format for a large quarto size, the magazine also featured a change in paper, one more suitable for advertising and the reproduction of half-tone illustrations; a stronger focus on formal reviewing; the elimination of artistic content; the inclusion of half-tone photographs; and space for the kind of political commentary that it had previously eschewed as irrelevant to a magazine concerned with culture.[6] *The Chap-Book* also distanced itself from the kind of literature and art it, and little magazines more generally, were associated with. An essay by Laurence Jerrold in the newly revamped *Chap-Book* offers what might be taken as an allegory of the magazine's coming of age. "The Literary Pilgrimage and the Youth's Progress" recounts the maturation of the French man of letters. As a youth, he is "heroic ... refreshingly intolerant and an exquisite zealot," his tastes running to Poe, Baudelaire, Maeterlinck, Louÿs, and other favourites of the decadents (8). This is his reading matter before he "is fitted for the man's journey," where the narrative leaves off (11). While the narrative does not discount the favoured reading of the young man, the suggestion is that, while necessary, it is the stuff of youth and that, eventually, a turn from it is needed. The story of this youth, of course, parallels the journey of *The Chap-Book*, which itself accounted for its transition to a mainstream literary journal as a maturation.

Though Wendy Schlereth claims that the physical transformation of the magazine did not reflect a change in intellectual content (12), clearly it underwent an ideological shift. *The Chap-Book* couched its transformation in heroic terms, but the changes were largely driven, as Stone himself suggested, by financial need and commercial interests: "the advertisers" he told his brother, "won't take space in a small paper" (qtd. in Bergel 171). Content might also have been a concern. *The Chap-Book* did not, in the end, make the transition to the big time successfully, and its peers expressed cynicism at its change and eventual demise. William Ellis of *The Philosopher*, for example, offered a strikingly different allegory of its development to Jerrold's, cynically identifying a commercial motive. While acknowledging the "exuberant enthusiasm of youth that had shaped its course and marked its destinies," he noted that "later it became not so much a question of making it pay as of how much it could pay, and it was in attempting to set its sails to the trade winds that the craft, already become unwieldy and somewhat water-logged, capsized and plunged to the bottom" ("In the Smoking Room," *Philosopher* 4, no. 1, 71). In the end, *The Chap-Book* was a victim of its success, unable to balance the competing demands of art and commerce in its rapid rise. *The Chap-Book*, therefore, served both as model and warning for its successors.

Thomas Mosher's *Bibelot*: The Little Magazine That Could

The success of a quarterly like *Modern Art*, the demand that has gone out for *The Chap-Book*, the publisher's own experience with his BIBELOT SERIES, all favor the belief that such beautifully gotten up affairs have created a republic of their own.

– Thomas Mosher, "*The Bibelot*," *Bibelot* 1, no. 1 (1895)

Like Stone and Kimball and those of the Cambridge/Boston bohemian set, Thomas Mosher, of Portland, Maine, was a devotee of the book arts exemplified by William Morris's Kelmscott Press and the British arts and crafts movement. He, too, would play a role as a literary publisher in the revolution in fine printing and establish an important and influential little magazine, *The Bibelot*. Like his counterparts, his aim was to provide beautiful print material at an affordable price, to demonstrate, as he said in his manifesto for the first number, "that choice typography and inexpensiveness need not lie far apart" ("*The Bibelot*"). Both his publishing operation and his magazine were more successful than Stone and Kimball's in terms of longevity. He published books from 1891 to his death in 1923, a list that eventually numbered 730 titles and 240 issues of *The Bibelot*, which, with its twenty-year run, equaled that of *The Philistine*.[7] Mosher's magazine was launched in January 1895, eight months after *The Chap-Book*. Like its predecessor, it was initially priced at five cents per issue, fifty cents for a year's subscription, later increasing to ten cents, a dollar a year. It represented a unique type within the genre of the little magazine and, more specifically, within the narrower field of the aesthetic little magazine. Though less imitated than *The Chap-Book*, it was much admired by little magazinists. Mosher's efforts to bring beautiful publications and an appreciation for choice typography to a culturally aspiring professional middle class were more successful in balancing the tensions between art and commerce than those of Stone and Kimball. A key to his success, it seems, was to keep his focus within reasonable limits. His circulation never exceeded 4,000 and he did not have to adapt, as *The Chap-Book* did, to sudden success. Mosher ran his small operation himself, with the assistance of a clerk or two and a secretary. Like Stone and Kimball, Mosher was a "literary publisher" rather than a small press, so printing was done off-site. Mosher kept his distribution costs under control by conducting all his business through mail orders with subscribers and the trade.

Though Mosher's introduction to the first volume of *The Bibelot*, quoted above, acknowledges *The Chap-Book* as a source of inspiration, his publication was different. While taking the chap-book format, *The Bibelot* was distinctive in its aims and purpose and innovative in terms of the content it offered. Like his predecessors, Mosher was much inspired by the arts and crafts movement and its experiments in book-making and the book arts. Whereas Stone and Kimball had modernized these ideas, Mosher was more loyal to the aims of the original movement. *The Hobby Horse* in particular, William E. Fredeman argues, exerted a profound influence on Mosher, "shaping his literary taste and his conception of the book beautiful," and informing his understanding of the function of literature to impart "rapture" (13, 14). Along with his commitment to the ideals of the private press movement, Mosher was also more traditional in his conception of literary culture and taste, his understanding of the book beautiful, and of the function and value of literature. He establishes this difference from *The Chap-Book* and its ilk in his opening issue, asserting that his publication "does not profess to exploit the new forces and ferments of *fin de siècle* writers" ("*The Bibelot*"). Indeed, only 35 per cent per cent of its content consisted of post-1850 literature (Fredeman 19). Mosher's publication, rather, as its subtitle indicates, was a "reprint of poetry and prose for book lovers, chosen in part from scarce editions and sources not generally known." His typical content provision is exemplified by his inclusions in the first year: William Blake's lyrics, François Villon's ballades, Medieval Latin students' songs, a section from Walter Pater's *Marius the Epicurean*, fragments from Sappho, sonnets of English dramatic poets, lyrics from James Thomson, D.G. Rossetti's "Hand and Soul," airs of Thomas Campion, an act from Percy Bysshe Shelley's *Cenci*, John Addington Symonds on the rose in poetry, and Robert Louis Stevenson's story about Villon, "A Lodging for the Night." Mosher's innovation, then, was to find the new in the old or familiar – to explore the byways of literature and bring forward, as he said, the "exotics … that might not find a way to wider reading" (Mosher, "*The Bibelot*"). There are familiar names, but the works Mosher chose were lesser known and not widely available. If his magazine was more conservative overall than *The Chap-Book*, it also exuded a different kind of cultural authority, one more in keeping with the genteel tradition and the culture of character than a culture of personality. Certainly, the magazine might still draw the same kind of young intellectual and professional middle-class readership as *The Chap-Book*. Savvy readers, for example, would recognize many of these authors as fundamental influences on the latest literary trends: Sappho, Rossetti, Villon, and Pater, for example, were figures of significant interest for late-nineteenth-century aestheticism and decadence. At the same time, the alternative nature of Mosher's selections within a recognizable literary tradition offered a particular kind of cultural distinction. The magazine might also, however, draw an older, more genteel, readership, in tune with the rather Arnoldian thrust of his project to offer "an aid to self-culture in literature" (Mosher, Foreword xi).

An additional innovation of *The Bibelot* was Mosher's packaging of content. Whereas *The Chap-Book* was, as its subtitle indicated, a miscellany, *The Bibelot* eschewed typical magazine form. With each of its issues focused on a particular author or text, it presented itself, rather, as an anthology. Though Mosher himself did not use this term, he did invoke the etymology of the word (coming from the Greek for flowers [*anthos*] and gathered [*legeín*]) in his description of the magazine as a "bring[ing] together of the posies of other men" ("*The Bibelot*"). Others, however, have readily identified it as an anthology. Mosher bibliographer Philip R. Bishop, for example, describes it as a "twenty-year anthology of Mosher's own making" (94), while Jean-François Vilain declares it a "very personal anthology," a "faithful alter ego of its creator" ("*Bibelot*" 49, 48). Though comprised almost entirely of the works of others, with only very short introductions by Mosher, the magazine is, nevertheless, as Bishop and Vilain suggest, highly personal. Mosher, after all, is identifiable as the creative force in the making of the magazine both in terms of content and form for, as he says, the "posies" he provides are "bound up by a thread of [his] own making" and "resown in fields their authors never knew" ("*The Bibelot*").

While the introductions to each issue of the magazine provide a sense of Mosher's personal intervention more broadly, *The Bibelot*, as twenty-year anthology, has a wider purpose that is connected to his investment in self-culture. William Marion Reedy identified this purpose in quasi-mystical terms, saying that *The Bibelot* aimed to "touch the soul to finer issues, to acquaint it with the ecstacies [*sic*] of life lived and contemplated" ("Ending" 190). It could be argued, also, that part of this higher purpose is an engagement in canon reshaping, through a focus on the byways of literature. An important part of this project, especially with respect to its position in the little magazine movement, is its incorporation, into a broader literary tradition, of contemporary writers. Though these writers accounted only for a small proportion of content, what is notable about Mosher's inclusion of writers like Yeats, Symons, Dowson, Wilde, and Carman, is that by placing them in the company of classic authors going back to antiquity, he confers canonical status on them at a time when they had not achieved this in their own countries. Framed within Mosher's little magazine, these writers become part of a tradition, while in the more modern *Chap-Book* they register as avant-garde and controversial.

Constructing an anthology that places particular writers and texts in relation to each other is, of course, one way that Mosher "resow[s]" them "in fields [they] never knew." So, too, of course does the package they come in – another sense of the "fields their authors never knew": first, as a kind of serial anthology, and second, as an 1890s little magazine. In thinking about Mosher's magazine as serial anthology, it is important to recognize how it fit into his larger publishing scheme, which was organized, Vilain argues, around the concept of series: "Mosher understood that people who like books tend to like their sets complete, and by packaging his publications in series, as well as making some volumes available as sets, he catered to this passion" ("Mosher's Concept" 8). As an anthology issued in monthly parts, *The Bibelot* functioned as a series within this larger scheme, becoming a collectible in its own right, serving as an advertising and marketing tool for his broader list, and also having a synergy with his other series. Indeed, much of the work printed in *The Bibelot* would go on to be issued in book format in his various series.

Mosher also contributed to enhancing the status of the 1890s little magazine as collectible in ways different to Stone and Kimball. Mosher, as I have said, appropriated the form innovated by *The Chap-Book*, which he maintained unchanged throughout the long run of the magazine. Measuring 6 × 4.5 inches, it was printed on Van Gelder paper bound in blue printed wraps, with printing in black and red (title, contents, price) on the front cover and a red fleur de lys design on the back (see Figure 3.2). Issues ranged between twenty-four and forty pages with advertising – limited to publishers and other little magazines – at back and front. Mosher, however, made innovations to the *Chap-Book* model in ways that emphasized the collectible status of the little magazine in this period. If the term chap-book applied to a specific kind of collectible print object, Mosher's term, bibelot, meaning "a small curio or article of *virtù*" (*OED* s.v. "Bibelot"), was more general, but certainly germane to the wider world of collecting, which was increasingly accessible to the middle classes. Like the term "chap-book," "bibelot" would also develop currency in this period, serving, for example, as Faxon's preferred term for the little magazine. Mosher reinforced the collectible status of his publication by offering it in a range of volume formats for subscribers of different means (Bishop 63). Standard binding consisted of blue boards with white paper spine (see

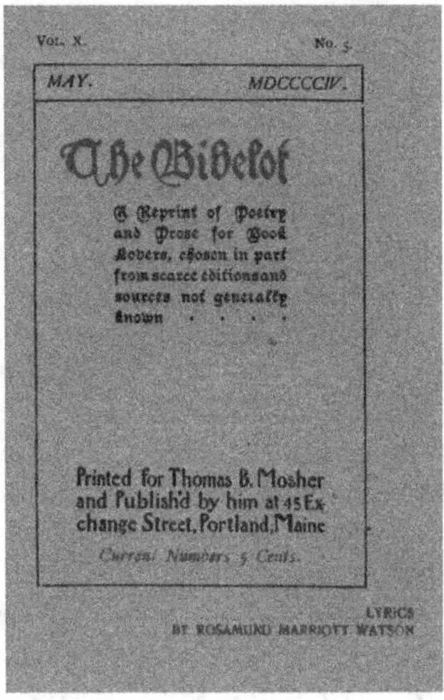

Figure 3.2 Cover of *The Bibelot*, January 1895. The standard cover design throughout its run, with rubricated title. In possession of author.

colour plate 11, second from left), with blue dustwrapper and slipcase, or, for libraries, sturdy blue buckram (see colour plate 11, extreme left). Mosher also offered options for serious and wealthy collectors. One hundred sets were produced with levant leather bindings in red, green, or brown with gilt tops and uncut pages at a price of $125, with extra gilt tooling available for $150 a set (see colour plate 11, third and fourth from left). Rarer still were twelve copies (only six from 1910) of a premium edition on Japan vellum (see colour plate 11, extreme right). One of Mosher's key innovations in the little magazine field, then, was to maximize the relationship between these publications and the world of fine press printing. While *The Chap-Book* offered attractive, if generic, bindings for subscribers, Mosher took the concept of the magazine as book a step further with his packaging of the little magazine and his presentation of it as a kind of literary anthology.

While few subsequent little magazines adopted the anthology format that Mosher devised, or packaged their magazines in such a variety of ways, his modest but successful publishing enterprise served as a more realistic model than Stone and Kimball's for many of the small presses and publishers that would issue little magazines and books in the spirit of fine press printing. While *The Chap-Book* had an ambivalent status within the field of little magazinists, Mosher was much respected, a reflection of his ability to balance the tension between art and commerce. Unlike Stone and Kimball, Mosher offered a consistent product and maintained it for twenty years; it survived to take its place, for a brief time, alongside a new generation of little magazines in the modernist period. His influence lay in the field of graphic design and in the shaping of literary taste through his construction of an alternative canon. As private press scholar Will Ransom noted, "He introduced 'fine writing' as well as 'fine printing' to many who met it for the first time" (127). With his enterprise, Mosher achieved what Morris aspired to, but did not realize – the production of beautiful publications at affordable prices, catering to those of the middle classes with high cultural aspirations. Moreover, his publications served as an inspiration to book designers of the early twentieth century and an education for emerging writers and intellectuals. Disciples included Bruce Rogers and Frederick Goudy, for example, but his style also strongly shaped twentieth-century book design in the commercial trade (Newton 124). At the same time, his literary tastes informed modernists who were exposed to his eclectic offerings. Ezra Pound acknowledged being "guided by Mr. Mosher of Bangor [*sic*]," thanking him for bringing to his attention "various fine things which I should not otherwise have come upon so soon" ("Lionel Johnson" 365). John Espey, meanwhile, has described *The Bibelot* as a "source book for Pound" (323).[8] If Mosher's magazine did not achieve the more popular status of publications like *The Chap-Book* and other faddish little magazines, its longevity assured him an influence that his counterparts would not achieve.

The Little Magazine Made Big: Elbert Hubbard's *Philistine* (1895–1915)

When I think of you, I rejoice that there is a man in the world that can keep up a small independent monthly howler without dying, going broke, or becoming an ass.

– Stephen Crane to Elbert Hubbard, 1 May 1899, in Crane, *Stephen Crane: Letters* 220.

Launched in June 1895, just over a year after *The Chap-Book* and five months after *The Bibelot*, Elbert Hubbard's *Philistine* is another major little magazine of the period, establishing a model for the "periodical of protest" and "one-man magazines" subgenres. Like *The Chap-Book* and *The Bibelot*, *The Philistine* was a product of an enthusiasm for Morris's Kelmscott Press and the revival of fine printing in Britain. In 1892, Hubbard abandoned a successful career as a soap salesman to pursue literary ambitions, attending Harvard as a special student and publishing a few novels before taking part in the revolution in fine printing by founding the Roycroft Press in East Aurora, New York. His enterprise differed from both that of Stone and Kimball and Mosher in combining a printing and publishing establishment. Hubbard's Roycroft Press typifies the more commercial form that fine press printing and little magazines would take in America. As a self-confessed "business man with a literary attachment" (Balch 103), Hubbard brought art and commerce together in a way that was more successful, commercially, than Stone and Kimball or Mosher. Hubbard developed a self-sufficient arts and crafts community, numbering five hundred at its height (Rust and Turgeon 7), based on the printing and publishing of books and magazines; artistic binding; Hubbard's free-lance writing and lecturing; and blacksmithing, carpentry, terra cotta, and weaving in the production of arts and crafts goods, furniture, and decorative objects. The most successful aspect of his enterprise was always, however, printing and publishing. Many have argued that the artistic merits of his productions were poor. Even Dard Hunter, who served for nine years as Director of Art at Roycroft, was unkind about the bourgeois, industrial, and commercial nature of the publications, mocking the features that made them widely popular in middle-class homes across the country:

> Hubbard … undertook to place limp-leather bindings on the golden oak tables of every sitting room in America. Books in their window-cleaner … covers were turned out in mass production; the dozen or more Roycroft presses were kept humming night and day; hand-made paper was imported by the thousands of reams; red and black ink was purchased by the barrel, and every goat in the world was a potential limp binding. (30)

Hubbard, however, demonstrated, in no uncertain terms, and on a much larger scale than Mosher, that book and magazine publishing based on private press ideals could be a big business indeed. A celebrity who understood that all publicity is good publicity, he defiantly advertised negative criticism, including the *Hartford Courant*'s suggestion that he was "the P.T. Barnum of art" (front matter, *Philistine*). He used his notoriety to popularize and democratize arts and crafts, reaching a broader segment of the middle class than any other little magazinist. As William Marion Reedy noted, Hubbard "makes lovers of books out of people who never knew books before. His [writings] ... are the beginnings of humanism for hundreds of thousands of people" ("Little Journey" 14).

The origins of *The Philistine*, which would become the jewel in the crown of the Roycroft enterprise, are somewhat unclear.[9] Begun, apparently, as a whim, with little intention of continuing beyond the first issue, *The Philistine* was initially a collaborative effort involving Hubbard, William McIntosh, and Harry Taber. Taber served as editor for the first months, but, by early 1896, the magazine was under Hubbard's sole control. Though the magazine would take time to establish its identity as a periodical of protest, it was successful from the first, its circulation increasing year upon year. The first number, priced at ten cents, was issued in a run of 2,500 copies, about typical for a little magazine of the period, and more modest than *The Bibelot*. By 1896, circulation reached 10,000, well surpassing *The Bibelot* and nearly attaining the level of *The Chap-Book* in this period. By 1897, with a circulation of 20,000, it had outstripped *The Chap-Book*. Sales more than doubled the following year and, by 1904, it was selling over 100,000 copies, a circulation it sustained until ceasing publication with Hubbard's death in 1915.[10]

Hubbard's *Philistine* is notable, then, as the most popular and longest-running little magazine, but also for its importance to small press publishers for whom the publication was either inspiration or abomination. Its production within the context of an arts and crafts community links it also to other such publications. *The Philistine*, however, was never as much a promotional organ for the Roycrofters as *The Artsman* and *Country Time and Tide* were for the Rose Valley and New Clairvaux colonies. More importantly, *The Philistine*, in its early guise, was competitive with *The Chap-Book*, making contributions to the development of the aesthetic little magazine. The most significant innovations that *The Philistine* would make, however, were not literary and artistic. Rather, it was Hubbard's use of the little magazine as a vehicle for social protest and his popularization of a highly personal, idiosyncratic, and vernacular style that would revolutionize the form.

Though established initially as an aesthetic little magazine along the lines of *The Chap-Book*, *The Philistine*'s spirit of protest was evident from the first issue. As opposed to the more serious-minded and idealistic intentions of *The Bibelot*, *The Philistine* took an aggressive, oppositional tone for its manifesto, following *The Chap-Book* in its attitude towards the mainstream press: "It is because we cannot say what we would in the periodicals which are now issued in a dignified manner in various places, that we have made this book," the editor declared in the first issue (probably Harry P. Taber, but writing as the "East Aurora School of Philosophy"), going on to attack the editors of *The Century*, *Harper's*, and *Ladies Home Journal* (17). This motivation was later reiterated by Hubbard: "We called it *The Philistine* because we were going after the 'Chosen People' in literature ... When you call a man a bad name, you are that thing – not he. The Smug and Snugly ensconced denizens of Union Square called me a Philistine, and I said, 'Yes, I am one if a Philistine is something different from you" ("An Interesting Personality" 312). Hubbard's critique highlights his discomfort not only with the mainstream, but with the intellectual literary and artistic milieu that *The Chap-Book* set represented. Hubbard was self-educated, a man who profited from the Chautauqua movement, and was contemptuous of the frigid intellectualism he had encountered at Harvard, where he took classes in the 1890s. *The Chap-Book*, for him, was part of this culture and served as a frequent target of attack in *The Philistine*, where it was referred to derisively as *The Chip-Munk*. Like the Roycroft enterprise more generally, Hubbard's magazine had a broader reach, aiming to appeal, as Paul McKenna argues, "to the unsettled, the creatively unsatisfied ... [t]he clerks, office managers, supervisors, and self-employed" (43). *The Philistine* was, in its early days, the poor man's *Chap-Book*, proudly and defiantly so. Hubbard, however, also had his share of admirers among artists, intellectuals, professionals, capitalists, the middle classes, and other little magazinists who were drawn to his charismatic personality.

In its early days as an aesthetic periodical, *The Philistine* had an ambivalent relationship to *The Chap-Book*, with which it was inevitably compared. Physically, it adopted the chap-book format, measuring 6.25 x 4.75 inches, later 6.25 x 4.5, going through minor design variations before settling on its signature look by 1898. It is notable that a virtually identical print object was created using a variety of production methods as the magazine's circulation increased. While it began quite literally in the spirit of small press ideals – as a hand-press printed, hand-folded and stitched magazine – its homely effects were eventually created through machine printing, folding, and stitching, to accommodate the magazine's large circulation (McKenna 39–42). A butcher paper cover in mustard yellow gave it pungency, distinguishing it from the more refined paper of *The Chap-Book*'s cream, and *Bibelot*'s blue, covers. Like its counterparts, however, *The Philistine* employed rubrication in the title, for lines framing a changing monthly epigraph, aphorism, or quotation, and for the decorative seahorse device, designed by W.W. Denslow, at the bottom left corner, which featured volume and number information (see colour plate 2, second row, left). The back cover was reserved for a serious or witty motto or quotation in decorative font framed with an ornamental border (see Figure 9.2), or accompanied by cartoons or satirical drawings (see Figure 3.3). Inside, content pages appeared on natural laid paper, remaining consistently at about thirty-two pages through the run of the magazine.

Its advertising pages, however, document its transformation from niche aesthetic periodical to popular periodical. Like many other aesthetic little magazines, *The Chap-Book* included, *The Philistine* initially limited advertising to small presses, publishers, and other magazines. Mosher, for example, was a notable advertiser in early issues. There was also joke advertising, a practice adopted by other little magazines of the period. In *The Philistine*, Stone and Kimball come under fire, for example, as Rock and Bumball, literary undertakers ("Advertisements" 72). As the magazine increased in popularity, it, like *The Chap-Book*, began to take advertising for more commercial products – bicycles, typewriters, breakfast cereals, medicines, etc., as well as Roycroft products. Though *The Philistine* never changed its size or number of content pages, it did change the paper upon which it printed advertisements, paper more suitable to reproducing half-tone images. At the height of its popularity, there would be as much advertising, front and back, as content between. Hubbard would become renowned for his skill at transforming advertising into content.[11]

In terms of content, *The Philistine*, in its first years, was much akin to its competitor, *The Chap-Book*, filling its thirty-two pages with a mixture of poetry, literary essays, fiction, and a notes section treating the world of magazine and book culture. Occasionally, the kind of social commentary that would come, eventually, to characterize the publication, appeared in the way of an essay critiquing religious and social custom and hypocrisy. Though this social commentary distinguished *The Philistine* from *The Chap-Book* in the early 1895–7 period, the publications shared as many as twenty-five contributors (Bruce A. White 36). Many of these contributors were also associated with other important little magazines, such as Carolyn Wells (*Lark*, *Bradley His*

Figure 3.3 Cartoon back cover, February 1899, featuring lines by Stephen Crane and an illustration by W.W. Denslow. The square frame surrounding the figure is rubricated. Courtesy of HathiTrust.

Book, Criterion), Gelett Burgess (*Lark, Criterion*), Yone Noguchi (*Lark*), Walter Blackburn Harte (*Fly Leaf, Lotus*), and Michael Monahan (*Papyrus*). *The Philistine*'s reprinting of work by Walter Crane, William Morris, and John Ruskin in this period, the kind of content that might appear, for example, in *The Bibelot*, further demonstrates the degree to which *The Philistine* was, at first, much more like, than unlike, aesthetic little magazines.

The Philistine, however, did have distinction in its tenure as an aesthetic little magazine, notably in its association with two important figures: Stephen Crane (1871–1900) and W.W. Denslow (1856–1915). While it might be expected that Crane's avant-garde poetry – "lines" as he preferred to call them – might be welcome in the pages of little magazines, he was more often a subject of mockery, a topic considered in more detail in chapter 5. Though *The Chap-Book* published Crane's verse too, it was *The Philistine*, of all the 1890s little magazines, that did most to showcase his work, printing twenty of his works of prose and poetry, many as first appearances, between 1895 and 1900. Indeed, Crane was the literary figure most represented in the magazine. Many Crane scholars have characterized Hubbard's relationship with the writer as exploitative, pointing as evidence to the infamous Philistine dinner in his honour that turned into a roasting of Crane, while serving as excellent publicity for Hubbard.[12] Though Hubbard may have profited more from the association, he did provide a rare supportive platform for Crane at a time when he was much derided. Hubbard and Crane were kindred spirits. Both, as Bruce A. White notes, were self-educated, anti-establishment, bohemian, and iconoclastic, with a shared sense of humour and an interest in journalistic prose (63). While Hubbard's admiration for Crane's writing was not unqualified – indeed, he took the opportunity occasionally to mock it – he identified with its individualism; as he wrote to Crane in 1895, "Your work is of a kind so charged with electricity that it cannot be handled. It is all live wire" (Crane, *Correspondence* 115). It makes sense that Crane was the most represented literary writer in *The Philistine.* Hubbard regarded him as "a coming man," like himself (Crane, *Correspondence* 109).

Another figure that provided *The Philistine* with distinction in the realm of aesthetic little magazines was W.W. Denslow, who was associated with the Roycrofters from 1896 to 1900, and would go on to achieve fame as the illustrator of the *Wizard of Oz* books.[13] Unlike a number of aesthetic little magazines of the period, *The Philistine* did not give much attention to visual art in the way of woodcuts and poster-style art, but Denslow's cartoons, which appeared regularly in the early period as back covers, were a unique contribution to the visual art of little magazines. Among his best works for the periodical were the cartoons that featured Crane or illustrated his lines (see Figure 3.3). While much of the poster-art style work in the aesthetic little magazines of this period was in the art nouveau vein and largely imitative of Beardsley and French poster artists, Denslow mostly bucked these trends, using a cartoon style to humorous effect and drawing inspiration from British children's book illustrators, such as Randolph Caldecott and Walter Crane, and from Japanese prints (Greene, "W.W. Denslow" 69; Greene, "W.W. Denslow: Illustrator" 88). In this respect, his work differed significantly from that of Will Bradley and Frank Hazenplug, favourites of *The Chap-Book*, a magazine Denslow referred to dismissively as the "Pap Book" (Greene, "W.W. Denslow, Illustrator" 89).

Despite *The Philistine*'s association with Crane and Denslow and its impressive roster of contributors drawn from the broader little magazine network, Hubbard did not have the connections or literary talent to sustain an aesthetic little magazine of the first rank; and, though sales of *The Philistine* were strong and ever increasing, Hubbard likely recognized this weakness, which might explain his attempts to collaborate with others he identified as "coming men." In 1896, after his falling out with Taber, for example, he proposed a partnership with Walter Blackburn Harte, an important rising figure in the little magazine world who had just established *The Fly Leaf*. The collaboration lasted a mere two weeks and might well have been designed, as some claim, to kill off the competition (Mott, *History* 389; Bruce A. White 45).[14]

Though the Roycroft Community would continue to be a magnet for little magazinists and potential partners, by 1897 the character of *The Philistine* as a vehicle for Hubbard's own views was taking firmer shape. Hubbard realized that his idiosyncratic and homespun style of commentary filled an important niche in the field of little magazines. Where *The Chap-Book*'s insouciance and spirit were attributed to youth, for example, the older Hubbard's brash boldness was more clearly in keeping with the emerging culture of personality and its interest in the charismatic individual. At the same time, Hubbard must also have recognized that this highly personal style was better put in the service of topical social and political commentary than literature and the arts, areas well addressed by the ever-expanding field of little magazines. From 1897 on, then, literary content takes a back seat to Hubbard's opinionated writing on social, political, and cultural issues, views, which, from a twenty-first century perspective seem somewhat irreconcilable. His thinking represented a blend of populism, socialism, progressivism, individualism, and corporatism. He was an admirer of Tolstoy and Christian anarchism, and of Ruskin and Morris and their views on the dignity of labour. He was against religion, more particularly the corruption of it by churches, and supported the principles of free love and women's suffrage. He was a strident pacifist and anti-imperialist. Hubbard was also anti-government. Though a self-declared socialist, Hubbard was anti-union. Believing neither in unions nor government, he put his faith in corporations, trusts, and big business, arguing, for example, that "The Trusts are getting things ready for Socialism" ("Heart to Heart Talks with Philistines" *Philistine* 14, no. 2, 42). Hubbard was also, however, an opponent of orthodoxy of thought and encouraged his readers to think for themselves, even if it meant disagreeing with him. His rhetorical style, touched on more fully in chapter 8, was personal and intimate, a combination of vituperation, frankness, homespun wit, folk wisdom, and optimistic idealism in a highly vernacular style.

It was this perspective and voice that would inform the transformation of *The Philistine* from aesthetic periodical to periodical of protest, a genre of little magazine that Hubbard would pioneer. The structure of *The Philistine* in its mature guise typically began with a quatrain or a motto, followed by an essay or two, but the bulk – often the entire issue – was devoted to Hubbard's "Heart to Heart Talks With Philistines by the Pastor of His Flock" or some variation on this title. This column was a mish-mash of essays and commentary on social, religious, and political issues, reflections, Hubbardian epigrams, gossip, satire, and jokes. The transformation of the magazine reached its apotheosis in 1899 with the publication, in January, of a manifesto declaring new intentions for the magazine, and, in March, of Hubbard's most famous contribution to American cultural life, "A Message to Garcia." In "Manifesto!," writing as "The Pastor," Hubbard declares his intention "to write every article and paragraph … including advertisements and testimonials of Roycroft books," attacking a number of contributors whom he had fed and boarded, notably former collaborators and contributors Taber, McIntosh, and Harte, as well as Crane (33). Like much that Hubbard wrote, this manifesto was not meant in full seriousness. It was not quite true, for example, that he was the sole contributor to the magazine from then on, though he was for most issues.[15] In spirit, however, the magazine had become, in effect, a one-man magazine, identified strongly with the larger-than-life persona of Hubbard.

Hubbard's wide fame and that of the magazine was brought about quite unintentionally by his publication of an untitled 1,500-word essay in *The Philistine*, a timely inspirational piece celebrating self-reliance and initiative on the part of the worker that was based on the exploits of Lieutenant Rowan in the Spanish-American War. The essay, later to be titled "A Message to Garcia," sparked an instant sensation, notably taken up by business and corporate leaders, churches, schools, and the military (Bruce A. White 126).[16] Unable to cope with the demand for the essay in its *Philistine* format and without the resources to mass-produce it through the Roycroft Press, Hubbard gave reprint rights to George Daniels, of New York Central Railroad, who issued 2,000,000 copies. Though Hubbard had long since established his homespun, slangy, and vernacular voice, "A Message to Garcia" transmitted it to the mainstream and he became a celebrity. In the first years of the twentieth century and up to his death in 1915, he was one of the most sought-after and highest-paid lecturers in America, earning an additional $30,000 a year as a writer for the Hearst syndicate (Balch 268; Bruce A. White 3). It may be argued that with the massive circulation boost and increased commercialization of *The Philistine* in the wake of the "Garcia" phenomenon, it ceases to be a little magazine. In many respects, this is a moot point. Whether we consider *The Philistine* little or not after this moment, the controversy led to a reinvigoration of the little magazine movement that had been on the wane since the demise of *The Chap-Book* in 1898. The controversy not only drew increased attention to *The Philistine*, but also demonstrated how the little magazine could function effectively as a vehicle of social protest for charismatic figures. In this revival of the movement, then, it would be the periodical of protest and the one-man magazine that would come to dominate.

Larking About: Gelett Burgess and His Little Magazines

We had been watching the literary movements of the time very narrowly, and the impulse to strike for California grew in us. There was a new note of personal expression then becoming dominant, but not in the *Revue Blanche*, not in the *Yellow Book*, nor in the Chicago *Chap-Book* did we seem to hear the tune ring true. Yes, we must demolish Decadence and its 'precious' pretensions, and careless of the outcome so long as we had our stroke for freedom, we sent forth our *Lark*.

– Gelett Burgess, *Bayside Bohemia* 19–20 (1954)

The most experimental and innovative little magazinist was undoubtedly Gelett Burgess, the presiding genius behind four little magazines, *The Lark* (1895–7), *Phyllida, or the Milkmaid* (1897), and two one-off publications: *Le Petit Journal des Refusées* (1896) and *L'Enfant Terrible* (1898). Unlike *The Chap-Book*, *The Bibelot*, and *The Philistine*, Burgess's magazines were not linked to a larger fine press or literary publishing enterprise, though aesthetically they would be among the most interesting. Burgess was especially interested in the magazine format, as his comments about *The Lark* and his restless experimentation suggest. Overall, he saw the little magazine as a vehicle for "personal expression" and, in a period just before Hubbard would so cleverly exploit the form to this end, he felt that no existing fin-de-siècle magazine in France, England, or America had captured the spirit he aimed for. Like Hubbard, Burgess was motivated by an impulse to "overthrow the staid respectability of the larger magazines … in a protest of emancipation from the dictates of the old literary tribunals" and was "disgusted with the sophistication of the *Chap-Book*" (Burgess and Porter; Wells, "What a Lark"). Where Hubbard, however, was animated by contrarian and splenetic impulses against the cultural dominance of the East Coast intelligentsia, Burgess and his coterie involved in his publications, known as "*les jeunes*," were removed from that atmosphere. The San Francisco Bay Area context was central to informing the ethos of these publications. Burgess and his San Francisco set made much of the fresh and primal atmosphere of this area, and *The Lark* was conceived in the redwood forests outside San Francisco at Camp Ha-Ha, where "*les jeunes*" congregated. The names of this camp, and of his first little magazine, are indicative of the particular "note of personal expression" that Burgess and his collaborators adopted – one of devilment and fun. Burgess's publications contributed significantly to the development of the little magazine through their injection of irreverence and a spirit of play, demonstrating how the genre could be exploited for comic purposes.

In many respects, "*les jeunes*" were the West Coast counterparts of the Boston and Cambridge coteries responsible for *The Mahogany Tree*, *The Knight Errant*, and *The Chap-Book*. The group comprised writers and artists with interests across literature, visual art, architecture and design, the book arts, and the decorative arts who were involved with the local arts and crafts scene. Contributors to *The Lark* initially came from this tight-knit, exclusively male circle, though some outsiders were eventually welcomed, notably Yone Noguchi and, when Burgess saw fit to allow women, Carolyn Wells and Florence Lundborg. Despite the group's name, they were not so young, closer to thirty than to twenty and yet, overall, they were less serious than their Eastern counterparts. They were enabled in their efforts by a thriving arts and crafts culture in the area that included a network of booksellers, printers, binders, publishers, and engravers interested in fine press production. Over and against art for art's sake, *The Lark* was, rather, fun for fun's sake. Like *The Philistine*, *The Lark*, launched in May 1895, was embarked upon apparently with little thought of continuing. Certainly, its producers seem not to have wanted subscribers, as the first two issues list a cover price of five cents for a single monthly issue, but a subscription price of a dollar a year – a cost that was adjusted by the third number to sixty cents. By this time, *The Lark* had secured a proper publisher in the form of William Doxey, also a prominent local bookseller. By the second and final year of its existence, the price had been raised to the standard monthly little magazine price of ten cents an issue with a subscription price of a dollar a year.

Though setting out to "demolish Decadence and its 'precious' pretensions" (Burgess, *Bayside Bohemia* 19), *The Lark* did not do so, as Burgess claimed, through satire or parody, as many another little magazines based on humour would do. It was wholly "original," as Burgess told Wells, not "dependent on others' work" (Wells, "What a Lark"). Certainly, it stood outside of decadent/anti-decadent, realist/anti-realist debates of the era by being, quite simply, absurd. More Lewis Carroll and Edward Lear than Oscar Wilde and Aubrey Beardsley, more Dada than decadence, the appearance and content of *The Lark* reflected this absurdist view. If *The Lark* does not base its humour on particular movements or figures, however, it does demonstrate a sophisticated self-consciousness about genre that might be regarded as a parody or satire on the form of the little magazine itself, that would become even more apparent in Burgess's one-off spoof *Le Petit Journal des Refusées.*

Key to this self-consciousness about the emerging genre of the little magazine was *The Lark*'s eccentric dress. If so many other little magazines fetishized a more traditional Morrisian appearance, *The Lark* broke the mould. Kevin Starr argues that the fine press movement in San Francisco was less based on the Kelmscott model than it was on its own "local tradition favoring the elegantly unlaboured" (255). *The Lark*'s printer, Charles Murdock, was one of a number of Bay Area printers who "had experimented with the pre-industrial Franklin Old Style type used in conjunction with engravings, generous spacing and margins, and an uncluttered layout … achiev[ing] a style which combined assertive modernity with graceful nostalgia" (Starr 257). It is the assertive modernity that comes to the fore in *The Lark*, though one certainly founded on an underlying interest in historical typography, illustration, layout, and design. Though printed by Murdock, Burgess and Porter were involved in the process, which was experimental. One of the features that most distinguished *The Lark* from its hand-made and imitation hand-made paper contemporaries was its use of bamboo paper that Burgess and Porter purchased in Chinatown (Wells, "What a Lark"). This paper caused problems in printing. In some batches, the paper was so thin that text and images could only be printed on one side of the paper. With others, the paper was grainy, leading to smashed type on the page (see Figure 2.3). This problem was ameliorated when they introduced electrotyping into the process (Wells, "What a Lark"). Burgess and Porter also experimented with format, type, and layout. They deviated, in certain respects, from the standard chap-book format. Though its paper covers and sixteen-page format were in keeping with the chap-book aesthetic (see Figure 3.4), its pages were book size and, when subscribers opted to have them bound in decorated publisher's bindings, it looked like a book (see Figure 3.5). For design, *The Lark* employed different fonts and specially designed decorative initial letters. Type was not justified – "too expensive," Burgess claimed, but also because they thought it was "artistic and dégagé" (Wells, "What a Lark"). Significantly, *The Lark*, along with *The Echo*, launched the same month, were the first little magazines to feature a changing monthly poster-style cover, preceding even *The Chap-Book*, which featured such covers, sometimes, but not always, from October 1895.[17] Though innovated by little magazinist Will Bradley for a trade journal, Bradley himself would not bring it to a little magazine until he launched *Bradley His Book* the following year. Following *The Lark*'s lead, a number of little magazines were issued with changing monthly poster-style covers in 1895 and 1896, including *Whims*, *The Lotus*, *Miss Blue Stocking*, *Alkahest*, *The Clack Book*, *The Black Cat*, *M'lle New York*, *Quartier Latin*, and *What to Eat* (see colour plate 12).

The aesthetic eccentricity of *The Lark* was enhanced by drawings, woodcut and woodblock illustrations, cartoons, satires, absurd and fantastical verse and prose, and mock advertisements. Notable features of the art were the japonisme of Lundborg and Porter, the impressionistic style of Peixotto, and the cartoonish figures of Burgess, notably his Goop characters, who would later become the subject of a series of children's books. Literary content was provided largely by Burgess, along with regular contributions from other members of the coterie. Burgess's own "Purple Cow" poem, later to become a children's classic, is the magazine's claim to fame (see Figure 3.6). Other notable content by Burgess includes his Richard and Vivette stories, later developed in book format, based on characters who work for a company that bring the kind of romance and adventure of novels into people's real everyday lives. The magazine, however, was not all nonsense, as is often claimed. There was sufficient interest in poetic trends of the day, notably blank verse, symbolism, and fixed forms. Burgess himself wrote such poetry for the magazine as did Yone Noguchi, a Japanese poet who would influence Ezra Pound's development of imagism. Noguchi's poetry was described by fellow *Lark* contributor, Carolyn Wells, as bringing a Whitmanesque sensibility to a Japanese spirit ("Latest Thing" 302). In their interest in Noguchi, the eccentricities

Figure 3.4 *Lark* in paper-bound monthly format, October 1896. In possession of author.

Figure 3.5 *Lark* in publisher's binding, in three colours, Book 1 (May 1895–April 1896). In possession of author.

Figure 3.6 Gelett Burgess's "Purple Cow" poem as it first appeared in *The Lark*. In possession of author.

of Burgess and Hubbard coincide, as Hubbard was the only other little magazinist to publish his work, though Noguchi would establish his own short-lived little magazine, *Twilight*, in 1898. Overall though, Burgess's whimsical nature and that of his co-contributors resulted in a magazine that reflected a bohemianism quite different to that of other little magazines.

Unlike Stone and Kimball, Mosher, and Hubbard, whose magazines were part of a broader printing and/or publishing concern, Burgess could devote his full attention to thinking about his little magazines as a means of "personal expression." With Burgess, "personal expression" means something different than it might for Mosher and Hubbard, whose magazines can also be thought of as vehicles for personal expression – the expression of literary taste and culture in the first instance, and of social and political views in the latter. For Burgess, meanwhile, personal expression was creative, and his interest in the magazine as a particular kind of venue for such thought led to a greater self-consciousness about, and a greater experimentation with, the genre of the little magazine, a form that, in his hands, constituted a work of art in itself.

While the magazine was, in many ways, an ideal form of self-expression for Burgess, it had limitations also. Magazines, after all, develop distinctive identities, and his restless creation of one-offs can be attributed to the constraints each of his productions set on him. *The Lark*, freeing as it was at first, did not provide enough scope for further experimentation once it became successful. Burgess felt "irritated," Hart argues, "by [*The Lark*'s] reflection of his own cleavage between quaint aestheticism and ludicrous fantasy" (introduction vii). This frustration led him to create two new and distinctive publications, one devoted to each of these qualities. Both journals were issued while *The Lark* was still running. Indeed, Burgess self-reflexively comments on the problem in one of his Richard and Vivette stories in *The Lark*. In this story, Richard and Vivette decide to start a little magazine called *Phyllida, or the Milkmaid*, to publish Vivette's work, which has been rejected by numerous magazines. As Richard describes it, her writing is experimental in nature, going beyond "the conventional problems of versification" to tackle "Greek and Latin Quantities ... Welch [*sic*] and Siamese rhyme-forms ... antediluvian anapests of Tertiary Man ... 17 syllabled *Ho-Ku's* [*sic*] and the 31 syllabled imperial U-ta's [sic] of Japanese poetry," etc. ("Avocations of Vivette"). They soon grow bored, however, because the magazine has established a "policy" that constrains their endeavours. So they start another one – *La revue jeune* – that will go back, Vivette says, to "Addison – to Montaigne – to Chaucer, if need be" and will be printed in "that fascinating 8 x 10 size of the *Tatler* – with square wood-cut initials and double columns, the proper names in small caps ... It will make the heathen rage" ("Avocations of Vivette"). When that magazine fails, they plan another, *The Anthropophagian*, to be printed on "real sheepskin rolls set from types cut to the faces of the 8th century Irish miniscules" ("Avocations of Vivette").

Though played out humorously in this story, the trials and tribulations of the little magazinist reflect Burgess's own experience. He already had, in fact, launched a periodical called *Phyllida, or the Milkmaid* a few months before printing this story, though, in practice, the magazine resembled what was called in the story *La revue jeune*. *Phyllida* was a more or less serious attempt to establish a literary periodical that would help build a coterie in California, though it was decidedly whimsical in form. Through this publication, Burgess, as Hart suggests, explored his interests in "quaint aestheticism" (introduction vii). The four-page folio magazine aimed to revive the personal essay style of Addison and Steele. It was printed on smoke-coloured imitation handmade paper in the style of the old *Tatler* down to the typographical style with its small caps, italics, and long "s." Unlike *The Lark*, it was to treat the topical, containing "lithe and sinewy comment, gossipy chatter, causerie, and reviews, 'devoted to literary topics, and reflections upon the doings of the town'" (Burgess, *Bayside Bohemia* 31). Having no interest in writing such material themselves, Burgess and his partner, Porter Garnett, sought outside contributors who failed, they claimed, to provide them with adequate material. The magazine came to an end after two issues, but was memorialized in Burgess's Vivette episode.

Burgess's experiment with what Hart terms "ludicrous fantasy" was played out in *Le Petit Journal des Refusées* (introduction vii). Mention of this magazine first appeared in *The Lark* in October 1895. The notice itself functions as a playful jibe at the little magazine genre, mocking its eccentricities and the vanity publishing aspect of some of these publications. "It will be the smallest and most extraordinary magazine in existence," the notice declared:

> It will be printed on Black paper with Yellow ink. The margins will be very, very wide, the cover almost impossible.
>
> The rates for insertion of prose articles will be only five dollars a page; poetry, ten dollars a page; but no manuscript will be printed unless accompanied by a letter of regret at not being able to find the same available, from some leading magazine. *No manuscripts will be refused.* Terms are cash, invariably in advance.
>
> Every article in every paper will be blue penciled, and the author's signature underlined.
>
> Each contributor will be allowed one hundred free copies of the number in which his article appears.
>
> Subscription to the *Petit Journal des Refusées*, will be five dollars a year; single copies, ten cents.
>
> Address all subscriptions and manuscripts to the editor, Gelett Burgess, San Francisco. (Burgess, "*Petit Journal*")

What may have started as a joke, however, became a challenge for Burgess, who aimed to create a magazine that would not only "out-Lark the *Lark*," but would also be the "reductio ad absurdum of the 'freak' journal" (Burgess, *Bayside Bohemia* 25, 26). And so it was, in every respect. In design terms, it took the little magazine fetish for quaint aesthetic effects to the extreme. Printed using woodcuts on both sides of wallpaper, the sixteen-page *Petit Journal des Refusées* was trapezoidal in shape (see colour plate 1). Beardsleyesque figures as well as Burgess's Goops and other fantastical types frame the texts. These poems and prose works, all purportedly by women and rejected by at least three magazines, were written by Burgess in imitation of the content found in little magazines. They include a Symbolistic prose sketch called "The Ghost of a Flea," which, as Drucker notes, has a "remote relation" to Blake's miniature painting of that name ("Bohemian by Design"); a poem set to music; a poem that is typeset to reflect the typographical experimentation of little magazines; a dialect piece; and an alphabet poem in rhyming couplets, occupying four pages. The poem, quoted here in full, is a notable documentation, a "blueprint," as Evans calls it ("*Vogue* and Ephemera" 34), of what constituted "little magazineness" in 1897, one that would certainly have pleased fans of the genre for whom it would serve as a test of their "knowingness" of the field:

A is for Art of the age-end variety;
We Decadents simply can't get a satiety.

B is for Beardsley, the idol supreme,
Whose drawings are not half so bad as they seem.

C is for *Chap-Book*, the pater familias
Of magazines started by many a silly ass.

D is for Darn it–it's awfully shocking
Your Dekel-edge Hosiery, Mistress Blue Stocking.

E is for Editor; what does it mean?
Everyone now runs his own magazine.

F is for Freak: see the great exposition
Of freak magazines–5 and 10 cents admission.

G is for Goup; I would much rather be
A nice Purple Cow than a G-O-U-P.

H is for Humbug attempts to be Horrid!
(See *Mlle. New York*, she's decidedly torrid.)

I am an Idiot, awful result
Of reading the rot of the *Yellow Book* cult.

J is for JENSON the TYPE of the day,
Some people can't read any other, they say.

K is for Kimball, assistant of Stone;
I wonder how he will get on all alone.

L is for *Lark* and the fellows who planned it
Say even they cannot but half understand it!

M is for Magazines recklessly recent
I know of but one that is anyway decent.

N stands for Nothing; I wish it had stood for
A little bit more than the *Fly-Leaf* was good for.

O's for Oblivion–ultimate fate
Of most of the magazines published of late.

P is for Poster; the best one, by far,
Is the one that was made for our own P.J.R. (Price 4 bits.)

Q is for Quarrel; Harte, Hubbard and Taber
To run the *Philistine*, each other belabor.

R is for Rubbish; are you looking for some?
Just open the *Bauble* and put down your thumb.

S is for Stevie Crane, infant precocious,
Who has written some lines that are simply ferocious.

T is for Thomas B. Mosher of Maine
Whose dinkey toy prefaces give me a pain.

U is for Useless and far beneath notice;
But I don't want to say all of that of the *Lotus*.

V is for Versification and Verse;
We thought *Chips* was bad, but the *Olio*'s worse.

W's for Woman, whom editors humor:
In the new field of letters, perennial bloomer.

X is for Something Unknown–let us say
How in the world do these magazines pay?

Y is for Young, and I marveled to learn
That fifty's the average age of les Jeunes.

Z is for Zounds! What unspeakable deco-
Rativeness Bradley has furnished for *Echo*. ("Our Clubbing List")

Having achieved the *reductio ad absurdum* in the realm of the little magazine, Burgess effectively retired from the field. He moved to New York where he produced only one more little magazine, *L'Enfant Terrible*, for April Fool's Day 1898, including a typical Burgess nonsense poem and a poem mocking the Boston bohemian set. But while he may have had nothing left to express through the little magazine, his establishment of the medium as a vehicle for humour would have an influence on satirical and comic little magazines, almost none of which would live up to Burgess's inimitable models.

The magazines discussed in this chapter – *The Knight Errant*, *The Chap-Book*, *The Bibelot*, *The Philistine*, *The Lark*, and Burgess's other periodical oddities – provide an indication of the development and evolution of the little magazine genre as it emerged in the last decade of the nineteenth century. Though, as these examples alone indicate, there was a remarkable range within the field in terms of styles, aims, and size of audience, they serve as representative types against which most any other little magazines of the period can be assessed. *The Knight Errant*, of course, represents a rare but important stereotype of the little magazine born of purist ideals. Its successors, *The Bibelot* and *The Chap-Book*, register an evolution of the elitist and purist nature of *The Knight Errant*. Both, though in differing ways, bring a democratizing and commercial spirit as applied to the little magazine and the dissemination of culture, a spirit that largely animated the movement as a whole in America. *The Philistine* achieves this commercialization and democratization of culture on a much bigger scale while, at the same time, establishing a precedent for the little magazine as a vehicle for social and political, rather than strictly literary and artistic, commentary. *The Lark* and Burgess's other publications, meanwhile, represent the high point of a trend in the broader movement to comic and parodic manifestations of the form. Other magazines could profitably have been discussed in this chapter: *Bradley His Book*, for example, an exquisite and ambitious embodiment of fine press ideals and poster art, and *M'lle New York*, the only really truly "decadent" American little magazine in a period when the term was rather loosely applied to these publications. There will be occasion to say something about these and other notable publications, however, in the ensuing chapters dealing with the content of little magazines.

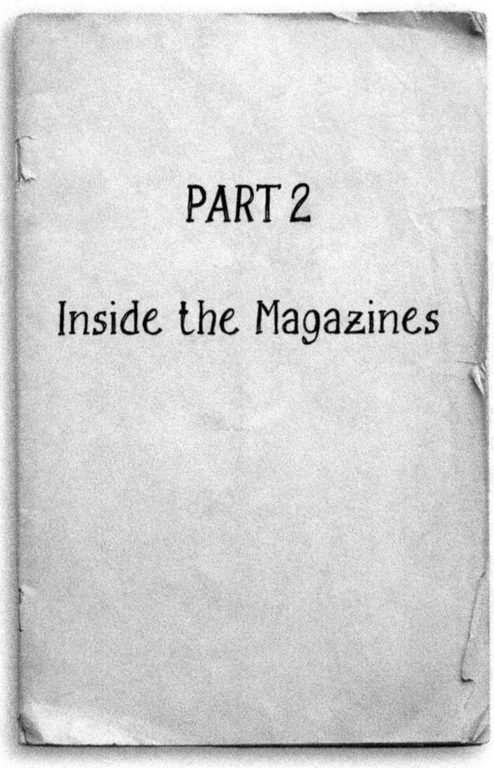
PART 2
Inside the Magazines

CHAPTER 4

Fiction: "Literature Staggering Blindfold"

But is it not true that the best thought and energy of American writers to-day goes into periodical literature instead of novels? The magazine or periodical press is a newer mode of expression, has a wider audience.

– Frances H. Bardeen, "Romance in Fiction," *Philosopher* 1, no. 4, 113 (1897)

The magazine revolution of the 1890s played a role in the development of American literary culture, more so, little magazinist Bardeen would claim, than the novel. More modern and more democratic a medium than the novel, the magazine of the 1890s was an ideal venue for the rise of a new genre of fiction – the short story – itself considered a democratic and modern form (Levy 40). The short story was not new. It was a development of what, earlier in the century, had been called "tales" or "sketches." These forms had a tradition in America, going back to Edgar Allan Poe, Herman Melville, and Nathaniel Hawthorne. In the 1880s, however, just as Henry James and Walter Besant were engaged in debates about the cultural status of the novel in Britain, in America, Brander Matthews was seeking to assert the artistic authority of the short story (Valerie Shaw 4). At the same time, Guy de Maupassant was coming to exert influence on the form in America.[1] The establishment of the International Copyright Act in 1891 and the growth of the periodical press meant increased opportunities for aspiring American authors and a demand for content that could be produced quickly. These factors spurred the rise of the short story as an important literary genre.

The short story was a versatile medium, capable, as Henry Mills Alden noted, of achieving many effects: "the character sketch ... a single dramatic situation, a succession of humorous incidents ... a quick comedy ... an equally quick tragedy ... a brief glimpse of special life ... a spiritual revelation ... a picturesque view of some old time" (170). It was also suited to the conditions of modern-day life. G.K. Chesterton, for example, felt it captured the "fleetingness" and "fragility" of the modern consciousness (85). Its versatility meant that it functioned as both a high and popular art form. It was, as Winnie Chan notes, a "product of both mass culture and the backlash against it" (xi), exploited both by writers seeking to engage readers in short, exciting, plot-driven narratives and by an avant-garde interested in its potential for exploring impressions and moods. At the same time, it was appealing to readers, who expressed a preference for magazines with material in this vein, and to writers for whom the form seemed an easy one (Mott, *History* 113, 429). The short story performed important cultural work. Ohmann, for example, sees it as a form catering to the desires and aims of the emerging professional middle class through its symbolic engagement with the "ideological motifs" of "modernity, class confidence, and the absence of social conflict" (*Selling Culture* 287). Periodicals were an ideal venue for short fiction, none perhaps more so than aesthetic little magazines and the related fiction-focused story publications that, at this time, were considered part of this broader little magazine movement. Where short fiction might be easily lost in what Harte referred to dismissively as the "bulky literary sandwich" magazine ("Bubble and Squeak," *Lotus* 2, no. 8, 298), the small format of most little magazines, prided by Harte and McIntosh, was better suited to showcasing the form. Though larger in format, story magazines, too, privileged the form by specializing in the genre. In these venues, serialized fiction, the mainstay of mainstream magazines and newspapers, is rare, while the short story is given prominence and authority.

The American little magazines of the 1890s are by no means a trove of lost literary classics. It cannot be claimed, as it is of their modernist counterparts, that they published 80 per cent of the most important modern writers (Hoffman, Allen, and Ulrich 1). The 1890s little magazines were venues for aspirants and amateurs, most of whom did not achieve posterity, even if they made a living as workaday magazinists. Given these circumstances, conventional literary approaches that focus on exemplary, notable, or prolific writers are not suitable for considering this fiction. While there were important canonical contributors, including Henry James, Jack London, Israel Zangwill, H.G. Wells, and so on, such writers are not *representative* little magazinists and do not yield an understanding of typical little magazine fiction. A consideration of *prolific* little magazinists might prove more fruitful but, in the case of fiction, there are no such figures. Yet, clearly, attempting an analysis of all the fiction in hundreds of little magazines is impossible. Instead, this chapter aims to provide a flavour of short fiction in little magazines through a form of distant reading. This analysis involves what Cohen has called "reading for patterns" to identify the key themes, genres, structural principles, and styles of short fiction in little magazines. In addition, it considers how this fiction might be read in relation to the broader literary and/or social contexts – the kind of cultural work it performs – as well as any significant distinctions in content across the various genres and subgenres of little magazines. As it aims for breadth of coverage, the chapter does not attempt in-depth or exhaustive treatments of the stories it covers, nor does it suggest that its readings are definitive. Rather, it proposes ways of understanding this fiction in terms of the cultural and media dynamics and literary contexts that are mapped out in the book. The discussion in this chapter is based on an analysis of a sampling of single issues of available little magazines published between 1894 and 1903 that contain fiction. The sampling, comprising sixty-five little magazines in total, includes two hundred pieces of fiction.[2] Not all of these are discussed, but this broader sampling has served as the basis for identifying key themes and trends that are treated in considerations of representative examples.[3] Story magazines, though more generally treated as a subset of aesthetic little magazines, are considered as a distinct category here because of the differences in their treatment of fiction. On this basis, aesthetic little magazines (not including story magazines) constitute 58.5 per cent of the titles considered and 50.5 per cent of the stories; story magazines represent 9.5 per cent of the magazines considered, but as much 26.5 per cent of the stories due to their longer format and fiction-focus. There are more stories per issue in these magazines than in typical aesthetic little magazines. Hybrid magazines, meanwhile, account for 18.5 per cent of the magazines sampled and 13.5 per cent of the fiction. Finally, periodicals of protest make up 14 per cent of the magazines sampled and 9.5 per cent of the content. In terms of content, the fiction falls into the following broad categories, with some stories occupying more than one. Stories with love and romantic or sexual intrigue as a key theme make up 38 per cent of the sampling;

23 per cent of the fiction takes a short short form – prose poem, parable, sketch, fable, etc; 17 per cent deal with the macabre, mystery, or forms of spiritual, mystical, or transcendent revelation; 15 per cent are concerned with artistic or bohemian life or have aesthetes or dandies at their centre; 12 per cent engage with local colour or dialect fiction; 11 per cent are historical romance, legends, or yarns; 9 per cent are miscellaneous in nature, none significant enough to constitute a distinct category.

At a basic level, this survey confirms what has been suggested about little magazine content more generally: that there is not as much distinction as might be expected between its types of content and those found in mainstream magazines. Little magazines engage with popular genres and they often do so in conventional ways. The most popular little magazine story genre, revolving around love and romantic or sexual intrigue, is also the most popular form in mass-market magazines, as Ohmann's work on what he terms "courtship stories" has shown (*Selling Culture* 297–329). Dialect and local colour stories, mystery and horror, and the historical romance/adventure story were also popular fictional modes in mainstream magazines and novels. Closer attention to particular trends within little magazines, however, does help to establish generalizable distinctions that might be said to set the little magazine story apart from its mainstream counterparts. Little magazines developed and were strongly associated with particular trends and genres. For example, while little magazines featured stories of all the types suggested by Alden, comedy is less prevalent than tragedy or the character sketch. Short, dramatic sketches, suggestive, ambiguous, and thought-provoking in nature, take precedence in many little magazines over the more detailed plot-driven short stories that dominated mainstream publications (with the exception of story magazines). Indeed, forms of the short short story, including prose poems, sketches, fables, and parables, thrive in little magazines, constrained as these publications generally are by size and format. Irony, a major component of the Maupassantian short story, is much in evidence in little magazine fiction. Further, there is a strong interest in subjectivity and psychological interiority, notable in the prevalence of first-person narration and free indirect discourse in these stories. About 20 per cent of the sampling includes stories narrated in the first-person or that make considerable use of free indirect discourse in a manner that emphasizes psychological or character study elements. This interest should not be surprising in a magazine genre understood by many as a vehicle of self-expression, one that catered to a readership that valued individualism and would be drawn to narratives that privilege interiority. Finally, there is notable evidence of writers undermining generic conventions in ways that challenge not only literary norms but broader social and cultural values as well. All in all, these qualities are suggestive of fiction of a modernistic, possibly avant-garde, bent. Certainly, this is a perception some commentators of the period had of these magazines, which they expressed in antagonistic terms. *Western College Magazine*, for example, took a dim view of little magazine stories, claiming "their tone is melancholy, and their typical stories are vague, inconsistent, bombastic ravings" (qtd. in [Harte], "Bubble and Squeak," *Lotus* 2, no. 8, 295). I would not, however, want to overstate the case that little magazines were a venue for progressive and avant-gardist trends. Not all little magazine fiction is challenging in this way, nor is this kind of challenge necessarily the sole purview of fiction published outside the mainstream. Still, little magazines may be said to include a greater preponderance of fiction that breaks with conventions than mainstream magazines.

This claim, in fact, is borne out by a comparison of little magazine love-centred fiction – which features a significant proportion of unhappy or troubled scenarios – with mass-market stories of this type, in which, as Ohmann outlines, the happy ending prevails (*Selling Culture* 311–12). Though love stories, broadly speaking, are the most popular form across mainstream and little magazine fiction, they offer different perspectives on the relations between the sexes and changing gender roles for a self-consciously modern professional-managerial class readership. This audience certainly overlaps in some instances and the love-themed stories that appear in little magazines are part of a broader field of stories around 1900 that, as Ohmann says, "were in dialogue with one another, registering through character and event a kind of statement and counterstatement about gender, conduct, feeling, social rank, and other important matters" (*Selling Culture* 313). While little magazines contain their share of conventional and sentimental tales, there is a marked trend towards the "sex-problem" story that explores controversial themes in an often cynical or risqué manner. This perspective makes these love stories, though often understood as a female genre, potentially more appealing to male readers. A dominant theme in this fiction is the love triangle – a feature of about 33 per cent of the love stories in the sampling – a structuring principle that David R. Shumway has argued is "fundamental to popular fiction of the turn of the century" (45). As in much of this fiction, the triangle serves, in little magazine stories, as a means to complicate a courtship or wooing plot. More controversially, however, and less usual in the mainstream, little magazine fiction exploits the triangle to explore infidelity, betrayal, jealousy, and the problems of "modern" love. Such fiction would appeal to the young professional readership that considered itself sophisticated and progressive and that was navigating an increasingly complex path to and within marriage. Indeed, as against the convention of popular stories focused on the courtship narrative, a number of these stories deal with marriage. Many also show an interest in the psychological processes or effects of betrayal and exploit first-person point of view, interior monologue, or free indirect discourse, modes of narration in keeping with the little magazine's intimate and highly personal quality.

Gertrude Atherton's "One of the Problems" (*Goose-Quill*), for example, is among the most risqué stories in the sampling, reflecting the *Goose-Quill*'s broader interest in socially and culturally radical and controversial topics. The story details the thought processes of a man, torn between two women, reflecting on his unhappy marriage as he lies in bed with his mistress. Ultimately, hate proves a more powerful bond than love and he chooses his wife, a choice represented in the narrative not as a sign of strength and integrity, as might be expected, but, more radically, as a sign of weakness. Leonora Beck's "Two Women" (*New Bohemian*), meanwhile, explores a similar theme in a pared-down sketch of less than five hundred words. Though *The New Bohemian* was a more conventional magazine than *The Goose-Quill*, situating itself, as Levin claims, between mass-market and little magazines (269), this tale actually creates more ambiguity than Atherton's.[4] In the story, Gareth, on the eve of marriage to Lily, is visited by an old lover (possibly wife), with his children in tow. She kills him, and the reader is left with a beatific and sentimental image of Lily, "not bride, nor widow, yet more than both" (213). Though the narrative ends with a suggestion that Lily and Gareth will meet again in heaven, much is left unknown about his conduct towards his former partner, and the story raises more questions than it answers. Betrayal is also the theme of Julian Harris's "A Double Deception" (*Alkahest*), a story that previously appeared in the *Chicago Times Herald*, indicating that controversial treatments of romance were not limited to little magazines. The story consists primarily of the interior monologue of a dying man who believes the "deception" of his wife and best friend lies in pretending that he is not dying. A coda to the story, however, reveals the "double" nature of the deception: after his death, his wife and friend become lovers. Though, technically, wife and friend have not been unfaithful in the man's lifetime, the title directs readers to reflect carefully on the coda, in which the friend's discomfort is evidenced when the wife blithely declares her love for him, while invoking her dead husband: "Men cannot talk of such matters in the restful fashion that a woman finds natural" (15). It is he, not the wife, who considers their relationship a deception. These stories, with their male-centred narrative focus and their treatment of male anxieties about relationships, demonstrate the ways in which romance fiction in little magazines might speak as much to men as women.

Women's perspectives on modern love and betrayal are also explored in these triangle stories. Henry James's "The Way It Came," featured in *The Chap-Book* in the same month as Harris's story, offers a variation on its theme of a love triangle involving a dead person. James's story is longer than usual for American little magazine fiction of this period, but he preferred this mode, and *The Chap-Book* accommodated him because of his high profile. In this instance, the unnamed female narrator is obsessed with the relationship between her fiancé and dead friend and where, in Harris's story there is merely a sense of foreboding in the man's discomfort, in James's the woman breaks off the engagement, unable to overcome her feelings of jealousy. While Harris's and James's stories both centre on dead people, symbolically, of course, the dead can serve to represent past loves and these stories, therefore, are a means through which readers might work through their own particular anxieties about their romantic lives.

Women's lack of desire for their husbands and erotic interest in other men is also explored in the little magazine love triangle story. Kate Chopin's novella *The Awakening* (1899), published, incidentally, by Herbert Stone, and her short story "The Story of an Hour" (1894), first featured in a racy, sophisticated women's magazine called *Vogue*, are among the most famous treatments of this theme from this period. Her fiction, however, was part of a much larger body of controversial work of the day engaged with female sexual desire. Within the sampling, "Parilee's Dream" (*Fly Leaf*), by Olga Arnold, opens with a husband watching his sleeping wife, imagining she is dreaming of him. The narrative perspective, however, slyly shifts to the woman and it is revealed that she is dreaming of a former lover. Upon awakening, she realizes that the shine on her marriage has gone – that the "dream kiss is still on her lips," while her husband's seems "slightly insipid" (17). She tries to justify her feeling, but is unsatisfied, her thoughts drifting back to her former lover. Instead of the happily ever after ending, the reader is left with "and she mused on" (17). While Parilee is no *Doll's House* Nora, the story is controversial in its depiction of female dissatisfaction within married life and the role fantasy plays as a sop to boredom.

Transgressive desire is played out also in less controversial contexts in little magazine triangle stories in which widows reflect on their new-found freedom to reunite with past lovers (Hoadley; Nathan). Like Chopin's "Story of an Hour," in which the woman dies from joy upon hearing of her husband's death, these stories have an ironic turn that plays on the conventional notion of women as self-sacrificing. In Ray Trum Nathan's "Renunciation," for example, in the story magazine *The Bohemian*, a woman reunites with a former lover only to renounce him for the sake of her children when he slanders her reprobate dead husband. In Francis A. Hoadley's "Triangular Irony," meanwhile, a woman's insistence on being true to a dissolute husband whom she has been forced to marry backfires. She tells her former lover to find happiness elsewhere and, just after her husband has died, she discovers he has – by marrying someone else. Nathan's treatment is slightly more conventional. Though allowing for the possibility of female desire, "Renunciation" ultimately reinscribes the socially conventional ideal of woman's self-sacrificing nature, while Hoadley's story hints that such a nature is an unnecessary form of self-punishment.

It is in these "sex problem" stories that little magazines come closest to dealing with issues facing modern or "new" men and women: desire outside of the married state, sexual jealousy and betrayal, women and men with a past, etc. These stories also come closest to voicing feminist perspectives that are otherwise largely absent from the medium of the little magazine. The first-person oriented nature of many of these stories and their embodiment in the highly individualised form of the little magazine bring a personal, intimate quality to the problems and themes they treat. Even if the stories do not ultimately depict women breaking free from conventional gender roles, they do create a fantasy space through which women readers might imagine things otherwise. At the same time, they appeal, perhaps, to new, modern, progressive men, those who might help to make things otherwise.

Beyond this bulk of triangle stories are others that deal with modern lovers – new women and bachelor aesthetes and dandies with world-weary, blasé, and sophisticated views. In these stories, romance and courtship are often treated with cynicism and irony, speaking to issues raised by transforming gender roles in this period of urbanization and modernization in American cultural life. Sometimes these modern types are mocked, their sophistication exposed as mere posturing in ways that speak to anxieties about the disappearance of genteel courting rituals and the problems posed by the "new woman." Sometimes, however, they glorify the sophisticated, independent, and knowing woman or girl.

Cynical wisdom and sophistication are especially prominent in some little magazines. *The Bachelor Book*, for example, was one of these, a magazine edited by Marion Thornton Egbert and Page Waller Sampson, women who, as discussed in chapter 1, were controversially bohemian and modern in their ways. Another was the New York-based story magazine *The Smart Set*, a magazine not acknowledged by Faxon but included in Moss's bibliography and in other works which consider it in a little magazine context.[5] Subtitled "a magazine of cleverness," *Smart Set* cultivated an image of urbanity and sophistication and was "by, for and about The Four Hundred," a term commonly used to denote New York's social elite of this era (Dolmetsch 22). In its early days, it was considered part of the efflorescence of upstart avant-gardist magazines, "burst[ing]," as one of its first editors said, "upon the literary horizon with something of the theatrical sensation of *The Yellow Book* in London or *The Chap-Book* in Chicago" (Towne 49). Catering to a professional urban elite and to university students (Sharon Hamilton 226), it drew criticism for its subject matter and treatment, even within the world of little magazines. The Nebraska-based *Kiote*, for example, complained of its "salacious exhibits of high society" ("Yelps," *Kiote* 3, no. 6, 133).

Stories from these magazines in the sampling indicate how these themes operated. These stories may celebrate the new woman, showing how she glories in the power she wields on the marriage market, how she plays the courtship game with wit and sophistication, coming out as equal to, or triumphing over, men, in the game of love. At times, however, they register ambivalence about these women. H.C. Chatfield-Taylor's *Smart Set* story, "If at First You Don't Succeed," is a telling example. Though his heroine, Mabel Wainwright, is a charming, witty, modern woman, her authority is undermined by the narrator in subtle ways. The narrator suggests that Mabel's sense of herself as sophisticated is a delusion and that her view of love as "merely a distemper, like measles or the whooping-cough" is but a pose (97):

she "*fancied* herself a woman of the world; her worldly experience, however, had been confined to the pages of French novels" (97). In the story, Mabel becomes engaged to Captain Wardour, a freewheeling bachelor type, who gets cold feet and jilts her at the altar. They meet the following year, and she is breezy, polite, and witty with him, asking for her chance to reject him at the altar. She tricks him, however, seeing the ceremony through. They are wed – "his doom was sounded" but, "strangely enough," we are told, "he never regretted it" (105). Though the modern girl in this story triumphs through her canny wit, her modernity functions, ultimately, in the service of a conventional outcome.

A story from the *Bachelor Book* sampling offers a slightly more controversial take on the same theme. The story, titled, "An Inconsistent Philosopher," is focalized initially through the perspective of a Captain Wardour counterpart – a freewheeling, pipe-smoking aesthete, who quickly renounces his bachelor ways upon falling in love. But where Chatfield-Taylor's *Smart Set* story forecasts a tamed Captain Wardour and a happy future for him and Mabel, the cynical narrator in this story indicates that this convert to matrimony has chosen "the path to the divorce court" (McIntire 7). Characters, therefore, may be exposed as sentimentalists at heart, but narrative strategies can function to direct readers to more "knowing," sophisticated, and cynical perspectives.

Like the romances Ohmann treats in *Selling Culture*, these stories, while acknowledging "new social arrangements in new social space" (317) in their representation of couples engaged in game-playing and charade in courting rituals, often end up affirming the traditional convention of marriage. Those that centred on modern women catered, in various ways, to the mixed desires of a middle-class female readership of the period, women that may have wanted romance and marriage but also desired the freedom available to the often wealthy or independent-spirited "new women" that featured in this fiction. This freedom was becoming increasingly available to women of the middle classes through greater access to education and to professional careers, transforming gender relations in the period. The witty and sophisticated women in these stories reflect a particular type of new womanhood idealized by the emerging professional middle class, one that has, in Ohmann's terms, "been released from old social confinements" (*Selling Culture* 329). Tellingly, though, this freedom did not, in fiction at any rate, generally extend to representations of liberated women who unequivocally reject marriage and are happy in so doing.

If little magazinists, like their mainstream counterparts, rarely explored the happy bachelor girl, they were not unwilling to engage with the dark side of the "sex problem," as has been suggested already through the discussion of the love triangle plot. Against the pose of world-weary cynicism displayed in Chatfield-Taylor's "If at First You Don't Succeed," the new woman speaker in another story in *The Smart Set* offers a bleak contrast. Narrated in free indirect discourse, Sadie Martinot's "Dream of the Ideal" is a psychological character sketch comparable in its cynicism to Atherton's *Goose-Quill* story, "One of the Problems." In this instance, however, the speaker is a woman whose experience of betrayal has left her disillusioned, with a belief that "It is the Law. *There can be no perfect sympathy*" (109). This kind of cynicism about relations between the sexes is much more strongly associated with the cultural avant-garde and appears more regularly in the more radical little magazines. Most markedly, this view is characteristic of *M'lle New York*, the most decadent of the little magazines, which freely explored controversial topics including sexual obsession, incest, prostitution, fetishes, bestiality, and adultery. The issue of *M'lle New York* in the sampling, for example, includes an unattributed Poesque tale in which a deranged speaker, who early on expresses distrust of his lover, thinks he is being tormented by a spider. Confusing his lover for the spider, he murders her, later insisting that she was, in any case, "a female fiend sent to snare my soul" ("The Spider"). This story is just one of many in *M'lle New York* over its broader run in which love, rage, violence, and madness go hand in hand.

The macabre element of *M'lle New York*'s treatment of love and sex draws attention to the close relationship between the sex problem genre and tales of murder, the macabre, and the mystical. This theme was second only to love-and-sex-problem fiction in aesthetic and story magazines. When combined, these themes figure the domestic/romantic sphere as a site of horror and crime. The popular down-market equivalent of such tales appeared in dime novels and cheap sensational periodicals and newspapers such as *The National Police Gazette*. It was also notable, however, in fiction aimed at a middle-class market. For today's readers, the best known tale of this type from the era is undoubtedly Charlotte Perkins Gilman's "The Yellow Wallpaper," published in the mainstream literary periodical *New England Magazine* in

1892. Like Gilman, some of whose work was published in little magazines, many little magazinists were interested in subjectivity and the psychological aspects of crimes of passion, features that distinguished their tales from sensationalized plot-oriented cheap fiction. This was sensationalism intellectualized and rendered artistic for an educated and aspirational professional middle-class readership. Writers of these tales were influenced by earlier American exponents of the genre, such as Poe, and also by recent masters, like Maupassant, whose work focused on subjectivity and psychological abnormalities. Domestic horror, centred on crimes of passion and the psychological effects of extreme love and hate, feature in about 27 per cent of the stories foregrounding murder, mystery, and the macabre in the sampling. In culturally symbolic terms, some of these stories, like Gilman's "The Yellow Wallpaper," represent the flip side of positive representations of modern gender relations. Murderous women seek revenge on male betrayers in Katharine J. Smith's "The Month of Mary" (*Bohemian*), Eden Phillpotts's "In the King's Chamber" (*Smart Set*), and the already discussed "Two Women" (*New Bohemian*). While these stories show justice being served upon men who betray women, they also speak to anxieties about women's potentially unbridled passion. Femmes fatales in another guise, meanwhile, provoke murder in "The Spider" (*M'lle New York*) and Michael Kinmarck's "What Did She Do With Her Left Hand?" (*Blue Sky*); murder-suicide in Charles Nobel's "Doctor's Argument" (*Miss Blue Stocking*); suicide in A.T. Swinburne's "Heart Stress" (*Lotus*); and death of a broken heart in Rodrigues Ottolengui's "For Fame, Money, or Love?" (*Black Cat*) and May Ethelyn Bourne's "A Black Cat" (*Gray Goose*).

These stories provide perspectives on the dangers of loss of self-control in men when they fall prey to emotion. This danger besets men of different types in these stories – aesthetes, professional men, and conventional men – in ways that might be read in relation to anxieties brought about by the shift from a culture of character to a culture of personality. While the dandy aesthete can and does sometimes serve as a model of new manhood, one based on a charismatic personality, the manliness of this type is also often questioned. Swinburne's "Heart Stress" (*Lotus*), for example, registers this dilemma, pitting two men as rivals for the love of Mary: Roger, the apparently soulful, emotive, and "picturesque" new man, an artist type, whose interiority we are given access to by the narrator; and Arthur, who is described as "formal," "correct," "a gentleman," "punctilious," "quiet," "conventional," "somewhat literal," and "slightly commonplace" (329). No access is given to his interiority. Instead, the narrator reports: "No one could imagine ... Arthur Lindale dying of a broken heart, but all were confident he would make an estimable husband" (329). Both Mary, his fiancée, and her friend love the more charismatic Roger. It is ironic, then, that Arthur does kill himself upon discovering that his fiancée loves Roger. This story suggests, on the one hand, that there is more emotional depth to the seemingly composed old-fashioned type of man but, on the other, that this type is a dying breed in the context of the emergence of a public-facing identity based on personality.

These crime of passion tales are part of a broader grouping of stories about spiritual or mystical experiences that include James's paranormal romance "The Way It Came" (*Chap-Book*) but also, more characteristically, tales informed by an aesthetic, decadent, orientalist, and/or symbolist mode that recount engagements in occult rituals of various types. Though such tales were less prolific than marriage and courtship tales, they were strongly identified with little magazines, such that, among the terms used to describe these periodicals were "decadents" and "greenery-yallery" (an allusion to Gilbert and Sullivan's term to mock aestheticism). These tales accrued cultural capital in comparison with their dime novel counterparts through their appropriation of the avant-garde themes and aesthetics of these European movements. Influences included recently published horror tales, such as British author Arthur Machen's *Great God Pan* (1894), issued by the notorious Bodley Head, publisher of the *Yellow Book* and of controversial New Woman and decadent writers which circulated transatlantically; Robert W. Chambers's collection *The King in Yellow* (1895); and J.-K. Huysmans's *A rebours* (1884). These books appealed to a sophisticated readership seeking cultural distinction, one knowledgeable about decadence beyond the more popular figure of Wilde. Arnold M'Causland's "As Told by the Persian" (*Lotus*), for example, is highly reminiscent of Machen's *Great God Pan* in its treatment of an occult ritual that fuses a man and woman into an androgynous being. A. Lawrence Gnichtel's "From a Hall Window" (*Bohemian*) and John Regnault Ellyson's "Habelais" (*Smart Set*), meanwhile, capture the "weird" quality popularized by Chambers's dream vision stories in *The King in Yellow*. Gnichtel's bohemian protagonist falls asleep in his New York tenement after his evening smoke to dream of a venom-drinking snake-charmer, while Ellyson's artist protagonist is taken on a trance adventure by a sorcerer in Paris to encounter an exotic and intoxicating woman. Finally, echoing the synaesthesiac experiments of

Des Esseintes in *A rebours*, a musician in "For Fame, Money, or Love?" (*Black Cat*) creates an instrument that translates musical notes into words that ultimately recount his death of a broken heart.

Interests in decadence, aestheticism, and bohemianism manifested themselves in a notable representation of artists and dandies in little magazine fiction, accounting for 15 per cent of the stories in the sampling, predominantly in aesthetic little magazines. The interest in the artist figure in this period has been attributed to a number of causes: the popularity of novels such as George du Maurier's *Trilby* (1894) and Henri Murger's *La vie de bohème* (1851), a novel popular throughout the century; the development of introspective and self-reflexive art forms such as aestheticism and decadence; the expanding literary and artistic marketplace, which generated interest in these professions and in the lives of writers and artists; and anxieties caused by changing conditions to the literary marketplace (Keating 79; Stetz 171–5; MacLeod, *Fictions* 57–8). At the same time, in a specifically American context, Levin has documented the role that concepts of bohemianism played in the construction of middle-class identity. Flexibly mobilized notions of bohemia, she argues, served to "challenge dominant ideologies and to mediate a series of social and cultural divides" in nineteenth- and early twentieth-century America (3). Like the arts and crafts movement, concepts of bohemianism were a means for a professional-managerial class "to compensate for, and thus accommodate themselves to, the demands of modern capitalism" (Levin 203). The artist was a useful, if not unproblematic, figure in this context. For a class invested in harmonizing culture and commerce, artists posed a challenge. On the one hand, the artist who rejected the marketplace undermined this aim, while, nevertheless, representing an appealing purity. On the other, the commercial artist threatened this ideal, representing a kind of crass vulgarity. The ideal artist, like the ideal of the professional-managerial class, was one who harmonized culture and commerce. At the same time, in the emerging context of the culture of personality, the new celebritized artists of various types might or might not serve for a professional middle class as models for identity self-fashioning and formation.

Artists, bohemians, and dandies appear in a wide range of story types in the sampling. They include stories that glamorize artists, catering to a readership with a fascination for this lifestyle who might, themselves, be living a version of this life or imagining themselves as embodying the distinction and cultural superiority of the artist.

Bill Hill's "Quat'z' Arts Ball" in *Quartier Latin*, a Paris-based magazine created by expatriate American art students and their teachers, offers an account of this joyful bohemian world for American readers and is framed, in narrative terms, as a letter from an artist abroad to his male friend back home. The romance, passion, and danger of this world, meanwhile, are explored in A.H. Shirk's "In a Studio" (*Muse*), Rodrigues Ottolengui's "For Fame, Money, or Love?" (*Black Cat*), Julian Sinclair's "Rhapsody in Red" (*Les Jeunes*),[6] and Eugene Eble's "Game of Chess" (*Whims*). These latter two stories also treat the relationship of the artist to his/her muse and art, as do Maurice Hewlett's "Quattrocentisteria" (*Bibelot*), about Botticelli, and Florence L. Holmes's "Woman Who Understood" (*Gray Goose*). In these stories, artists are represented as possessing a greater capacity for passionate love and intensity of feeling.

Highly glamorized stereotypes of the artist's life are countered with more critical representations of the artist as dangerous type, inimical to the social order desired by America's middle classes. Edmund Yarrow's "Merely an Experiment" (*John-a-Dreams*), for example, represents artists as socially disruptive, literalizing the notion that they exploit others for their art. The artist in the story interferes with the lives of people in a small town, stage-managing events, in effect, for the purposes of his novel. He is a modern-day devil – "the man who, for his art's sake, will vivisect his victims without anaesthetics, and will hold up the quivering members for the delectation of the wondering crowd, among whom none can tell who is marked out for the next victim" (3). In another story, the first-person account "Change of Thought" (*Moods*) by G. Frederic Russell, the social and moral redemption of a cynical, aspiring, unsuccessful artist is brought about by love. A visiting friend gushes to him about her fiancé, a young man making his way in the professional world and saving up for marriage. This discussion prompts the artist to a sudden realization of his love for a girl back home. The implication is (though it is only an implication) that he will return home, give up his dalliance with art to find a "real" profession, and settle down with his sweetheart. Here, a young man experimenting with the modern dandy-artist identity finds it wanting and turns, it would seem, to a model of masculinity more suited to the new professional ethos of his class.

The varied and contradictory representations of artists in the little magazines of the period reflect the complex ways in which the popular notion of bohemianism was exploited to various cultural ends.

It has been understood both as a striking opposition to bourgeois life and as bourgeois. Levin's work traces how the concept was used flexibly in late nineteenth- and early twentieth-century America as a means of negotiating and transforming bourgeois ideals, values, and cultural life (Levin 2–3). The appeal of the bohemian in America is indicated, in part, by the number of magazines exploiting the term in this period, many of which can be considered part of, or related to, the little magazine phenomenon. Magazines titled *The Bohemian* issued from New York, Boston, Buffalo, Fort Worth, and Philadelphia. There was also a *New Bohemian* from Cincinnati and an *Amateur Bohemian* of Oakland, California. As Albert Parry indicates, most of the magazines that capitalized on the appeal of bohemianism offered a watered down, genteel, domesticated version of the lifestyle, collapsing the distinction between bourgeois and bohemian (98). So, for example, *The Bohemian* (Boston), a title included in Faxon's list, sought to enlarge the scope of the term beyond those "who love pleasure without regard to conventionalities" to include "all who appreciate good fellowship" (front matter). *The New Bohemian* similarly offered itself as a "wholesome, pure, and refined" magazine, one that was "ideal … for the home" ("Advertisements" iii). The anonymously authored story, "A Night in Bohemia," from the first issue of this magazine (a title outside the sampling), provides a flavour of the aims of the magazine in its representation of Bohemia. In it, the protagonist reflects on the Bohemian gathering before him as he enjoys a party with an old man who is a writer, the old man's wife, an actress, an artist, and a journalist: "It was not the Bohemia of unshaven faces and frayed cuffs – although the personal appearances of Scoopum and the artist were frequently not up to the mark when they were in hard luck, which was sometimes and usually, respectively – nor of long hair and soiled finger-nails and vulgar grisettes, but a cozy home-like Bohemia, with the Little Woman to do propriety" ("Night in Bohemia" 19).

While these examples seem to support Parry's contention and suggest that these publications be understood as part of the mainstream, Levin's more nuanced analysis argues for their oppositional nature and the difficulty of setting strict parameters for the field of little magazines. She argues that, in the case of a regional publication like the Fort Worth *Bohemian*, though its bohemianism may come across as rather bourgeois, its antagonistic force is directed at the bourgeois Northeast and its publications (263). Regional magazines, then, did function to give voice to the cultural interests and identity of the margins in relation to a dominant centre. Here, we see evidence of those who are culturally at the margins appropriating and redefining bohemianism to assert their authority.

The magazines of this period that engaged explicitly with bohemianism, however, were not only defining themselves in relation to the mainstream. In the 1890s, after all, the bohemianism that the *New Bohemian* rails against, that of "long hair" and "vulgar grisettes," was linked with the decadent avant-garde extolled by many little magazinists. Publications like the *New Bohemian*, then, exist, as Levin argues, somewhere between mainstream and little magazines and they do so self-consciously (270). *The New Bohemian*, for example, valorized publications that find a "mean … between the jejune inanity of Bokish exploitation [a reference to Edward W. Bok and his editorship of *The Ladies' Home Journal*] and the hectic apex of decadent ribaldry" that it located in more extreme little magazines like the controversial *M'lle New York* ("Between the Covers" 226). Little magazines, then, offered a range of representations of bohemianism, a tendency noted by the magazines themselves. Magazines with a decadent bent may have promoted a bohemia that, in the words of *The Lotus* editor, represented "an alluring and subtle danger which threatens the morals and manners of the great musical, literary and artistic world" ("Comment" 90): in other words, the "unshaven faces" and "vulgar grisettes" deplored by *The New Bohemian*. Meanwhile, those with an earnest and idealistic strain, such as *The Lotus*, which characterized itself as "Unconventional but not Decadent," might want to emphasize a battle against "the enemies of Art," disassociating bohemianism from its negative connotations (*The Lotus*, advertisement; "Comment" 90).

Given the large number of aspiring writers producing these stories, narratives of artists and bohemian life can also be understood, of course, as a way of asserting cultural authority. So too, can the considerable body of short short forms of fiction (22 per cent of the sampling) found in little magazines that include sketches, parables, fables, and proems. While consummate artists such as Henry James interested themselves in the "long" short story, extreme brevity was also touted as a sign of artistry in the short story of the day, much in the same way that "littleness" gave cultural value to the little magazine. The higher artistry ascribed to short short forms lies in the fact that they rely on poetic effects and/or leave more to the imagination. They draw attention to themselves as highly polished aesthetic prose objects. Indeed, sometimes their authors strive explicitly to associate their written work with other artistic forms, notably the visual and musical arts.

This interest in the transposition of the arts was an important feature of late nineteenth-century European art movements, especially impressionism, aestheticism, and decadence. Little magazinists shared this interest, drawing on music, sculpture, and the visual arts. Stories from the sampling are identified, in some cases, as sketches, etchings, engravings, mosaics, pictures, or rhapsodies (Moorehead; Frederic C. Bennett; Mary Lenox Morris; Deland; Sinclair; Davis). The term sketch, of course, does not automatically indicate a connection to visual arts. The genre of the literary sketch was prevalent in America from the early nineteenth century and denoted a descriptive piece (of character, scene, incident, recollection, or reverie) as distinct from a plot-oriented short narrative or "tale" (Kristie Hamilton 2). At the same time, writers earlier in the century had exploited a wide artistic vocabulary in their development of this genre, using terms like jotting, inkling, outlines, and so on (Kristie Hamilton 2, 3). Certainly, this practice continued through the century and was taken up in the little magazines, where the evocation of terms from the visual arts is often as much a literary conceit as it is an attempt to transpose the arts. There are, however, striking instances in the sampling where experimentations with this aesthetic and decadent practice are in play. One of these is by Richard Harding Davis, whose position in the field of mainstream journalism makes him a rather unlikely proponent of decadent aesthetics. Nevertheless, "At the Opera," one of a pair of self-identified "sketches" published in *Bradley His Book*, evokes the mood and imagery of impressionist paintings by Manet, Degas, and others. In Helen G. Moorehead's "Wood Engraving" (*New Bohemian*), meanwhile, the invocation of this form of visual art, regarded as old-fashioned and folky by the end of the nineteenth century, and a popular form in the little magazine, is particularly suited to the content – a short idyll of gypsy life.

The aesthetic prose object is also notably represented in little magazine content in the form of the proem or prose poem. This form had cultural prestige in this period as experimental and innovative and was popular among European aesthetes, decadents, and symbolists. The prose poem, of course, represents another kind of transposition of the arts, one restricted to the literary sphere, where the rhythmic and metrical effects of poetry are brought to the prose realm. Wilde, Baudelaire, Mallarmé, and Maeterlinck were important European innovators, along with the American symbolist Stuart Merrill. This form, one described as a "peculiarly modern invention" by William Dean Howells in his introduction to Merrill's translations of French prose poems (v), was a means of showcasing a jeweled prose style and exotic themes, drawing attention to the work as art object. In addition, proems were often visually displayed as artistic objects on the page. In an instance from the sampling, a proem about the lotus flower by Philemon Garrique (*Lotus*) appears in a single column, centred on the page, in full caps, justified, and in old-style Jenson font, a typographic embodiment of the lotus which, in the poem, declares itself "the capital of columns in the temple of the soul" (see Figure 4.1).

This proem, with its oracular style, also functions as a fable about the lotus, and is thus part of a larger body of symbolic fiction in the way of fables, parables, and allegorical tales that constituted the majority of short short forms in little magazines. The didactic nature of fables and parables might seem contradictory to the art-for-art's-sake ethos of aesthetic little magazines. These forms were, however, popular with European decadents and symbolists and gained prestige in this period. Wilde for example, was as drawn to the fable, fairy tale, folk tale, and parable as he was the prose poem. Indeed, he, and other writers, often combined these forms, especially the parable in prose poem form. At the same time, the fable, parable, folk tale, and fairy tale were germane to the chap-book format that so many little magazines adopted, as this was precisely the type of content that appeared in the historic form. Allegory, meanwhile, offered a more complex manner of dealing with moral, ethical, and spiritual matters. The symbolism of Maeterlinck, for example, with its interest in mysticism, nature, and the occult, engages with allegory in complex ways in considering metaphysical matters of the soul, death, and the meaning of life. In this mode, allegorical meaning, as little magazinist Richard Hovey argued, is meant to be "suggestive" rather than "cut-and-dried": "Its events, its personages, its sentences rather imply than definitely state an esoteric meaning" (6, 5).[7] This mode was popular with little magazinists who had interests in the European avant-garde, especially those writers associated with *The Chap-Book*. Indeed, Stone and Kimball dedicated a book series, the Green Tree Library, to translations of European decadent texts that included Hovey's translations of Maeterlinck.

The more suggestive, enigmatic mode associated with symbolism is exploited by little magazinists in a number of parables that take the form of proems in the sampling. E. St Elmo Lewis's "Life's Quest"

IN THE BEGINNING I WAS
THE MYSTIC OF THE SUN. I
LOOKED UPON THE MOTHER
BREASTED NILE WITH PAS
SION. I SAW MY IMAGE GROW
WITHIN HER FERTILE, SOUND
LESS EYES. SHE LOVED ME,
CONCEIVED OF ME, BORE ME
CHILDREN; CHILDREN MULTI
TUDINOUS, WHITE, CHASTE,
BEAUTIFUL; THEY REST UP
ON THE BILLOW OF HER BOS
OM. THE FIRST BORN LEFT
HIS MOTHER. I WATCHED
HIM EAST, THEN SOUTH
WARD UNDER THE PROCES
SIONAL STARS. LOVE SHOT
HIM, AND HE BECAME ORI
ENT, ORIFLAMMED, BROAD
RED. I SAW HIS CHILDREN
KISS THE FEET OF WOMEN
AND THERE WOMEN ARE
THE LILY-FOOTED TO THIS
PRESENT HOUR, THEIR
SOULS STAR-PETALED; LIKE
A WHITE EVENING. I AM
THE SUN. I AM THE WORLD, I
AM WOMEN BEAUTIFUL. I AM
THE CAPITAL OF COLUMNS
IN THE TEMPLE OF THE
SOUL. A GOD ROSE OUT OF
THE SEA, THRONED AND
FLOATING ON ME. MY
ODOUR ESCAPED OUT OF
PARADISE. I AM THE CUP OF
ALL PEACEFUL WATERS, PRO
CHEIN SIB OF REST. I AM THE
LOTUS. WORSHIP ME, O MUS
ARD.—PHILEMON GARRIQUE

Figure 4.1 "Proem" by Philemon Garrique in *The Lotus*, May 1896. Courtesy of HathiTrust.

(*Moods*) and Brainerd Prescott Emery's "Shadow of the Sphinx" (*Clique*) take place in a timeless, spaceless void from which their speakers reflect futilely on metaphysical questions of life, death, pain, and suffering. In "Life's Quest," the speaker is tormented by an inability to reconcile the conflicting demands of soul and heart: "the World seems to have gone on without me, leaving me here on these shifting sands of mortality and the passersby tell me that Love and Truth are with the World/Yet my heart weeps for Love/While my Soul yearns for Truth." Though the speaker in "Shadow of the Sphinx" has a lover, his world is just as bleak. They die together trying to "solve Death's strange enigma," while the Sphinx looks "coldly over death and silence to the horizon's rim." This form of symbolism, though highly esoteric, was not restricted in its interest, necessarily, to an artistic elite. As Stone and Kimball's dedication of a portion of their book publishing enterprise to this genre suggests, it was of interest to those among the professional class seeking self-culture and cultural distinction. For this class, these proems engage in abstract, philosophical, and symbolic terms with precisely the issues of alienation, loneliness, social disconnection, etc. that were germane to their experiences in the context of fin-de-siècle modernity. They might function, therefore, as a literature of self-reflection and soul-searching.

Little magazines also featured more straightforwardly didactic fables and parables. A number of these, significantly, are part of the body of fiction depicting artists, and contribute to broader critiques of aestheticism and decadence, even while invoking its tropes and motifs. Ernest Thompson's "Pack-Rat" (*Quartier Latin*) for example, is a conventional fable. Though represented as a beast fable, the "pack-rat" is aligned with a specific kind of hoarder through word choice and accompanying image. The bits of pine cones, scraps of soap, snake-skins, etc. that he accumulates are described as "bibelots," and his abode a "museum," identifying him as an aesthete collector (25). This connection is reinforced by an illustration of an artist in a bric-a-brac filled studio replete with Japanese lanterns, a parasol, Persian rugs, sketches, books, vases, pedestals, etc. (Pemberton 26). More scathingly, Ernest Crosby makes a link between sin and art, evoking tropes of decadence in his parable and prose poem, "A Vision of Art" (*Whim*). The speaker in this poem encounters art in the guise of "a fair oriental princess, reclining on a deep cushioned divan, and yawning indolently while her handmaidens and eunuchs fan her" (97). Deploying all the trappings of a decadent jeweled prose style, Crosby ultimately renounces such art in revealing that the initially highly seductive princess, who declares "languorously," "I am Art … and I am for my own sake," is actually "sallow" and overperfumed (97).

The decadent and symbolistic treatment of allegorical fictions was one prevalent in aesthetic little magazines that privileged these forms as high art. Allegorical literature, however, was even more important in periodicals of protest and hybrid magazines with a protest agenda, where it functioned differently. In these magazines, fables, fairy and folk tales, and parables served political ends, offering commentary, for example, on the fractious labour issues of the period that were relevant to the interests of a largely progressive readership. These little magazinists eschewed the jeweled style and deliberate ambiguities favoured by those exploring the form in decadent or symbolistic terms. Instead, they foregrounded the moral and didactic function of these forms, often signalling their intentions with cruder and more simplistic "once upon a time" openings, and "the moral is" endings.

Much of this content engaged with the problems of capitalism, adopting the progressive, reformist, and even socialist stances at the heart of the professional-managerial ethos of the period and reflecting this class's complex positioning between capital and labour as reformers and healers of class conflict (Ehrenreich and Ehrenreich 19). Much of this allegorical content, as demonstrated in the sampling, is critical of employers, blaming them, not workers, for labour unrest. Sometimes this critique is general in nature, as in the depiction of wealth and greed in Minnette Isbell's "The Mountain" (*Optimist*), which juxtaposes the artist who immortalizes the mountain in his art with the greedy owner who glories in his possession of it. The mountain also figures symbolically in a parable about greed by J.C.W. (likely J. Cal Watkins) in *The Ghourki*, in which the "Mountain of Wealth" is populated by those struggling, trampling, and crushing each other in efforts to reach the top. Others, especially those in the socialist magazines that were part of the body of periodicals of protest, target capitalism more explicitly: Dorothy Dix's "The Bear Who Found Nothing in Economy" (*Wilshire's*) attacks the credit system, while Polly Dawson's "Into the Deeps" (*Conservator*) offers a scathing critique of the exploitation of cigar factory workers who suffer on behalf of the "torpid, indolent rich" who, as they smoke their cigars, "dream of fat bank accounts and wondrous women" (5). Some of this content is utopian in spirit, as in Harold C. Robinson's "Third Lesson" (*Comrade*), the story of Sfinx, who becomes a hero when he breaks the multibillion-dollar trust and puts power in the hands of government. More famously, this issue of *The Comrade* also includes an installment of William Morris's utopian novel *News From Nowhere*, which imagines a society based on Ruskinian and Marxist principles. This didactic content is well beyond the realm of the art-for-art's sake material that little magazines were associated with. If aesthetic, decadent, and symbolist content served a readership invested in self-culture through high art, the socio-political activist elements of the fiction in periodicals of protest fed its equally strong interest in reform. This reformist impulse would be further engaged with in other kinds of content in periodicals of protest and hybrid magazines that will be explored more fully in subsequent chapters.

Though little magazines were associated in the popular imagination with aestheticism, decadence, and symbolism, they also engaged with realist trends of the day and 12 per cent of the stories in the sampling are of this type. Popular forms of realist fiction included local colour stories, urban slum narratives, regional fiction, and dialect stories. Ohmann uses the term "elsewhere" stories to refer to this fiction, defining its focus roughly as "why people in other cultures or subcultures do what they do" (*Selling Culture* 322–3). Much of this fiction approached its subject matter with a sentimentalizing or moralizing gaze, though, by the 1880s, this was being replaced by ethnographic or aestheticized treatments. Ohmann notes a key distinction between stories about people "like us" (i.e., the professional-managerial class) and "elsewhere" fiction: "Writers bring philosophy or psychology to bear in explaining the conduct of people 'like us'; they often shift to a *sociological* understanding when representing uneducated rural or provincial or immigrant folk" (*Selling Culture* 322). His insight holds equally true with respect to little magazine fiction where people "like us" stories across a range of genres privilege interiority, often from a psychological or philosophical point of view. In turning to regional and dialect fiction, by contrast, the ethnographic gaze prevails, though aspects of an old-fashioned sentimental or moralizing gaze and of aestheticized representations of the lives of others are also evident.

Within the broader genre of regional and dialect fiction in little magazines, slum fiction accounts for a significant proportion, representing over 20 per cent of stories of this type. New York's tenements were a favourite topic in the 1880s and 1890s and much of this fiction, as Keith Gandal argues, adopts an ethnographic or aesthetic gaze and is characterized by sentimentalism and a Protestant moral ethos (39–60). Stephen Crane's *Maggie: A Girl of the Streets* (1893), he argues, was one of the few works to resist the moralizing impulse, seeking to understand the ethics of tenement life on its own terms instead of through the lens of bourgeois morality (50). Little magazines engage, in various ways, with the subject of the slums. Unsurprisingly, those that most exploited the fad were New York-based publications. In these stories, the slum dwellers and setting function as a means for these writers to provide "local colour" description or dialect. Louise Betts Edwards's "Mary the Prig" (*Criterion*), for example, casts a voyeuristic and sentimentalizing gaze on the courting rituals of Irish tenement dwellers in New York from the perspective of a wry narrator. Mary, initially too genteel in her ways for her community, learns to act like others of her set, drinking, stealing, and gallivanting, in order to win the heart of Thorny Wood, the man she loves. The story is not moralistic. Indeed, it rejects the cosy fireside image of the bourgeois marriage, referring to it as a "hateful spectre of Ennui" (9). Thorny Wood will, it is suggested, have a much happier life with the lively Mary. Nevertheless, the story is patronizing in its treatment and in its reinforcement of a social divide. The narrative privileges the naturalist understanding of environment as fate, rather than the aspirational ideals of white Protestant American life. Thus, though Mary's bourgeois ways make her unsuited to her environment, she must adapt to it. Like the dialect fiction Ohmann considers, this story represents "human possibility trapped" (*Selling Culture* 324), even while it treats the subject matter in a humorous vein, and reinforces the social divide between "us" and "them."

A similar message is projected, in a more depressing register, in Joseph von Whalen's "Sputterings of a Seething Cauldron" (*Whims*). The main character in the story is, like Mary, a misfit within his class. A strident socialist, he launches into a speech about capitalism and the oppression of the working-classes to an audience of slum dwellers at a café. The hopeful note he ends on, a utopian vision of the triumph of "industrial freedom," is undermined, however, as the speaker collapses in exhaustion, his audience indifferent to his efforts. The title of the story, the representation of the slum dwellers in animalistic terms, the narrator's dismissal of the socialist's rhetoric as "jargon," and the sense of futility of the ending, suggest a high degree of cynicism about the socialism being preached and the ability of slum dwellers to take action to better themselves. While, like "Mary the Prig," the story is neither moralistic nor sentimental, its sociological and ethnographic perspective offers an explanatory narrative that reinforces middle-class prejudices about immigrants and the working classes. Both stories show that against the progressive, forward momentum of middle-class Americans with a belief that they can control their lives, lies an immigrant population trapped by their conditions.

Little magazine slum narratives also explore the interaction of middle-class people with the immigrant poor, providing contradictory views of the efficacy of middle-class intervention. Though the reformist impulse, as indicated in chapter 1, was strong in middle-class culture, it was not uncontroversial, as differing perspectives in little magazine stories show. Margaret L. Knapp's "A Moment Musical" (*Chips*) is relevant in this context. In this story, a middle-class girl wanders into a working-class tenement community where she begins to play her violin. As in Von Whalen's story, the immigrants are presented in animalistic terms: they are "dirty, patched, all but ragged ... wild creatures of the woods" (120). In addition, while the girl's interiority is made accessible in the narrative, the slum dwellers remain unknown. The story functions as a fantasy of middle-class reformist ideals, presented as a win-win scenario. The charitable act of a middle-class woman brings culture to the uncultivated, while serving, simultaneously, as a means for her own transcendence. Virtue becomes its own reward.

By contrast, this kind of middle-class charitable reform is looked upon with scepticism in another story from the sampling – Edward W. Townsend's "By Whom the Offence Cometh" (*M'lle New York*). Like Crane in *Maggie*, Townsend resists aestheticisation and moralizing in his tale,[8] a feature of much of the fiction of urban life in the radical and anti-establishment *M'lle New York* more broadly speaking. Though not wholly unproblematic in its representation of ethnicity and class, the stories in *M'lle New York* do much to celebrate the city's immigrant life. In his story, Townsend turns the tables on conventional understandings of immigrant culture. The narrative avoids judgment in its representation of an immigrant girl's turn to thieving, drug addiction, and prostitution, reserving its condemnation for the middle-class religious social missionaries – those "by whom the offence cometh" – who are depicted as ignoring her dead body on the street at the end of the tale.

Beyond the urban realism preferred in New York-based publications, little magazines also engaged with regional or local colour writing and/or dialect fiction centering on rural areas and small towns – a form of "elsewhere" writing for some, but not all, as little magazinists and their readers were neither necessarily urban-born nor urban-based. Though regional writing is found in little magazines, it was a form regarded with ambivalence by established and emerging literary elites. This ambivalence was rooted in the sense that, on the one hand, as noted regionalist writer Hamlin Garland acknowledged, it could be exploited to draw on the unique character and variety of life in America towards the creation of a distinctively national literature, about which he wrote passionately in his essay collection, *Crumbling Idols* (1894). This potential was important to those who believed that America should develop its own literary forms and traditions rather than imitate European models. On the other hand, however, there were those who felt that local colour writing was a low, inartistic form, indicative of a kind of provincialism and parochialism that was oversaturating the literary market.

In general, local colour writing was most favoured, understandably, by regional aesthetic little magazines that often promoted local writers. *The Kiote*, for example, was proudly Nebraskan, contemptuous of the East and its anglomania: "The critics of the east," it complained, "have made it their business to keep down the writers of the west ... *The Kiote* and the Kiote books are not sent east to be reviewed. If an eastern critic wants to take a fall at us or our work he can do so only by paying the regular price of the magazine or book for the privilege" ("Yelps," *Kiote* 3, no. 3, 69–70). For *The Kiote*, then, regional and dialect fiction centred on Nebraska and the west represented an aesthetic revolt. Its readers are discouraged from reading with eastern anglomaniac eyes that will view the local colour as trite and quaint. This is the frame it establishes for considering the local-based fiction in its pages, such as Eva Mary McCune's "What's in a Name?" from the sampling, a slice-of-life piece in which residents of a new settlement argue over what to call their town. Such subject matter is clearly unique to America, a nation still engaged in settling new territory. Other region-proud little magazines included *The Dilettante* of Seattle, which strove to be "*the* literary publication of the Northwest" and "to be local but not provincial" (front matter), and *The Alkahest*, which made much of its Southern identity, aiming to demonstrate that "the genius of the South is equal to any section" (front matter, *Alkahest* 4, no. 1).

The celebration of regional identity in these magazines functioned much in the same way as did appropriations and adaptations of notions of bohemia as described by Levin: the representations of local writers and topics serve as an indication of how these magazines negotiated their marginal identity in relation to a dominant centre. Celebrating regional literature might function as a way of resisting an Eastern-dominated literary culture; alternatively, it might serve as part of an interest in expanding the parameters of that culture. Certainly, editors of regional little magazines were keen to situate local writers within a wider national and international cosmopolitan literary context. William Ellis, of *The Philosopher*, for example, insisted that literature should be "un-national" ("In the Smoking Room," *Philosopher* 1, no. 1, 27), and his magazine and other regional publications mixed the work of locals with writing by, and discussions of, national and international figures.

The ambivalence towards local colour writing is well illustrated by *The Chap-Book*'s treatment of it. Though it regularly featured local colour stories by authors such as Hamlin Garland, Alice Brown, Maria Louise Pool, and Katherine Bates, its editor mocked the notion that "to be indigenous is to be artistic" ("Notes" *Chap-Book* 3, no. 10, 402). *The Chap-Book* presumably made an exception for the writers it included. Wendy Schlereth, for example, has argued that while Garland's local colour writing might, at first glance, seem inimical to the aesthetic ideals of *The Chap-Book*, it exhibits a strain of romanticism that brought his work closer to the more avant-gardist interests of the magazine and its editors (69–76).

Regional fiction, then, could be accorded a high cultural status, particularly if understood within the context of the anti-modern trends and the romance vs. realism debates of the period that tapped into anxieties about the enervating and effeminizing effects of modernity. Regional fiction was sometimes couched in these terms, representing particular locales in idealized and nostalgic terms. A story from the sampling by popular novelist Ralph Connor is in this register. "Beyond the Marshes," which appeared in the belletristic *Bibelot*-style *Cornhill Booklet*, concerns a missionary's visit to a Canadian prairie settlement. An introduction to the story by Ishbel Hamilton-Gordon, Lady Aberdeen, wife of the Governor General of Canada, promotes its power to bring about a transcendent experience for a world-weary reader:

> And this sweet prairie idyll is surely one of these fragrant messages which lays its hold on us as we pause for a moment in the midst of our fevered lives and anxious thoughts, and step across the threshold of that chamber where we must needs put our shoes from off our feet, for the place whereon we stand is holy ground. And, as we press on again to life's duties, may we bear with us something of that precious perfume diffused by plants which are divine in their origin and which must be divine in their influence. (330)

In Aberdeen's terms, the story is art sacralized, providing the solace and escape from modernity ardently desired by the genteel middle and professional managerial classes in the context of increased commercialism and industrialism.

Regional fiction might also occupy high cultural ground if imbued with the qualities of adventure and historical romance that, in literary debates of the period, were seen as antidotes to effeminate modes of realism. Little magazinist Bliss Carman, for example, endorsed what he called "the new romance movement," touting it as more artistic than realism, which, to him, was "mere self-portraiture" ("Mr. Gilbert Parker" 340, 342): "We demand in art something better than we can find in ourselves" (342). Carman's comments originate from an article on fellow Canadian author Gilbert Parker and his famous Pierre stories about a French-Canadian trapper, one of which, "Across the Jumping Sandhills" (*Pocket Magazine*), is in the sampling. For Carman, Parker's stories of a "reckless, gambling, adorable half-breed" with his own moral code embody the "new romance movement" and are at once popular and artistic (339, 340). These stories were certainly popular with the mass-market, and, indeed, *Pocket Magazine*, a story magazine, was most definitely at the commercial end of the little magazine spectrum. Parker was also favoured, though, by the little magazine elite, contributing, for example, to *The Chap-Book*. While these stories might have appealed to the masses for their regional trappings, Parker himself preferred to understand them as universal in their import and therefore timeless and artistic rather than topical and ephemeral (Parker, Introduction viii–ix). Though far removed from the introspective fiction more characteristic of little magazines, the new romance was another significant trend, endorsed and enjoyed by an educated elite within the broad anti-modern movement of the period that T.J. Jackson Lears has documented (103–7). This type of fiction represented the spontaneity, vitality, and rejuvenation that were viewed as necessary in the context of an increasingly fast-paced modern life – the "fevered lives" invoked by Aberdeen (330).

While region-oriented fiction might serve the purpose of providing solace or rejuvenating jaded and weary Americans caught up in the travails of modern commercial and industrial life, it was the historical adventure romance that was more often thought of in this respect. Popular historical romance of this era encompassed a broad range of periods, styles, and geographical locales and included James Barrie's and Ian McLaren's tales of rural Scottish life, novels about the French and American revolutions, Southern plantation stories, stories of early New England and New France, swashbuckling romances of the *Prisoner of Zenda* type set in imaginary kingdoms, tales of ancient Rome and early Christian-era romances inspired by the success of *Quo Vadis*. Interestingly, historical romance, despite its popularity, was not, Ohmann attests, prevalent in mass-market magazines, where westerns were the key form of adventure romance (*Selling Culture* 330). Little magazines, by contrast, contain more historical romance than westerns, though the number is again quite small, and adventure stories not set in the past are more likely to take place in exotic, foreign locales than in the west. The limited representation of the historical romance in mass-market and little magazines may be due to the fact that the short story form, privileged increasingly by these magazines, was less amenable than the novel to the epic scope and plot-oriented nature of the adventure genre. As a consequence, within the realm of little magazines, it is mainly story magazines, which allowed for longer content, that feature adventure romances of a more popular type. These magazines included several popular masters of the genre, such as Stanley J. Weyman, whose "Flore" (*Pocket Magazine*) is representative of his specialization in historical romances set in sixteenth- and seventeenth-century France (Simmons); Carlton Dawe, whose "Silken Cord" (*Smart Set*) is characteristic of his exotic Far East tales ("Carleton Dawe" 91); and Eden Phillpotts, a prolific writer across a range of genres (Ferns), whose "In the King's Chamber" (*Smart Set*) offers historical fiction in an orientalist decadent mode in its account of a murderous love triangle set in an ancient Egyptian harem. Stephen Crane, meanwhile, demonstrates his willingness to cater to the popular interest in sentimental Civil War era romances in "A Grey Sleeve" (*Pocket Magazine*), a marked departure from his obscure and outré poetry. Beyond these story magazines, the aesthetic little magazines in the sampling include, in the way of historical romance, a variation on the *Zenda* theme, a parody of Bertha Runkle's bestselling *Helmet of Navarre* (1901) called "The Stovepipe of Navarre" (by "Poeta Pants"), as well as stories set in Civil War–era America, Renaissance Italy, Medieval and Arthurian England, ancient Rome, seventeenth- and eighteenth-century France, and ancient Arabia.

Like local colour fiction, historical and adventure romance can be considered forms of what Ohmann calls "elsewhere" fiction, whether that elsewhere is temporal, as in historical fiction, or geographical, as in the case of exotic adventure romances. While these worlds may, like slum fiction, enable a consideration of "otherness" in class and racial terms, they might also feature people "like us." Adventure fiction was a malleable genre, rooted in the socio-political contexts and ideologies of the turn of the century, where it performed various kinds of cultural work germane to its largely professional-managerial audience. Lears, for example, situates the rise of historical romance within the anti-modernist trend of middle-class life in the period, seeing it as a reaction, in literary terms, to realist fiction and, in cultural terms, to modernization (97–140). Both realist literature and fin-de-siècle modernity were associated by proponents of romance with overcivilization, morbid self-consciousness, ennui, and the feminization of culture. As a "literature of action," the romance remasculinized literature, addressing the desire for "intense, immediate experience" and it was understood as serving a revitalizing, therapeutic function, reaffirming, Lears argues, "the bourgeois ethic of autonomous achievement" (107, 104). Shumway, meanwhile, considers the importance of historical romance from a gendered perspective, stressing the centrality of the romance/courtship plot in this fiction and a discourse that spoke to contemporary issues around gender and sexuality (34–52).[9]

Given the dominance of the love story in little magazines, it is hardly surprising that its central themes are explored in historical fiction also. In contrast to modern, realist treatments of this subject, adventure stories offered exoticised and abstracted representations that could explore taboo aspects of love and desire and locate them elsewhere. It is telling, for example, that two of the historical romances in the sampling concern cross-class relationships, when this theme is not prevalent otherwise in the little magazine love story sampling, nor, indeed, in Ohmann's mass-market sampling. Cross-class love stories, Ohmann argues, were carefully contained: "the courtship story confers its ideological blessings on socially disparate couples only if both partners belong or are about to belong or have the right to belong to one of the reputable classes" (*Selling Culture* 319). Historical fiction, however, may have represented a safe way of exploring this controversial theme. So, for example, Sophie Earl's "A Prophecy" (*Bohemian*) is a fictionalized moment in the life of Marie Leczinski when a clairvoyant reveals to her her seemingly improbable destiny as future Queen of France. In neglecting to mention that the real life Leczinski is the daughter of the deposed King of Poland, the narrative emphasizes her humility and obscures her class suitability. Though clearly, in Ohmann's sense, Leczinski has the right to belong to the nobility she is destined for, and the story is, therefore, carefully contained, it nevertheless caters to the powerful American democratic myth that class barriers can be transcended, one central to the ethos of an aspirational professional middle class.

A similar theme is treated in Carlton Dawe's "Silken Cord" (*Smart Set*), in which a court official in Imperial China concocts an elaborate plan to elope with the Emperor's sister. Though rather conventional as a cross-class love story, "The Silken Cord" offers a complex representation of manhood if considered from the perspective of Lears's understanding of the function of "literature of action" for its middle-class readership. Indeed, this story, along with at least five other historical romances in the sampling, can be read as allegories for the working lives of middle-class men of the day. They play out, in symbolic terms, and through the medium of a "literature of action," the psychic drama of the professional workplace or business environment. The positions of the protagonists in these tales in relation to figures of benevolent or corrupt authority parallel those of professional men in turn-of-the-century America. In the stories, the protagonists are courtiers who are well, albeit precariously, positioned within a hierarchal structure, and, like turn-of-the-century professional men, dependent more upon wits than brawn in navigating the potentially treacherous environment in which they find themselves. In two instances, these protagonists are fools, figures who, traditionally, serve not only to amuse, but to criticize their betters, a position akin to that of the professional-managerial class vis-à-vis the capitalist class in American life as defined by the Ehrenreichs. The tales deal variously with themes of loyalty, bad and good models of leadership, and betrayal and treachery in court life.

Dawe's "Silken Cord" speaks complexly to a number of these issues. A postcolonial reading might see the tale as an "elsewhere" narrative in racial terms that emphasizes the superiority of the British white first-person narrator over that of Loh, the Chinese courtier whose story he tells. Loh, after all, is represented in terms of racial stereotypes – impulsive, prone to emotion, "somewhat profligate" – while the narrator functions as the voice of wisdom, putting the pieces in place that enable Loh's elopement with the Princess (127). The narrative, however, offers the possibility of another reading, a "like us" one in which Loh serves as a type of potential young professional man. The narrative attends to Loh's character in this respect. The narrator notes, for example, that he "is an accomplished gentleman," "a general favorite at court," "a scholar of some pretensions," and says, "I believed that he had it in him to rise to distinction if he would only go to work in a proper manner" (127). Loh, however, is cynical and lacks ambition and, though he prevails in the romance plot, his entanglement has prevented him from achieving his professional potential in court, where it was predicted he might gain a viceroyalty.

Variations on the theme of professional manhood and issues of risk, trust, and loyalty also play out in other adventure romances, without the complications of love plots. The protagonists in Stanley Weyman's "Flore" (*Pocket Magazine*), Richard Gorham Badger's "The Slight Forgetfulness of the Knight of the Four Oaks" (*Miss Blue Stocking*), and William Aspenwall Bradley's "Dagonet" (*Morningside*), for example, are caught up as pawns in battles for power between their superiors in which loyalty is tested. Helen Sterling Thomas's "Heart's Desire (A Fable)" (*Blue Sky*) is a more complexly structured historical adventure romance in the form of an allegory that speaks to power relations and hierarchy in court structures. In it, a fool is led astray by a merrymaking king's son and his "gay comrades" on the Highway, becoming lost for a time in a great, dark wood before emerging back onto the road where, with newfound wisdom, he abandons his fool's cap and bells and sets forth eastward and into the dawn.

Read as allegories of professional middle-class identity, these stories are structured as progress narratives in which autonomy, self-fulfillment, and control of one's own destiny, core values of this class, are threatened by the hierarchical and anti-democratic social structures in which the protagonists operate. Though professionals in a democratic America had a high degree of autonomy, anxieties about bureaucratization and monopoly capitalism, for example, represented challenges to middle-class professional identity. In Lears's sense, these stories indeed affirm "the bourgeois ethic of autonomous achievement" as a desirable goal (104), though the protagonists are not always capable of achieving it.

If the adventure story in little magazines addressed, in symbolic ways, the interests and ethos of its professional-managerial class readership, it also functioned to consolidate a notion of "little magazineness" and to assert the artistic legitimacy and value of the medium, notably through an engagement with European high art trends. In keeping with its other forms of fiction, the stories qualifying as adventure or historical romance are often very short, indeed, impressionistic in nature, providing colour and tone more than the action-packed adventure associated with the genre. "The Heart's Desire" (*Blue Sky*), discussed above, for example, while sharing, in general terms, the themes and tropes of popular forms of historical fiction, is not in the same register. Its archaic language, self-consciously allegorical form, pseudo-medieval style of illustration by artist Harry Townsend, and typographic presentation place it strongly within a Pre-Raphaelite and arts and crafts context. This effect is enhanced by the story's inclusion in *Blue Sky*, a magazine that specialized in fables and stories of chivalric romance, usually including a story of this type along with a sophisticated modern story in its pages. This was in keeping with the spirit of the publication, which sought "to bring sometimes the sound of an old chivalric song over star-strewn waters tuning the Elder elemental note to the sweetest harmonies of the New" (Stevens, "Stray Clouds," *Blue Sky* 3, no. 5, 263). Understood in this context, the story accrues a particular kind of cultural distinction that sets it apart as an artistic form of historical romance for an educated and aspiring elite. A similar claim can be made for the historical fiction in *John-a-Dreams*, an aesthetic little magazine that, like *Blue Sky*, had a strongly focused aesthetic vision and identity rooted in arts and crafts ideals. Its historical tales and vignettes, which range from the French medieval and Renaissance periods to eighteenth-century British coffee-house culture, are fundamental to setting tone and lending colour and flavour to the magazine. The issue sampled includes an atmospheric vignette of tavern life in sixteenth-century France by Edward W. Bryant, "The Stirrup Cup," which, like its other historical sketches, centres on the bohemian themes of wine, women, song, and vagabondage that were central, as Levin argues, to establishing professional middle-class identity in the period, notably as compensations for "the demands of modern capitalism" (203).

Other inclusions in the sampling indicate the degree to which, in more self-consciously artistic little magazines, the historical sketch promoted the aesthetic interests and ideals regarded as more typical of these publications. Conceptualized as a vehicle of personal expression and crafted in a manner that asserted individuality, the little magazine privileged fiction that explored psychological interiority, a mode relevant to a class for whom individuality and personal subjectivity were increasingly valued. If the historical romance, in its popular form, was resistant to the introspection and analysis of realism, some little magazines featured stories that brought together these trends. These stories often featured the kind of philosophical, psychological, or aesthetic perspectives that were characteristic of other genres of its fiction and were less plot-oriented, more impressionistic in nature. In the sampling, three of the historical fictions engage, in a concerted manner, with the interiority of their protagonists: G.W. Stevens's "An Hour With Caesar Augustus" (*Philistine*), a humorous manifestation of the form that provides an interior monologue of the Roman Emperor; Hewlett's "Quattrocentisteria" (*Bibelot*), which imagines the relationship between Botticelli and his muse; and

Frederick Maynard's "The Revenge of Izzedin" (*Rubric*), an orientalist sketch about an Arabian warrior.

Of these, the latter two are most germane to the little magazine's promotion of a more self-consciously artistic form of historical fiction and its connection to arts and crafts, aestheticism, and decadence. Hewlett's tale, for example, takes the form of an imaginary portrait, an impressionistic genre associated with British aesthete Walter Pater. For Pater, the imaginary portrait did not present "an action, a story; but a character, personality, revealed especially in outward detail," seeking to understand the "living personality behind the philosophic idea or work of art" (Monsman 73). Hewlett's story is in this vein, providing a psychological drama around, and insight into, the paintings of Botticelli in treating the legend that the artist's muse was Simonetta Vespucci. The result is a philosophical rendering of historical fiction, appealing to a professional-managerial class that might well enjoy more popular forms of the genre, but might also look to little magazines for culturally distinctive fare.

"The Revenge of Izzedin" (*Rubric*), meanwhile, demonstrates how the "literature of action" might be combined with an introspective decadent mode. This very short sketch, in two parts, concerns a man seeking revenge on his son's killers. The first section is in the psychological and introspective first-person mode characteristic of little magazine fiction, bringing the reader into the mind of the warrior as he prepares to fight. This interiority is denied the reader, however, in the second section, which is a third-person description of the battle in dramatic language. This juxtaposition is jarring and the narrative is confusing from this point, as the outcome of the battle is unclear. While the story, with its celebration of the lone warrior heroically confronting a mob, is ideologically in tune with the popular "literature of action" of the period, its introspective and difficult qualities align it with the effete realism against which the popular romance was defined. The little magazine, then, allowed for a hybrid form, one that might satisfy its readership's interest in tales of adventure that promised a certain kind of psychic comfort, while also appealing to its desire for a philosophically or psychologically oriented literature that offered sophistication and cultural distinction.

If this chapter began by asserting that the fiction in little magazines was much like that found in mainstream magazines, the analysis undertaken may seem to belie this claim. Yes, in terms of genre and the popularity of particular genres there is certainly commonality. Yet little magazines, as the chapter has insisted, often gave distinctive treatment to particular themes. I remain reluctant, however, to assert that little magazine fiction is categorically more avant-garde, progressive, or experimental than fiction that appears in mainstream magazines, even if these findings seem to suggest as much when compared with Ohmann's. Little magazines did not have a monopoly on such fiction. After all, plenty of proto-modernist and modernist fiction that is considered within a canonical high art tradition made its first appearance in mainstream magazines. At the same time, interpretation is relative and popular fiction is certainly amenable to resistant reading that troubles seemingly straightforward and conventional narratives. If interpretation is relative, it is also, however, contextual. If Ohmann does not engage in resistant readings of his magazine fiction, it is because he is accounting for this fiction with a view to the material conditions of its production and reception, considering the context of the rise of the mass magazine, national advertising, and an increasingly aspirational, socially mobile, and urban professional-managerial class whose emerging values, he asserts, are being negotiated and reflected in the fiction. If we regard magazine stories, as Ohmann does, as "in dialogue with one another, registering through character and event a kind of statement and counterstatement" about issues and values (*Selling Culture* 313), little magazines were certainly more likely to be registering resistant counterstatements to cultural norms. Little magazines represented another context for fiction of the period, one in which materiality, as I have insisted, matters. The conditions of production and reception, the particular format of the little magazine, and the meanings that this materiality generated to make the medium an alternative form of cultural capital, incline readers to bring a particular mindset to their consumption of these magazines and its fiction. Read in the little magazine context, this fiction seemingly places emphasis on and brings greater intellectual and artistic seriousness to the sex-problem, bohemian lifestyles, self-reflexive interiority, and the tensions of commercial and industrial modernity.

CHAPTER 5

Poetry: "Literature on 'a Drunken Spree'"

Poetry is the spirit tongue. A link connecting man with the unseen life awaiting him. It deals with the "true realities," as distinguished from the materialities of his existence. And its proper function is, to arouse his spiritual energies, and inspire him with strength and courage to strive after meekness for his high destiny among the Immortals.

– H.E. Belin, "What Is Poetry?" *Optimist* 2, no. 3, 145 (1901)

Like fiction, poetry was popular magazine and newspaper fodder at the end of the nineteenth century. If this era is notable, however, for the flowering of the short story as a popular and avant-garde medium, for poetry it has been deemed a "twilight period" (Mott, *History* 120–1; Perkins). David Perkins attributes the so-called poor quality of verse in this period to the following causes: first, many American poets were isolated and self-taught, seeking to emulate great poetry, looking especially to the Romantics and the lyric poem, and aiming to perfect their skill in fixed forms rather than to innovate new ones; second, "handyman" poets, amateurs, "do-it-yourselfers," and poets by avocation abounded, flooding newspapers and magazines with occasional verse; third, American writers were intimidated by the British tradition, which resulted in poor imitations of, or immature revolts against, it; fourth, the genteel tradition – idealized, for example, by Belin above – which privileged "elevating" poetry and sentiment, remained a dominant force; finally, the poetry market catered to an unsophisticated audience, depriving talented poets of opportunities to publish (85–99). These aspects of the poetic field, Perkins claims, were challenged only to a minor degree. Homespun, regional, and dialect verse, for example, represented a revolt against genteel poetry; poetry of social protest emerged, an extension of the reformist interests of this era's middle class; free verse forms, inspired by symbolists in Europe and Whitman and Dickinson in America crafted a new language for poetry – one that was, on the one hand, divorced from the constraints of form and, on the other, asserted a distinctively American poetic idiom.

Despite his clear bias for modernist poetry and its innovations, Perkins astutely identifies the main features of the American poetic field of the 1890s: the prevalence of the amateur, the importance of the poetic tradition and established poetic forms, and the interest in poetry of social protest and moral uplift. In contrast with the modernist emphasis on the intellectual and abstract, the cultural elite of the 1890s did indeed privilege the sentimental, spiritual, and the emotive power of poetry and the social mission of the poet. These characteristics are a consequence of the more public role poetry played. Whereas modernism abstracted poetry and the poet from everyday life, reifying and intellectualizing the poem, nineteenth-century poetry was grounded in, and was a part of, everyday life for many Americans.[1] In this respect, poetry was not, as Perkins and Mott suggest, simply "filler," but addressed the social and cultural interests of middle-class Americans who quoted newspaper and magazine poetry in letters, clipped and pasted it in scrapbooks and commonplace books, hung it on their walls, read it aloud in their homes, and memorized and recited it in school. More importantly, Americans were significant consumers of such poetry, attending poetry readings and purchasing volumes of poetry in vast quantities. Sentimental poet James Whitcomb Riley, for example, was hugely popular, his works selling over three million copies between 1893 and 1949. Edwin Markham, a poet with reformist and spiritualist ideals, was popular also, earning over $250,000 in his lifetime for his protest poem "The Man With the Hoe" (Perkins 117, 99). At the same time, as Perkins indicates, Americans were prodigious producers of poetry. Magazines and newspapers were full of verse by would-be poets, amateurs, and those who practiced poetry as a vocation, some of whom gained significant local, national, and international followings.

This broader context informed the poetry of the little magazines of this era. Thus, while there were inklings of the modernist poetics that would develop in the early twentieth century, they were not as pervasive as one might expect. Certainly, there were magazines, such as *M'lle New York*, that featured European avant-garde and proto-modernist poetry, but these were exceptional. Little magazines were not, actually, a major venue for aesthetic revolt in poetry, in a modernist sense, in this period. The values of the genteel tradition prevailed, combining, in some instances, with the reformist interests of the emerging professional-managerial class of the Progressive Era. Unlike their modernist "make it new" counterparts who valorized "difficulty" and intellectualism, many little magazine poets of the 1890s and their readers valued the emotive quality of poetry. These poets often sought to "make it old" – i.e., to emulate the great poetry of the past, to experiment with fixed forms such as the rondeau, triolet, sonnet, villanelle, ballade, and quatrain. Middle-class readers, meanwhile, looked to poetry for its expression of "intense experience" in the context of an increasingly "bureaucraticized, impersonal society" and sought in it relevance to their everyday lives (Rubin 135). Little magazines of the period addressed these interests in publishing poetry that was sentimental, lyrical, or homespun, focused on nature, harmony with nature, transcendent experiences, or the everyday. Though there was a self-consciousness that these forms were "out of date," they are a prevalent feature in aesthetic little magazines, especially those of the arts and crafts tradition, such as *Blue Sky* and *John-a-Dreams*. *Blue Sky*, for example, featured a regular section called "In Formal Measure," devoted to publishing fixed verse forms. *John-a-Dreams* was also interested in traditional verse forms, innovating through layout and typography rather than in formal poetic terms. In one example of Nicholas Senior's regular column, "The Print Shop," for example, a triolet was printed in ten different typefaces, and readers were asked to consider which was most appropriate for the poem. In the subsequent issue, Senior commented on the responses, commending readers for preferring French Elzevir, a typeface light and delicate like the manner and matter of the poem ("In the Print Shop" 179–83). In the context of the revolution in fine printing, innovation in form in poetry was often material in nature.

In the main, then, little magazine poets were themselves part of the broader context mapped out by Perkins. Indeed, it is inaccurate to speak of a "little magazine poet," as these publications were rarely the sole venue for these writers. Little magazine poets included newspaper and magazine poets, popular poets of region or nation, amateurs and poets by avocation, "handymen" and "do-it-yourselfers." As a market for poetry, little magazines were less a reaction against, than an extension of, mainstream newspapers and magazines, as well as a publicity venue for poets who issued volumes from some of the small presses that published little magazines. In terms of poetic content in the aesthetic, hybrid, and protest little magazines of the period, there is much crossover, in terms of themes, with fiction. In a survey of eighty-one issues of little magazines featuring just over three hundred poems, love poetry, like fiction centred on love, dominates, accounting for 25 per cent of the titles in the sampling.[2] Most of this poetry is in aesthetic and hybrid magazines and takes sentimental, chivalric, and cynical or modern approaches to the topic. Topical political poetry follows, in about 16 per cent of the sampling, a feature dominant in protest and hybrid magazines and notably absent from aesthetic little magazines. Falling out in almost equal numbers beneath these top themes are poems addressing philosophical, spiritual, and mystical issues, especially death, hope, time, and transcendent experiences in nature (10 per cent); poetry about art and artists (11 per cent), bohemianism, vagabondia, and chivalric poetry (10 per cent), including a notable body of poetic imitations of and tributes to the *Rubáiyát of Omar Khayyám*, which popularized the quatrain form as well as the subject matter of wine, women, and song in exotic settings.

Rather than revisiting the terrain of the previous chapter in an analysis of the cultural work effected by recurring themes and their variations on the basis of a broad sampling, this chapter adopts a different methodology to treat poetic content. In the first section it focuses on prolific little magazine poets: Stephen Crane, Bliss Carman, Clinton Scollard, Ella Wheeler Wilcox, and Sam Walter Foss. This approach is more suitable for poetry than fiction because, whereas there are no clearly identifiable representative or prolific writers of little magazine fiction, there are such figures in the domain of poetry. At the same time, the versatility of these poets enables a discussion of dominant themes and a comparison of their treatments. The chapter uses sampling in the second section, which accounts for political uses of poetry, a trend absent in art-for-art's sake inflected aesthetic magazines, but dominant in periodicals of protest and some hybrid little magazines.

Among the most well-known writers associated with the little magazines of the 1890s was Stephen Crane (1871–1900), whose poetic output in this period included *Black Riders and Other Lines* (1895) and *War is Kind* (1899). These works represented a distinctive break with conventional poetic forms, published in volumes that were exemplars of the art nouveau style in fine bookmaking and of a difficult style appreciated by modernists of the next generation. In his day, however, Crane's gnomic, impressionistic free verse, printed in upper-case letters, with its concerns about the nature of god, man, and the universe, was derided by the mainstream press as "poetic lunacy" and "trash" (*Daily Inter Ocean* [Chicago] and *Daily Tribune* [New York], qtd. in Monteiro 13, 15). Crane was described as Maeterlinckian, "an American Decadent," and the "Aubrey Beardsley of poetry" (*New York Recorder* and Harry Thurston Peck, qtd. in Monteiro 12, 11). He was also associated with the poster movement, partly because of the art nouveau design of his poetry volumes, but also for the exploitation of colour effects in his writing. Little magazinist Jonathan Penn, for example, writing of Crane in *The Lotus*, dubs his work "poster literature" and criticizes his "fondness ... for chromatic effects" ("Little Study" 208, 211). Marco Morrow likewise complained of Crane's "bad habit of laying gaudy chromo colors over everything he touches" (qtd. in Monteiro 113).[3]

Aspects of these influences are apparent in his "Lantern Song," which appeared first in *The Philistine* and, later, untitled, in *War Is Kind*:

EACH SMALL GLEAM WAS A VOICE
– A LANTERN VOICE –
IN LITTLE SONGS OF CARMINE, VIOLET, GREEN, GOLD.
A CHORUS OF COLORS CAME OVER THE WATER,
THE WONDROUS LEAF-SHADOWS NO LONGER WAVERED,
NO PINES CROONED ON THE HILLS,
THE BLUE NIGHT WAS ELSEWHERE A SILENCE
WHEN THE CHORUS OF COLORS CAME OVER THE WATER,
LITTLE SONGS OF CARMINE, VIOLET, GREEN, GOLD.

SMALL GLOWING PEBBLES
THROWN ON THE DARK PLANE OF EVENING
SING GOOD BALLADS OF GOD
AND ETERNITY WITH SOUL'S REST.
LITTLE PRIESTS, LITTLE HOLY FATHERS,
NONE CAN DOUBT THE TRUTH OF YOUR HYMNING
WHEN THE MARVELOUS CHORUS COMES OVER THE WATER,
SONGS OF CARMINE, VIOLET, GREEN, GOLD. (124)

Crane's impressionistic prose poem operates in the "suggestive" rather than "cut and dried" manner that Hovey equated with the

Maeterlinckian symbolist style (6). While there is undoubtedly a spiritual element to the poem, its focus on coloured lanterns as the bearers of this message secularizes it. At the same time, Crane's images of a "chorus of colours," and "songs of carmine, violet, green, gold" at once invoke the chromatic schema of contemporary poster art and exercise a decadent transposition of the visual and musical arts.

With such a gnomic style, Crane, we might expect, would be looked upon favourably by little magazinists, especially those of the aesthetic school, with their interests in symbolism, decadence, and art nouveau. Appreciation for Crane, however, was the exception more than the rule. A terse set of lines printed in red, appearing on the back cover of *The Ishmaelite* for January 1897 and titled "Stephen Crane," encapsulates the largely negative response he received among little magazinists: "He writes his words in upper case/All straggling down the page/And thinks that he has set the pace/For poets of this age." Overall, the reaction of little magazinists to Crane's poetry highlights the degree to which traditionalist values prevailed. Ironically, then, while Crane was much discussed and much parodied in little magazines, he was not much published in them. Those that did included *The Chap-Book*, which published one poem that would later appear in *War Is Kind*, and *The Philistine*, which included fifteen Crane poems between 1895 and 1899.[4] Even Elbert Hubbard, however, as I have indicated, was equivocal in his view of Crane, noting the challenge the work presented for critical analysis: "it eludes all ordinary criticism … What is left? I'll tell you, we can stand off and hoot – if we have columns to fill we can fill them with plain hoot" (Crane, *Correspondence* 115). Hubbard accurately characterizes how Crane was regarded by many little magazinists who, not knowing what to make of his strange poetry, resorted to hooting. Jonathan Penn, for example, described Crane's poetry as "ludicrous" and "irrelevant" in articles in *The Fly Leaf* and *The Lotus* ("A Little Study" 208).[5] Walter Blackburn Harte, editor of both these magazines, endorsed Penn's views, presenting a more measured but, nevertheless, uncertain response:

> His mystic, weird lines outrage all the laws of prosody, and can only stand as the audacious flings of a fantastic and untramelled imagination, that is impatient of form and loves the hot splash of thought. But it must not be rashly judged that any fool can do this sort of thing. It demands a feeling for words and an abundant, bubbling imagination. Still, the grave critics who have seriously accepted Mr. Crane's little book of verses as

> poetry and literature of a high order appear in a rather ludicrous light. ("Bubble and Squeak," *Fly Leaf* 1, no. 1, 28)

This ambivalence characterized even those magazines that published Crane-inspired gnomic verse, such as this poem, "Repair," by Ivan Swift, in *Blue Sky.*

> A spiral soul drawn thin in growing circumference,
> Coiled again
> In the tight circle of faded faith.
> An artist, spilt from the mould of man.
>
> A webby attic –
> Crab-tangled fish nets.
> Quivering snake waves,
> Gossip of dust-mites,
> Misery of flies.
> A ragged gull, socket-eyed,
> Swung on a string.
> A chattering manikin,
> Misjointed.
> Rattle music of dead flowers
> Stuck from a shaving mug
> Gritty on a cold mantel.
>
> An ulster
> Jostling in the rumples of the world
> Obscure in the dream-freezing frolic of the market-place.
> A tender word,
> A small hand,
> A jewel.
>
> A parting ray,
> An uttering canvas,
> Dust mites floating silent gold,
> A white bird, swung by current incense.
> A rose-bloom, warm and eloquent,
> Leaning from a shaving-mug,
> Silver snake links,
> Soul of artist,
> Sense of man. (139–40)

In his discussion of the poem's style, editor Thomas Wood Stevens, while as ambivalent as Hubbard and Harte, comes closer to staking a claim for its importance as a new and significant mode: "If it had been written a hundred years ago we might read it in the next *Honey Jar* [a belletristic aesthetic little magazine], and be moved by it and say trite things about love and optimism" ("Stray Clouds," *Blue Sky* 1, no. 5, 149). Stevens acknowledges the traditionalism of the era's poetic taste, implying that Crane and Swift are ahead of their time. A more negative, but equally illuminating, response to this style appears in the fixed-form-loving *John-a-Dreams*, where Benjamin A. Schade recounts a conversation involving the magazine's key contributors in which the symbolistic style is likened to developments in poster art. Schade acknowledges the "modernity" of the modes but resists them heartily (123–4). The connection between Crane's poetry and the modern poster movement is implied also in *Miss Blue Stocking*, in which the editor's synaesthesiac response to *Black Riders* invokes a colour palette of modern visual art: "I [swore] in jagged green and crimson cusses, till I swooned in inky blackness. And after did I say to myself meekly with purple reverence, yes Crane is a great man" ([Badger], "Notes" 25). The implications of Crane's style for future poetry were worrying indeed to *The New Bohemian*: "But oh, the wonder as to what Twentieth Century poetry will be, that such forms are with us now" ("Borders of Bohemia" 282). Crane was, then, a major figure in the little magazine movement, discussed widely as a point of reference for trends in modern poetry, but in a negative way. While he could not be ignored, his verse was a subject of mockery and parody, just as it was in the mainstream press.

The reaction to Crane's poetry underscores the reverence for traditional verse forms in this period, even among those who considered themselves in revolt against the conventional and mainstream. The free verse that would become so central to modernist poetry was not yet a major form. Even while many little magazinists revered Walt Whitman, a major American innovator of free verse, they did not emulate him. His "influence" in this period was "not in form," as poet and critic Jessie B. Rittenhouse noted, "but in ethics" (464). He was looked to particularly as a role model for individualist and independent identity. As Hubbard remarked in 1899, "The number of people who admire Walt Whitman's work is increasing, but there is only one person who is possest [*sic*] of an ardent desire to write just like him" ("Heart to Heart Talks with Grown-Ups," *Philistine* 8, no. 3, 84). In contrast to Whitman, Emily Dickinson, another free verse innovator whose works were posthumously published in this period, was virtually ignored by little magazinists, though she served as an inspiration for Crane's experimentations.[6] Proto-modernist American decadent and symbolist poets, meanwhile, were few and far between and, of those, the most notable, Francis-Vielé Griffin and Stuart Merrill, resided in France. Beyond the avant-garde *M'lle New York*, the work of these expatriates was of minimal interest to little magazines.

A sense of this more traditional and popular aspect of little magazine poetry and some of the key poetic trends can be further gauged from an overview of some of the most prolific little magazine poets. Tellingly, three of the poets that Mott identifies as the leading magazine poets in mainstream media – Clinton Scollard (1860–1932), Bliss Carman (1861–1929), and Ella Wheeler Wilcox (1850–1919) – are also the most widely represented in little magazines (*History* 120). It might often be the case that the poetry of newspaper and magazine poets such as Scollard, Carman, and Wilcox was similar across mainstream and little magazines. Publication contexts and formats, however, as suggested in chapter 2, influence the meaning and cultural value accorded to the poetry. Little magazines often gave pride of place to poetry, whether through placement on the page or in formatting and design. At the same time, too, poets could exploit different venues for experimentation and variation, suiting their content to the particular nature of the magazines. This was common practice in a period when newspapers and magazines were an important first arena of publication for many poets. From a cynical perspective, little magazines, which would not have paid as well as mainstream ones, might have served as a dumping ground for work poets could not place elsewhere. Nick Mount, for example, claims that Carman regarded little magazines in this light (74), while Wilcox recounts her efforts in trying to place a poem with mainstream magazines before submitting it to *The Chap-Book* (*Worlds and I* 112–13).

Despite Scollard's status as a popular leading magazine poet of the day and author of over forty volumes of poetry, there is little scholarship on him. Though a self-acknowledged "minor poet,"[7] he was a versatile and able versifier, technically skillful, aiming to perfect received forms and traditions of poetry, such as the rondeau, triolet, and ballade. Major influences were Keats, Shelley, Dante Gabriel Rossetti, and Sidney Lanier, and late Romantic and Pre-Raphaelite strains are evident in his poetry. Thomas F. O'Donnell identifies Scollard's characteristic work as exploiting French forms, lyrics and tales of long ago, and "semi-mystical verse that reflects an outdated pantheism" (54), a description which accurately reflects his contributions to a range of little magazines, including *Lotus*, *Chips*, *Philistine*, *Little Chap*, *Clack Book*, *Criterion*, *Red Letter*, *Chap-Book*, *Four O'Clock*, *Philosopher*, and *Smart Set*.

Scollard's "Chant of Prester John," for example, one of his *Chap-Book* contributions, is a rollicking verse in rhymed couplets. In keeping with the Pre-Raphaelite and arts and crafts interest in medieval and orientalist subjects, it focuses on a popular legend about a Christian kingdom in the midst of a Muslim and pagan world. "The Dancing of Suleima" for *Smart Set*, represents a more decadent and exoticised treatment of orientalist subject matter in its depiction of the Salomé theme, one more famously treated by Wilde. In Scollard's poem, an Indian bayadère, whose very name is redolent of her Biblical counterpart, uses her seductive powers as a dancer to initiate revenge on the Grand Vizier. Scollard uses the same kind of decadent tropes as Wilde does in *Salomé*, notably repetition of phrasing and metrical rhythms (in Scollard's case rhyming couplets) to create a trancelike effect and sense of foreboding. His *Smart Set* contributions frequently invoke such exotic and orientalist themes, suggesting their popularity for this magazine's largely urban-based university and professional readership.

Scollard's interest in fixed forms is exemplified in two ballade contributions to *Chips*. The ballade form originated in fourteenth- and fifteenth-century France and had associations with François Villon, and later with Rossetti and Swinburne. Scollard uses the form to reflect on the mortality of poets and the immortality of poetry in "The Ballade of Dead Poets," a theme in tune with the overall interest of little magazines in the artist. In "The Ballade of Mid-Summer," meanwhile, he contemplates the langorous quality of this time of year. In addition to its exemplification of his interest in French forms, this poem also touches on the most characteristic aspect of his poetry and that of many little magazine poets: the power of nature to evoke moods of intensity. In Scollard, this is where his semi-mystical pantheism asserts itself most strongly. This mode is deployed in "The Walk," a *Chap-Book* contribution, in which the speaker and the "souls" who accompany him experience spiritual transcendence in nature, "find[ing] the chrism of bliss/ Upon the hills of morn" (183). In his orientalist sonnet, "Night in the Desert," in *Smart Set*, the desert likewise evokes an experience of the sublime – an "awful solitude, the imminence/as of some unimaginable thing" (115). In general, however, this mystical relationship to nature is far less evident in the poetry that he contributes to little magazines than it is in that of his contemporary, Bliss Carman.

More characteristically, Scollard explores the affective powers of nature on the human psyche, another theme that recurs widely across little magazine poetry of the era. But where much of this poetry in little magazines deploys the traditional trope of pathetic fallacy to emphasize the speaker's sense of oneness with nature in spiritual terms and to lend a transcendent quality to the experience, Scollard tends to opt for a secularized approach. In line with the interests of an emerging professional-managerial class in interiority, his poems often forgo a spiritual/mystical perspective for a modern psychological one, as in "Autumn Twilight" (*Chap-Book*), "Homesick" (*Chap-Book*), "A Dark Day" (*Chips*), "A Grain Field" (*Clack Book*), "The Turning of the Tide" (*Lotus*), "Roses" (*Smart Set*), "In an Egyptian Garden" (*Smart Set*), "Fog in the City" (*Smart Set*), and "Moods" (*Philistine*). In many of these poems, Scollard's speakers' interactions with nature culminate in a sense of alienation or despair. In his short, two-stanza quatrain poem "A Dark Day," for example, the external world is a reflection of the bleak psychological landscape of a couple in an unhappy marriage, reminiscent of George Meredith's style in his sonnet sequence, *Modern Love* (1862):

We woke. No solitary ray
The mist banks struggled through;
The heaven was a wall of gray,
And chill the east wind blew.

A dream! – an evil dream! – but no;
The fetters would not part;
They closed the tighter round, and so
Gloom revealed in the heart.

In a less serious mode, his *Philistine* contribution, "Moods," uses a four-stanza model to play on pathetic fallacy. In the first two stanzas, the wind, characterized as "the echo" of the speaker's "soul," brings upon him a dreary mood, which is quickly dispelled by the sudden mirth of the wind to reveal that "as shifting as the freaksome wind/ The many moods of man!" (141).

Scollard's themes and style are similar to those of his now more famous contemporary, Bliss Carman. Indeed, the work of these poets, who were friends, was often compared, and they were considered among the best young poets of the day. A review of their poetry in the little magazine, *The Shadow*, perceptively noted the distinctive qualities of each, describing Carman as having a more "vital energy" and Scollard as endowed with "greater refinement, a smoother finish" ("Two Minor Poets" 42). Certainly, Carman might be thought of as a rougher and more radical Scollard, dealing with similar themes, filtered through the lens of symbolism and decadence, and befitting his reputation as "the American high priest of Symbolism" (*New York World*, qtd. in Muriel Miller 154). At the same time, Carman might be situated midway on a spectrum that positions Scollard and Crane at opposing poles, as Carman also engages with Crane's themes, but in a less esoteric and outré fashion. Little magazinist Marion Daniel M'Connell noted that Carman embodied the qualities of both "lyrist" and "symbolist," writing poems that "haunt … the ear with … harmonies" and "appeal to the heart and intellect" (8).

Of the three, Carman was more important in the little magazine movement, as a contributor and influence, but also as a driving force behind the creation of early publications such as *The Knight Errant*, *Le Courrier Innocent* and *The Chap-Book*. Carman was published in *Courrier Innocent*, *Lotus*, *Modern Art*, *Kit-Bag*, *Chap-Book*, *Bibelot*, *Philistine*, *Criterion*, *Smart Set*, and others. He was the quintessential little magazine poet in terms of his own contributions, the forms he worked with, and his influence on others. Also, he represents the more modern, if not modernist, face of the movement. So, for example, where Scollard's little magazine poems about poets reference classical and traditional poets such as Keats, Shelley, Homer, Theocritus ("A Ballade of Dead Poets"), Andrew Lang ("Upon the Birth of a Babe"), and Henry Timrod, a poet of the American South ("Henry Timrod"), Carman's are devoted to avant-garde and modern contemporaries: adulatory poems to the decadent Paul Verlaine ("To P.V."), to Richard Hovey, friend and collaborator ("Along the Trail"), and, under the pen name "Slim Barcans," to contemporary poet and fellow *Chap-Book* contributor Eugene Field ("To a Portrait of a Western Poet"). Similarly, in contrast to the arts and crafts flavour of Scollard's "Prester John" sits Carman's symbolistic "Night Washers" (*Chap-Book*), a "study in the horrible," as he called it (qtd. in MacKendrick 138), based on the Brittany legend about evil river spirits who cajole passers-by to help them wash the linens of the dead. In decadent fashion, Carman's evil spirits speak of "sin[ning] the seven lovely sins/While wearing the virtue a cardinal wins" (63). His "Ballad of Saint Kavin" (*Chap-Book*) also differs significantly from Scollard's "Prester John." Against the Christian earnestness of "Prester John," "Saint Kavin" is an irreverent and risqué treatment of an Irish "holy man" from Tipperary who goes to war – "But not against the devil" – and is unsainted in his wooing of the fair Kathleen (560). This poem is in Carman's vagabondia mode, which brought together the vogue for bohemianism and Omar Khayyám with a popularized form of Whitman's thematics to celebrate wine, women, and song, the freedom of the open road, and the vagabond poet. These themes were highly popular in the poetry of the period.[8] "Saint Kavin" would go on to be included in one of a series of three vagabondia volumes Carman co-authored with Richard Hovey in the 1890s that would bring them considerable fame. Other poems of this type by Carman that were published in little magazines include "The Paupers" (*Lotus*), a saucy and suggestive appeal for love by an impoverished and self-confessed bad poet, and "In Philistia" (*The Philistine*), in which Carman again exploits the ballad form to comic effect. In it, he satirises philistine women who dote on bohemian poet types. There is also, however, a degree of self-mockery in it, as he pokes fun at his own decadent reputation in the lines "My unerratic life denies / My too erotic verses" (65).

Carman's other main theme was love, though his treatment is abstract not sentimental or cynically modern. Like Scollard, he is interested in nature, but as a backdrop to the mystical, spiritual, and pantheistic kind of love he documents. This work was informed by his Unitrinian philosophy, one that sought to "harmoniz[e] body, mind and spirit in everyday life," and was based on Delsartean principles (Sorfleet 208). As he explained, "[t]hey are primarily love poems … but the love passion is sublimated by imagination and meditation until it transcends the physical and becomes mystic … spiritual rapture, love with all its divine attributes, and intellectual elation, cannot divorce themselves wholly from the physical; they must forever be enamored of outward physical beauty, beauty of nature, and beauty of people" (*Letters* 190). "Little Lyrics of Joy – IV" (*Chap-Book*) explores the tension between an intellectualized imaginative form of love and a physical one:

I see the golden hunter go,
With his hound star close at heel,
Through purple fallows above the hill,

When the large autumn night is still
And the tide of the world is low.

And while to their unwearied quest
The sister Pleiads pass,
That seventh loveliest and lost
Desire of all the orient host
Is here upon my breast. (435)

Carman's invocation of myth and astronomy through the references to Orion and the Pleiads abstracts the physical and erotic undertone of the poem that is only revealed in the final line when the lover is identified as that elusive seventh sister – the star that cannot be seen in the sky with the human eye alone. In this poetry, then, the carefree attitude towards love expressed in the vagabondia poems gives way to more serious reflection. Carman published a number of poems of this type in *The Chap-Book* under the titles "Songs of the Sea Children" and "Little Lyrics of Joy." These would later be included in his Pipes of Pan poetry series.

Though Carman's style and themes influenced other poetic contributors to little magazines he was, like Crane, an easy target for mockery and parody. His "Little Lyrics of Joy," for example, were parodied in *The Bauble* as "A Lyric of Grief" by "Cliss Barman" and in *The Philistine* as "Little Delirics of Bliss" by "Joy Trolleyman" and "Joy Cartman." At the same time, Carmen's mysticism garnered comparisons with Crane. A parody in *The Clack Book*, "A Karmenokranian Idyl" by "Bliss Krayne," conflates the poets, emphasizing the obscure, gnomic, and morbid qualities of their work and the apparent popularity of such "modern" poetry. In it, the poet speaker appeals to devils to take him "off from the earth," offering to write verses for them – "verses soothful to fiends/Verses no man of the age is worthy to read/Verses hot with passion, verses cold with death!" – verses that are ultimately profitable for the poet/speaker: "I like to sell poetry/Like this/For/Thirty-five cents, or /Most anything I can/Get" (158, 159). Carman, however, was more "professional" as a poet than Crane, engaged with the literary marketplace and mindful of the necessity of catering to it in order to make a living through his writing.

If Carman's symbolistic mysticism was particularly suited to the ideals of aesthetic little magazines, there were other forms of spiritualism that appealed also, best represented in the work of Ella Wheeler Wilcox, another leading magazine poet of the day. Like Scollard, Wilcox is now largely forgotten, though she was hugely popular in the period. In addition to her numerous contributions to magazines and newspapers, she published over forty volumes of verse. Wilcox achieved a *succès de scandale* with *Poems of Passion* (1883), a collection that, though initially rejected by one publisher as "obscene," would go on to sell 60,000 copies (Wolosky 189). Like many poets of her day, however, Wilcox wrote in a variety of genres and combined the radical and innovative with the conservative and traditional. Thus, in addition to her scandalous sexual poems, she also wrote poems on social issues, including *Drops of Water* (1872), devoted to temperance interests; spiritual poems based on her interests in New Thought and Rosicrucianism; animal rights and vegetarianism; socialism; and sentimental poems of cheer and uplift. Her most famous poem, "Solitude," contains the now famous cliché, "Laugh and the world laughs with you; Weep and you weep alone" (*Poems* 131). Wilcox was not universally respected by little magazinists. Fellow Wisconsinite, Neal Brown, for example, associated with *The Philosopher*, castigated her for her "egotism," warning the editor of the magazine not to fall prey to this vice (16).[9] Others, however, admired her and her work appeared in *The Chap-Book*, *Noon*, *Papyrus*, *Optimist*, *Smart Set*, *Comrade*, *Quiet Observer*, *Crier*, *Erudite*, *Doctors' Magazine and How to Live*, *Tabasco*, *Vanguard*, and *Criterion*.

Two of Wilcox's *Chap-Book* contributions, "The Awakening" and "Illusion," demonstrate that her work could keep company with the mystico-symbolism of the Carman and Crane type. The shorter "Awakening" gives a flavour of her style in these poems:

> Out of the sleep of earth, with visions rife
> I woke in death's clear morning, full of life;
> And said to God, whose smile made all things bright,
> "*That was an awful dream I had last night.*" (289)

Both of these *Chap-Book* poems take place in a timeless dream space and involve an exchange with God, aspects reminiscent of Crane's work. The space of "death's clear morning," where she talks to God in "Awakening," becomes "in space alone" in "Illusion" (49). In "Illusion," however, this abstract void is identified as reality. In this space, alone with God, the speaker poses a series of questions about

Life, Heaven, Hell, and Judgment Day, all of which are said by God to be "but dreams" (49). At the end of the poem God reveals the true reality: "There are no such things as fear, or sin; / There is no you – you have never been – There is nothing at all but me!" (49). The gnomic elements of these poems, as well as the unorthodox presentation of Christianity, in "Illusion" particularly, resonate with the symbolistic types of poetry produced by Crane and other little magazine poets. By Wilcox's account, "Illusion" was too unorthodox for the numerous mainstream magazines that rejected it before it was accepted by the *Chap-Book* (*Worlds and I* 112–13). Certainly, in the context of *The Chap-Book*, a little magazine associated with modern and avant-garde art forms, these poems invite a symbolistic reading and a comparison with the likes of Crane and Carman. Wilcox's style, nevertheless, differs in key ways from the pagan spiritualism of Carman and the gnomic style of Crane. Where Crane's speakers, for example, often encounter an angry and vengeful God, that of Wilcox's poems is benevolent, presiding over an afterlife that is inspired more by Eastern religion than Christianity. Indeed, outside of the pages of *The Chap-Book*, "Illusion" might register very differently. Its basic premise of the individual's oneness with God and the illusory nature of matter and time, for example, are key tenets of the New Thought movement to which Wilcox ascribed. This New Thought context might or might not inform the perspective of a *Chap-Book* reader with interests in aestheticism and decadence, but would certainly come to the fore in other periodicals to which Wilcox contributed.

Wilcox, in fact, contributed more explicit New Thought poetry and prose to other little magazines, including *Papyrus*, a hybrid periodical with interests in alternative religious movements ("What Love Is"; "My Belief"; "Attainment"). "Attainment," for example, treats the spiritual, not in the gnomic or oracular style of Crane or Carman, but in plain speech that draws on self-help discourse:

> Use all your hidden forces. Do not miss
> The purpose of this life, and do not wait
> For circumstance to mould or change your fate.
> In your own self lies Destiny. Let this
> Vast truth cast out all fear, all prejudice,
> All hesitation. Know that you are great,
> Great with divinity. So dominate
> Environment, and enter into bliss.

Love largely and hate nothing. Hold no aim
That does not chord with universal good.
Hear what the voices of the silence say,
All joys are yours if you put forth your claim.
Once let the spiritual laws be understood,
Material things must answer and obey. (32)

Though written in iambic pentameter sonnet form, the poem is a prose poem, aphoristic in nature, an effect reinforced by the fact that it is positioned in the magazine in the midst of a series of self-help oriented aphorisms, including "That which was power is now impotence, but wait! it will soon be power again," and "Look back now over the long way and see if it be not Love that has led you so far!"

Though Wilcox published in art-for-art's-sake oriented little magazines that eschewed topical poetry and poetry with a purpose, her more conventional religious stance, her plainer style, and her interest in spiritual, moral, and social uplift made her work better suited to little magazines that promoted protest and/or alternative lifestyles than those with an art-for-art's sake agenda. Nevertheless, *The Chap-Book*, a vociferous opponent of topicality in its early days, did publish one of Wilcox's reformist poems in 1898, after it abandoned its purist aims and became a general literary magazine. In this contribution, "Goddess of Liberty, Answer," Wilcox tackles the controversial issues of the Spanish-American War and the treatment of the working poor in America, questioning whether Spain's slaves in Cuba could really be freed by a nation who treated its own poor as wage slaves.

Scollard, Carman, and Wilcox are undoubtedly among the most prolific little magazine poets, featuring in the most publications and serving as influences on their lesser-known counterparts. As professionals in the field, and contributors, in the main, to the most prestigious little magazines, however, they are not entirely representative of the little magazine poet whose ranks included a number of those Perkins dismissively terms "handymen" and "do-it-yourselfers," popular poets of region, amateurs, and poets by avocation whose work appeared in some of the lesser aesthetic little magazines as well as hybrids and periodicals of protest. Many of these published also in mainstream magazines and newspapers. Notable among the many such figures are William Reed Dunroy (1869–1921), a popular Nebraskan poet famous for celebrating the landscapes of the west and the lives of its people (contributor to *Lotus*, *Blue Sky*, *Optimist*, *Clack Book*, *Ishmaelite*, and

The Knocker, among others); Alonzo Leora Rice (1867–1946), farmer, schoolteacher and magazine and newspaper poet from Indiana, who wrote homespun, uplifting verse (contributor to *Muse*, *New Bohemian*, *Ghourki*, *Optimist*, *Whim*, etc.); and St George Best (1860–1936), bookseller and writer of poetry for magazines, newspapers, and little magazines (contributor to *Lotus*, *Muse*, *John-a-Dreams*, *Stiletto*, *Four O'Clock*, *Sothoron's*, *Quartier Latin*, *Smart Set*, and *Book-Lover*).

A good example of a "handyman" poet who enables a discussion of key differences between aesthetic little magazine poetry and that of periodicals of protest is Sam Walter Foss (1858–1911). Though Foss contributed to aesthetic little magazines such as *The Lotus* and *Fly Leaf*, his work was more usually found in hybrid magazines and periodicals of protest, namely *The Ghourki*, *Ye Quaint Magazine*, *Good Cheer*, *Socialist Spirit*, *Social Crusader*, and *Soundview*. Foss was a librarian by day and a prolific newspaper poet. He was famous for writing a poem a day and his poems were dubbed "scrap-book favorites" (W.H.H. 170). Foss was a poet of uplift, specializing in homespun verse, often in dialect, for the common man. His most famous poem, "The House By the Side of the Road" (1897), popular through the twentieth century, encapsulates his ethos of "being a friend to man."[10] This message and spirit animates, in various ways, his poetry that appears in protest and hybrid magazines. A *Ghourki* contribution, "Walk Right Up and Say Hullo," in which the speaker advises readers, "when you see a man in woe/walk right up and say 'hullo,'" takes a homespun approach to his "being a friend to man" theme, while "I Shall Not Pass This Way Again," in *Good Cheer*, is more serious and literary. Drawing on the words of the Quaker William Penn, the poem, again, appeals to its readers, asking them to "Strew gladness on the paths of men – /You will not pass this way again" (103). Foss's more pointed political poetry, meanwhile, brings a socialist bent to his overarching theme, with concepts of brotherhood and fellowship coming to the fore. In "Talking Horse and Talking God" for *The Socialist Spirit*, for example, a group of common men bond in fellowship discussing their love of the horse, but discord is bred among them when discussion turns to God.

Foss's contributions to two aesthetic little magazines, however, go against type in that they are highly self-reflexive poems about poetry. His contribution to *The Fly Leaf*, "The Wail of the Hack Writer," laments the lot of a poet who must "feed the million-throated swine / That gulps its garbage and then sleeps" (10), and is clearly appropriate fodder for magazines that situated themselves in opposition to the mass market. At the same time, it might well serve as a self-conscious reflection of Foss's own status, one that he can articulate better in the pages of a little magazine than in newspapers and magazines for the masses. *Fly Leaf* editor Harte acknowledges that the note of "revulsion and despair" in the poem will seem unusual coming from Foss, "who has been synonymous with the most bubbling humor and spontaneous, genial fun," and lauds it as a "new and serious" side of the poet that should encourage readers to think differently about him ("Bubble and Squeak," *Fly Leaf* 1, no. 2, 27–8). If we detect a sense of shame about popularity in Foss's *Fly Leaf* contribution, however, this mode is countered, though in an equally self-conscious manner, in "To a Poet" in *The Lotus*, another magazine edited by Harte. Here, in bouncing tetrameter couplets, Foss criticizes poets like Carman and Scollard, who treat Classical themes in poems that abound with naiads, sylphs, nymphs, Pans, graces, and muses – "Why our modern verse encumber / With this dead Olympian lumber?" – urging them instead to "speak the aspiration / of your place and generation," celebrating poets who, like him, "sing the heart-throbs of your neighbors" (197).

The self-consciousness Foss demonstrates about his status as a "friend to man" in poems for aesthetic little magazines attests to an increasing divide, in this period, between art-for-art's-sake and popular forms of poetry that included sentimental verse and poetry with a purpose – the kind of poetry Foss wrote for hybrid and protest magazines. These latter forms, though largely neglected in literary scholarship, were dominant at the end of the century, given a boost in 1899 with the success of Edwin Markham's "Man With the Hoe."[11] Based on Jean-François Millet's 1863 painting of a weary agricultural labourer, the poem first appeared in the San Francisco *Examiner* and was soon reprinted in newspapers across the country, becoming a rallying cry for the labour movement. Markham became an international celebrity as a poet of reform and, as Lisa Szefel notes, the poem "marked a turning point in the relationship between American poetry and politics … creating a current of verse that inspired poets and excited readers (59)." Markham was a frequent contributor to and topic of discussion in these new periodicals of protest, hybrid magazines, and related socialist publications in which literary content played a significant role.

The rise of politically charged poetry that Markham's "Man With the Hoe" inspired coincided with the second wave of the little magazine movement in which the periodical of protest came to the fore. While aesthetic little magazines were loathe to mix art and politics, periodicals of protest and hybrid magazines, by contrast, gave significant space to this poetry, such that this type is the second most represented in the sampling. The preponderance of such poetry speaks to the power of the reformist impulse on the part of the largely professional-managerial class readership of these magazines but also of the importance, to many, of the link between literature and social and political action that existed alongside the art-for-art's sake ethos of aesthetic little magazines. While poetry of protest could range generally across themes of tyranny and oppression in ways that *might* be read in the context of current events, it could also be explicitly topical, as a consideration of some of the poetry in the sampled periodicals of protest and hybrid magazines demonstrates. Markham's poem itself was topical, prompting thousands of responses (Stidger 143), some of them appearing in little magazines. W.A. Smith's "The Man Without the Hoe" in *The Schoolmaster*, for example, extends Markham's critique, identifying the "man without the hoe" as the exploiting employer. The Boer War and the crisis in Cuba that culminated in the Spanish American War in 1898 were also notable topics in this verse. In the sampling, Meredith Nicholson's "Cuba" (*Ishmaelite*) is a call to arms for Americans to "help rear, with practiced hand, / A new republic of the sea," while Lee Fairchild adopts a similar pro-intervention stance with respect to the Boer War, representing the Transvaal farmers as oppressed dwarves to the British Giant in "Friendship's Shame" (*The Thistle*).

The Socialist Spirit was particularly invested in topical literature, making a regular feature, in its poetry and prose, of framing content with brief reports on current events or excerpts from other newspapers and magazines. In the sampled June 1902 issue, for example, a piece called "Work" presents workers' views of labour in poems voiced by a miner, a weaver, and a sweater (8–9). These are framed as a response to Princeton professor Henry Van Dyke's poem "Work," recently published in the news and opinion weekly, *The Outlook*. Van Dyke's poem encourages workers to be content with their lot and to approach their labours with good cheer. His poem is reprinted at the top of the page, alongside a quotation from socialist W.J. Ghent's articles on "benevolent feudalism" that appeared in the *Independent* (New York) in April. This quotation from Ghent is an appeal to those in powerful positions between capital and labour (i.e., the professional-managerial class) to serve as agents for change. Addressing, in particular, teachers and clergymen, the quotation insists that "the teachings of the schools and colleges, the sermons" should "be persuasively molded" towards the "prevention of discontent" (8). The poems that follow respond bitterly to Van Dyke's plea, as the workers expose the impossibility of "cheerful[ly] greet[ing] the laboring hours" in the face of miserable working conditions (8). The miner, for example, contrasts his work "a thousand feet from daylight in the mirk / Bent double in a narrow vein of coal" with that of the poet, "a lady-handed shirk," who "writes poems of the sunshine of the soul / A-preaching what my tired heart should say" (8).

Alongside these sentimental and emotive responses to the plight of the oppressed were far more biting satirical and humorous attacks on oppressors. La Verne F. Wheeler's *The Jester*, in the spirit of its title, intersperses barbed prose commentary with verse critical of the imperialist greed underpinning the Boxer Rebellion (untitled poem), and the Philippine-American and Boer Wars ("The Banditti"). George McA Miller's "Uncle Ike on the War," in the reform-oriented *New Time*, meanwhile, deploys satire in a dialect poem that exposes the selfish motives of the American banking system in its response to the Cuba crisis, while likening the tyranny of Spain over Cuba to the financial system in America: "if we succeed in breakin' down the tyranny of Spain / To establish that of Rothschild, how much freedom do we gain?" (14). Politicians and captains of American industry, including Jay Gould, Theodore Roosevelt, Andrew Carnegie, Henry Clay Frick, Charles Schwab, and others also face judgment in the mock-apocalyptic "Bring on the Swab" by J.W. Stimson in *Comrade*, which envisages the triumph of socialism. Little magazine poets were not always of the same political stripe, however, as exemplified in differing treatments of the recently assassinated President McKinley across the socialist *Wilshire's Magazine* and the hybrid magazine *The Junk*. Harry M. Grooms's "Old Dinner Pail" in *Wilshire's* presents a defeatist and cynical view of how the American people were deceived by McKinley's "full dinner pail" campaign, while J.F. Mathieson, in the immediate aftermath of the President's death, memorializes him in "To Columbia" in *The Junk*, castigating the forces of anarchism and nihilism.[12]

Socialist publications, in particular, were invested in promoting an internationalist and historical perspective on the existing political situation in America, and in emphasizing the importance of literature and the arts in the class struggle. *The Comrade*'s manifesto, for example, declared its aim was "to mirror Socialist thought as it finds expression in Art and Literature" and "to develop the aesthetic impulse in the

Socialist Movement" ("Greetings" 12). This literature, in *The Comrade* and other socialist publications, might or might not be explicitly socialist, but, in a remediated context, invited a socialist interpretation. Reprint material from literary greats of the past whose works could be used to promote reform and revolution often served these aims. Within the sampling, reprint material by William Morris, John Ruskin, Robert Browning, Ralph Waldo Emerson, Lord Byron, and German radical George Herwegh on the themes of freedom, injustice, brotherhood, and oppression, positions the social and artistic ideals of these publications within this broader context. This material might serve, also, to illuminate aspects of the contemporary political situation in America. Relevant in this respect is *The New Time*'s reprinting of Canto 1, stanzas 86–8 of Byron's *Childe Harold* in July 1898 under the title "Hispanoila" [*sic*]. The stanzas, which focus on the war-mongering and bloodthirsty ways of the Spanish in an earlier historical period, take on a new and radicalized meaning when issued in this reformist magazine at the height of the Spanish-American War.

Even more significant than figures of radical romanticism such as Byron were Pre-Raphaelites, like William Morris, and their craft-informed and guild-based notions of brotherhood and community. Morris's poem "When the World Grows Fair," in *The Vanguard*, celebrates a utopian future in which all rejoice in their work and share the wealth equally. The Pre-Raphaelite idea that such values existed in an idealized past is one promoted by American Christian socialist, George D. Herron, who celebrates Bruges as a town historically rooted in "comrade-life" and fellowship in his poem "In Bruges Town" (*Comrade*). France, with its democratic revolutionary past also appeals as a model, valorized in an excerpt from muckraking journalist Charles E. Russell's longer poem "Picardy" (*Conservator*) that celebrates that town's tax revolt of 1790.

Inspirational songs and calls to arms, an important feature of the Chartist movement in Britain earlier in the nineteenth century, gained favour with American urban workers from the 1860s on and were a notable feature of socialist oriented little magazines. In the sampling, they are represented by "Comrades' Song" (*Comrade*), a translation of a song by George Herwegh, the German Romantic revolutionary poet, written originally for the General German Workingmen's Union. Often, however, these songs were popular American patriotic songs, or riffs on them, meant to prompt a consideration of the relationship between the nation's history and its present and future. Hamlin

Garland's "The Battle Hymn of the Wronged," for example, reprinted in *The New Time*, turns Julia Ward Howe's popular patriotic "Battle Hymn of the Republic" into a socialist protest poem that inveighs against the treatment of urban and rural labourers.[13] This poem was widely reprinted in a range of periodicals interested in labour issues and demonstrates another side of Garland, who was a significant contributor of regionalist and local colour writing to the aesthetic little magazine *The Chap-Book*. Garland's reformist side did not appeal to *Chap-Book* editor Stone, who urged the writer to forget "his 'cause'" and focus on his "art" (Wendy Schlereth 71–2). In this issue of *The New Time*, Garland's poem appears opposite a reprint of Frank Lebby Stanton's popular "Old Flag Forever," not a socialist song per se, but one that, in the context of the aims of the magazine, invites readers to see America's democratic ideals through this framework. This effect is reinforced by the inclusion in the issue of a poem by Richard Linthicum, written especially for the magazine, that posits the American flag as a symbol of the nation's commitment to ensuring the freedom of the downtrodden from tyranny. *The New Time*, in particular, couched its socialism in patriotic terms, where other socialist magazines such as *Comrade* and *Wilshire's* were more internationalist in perspective.

Spirituality played a key role in the socialism of this period, especially as it manifested itself in little magazines. A number of little magazinists were part of a network of Christian socialists and adherents to the social gospel movement, many of them clergymen. Poems that appear in these publications often equate socialist and Christian ethics. In Ernest Crosby's "The Great Joy" (*Social Crusader*), for example, renunciation of desires for wealth and political and social power are framed as positive socialist qualities but also ones that make one "part of the Divine will" and a possessor of the "life eternal" (24). Similarly, in J.H. Garrison's list poem "What We Stand For" in *The Vanguard*, "we" are both Christians and socialists, who stand for the "Christ of Galilee," "the church" "the right against the wrong," "the weak against the strong," "the New Earth," and "the heaven above us clearing" (9). Garrison's invocation of the apocalyptic New Heaven and Earth as the socialist future is characteristic of much of this poetry, including a reprint of British poet Lewis Morris's "The New Time" (*Vanguard*), which envisions the triumph of brotherhood in the post-apocalyptic new Heaven and Earth (17). Ernest Crosby's "New Creation," a quatrain, operates similarly. It, too, imagines a post-apocalyptic paradise:

The world to-day is without form and void, and darkness is upon the face
of the deep.
But lo! The Spirit of Love moveth upon the face of the waters of humanity,
And we shall ere long see a new heaven and a new earth.
And behold, it will be very good. (17)

Lacking the traditional diction and imagery of the class struggle, this poem might easily be read in conventionally religious terms. Its context in *The Social Crusader*, however, invites an allegorical reading, more so for its positioning immediately following an article documenting the partnership between two leading figures of the Christian socialist movement, George D. Herron and J. Stitt Wilson, to promote a great new religious and social movement for the twentieth century (J. Stitt Wilson 13–17). Such poetry represented the nadir of the reformist impulses of the progressive middle classes of America in this period. It assuages, in an idealist and spiritualist sense, anxieties about labour and capital in a form of missionary socialism that relies on an arts and crafts and aestheticist style to encourage social action and transformation.

In "Little Magazine, World Form," Bulson argues that all little magazines "share an interest in the present" and an "obsession with the 'NOW' of literary production and consumption" (268). Too bent on looking, in vain, for inklings of a twentieth-century modernism, modernist scholars since Hoffman, Allen, and Ulrich have neglected these magazines and what they might tell us about the history of poetry in America. If we stop looking for the future in them, however, and focus on the "NOW" that was then, they speak volumes, and we can begin to gauge the innovation and experimentalism of poetry, broadly speaking, in the period. Paula Bernat Bennett has characterized the poetry of this period as "seeking a 'new' which now knew itself to be 'new' but at the same time did not know what that 'new' was" (182). In part, as I have suggested, that new involved looking to the old – for aesthetic and socio-cultural reasons. Some, like Crane, dove boldly into the new – innovating form in what amounted to proto-modernist abstract and difficult poetry. But he was out of step with his time, while, at the same time, of his time. Considering Crane as a "poster poet," for example, roots him directly in the obsessions of the era and its sense of the modern. Scollard, Carman, Wilcox, and even Foss, meanwhile, and the thousands of poets like them, register similar concerns to Crane, in a more conventional manner, about the nature of the self, philosophically and psychologically. How to be and, in the case of socialist poetry, how to act in the world, are the concerns of this poetry, written and read by a self-identified "modern" and "progressive" class. This class was increasingly prone to introspection, but still wont to use poetry in, and to make sense of, everyday life. Along with other content, the poetry of little magazines was a barometer of a class negotiating what precisely the "new" of the "NOW" was in aesthetic, cultural, and political terms.

CHAPTER 6

Visual Art: "Art Running Amuck through Posterdom"

Few purchasers of fad periodicals ever get beyond the cover, and it is well for their peace of mind that they do not. The publishers know this, and put their best foot on the outside. The designs for these covers must be the result of nightmares – a succession of nightmares, perhaps. What they mean, who shall say? – for what they mean, who shall know?"

– "Fad Periodicals," *Critic*, 12 (1897)

While this anonymous journalist's remarks reflect poorly on the literary content of American little magazines of the 1890s, they are suggestive concerning key aspects of their appeal – their visual appearance and status as collectible objects for a culturally aspiring professional class. If these publications proved less successful than their twentieth-century successors in forging influential avant-garde fiction and poetry, it may be that their greater innovation was in the graphic arts. Linked to the contemporaneous fine press and poster movements, as discussed in chapter 2, little magazines were also connected to the origins of what have been acknowledged as the "golden ages" of illustration and advertising (Thomson, *Origins* 12; Mott, *History* 20–2). They served as a training ground for a number of artists and graphic designers who would go on to have careers in mainstream magazine and book illustration and design as well as advertising. These artists might be students or teachers at the many established and emerging art schools around the country, some of which were beginning to focus on commercial art. The artistic trends developed in little magazines provided a visual complement, thought not necessarily as illustration, to the themes explored in fiction and poetry. As in literary content, the influence of Pre-Raphaelitism, aestheticism, arts and crafts, and symbolism was prevalent. Little magazine artists looked both to the past for inspiration while exploiting the new, shocking, and modern of the art nouveau and poster art style. In art trends, too, there was evidence of anxieties about commercialization and a resistance to the manner in which mainstream magazines featured art.

While little magazines did sometimes exploit visual art in the manner of mainstream magazines – i.e., as illustration to accompanying text – there was a concerted effort to give art independence from written matter. Little magazines like *The Chap-Book* and, in Britain, *The Yellow Book*, sought to distinguish between literary and artistic content in reaction against profusely illustrated mainstream magazines. Those critical of popular illustrated magazines complained that this practice demeaned magazine art or, alternately, that the abundance of visual material subordinated literary content to pictures.[1] These critics insisted that giving each its own proper sphere foregrounded the "art" status of both media. At the same time, there was, in general, a reaction against photography and photographic realism in aesthetic little magazines, akin to the revolt against "local colour" realism within the literary avant-garde. One young artist, Henry Brevoort Eddy, interviewed for *Bradley His Book*, characterized this anti-realist trend as the "decadent" stance of a "minority" who "recognize there's a fight on between the draughtsman and the dry plate" (Frank R. Knight 90). These artists favoured forms that drew attention to the artist's hand in the work or to the craft involved, such as black and white pen and ink sketches or woodcuts. As Beegan argues, "the apparent speed, fluidity, minimalism, and roughness of the sketch became tokens of artistic sincerity, of an honesty that set it apart from Academic gentility or photographic literalism" (20).

The interest in old technology was also a resistance to mass production, prompting the valorization of woodcuts. The revival of the woodcut in this period, notable among European symbolists, was a "deliberate attempt to recapture a time and a craft that intimately conjoined the artist and his materials" (Field 23). While some artists of this period did produce woodcuts, they also used other processes to invoke the "idea of the woodcut" (Beegan 133), a demonstration of the versatility and innovation of the period that combined old and new. Notably, Beardsley's drawings, for example, though produced using a new photo-relief linecut process, were, nevertheless, much "indebted to the woodcuts" of fin-de-siècle French artists such as Félix Vallotton (Field 23). Photomechanical methods, then, might be used, even when the effect sought was some kind of pre-industrial authenticity. Photography allowed for original drawings to be transferred onto metal plates or wood blocks and then etched or cut so as to be printed alongside letterpress type (Beegan 8). Purist principles of hand craft were supported by new and commercial technological innovation and were embraced by a class of artists comfortable with the mediation of culture and commerce. Pen and ink drawings were associated with artistically legitimate forms such as the aesthetic movement and impressionism, and yet, at the same time, the commercial application of the form defined it as particularly modern, "immediate, accessible, and democratic" (Beegan 21). In the poster style, meanwhile, flat bold colour was used to achieve non-realistic effects. The styles employed, as Bogart notes, "signified uniqueness, 'refinement,' sophistication, 'daring invention,' and cachet" (83). In turn, knowledge about the latest trends in art was a sign of cultural sophistication (Bogart 327 n10). Where mainstream magazines were profusely illustrated, the principle of "less is more" prevailed in little magazine art, as it did for content more generally speaking. The choice and selective nature of artistic content helped to reaffirm the elite cultural status of little magazines that their makers sought to project and that their purchasers desired.

Because of the limited number of little magazines that featured art to any significant degree and the dominance of particular publications in this domain, little magazine art is treated in this chapter through a focus on three distinctive and influential publications that provide a sense of the broader range of artistic interests within the field. The chapter does not look to periodicals of protest, most of which did not feature art to any significant degree. Of those that did, namely socialist periodicals within the realm of periodicals of protest, art was generally in the way of illustration and cartoons, often after the manner of mainstream publications. The "little magazineness" of these socialist periodicals lay more in their literary than their artistic content. Chosen for consideration, then, are three aesthetic little magazines that represent the range of artistic interests of little magazines, exploited in different ways. *The Chap-Book* demonstrates the mediation between traditional and modern art forms and how visual art served in a predominantly literary magazine. *Bradley His Book* is indicative of an aspiration to make the magazine itself a work of art, while *M'lle New*

York bucks the arts and crafts trends of its counterparts as an urban, decadent periodical indebted to contemporary French magazine visual culture. In various ways, the art in these magazines, like the fictional and poetic content, addressed the aspirational and cultural ideals and values of an emerging professional-managerial class that regarded itself as modern and culturally sophisticated.

The magazine that established a precedent for others in terms of artistic content was *The Chap-Book*. Though conservative in its leanings in comparison with *M'lle New York* and *Bradley His Book*, it was able, as with fiction and poetry, to feature major European and emerging American artists. In its first few months of existence, its art reflects the magazine's origins as an advertising vehicle for Stone and Kimball's publishing house and its status as a self-styled literary journal. Art, in this context, was subservient to literature and was geared towards the promotion of the book as collectible object, catering to a bibliophilic segment of the professional classes. It played up its chap-book roots and its association with the fine press movement by featuring woodcuts in its "From Old Chapbooks" series that ran through volumes four and five in 1896. Further, its first issues featured designs and illustrations for books. Most of these were the publisher's own books and included a conventional floral and emblematic design by G.H. Hallowell for Maurice Thompson's *Lincoln's Grave*; Thomas B. Meteyard's illustration for Robert Louis Stevenson's *Ebb Tide*, with its elements of Japonisme and art nouveau ("Titlepage"; see Figure 6.1); and Aubrey Beardsley's eroticized grotesque illustration for Poe's "Masque of the Red Death" ("Design"). The magazine's broader interest in the promotion of the book beautiful is reflected in the inclusion of designs for books not published by Stone and Kimball, notably Charles Ricketts's for Wilde's *Sphinx*, which had been issued by the Bodley Head in 1894.

At the same time, portraits of writers were a dominant feature of the magazine in this early period, and would remain so. These generally appeared in conjunction with an article on the writer. In early numbers, *The Chap-Book* even included photographic representations of authors, a practice increasingly popular in mainstream magazines where authors were treated as celebrities.[2] Photographs, as Beegan argues, "played an important role" in the shift from a culture of character to a culture of personality, enabling "a direct connection between the reader and the subject of the photograph" (115, 117). In this respect, the halftone might have seemed well suited to magazines that privileged intimacy, personality, and subjectivity. Its association, however,

TITLEPAGE FOR "THE EBB TIDE" DESIGNED BY MR. T. B. METEYARD.

Figure 6.1 Thomas B. Meteyard title page design for a Stone and Kimball edition of Robert Louis Stevenson's *Ebb Tide*, *The Chap-Book*, 15 May 1894. Courtesy of HathiTrust.

with mass reproduction made it suspect, and little magazinists often frowned on photographic representation as inartistic, save for those who were seeking to promote photography as art, as Alfred Stieglitz would soon do in his little magazine, *Camera Work*. In this context, *The Chap-Book*'s early photographic representations of authors soon gave way to more artistic modes that accentuated the individuality and personality of their subjects in a different manner.

This transition is exemplified in the magazine's treatment of Paul Verlaine. A July 1894 issue features a photographic representation of the poet that emphasizes his gravitas in the reverent and conventional style of the period ("Paul Verlaine"; see Figure 6.2). In March 1895, however, *The Chap-Book* features a more unconventional representation, one informed by French artistic avant-gardism and produced by Verlaine's friend, F.-A. Cazals. Rather than providing a realistic image of the author's face, Cazals's "Portrait of P.V." seeks to capture his essence in an image from behind, depicted in a hat and large coat, strolling cane in hand, looking every bit the vagabond poet (see Figure 6.3).

Figure 6.2 Photograph of Paul Verlaine (1893), by Otto Wegener as reproduced in *The Chap-Book*, 1 July 1894. In possession of author.

Figure 6.3 "Portrait of P.V." [Paul Verlaine], by F.-A. Cazals, *The Chap-Book*, 15 March 1895. In possession of author.

The image challenges the reader's cultural sophistication, as it provides only a cryptic identification in the caption. The reader must know that "P.V." stands for Paul Verlaine and that *Epigrammes* is his book. At the same time, this image represents another instance of *The Chap-Book*'s use of art to promote books and a cosmopolitan bibliophilic culture – in this instance, a French limited edition book issued by a press associated with the avant-garde magazine *La Plume*.

Throughout the run of *The Chap-Book*, portraiture in a traditional style was featured. In early issues, these were often based on photographs. Later, they might take the form of realist artistic representations, as in the "Portraits of Contemporaries" series through volumes four and five. Traditional representations, however, appeared alongside avant-garde, modern, or impressionistic styles in sketches and caricatures. Swiss artist Félix Vallotton, member of the avant-garde Nabis group in France – a movement influenced by art nouveau, symbolism, and British arts and crafts – contributed this latter type of work, including portraits of Rimbaud, Zola, and Mallarmé ("Arthur Rimbaud"; "Portrait of Emile Zola"; and "Portrait of Stéphane Mallarmé"). These relied on minimal detail and the use of flat blocks of black and white (printed in red and white in the case of Mallarmé) to capture the essence of those represented (see Figure 6.4). Another image of the artist in this manner is a black and white self-portrait of Beardsley, "After Himself," dominated by somber black as if to emphasize his association with decadence. In a different mode, Paul Berthon's "Portrait of M. Andhré des Gachons" captures the spirit of the artist in a symbolistic mode, depicting him writing a text, "Vie de la Vierge," as an angel muse appears behind him. In addition, Max Beerbohm represented the lighter side of the European fin-de-siècle avant-garde scene, providing a series, "Chap-Book Caricatures," printed in colour and included as supplements from September to November 1896.

The Chap-Book's increasing emphasis on new forms of art and portraiture is indicative of how, as it developed, the magazine understood its mission as more than a literary one. In 1895, the editor commented that in aiming to capture the "spirit of [the] period," it was necessary to encompass the range of new "artistic as well as literary movements" ("Notes," *Chap-Book* 3, no. 12, 509). By this time, the magazine had demonstrated its commitment to art by dedicating a category in the annual index to "prints," alongside "poetry" and "prose." This treatment of art as its own category indicates that, like its British counterpart, *The Yellow Book*, and in opposition to mainstream magazine practices, *The Chap-Book*, asserted the independence of art from text.

Figure 6.4 "Portrait of Emile Zola," by F. Vallotton in *The Chap-Book*, 15 May 1895. In possession of author.

Key to the magazine's interest in promoting the modern "spirit of the period" in visual art was the poster. *The Chap-Book* exploited the poster movement early on and its inaugural poster, Will Bradley's "The Twins," has been heralded as the first American art nouveau poster (Wong 294). "The Twins" was one of sixteen advertising posters for the magazine issued between 1894 and 1897 in art nouveau or arts and crafts style, seven of them designed by Bradley (Kramer 213). Other *Chap-Book* poster artists included Frank Hazenplug, Claude F. Bragdon, J.C. Leyendecker, E.B. Bird, and Toulouse-Lautrec (likely a poster for European distribution). *The Chap-Book* also imported and sold French posters and, eventually, following the lead of competitors, it featured poster-style covers intermittently through 1896.

The Chap-Book's exploitation of the poster fad is in keeping with broader trends of the period, notably the use of women as iconic figures in the medium. Eleven *Chap-Book* posters featured women – indicative of the ubiquitousness in advertising of "the poster girl" phenomenon.[3] Unlike Beardsley's women or those of French artists, iconic American poster girls, Bogart argues, were "idealized, beautiful … rather unsensuous … rendered as decorative forms rather than as thinking, acting individuals" (83–5). Symbolically, however, the modern poster girl may have been more progressive than Bogart suggests. If the flat non-realist representations lent a static and passive quality to poster girls, they were, nevertheless, associated with modern, sophisticated, or intellectual activities: flirting, smoking, skating, writing, reading, and biking. At the same time, these women were represented in a modern medium linked with spectacle and designed for shock effect in its bold use of colour and design. In gendered terms, it was a medium, Ruth Iskin claims, associated with the streetwalker – garish, brightly coloured, and on public display (259). Even if American poster girls, then, looked quite tame, these contexts created unsettling ambiguities. Commenting on Bradley's "Twins" poster, for example, a reviewer for *The American Printer* deplored its eccentricity and ambiguity: "no man can possibly tell, without deliberately investigating, what it means or what it represents" (qtd. in Wong 296).

The Chap-Book posters variously reflect the controversial gender politics of the poster movement. In Bradley's pseudo-medieval Kelmscott/Beardsley-inspired "Poet and His Lady," the lady gazes provocatively at the viewer, while her lover is caught up in the reading of what looks like a modern-day little magazine with a poster girl on the back cover (see Figure 6.5). Another flirting woman is depicted in Frank Hazenplug's "Black Lady." In this poster, a woman casts a provocative glance back at a gang of menacing androgynous Pierrot figures whose faces resemble her own (see colour plate 13). Pierrot was a popular figure in decadent and symbolist art and in little magazines, associated, in this period, with the alienated and misunderstood artist and with violence and transgression (Storey 122, 126).[4] Hazenplug's "Red Lady," meanwhile, lurches bosom-first out of the frame (see Figure 6.6), an image derided by one critic who referred to it as "Idiot Undressing" (qtd. in Rhodes 417). It is Bradley's "May" poster though, which is the most provocative of *The Chap-Book* posters ("May"), depicting a nude bacchante with cymbals amid flowers and foliage that do not entirely conceal what they ought to (see colour plate 14). His bacchante, a figure associated with drunken revelry, suggests that women, too, can live the life bohemian.

Considered from this broader context, then, and in light of these *Chap-Book* examples, the American poster girl, if not as obviously racy as her European counterparts, may well be more radical than Bogart suggests. Indeed, the poster girl became a lightning rod for fashionable young women who signalled their modernity by dressing up in a poster style. If these "poster girls in real life," as one newspaper called them, were "not as weird as … Beardsley's nightmares in black and

Figure 6.5 Will Bradley. "The Poet and His Lady."
Chicago: Stone and Kimball, 1895. Art & Architecture Collection, Miriam and Ira D. Wallach Division of Art, Prints and Photographs. New York Public Library. New York Public Library Digital Collections.

Figure 6.6 Frank Hazenplug. "The Red Lady." Chicago: Stone and Kimball, 1895. The Miriam and Ira D. Wallach Division of Art, Prints and Photographs: Art & Architecture Collection, New York Public Library, Astor, Lenox and Tilden Foundations.

white," they were, nevertheless, "modernized Gibsonish edition[s] of the poster girl" ("Poster Girls in Life" 18). *The Chap-Book*'s posters, executed by leading artists in the movement, as well as the magazine's role in importing and selling European posters, identified it with an aesthetically and socially progressive modernity. While its book and author-focused art addressed a bibliophilic and book-collecting market, its poster art sought to reach a younger portion of the professional class, namely young women who may have identified with the modernity the poster girl represented. The poster style also catered to aspiring modern artists, ones who, as Theodore Dreiser would characterize in retrospect in his novel *The Genius*, "considered themselves connoisseurs of pen and ink and illustration," "subscribe[d] to *Jugend*, *Simplicissimus*, *Pick-Me-Up* and the radical European art journals," and "were aware of Steinlen and Cheret and Mucha and the whole rising young school of French poster workers" (cited in Bogart 327 n10).

Inside the pages of the magazine itself, though, and in addition to poster art, *The Chap-Book* promoted the fin-de-siècle revival of woodcuts, the black-and-white style, line drawing, lithography, symbolism, and art nouveau. Asserting its connection with the European avant-garde, *The Chap-Book* published work by major European artists of these movements: woodcut images by Félix Vallotton ("Le Bain") and Georges Pissarro ("In the Garden"; see Figure 6.7); European versions of the poster girl, including one by Beardsley in his black-and-white mode ("A Drawing"), and two in the art nouveau style, one by Paul Berthon ("Drawing for a Poster"; see Figure 6.8) and one, in colour, by Andhré des Gachons that appeared as a supplement for volume 4, number 7 ("Supplement for no. 7"); and symbolistic illustrations and images by des Gachons ("Illustration for a Poem by Jean Lorrain") and Alexandre Séon ("Douleur de la Chimère"). It also supported American exponents of these movements, including features on and work by Will Bradley and John Sloan, for example.

The most prolific contributors of art to *The Chap-Book*, however, were Fred Richardson, Claude F. Bragdon, Frank Hazenplug, and Raymond Crosby. Each of these artists represented, in particular ways, the dominant artistic trends of the era. Fred Richardson (1862–1937), whose little magazine work was a sideline to his main job as a newspaper illustrator with the *Chicago Daily News*, was a key contributor to the "Portraits of Contemporaries" series. Among the authors he drew were Joaquin Miller, Israel Zangwill, Anthony Hope, Stanley Weyman, William Watson, Ralph Adams Cram, Harold Frederic, Kenneth Grahame, F. Frankfort Moore, and John Fox Jr.[5] He displayed versatility in his style, often exploiting hatching to create elaborate tonal effects. His portrait of American decadent Ralph Adams Cram, however, shows him adept at the Beardsley technique of massing black and white ("Portrait"; see Figure 6.9) Though more realistic in mode than Beerbohm, who also provided a series of portraits of authors for *The Chap-Book*, Richardson occasionally employs caricature effects. He pictures Joaquin Miller, for example, as a dandy-aesthete cowboy ("Joaquin Miller"), and *Prisoner of Zenda* author, Anthony Hope, as a head on a platter à la John the Baptist ("Mr Hope"). Zangwill, meanwhile, is presented as a Jewish stereotype, his large nose cut off by a drawn frame ("Mr Zangwill"; see Figure 6.10). Other representations of artists are more reverential and aim for a realistic effect, in contrast with contributions by European artists. Many of Richardson's portraits are of Stone and Kimball authors. Richardson's images of William Watson, Harold Frederic, and Kenneth Grahame, for example,

Figure 6.7 Georges Pissarro, European contributor to *The Chap-Book*. "In the Garden." *The Chap-Book*, 15 September 1895. In possession of author.

Figure 6.8 Paul Berthon, European contributor to *The Chap-Book*. "Drawing for a Poster," in *The Chap-Book*, 15 January 1896. In possession of author.

Figure 6.9 Fred Richardson, portrait of Ralph Adams Cram, with Beardsleyesque black and white massing effects. *The Chap-Book*, 1 April 1896. In possession of author.

Figure 6.10 Fred Richardson, portrait and stereotyped caricature of Israel Zangwill. *The Chap-Book*, 15 September 1895. In possession of author.

coincide with the publications of books by them. In other instances, Richardson's images accompany celebrity-style articles on the subjects, as in the case of popular authors Stanley Weyman and F. Frankfort Moore ("Notes," *Chap-Book* 3, no. 11, 446–52; Picaroon 259–66). Richardson, then, served as a reliable staff artist, whose work functioned to promote the publishing enterprise of the firm and its ambitions as a high quality literary magazine that understood itself as a cut above the more popular *Bookman*, which *The Chap-Book* often positioned as a rival in its editorial commentary.

The contributions of Raymond M. Crosby (1876–1945) were more self-consciously "modern" than Richardson's, consisting of subject matter relevant to the experience of urban or cultured sophisticates and bohemian types. Against the more "finished" quality of Richardson's "portraits," Crosby provides "sketches" that foreground the mark of the artist's hand and suggest more hurried work. His work is rougher, less detailed, not aiming for realism as Richardson often does. Crosby's style, rather, is defined in resistance to the photographic realism of the period and is part of a trend in drawing that Beegan maps out, in which images were "more minimal and gestural" (132). It was a style regarded as suited to the modernity of the era insofar as its unfinished, hurried quality "evoked the transitory and individual nature" of modern, urban, experience (Beegan 138). This style, though regarded as modern, "innovative" and "contemporary" (Beegan 18), was not exclusively avant-garde. Indeed, it was a feature of both mainstream and self-consciously artistic magazines on both sides of the Atlantic, often used for satirical purposes. Crosby, himself, would become an illustrator for popular magazines, including *Life*, *Cosmopolitan*, and *The Saturday Evening Post*. If his work comes across as avant-garde or more "artistic" in the pages of *The Chap-Book*, it is due to the magazine's sparer use of art overall, its avoidance of art as illustration, Crosby's subject matter, and his use, generally, of the sketch in a serious, rather than satirical fashion. His "modern" subjects centre largely on artistic and urban themes, notably new women and bohemian men. His women are engaged in bicycling (see Figure 6.11), playing the piano, observing a park concert from a bench, while his men include an actor on a roof garden, smokers, and contemplative readers.

If Richardson contributed to establishing the gravitas of *The Chap-Book* as a serious literary enterprise and Crosby connected *The Chap-Book* with urban modernity and the new, Claude Fayette Bragdon (1866–1946) and Frank Hazenplug (1873/4–1931) supplied material that foregrounded *The Chap-Book*'s connection to aestheticism, arts

Figure 6.11 Raymond Crosby, "Drawing." *The Chap-Book*, 1 October 1896. One of Crosby's typically "modern" subjects. In possession of author.

and crafts, decadence, and art nouveau, movements that represented, according to Beegan, another kind of reaction against realism in art in their focus on fantastical, otherly worlds (132). Bragdon, an architect by profession, was a notable contributor of art, poetry, and prose to other little magazines, too. While two of Bragdon's posters are in a colonial style that was linked to the chap-book revival, most of his work for the magazine is simple, cartoonish, line work with no hatching or massing of colour, overall less connected to the artistic trends of the period than other contributors. His subject matter, however, is notably decadent, orientalist, and macabre in flavour, the visual equivalent of many of the tales of horror and mystery and the symbolistic prose fables in little magazines. His images include sphinxes, snake charmers, Ra, rope dancers, skeletons, and explorations of decadent themes: a soul rising from the dead body of a suicide; the representation of the decadent artist's muse as a skeleton angel; and an enigmatic depiction of a dead woman lying at the feet of a Pierrot ("Drawing"; see Figure 6.12), an image suggestive of the dangerous consequences of flirting with these

Figure 6.12 Claude F. Bragdon, "Drawing." *The Chap-Book*, 1 June 1896. An image typical of Bragdon's decadent, macabre style. In possession of author.

transgressive figures in the manner represented in Hazenplug's "Black Lady" poster of two months earlier (see colour plate 13).

Hazenplug, meanwhile, who was a staff artist for the publishing firm, did much of its book design, and was the most prolific contributor of art to the magazine, was more versatile than Bragdon. As *Chap-Book* editor Harrison Garfield Rhodes remarked: "Working entirely alone, Mr. Hazenplug put himself to the test of a constant change of style. One month saw him drawing like the most decadent of decadent Englishmen; the next saw him imitating the style of old woodcuts; and the third found him attacking the problems of poster-making which have been mastered only by the French" (414). Hazenplug's work demonstrates the influence of the Pre-Raphaelites, arts and crafts masters such as Walter Crane, art nouveau, and Aubrey Beardsley. Beyond his posters for the magazine, his main contributions were elaborate illustrated and decorative borders for poetry that appeared in the magazine, such as the one that accompanies John Davidson's "Ballad of an Artist's Wife" (Hazenplug, [Designs for]; see Figure 2.2). Standalone

Figure 6.13 Frank Hazenplug, "A Drawing." *The Chap-Book*, 15 September 1895. Hazenplug in his arts and crafts style. In possession of author.

works by Hazenplug in the magazine included black and whites in a decadent and symbolist vein: a convincing imitation of Beardsley ("A Drawing: With Apologies to Mr. Beardsley"); a poster-style girl ("Drawing," *Chap-Book* 4, no. 9); and a symbolistic allegorical image entitled "The Blind," featuring two nude figures groping their way through a forest. This picture may have been inspired by Maeterlinck's play *The Blind*, which Stone and Kimball had issued in translation the year previously.

His main work for the magazine, however, was in the arts and crafts and art nouveau style. Hazenplug had a straighter and more structured line than his British counterparts and his images had a lighter feel as he made less use of heavy black, giving his work a fairy tale quality. This style is exemplified in "Envious Black-Hair'd Queen" and in his image of a maiden accompanying a Mother Goose rhyme, "First of May," a poem about bathing in the dew of hawthorns on the first of

May in order to preserve beauty ("Drawing," *Chap-Book* 3, no. 7; see Figure 6.13). Hazenplug's May girl is conventional, in keeping with the styles of illustration found in children's books of the day. Notably, it stands in contrast to another *Chap-Book* image which might well be said to be a modern, up-to-date accompaniment to this poem for the new woman, i.e., Bradley's provocative May 1895 poster of the bacchante awash in hawthorns (see colour plate 14). Indeed, Bradley may well have had this proverb in mind when producing his poster.

Within a year of having produced his "May" poster, and eight months since his last contribution to *The Chap-Book*, Bradley launched his own magazine, *Bradley His Book*, an art and literary magazine and technical journal through which to realize his artistic ideals (front matter, *Bradley His Book*). Bradley, a printer, graphic artist, book designer, and typographer, was undoubtedly the most important artist in the little magazine movement. He was as versatile as Hazenplug and more talented overall, fashioning posters and contributing content to a number of publications. While his interests and tastes were in keeping with those of *The Chap-Book*, he had a different conception of the relationship between literary and artistic content. Bradley did not insist on the separation of literary and artistic content, believing that they could coexist in an artistic literary production. At the same time, and more controversially, he insisted that art and advertisement could be harmonized. These aims served as the foundation for *Bradley His Book*, a magazine targeted at a mixed audience: "Altogether, this magazine is intended to be one that will be sought for by women and welcomed in every home; a magazine that the artist and book-lover will prize; a magazine that will prove a help and inspiration to every amateur in art, and to the ambitious printer; and withal, a popular artistic and literary magazine in every sense of the word" (front matter).

Like *The Chap-Book*, Bradley's magazine reflected its position within a larger printing and publishing enterprise. It was issued from his Wayside Press, a commercial establishment, but one dedicated to small press ideals and artistic printing. *Bradley His Book* featured work by and about leading figures in the small press and poster movements. Bradley reproduced covers, title pages, and pages from exceptionally designed books and magazines, bookplate and initial letter designs, and the work of leading poster artists. He had ambitions, also, to promote aspiring graphic artists and those working in the decorative arts. In July 1896, for example, he announced his intention to sponsor a series of competitions for posters and magazine covers, book covers, wallpaper, head and tail pieces, embroidery designs, fretwork, printing and press work, etc. (front matter). The magazine, of course, was also a vehicle for his own work, which included elaborate illustrations and decorations for the literary and artistic content, such as his black-and-white Kelmscott-inspired design for Harriet Monroe's poem, "The Night-Blooming Cereus" (see Figure 6.14), and colour woodcut illustrations for Tudor Jenks's "Island Queen," a fairy-tale style romance (Designs for "Night-Blooming Cereus" and Designs for "Island Queen").

In many respects, however, Bradley's greatest artistic achievement was his conception of *Bradley His Book* as a print *gesamtkunstwerk* (total work). He oversaw every aspect of the magazine's design and production and each issue was a unique work of art in itself. Bradley was ambitious in his aims, featuring a new design and theme each month with different colours, papers, and types. A poster was issued in conjunction with each number, lithographed in four colours, offered at fifty cents for subscribers. Bradley produced a limited edition version of the first number, fifty large paper copies printed on Japanese parchment, bound in flexible Japan vellum wrappers, and accompanied by a small poster in two colours designed and engraved on wood ("*Bradley His Book*: Prospectus"). Among Bradley's monthly themes was his July 1896 "woman's issue," printed "daintily" on enameled paper with illustrations "chosen with special reference to their pleasing women" ("Features of July Number"). Newspaper- and poster-themed issues were planned, though not realized. While Bradley may have wished to emphasize the interrelationship between art and literature in his magazine, his illustrations often overwhelmed the texts they accompanied, making the literary content unreadable. Nowhere is this more apparent than in his August 1896 volume, which included "Beauty and the Beast," a theatrical extravaganza comprised of songs, scenes, and poster-style illustrations in black and white. The confusion lies in the fact that the play is interspersed throughout the issue alongside other content, with the play text set out along the bottom of pages, illustrations occupying whole pages or margins, with other content on the main part of the page. *Bradley His Book* is, in many respects, a magazine to be looked at more than read, a critique often made about small press publications, including Morris's Kelmscott books and the engraved texts of William Blake.[6]

The advertisements in Bradley's magazine were an important part of its artistic content and demonstrate his view of advertisement as

Figure 6.14 Will Bradley's design for Harriet Monroe's "Night Blooming Cereus," in *Bradley His Book*, May 1896, with rubricated title. In possession of author.

art. Bradley shared the beliefs of other graphic artists of the day who saw the advertisement as a means of democratizing art and of bringing beauty, as Bragdon argued, to the "commercial spirit" of the age (qtd. in Singleton 24). Bradley, for his part, endeavoured to make his advertisements a thing of beauty, referring to them as "illuminated advertisements" ("At the End of the Book"), thereby linking the modern medium of commercial advertising with the artisanal practices of the manuscript age. Recognizing both the need for "a liberal advertising patronage" for his magazine and the medium's decorative possibilities, he sought, as he said, to make his ads "a feature of the book" ("At the End of the Book"). Bradley was praised for his "revival of artistic printing and the development of decorative advertising," and his ads were declared by the *Chicago Daily News* to be "poems in themselves" ("End of the Book" 112). An example of his blurring of art and advertisement and his playful attitude towards the comments of admiring critics is represented in his ad for Ayer's Vigor, a treatment for thinning hair. The ad plays on the division between high art and the commercial by juxtaposing a beautifully designed graphic with a deliberately bad poem (see colour plate 15). In the ad, which could easily be mistaken for the literary/artistic content of the magazine, a Pre-Raphaelite "stunner" with lush red hair and medieval-style headpiece, done in poster style, frames the following poem, entitled "A Ballade of Baldness":

Sad is Decay, and saddest yet,
When it doth shear soft tresses, fair.
We know that we must pay the debt,
To Shylock Age, who doth not spare
When once he hath us in his net.
'Tis well to heed the oracles
That teach us we may save our hair
Till folly kills the follicles.

Naught is as vain as vain regret
For locks once gone beyond repair
We've passed the Rubicon that's set;
The dye is cast away; we'd tear
Our flowing locks, if they were there.
Alas! Nor boats nor coracles,
Can stem Time's river. Gone our hair
When folly kills the follicles.

Envoi.
Maiden, be wise, as you are fair;
Use Ayer's Vigor for the hair.
Fail not to heed this oracle,
Ere folly kills the follicle.

Punning aside, *Bradley His Book*, like this advertisement, had a dual status. Certainly, it was artistic, but the magazine might well have been called *Bradley His Advertisement* in its showcasing of Bradley's artistic talents across content and advertising pages, the latter of which outnumbered the former in the first issue. Like Stone and Kimball, whose *Chap-Book* functioned, in part, to advertise their book list, Bradley understood that his magazine could be used as a medium to sell the Wayside Press and the specific products featured in its pages in ingenious ways. Bradley, for example, used the papers he advertised, indicating in the ads on which pages particular papers appeared. He also advertised the ink he used, the photo-engraving and electrotyping company involved in the magazine's production, the printing press it was printed on, and even the electric motor that powered the printing press.

While *The Chap-Book* and *Bradley His Book* were steeped in small press and poster ideals in their presentation of art, *M'lle New York* drew artistic inspiration from fashionable illustrated French literary, artistic, and satirical magazines such as *Gil Blas*, *Le Chat Noir*, *Le Rire*, and *La Plume*, whose artists included Toulouse-Lautrec, Steinlen, Grasset, Pissarro, Vallotton, Mucha, and Odilon Redon (see colour plate 16). Significantly, too, it broke from the chap-book or pamphlet-size adopted by many American little magazines to take on the larger tabloid dimensions of its French models in a publication of sixteen pages. This format was best suited to the extravagant design of the magazine, described by one critic as "almost perfect as an example of the publisher's, the printer's, the papermaker's workmanship and ... certainly perfect as a sample of sure, skillful and inventive drawing and illustrating" (J.L.S. 4). Thomas E. Powers (1870–1939) and Thomas Fleming (1853–1931), professional newspaper illustrators, produced the bulk of artistic content, designing posters, poster-style covers in pastel, and providing interior illustration and decoration. Powers specialized in cartoon sequences, while Fleming's forte was in sketches of figures and creatures. Their work was supplemented by that of others, sometimes credited, sometimes not. These included the drawings of French artists and illustrators Henri Boutet and Albert Robida, lifted directly from the pages of *La Plume* and other French periodicals. The dancing girls along the left and bottom margins in Figure 6.16, for example, are by Boutet. Unusually, there was colour illustration throughout the magazine, the product of a new colour process, as co-editor James Huneker claimed, that gave the appearance of having been hand-tinted (qtd. in Schwab 95). This photo-relief stencil process is characteristic of the French periodicals that *M'lle New York* drew inspiration from.[7]

While this overall look of the magazine clearly linked it to the satirical French weeklies, the colour process, which emphasized "flatness and artificiality," was one associated, too, with the Japanese print (Beegan 142). Along with this hint of japonisme, the art in *M'lle New York* bore traces of the influence of other contemporary art trends popular with little magazinists. Fleming, for example, exploits the art nouveau curvilinear line to exaggerated and phantasmagoric effect in his drawings in an idiom different from the more conventional art nouveau style of Bradley, as in his depiction of a demi-mondaine and pig on the beach in the first issue (see Figure 6.15). As Vance Thompson, the magazine's editor, said, Fleming had a "marvelous command of line – he can be brutal, grotesque, gracile [*sic*], elegant, monstrous, expressive, or suggestive" ("Newspaper Illustrators" 546). The poster-style girls of Powers and Fleming, too, are nothing like the American ones of the period. Like their French counterparts they are buxom and racy, evoking belle époque decadence. Overall, though working under the same influences as many of their counterparts, Fleming and Powers deploy them to different effect in a publication that, in its unparalleled realization of the little magazine ideals of individuality and originality, is unlike any other of the era.

Unlike in *The Chap-Book*, art and literary content were not treated as distinct spheres in *M'lle New York*. Rather, like *Bradley His Book*, *M'lle New York* foregrounds a relationship between text and image. It does so, however, on distinctly different terms than *Bradley His Book*, creating a visual aesthetic that is in keeping with its decadent and symbolist literary content. In reading *M'lle New York* one experiences a bizarre visual feast. Some art serves as illustration for accompanying text; indeed, sometimes text is superimposed over images. Other sketches and drawings, however, appear randomly, seemingly distracted jottings riddling the margins of the page (see Figure 6.16). In effect, the visual page of the magazine captures the real and imagined world of the decadent flâneur, in its representation of the city and of a mental landscape of a particular type. Speaking of the mainstream illustrated magazine of this period, in Britain particularly, Beegan argues that it "was a form that allowed readers to make meaning of the city by creating what Patrick Joyce terms an 'imagined collectivity.' Like the pubs, music-halls, and theatres of the metropolis it provided a sense of a shared experience and a guide for how one might behave" (1). *M'lle New York*, it can be argued, performed this function for a very specific kind of "imagined collectivity," that of the bohemian or aspirational bohemian in the city.

Figure 6.15 Thomas Fleming illustration for *M'lle New York*, August 1895, demonstrating artist's curvilinear style and the magazine's use of pig imagery. In possession of author.

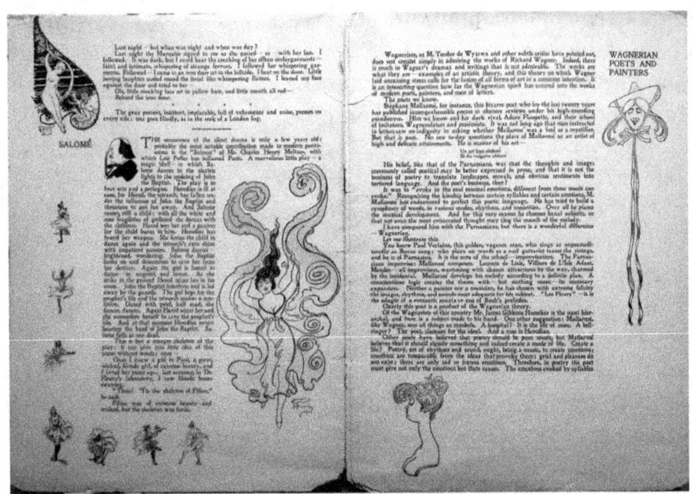

SALOMÉ

WAGNERIAN POETS AND PAINTERS

Figure 6.16 Page layout from *M'lle New York*, 23 August 1895. The image by Fleming accompanying the Salomé article is pastel tinted in pink and blue. In possession of author.

Powers's cover for the first issue sets the tone for a reader's encounter with the magazine (see colour plate 17). The viewer is positioned as a voyeur at the back of a smoke-filled club, perhaps occupying the position of the man situated bottom left in the frame whose cigar contributes to waves of tobacco smoke. Japanese lanterns decorate the crowded club, which is peopled with men in top hats and boaters, an androgynous new woman drinking beer, and a waiter. A female performer is on stage in the distance. Through this and subsequent issues of the magazine, the reader encounters, through cartoonish sequences, sketches, and illustrations, the elements of the decadent's urban and fantasy realms: New York cityscapes; naked and semi-clad ladies, ballet girls, exotic dancers, and demi-mondaines, including M'lle New York herself; fatcat industrialists smoking cigars and drinking champagne; louche men; demonic fairies; muses emerging from bottles, from cigarette smoke, or from smoke clouds; devils and demons; satyrs and nymphs; mystics and angels; skeletons and skulls; dwarves; pigs, birds, apes, and cats; Pierrots; racist caricatures of Jews, Chinese, and Africans; literary men, including Max Nordau, Baudelaire, Philip Hale, Charles Cros, and Verlaine. These images work in tandem with the content of the magazine, notably its urban realist stories, decadent horror tales, and symbolist poetry.[8] On the one hand, some of these images transport readers as armchair flâneurs to ethnic and bohemian New York – the Bowery and the French Quarter, for example – for encounters with their inhabitants. On the other, the grotesque and bizarre images reinforce the prevalent themes of madness, genius, and bohemianism considered in the literary content. The skulls, skeletons, and odd creatures are in a similar artistic idiom to the work of French symbolist artist Odilon Redon, but after the cartoonish manner of a French caricaturist such as Gustave-Henri Jossot.[9] The grotesque imagery functions as a visual equivalent of the absinthe, opium, or cigar-induced reveries of the decadent artist. The cat, meanwhile, one of the most prolific images in *M'lle New York* (see, for example, colour plate 12, bottom centre), and associated, in the French context, with hedonism, reinforces the magazine's decadent bohemianism.[10] Thus did content and images in the magazine work together to invoke a decadent reader, an effect described by Walter Blackburn Harte as one of "imprisoning the imagination in the stews, and banishing the mind and spirit out of life in a poetic mist of purely sensual existence" ("Bubble and Squeak," *Lotus* 2, no. 7, 256).

The "purely sensual existence" that the reader derives from *M'lle New York* is enhanced by the personification of magazine and city as demi-mondaines. *M'lle New York* thus embodies a sexualized notion of the intimacy privileged by little magazinists. In addition to turning the reader into a decadent flâneur, the magazine likens the act of reading it and of experiencing the city to sex with a prostitute. This metaphorical sexual encounter is narrated in a short prose sketch at the end of the first issue, "M'lle New York," quoted here in full:

> She is all feminine, this New York, of ours – the Helen of cities.
>
> At night when the supper candles are lurching in the sockets, and the dancing is over and done with, this sweetheart city gives you one kiss –
>
> *Dor' bien, p'tit rat!* [Sleep well, little rat!]
>
> *Bonne nuit, M'lle New York!*
>
> It is perfumed, this good-night kiss, with wines and spices, birds and truffles, and over-sea fruit, with the light incense of Bakchar tobacco, the fervor of champagne, and the exultant sweetness of chartreuse; withal something personal, feminine, perverse, wherein the cantharides of desire flicker faintly – all in this good-night kiss of M'lle New York. Oh, you know her very well at night, this laughing city, high-colored, decollete [sic], with warm flesh, rose-white and red-gold in the gaslight.
>
> Have you kissed her good-morning?
>
> She is haggard at daybreak, M'lle New York. The rouge and powder are smeared on her frowsy face; the dishevelled hair seems scant and coarse; the throat you thought so white is pallid yellow; the lips are swollen with sleep and wine. She gapes and yawns, stirring with amorous unrest. Even a woman finds one man who loves her – one whom her first kiss does not disgust; why not M'lle New York?
>
> Ho! lover of this Helen of cities. The housetops are reddening to the dawn; a sea-bred wind rides down the foul odors of street and alley; the squares are desolate, the tall haggard city crowding down on them – bleakness in the streets, gray houses and blank distances, an oppressive lack of color, save where a forgotten street-lamp sputters feebly or the electric lights shine white and wan in deserted shops. A tired cab-horse goes up Broadway, his head between his knees; the cabman drowses on the box; inside the 'fare' is asleep, with one knee on the window ledge; a cable-car passes –
>
> *Bon jour, M'lle New York!*
>
> *Eh! Saperlipopette – b'jour, petit rat!*
>
> M'lle New York is awake. You have indulged in the innocent depravity of her morning kiss. Now ring the bell and bid your man bring you a tooth-brush and a glass of water.

In its use of personification, the sketch deftly blurs boundaries. M'lle New York is at once the city, a demi-mondaine, and the magazine itself

– and the reader ("you") is implicated in a one-night stand. The small drawings accompanying this prose sketch are, in the main, not illustrations for the text. The encounter with the demi-mondaine, for example, is not represented, nor is M'lle New York in her human female guise. Instead, the drawings are suggestive of various aspects of the New York demi-monde. A pig head serves as headpiece. The pig is a recurring image in the magazine, often personified as a fat, louche, wealthy man in the company of a demi-mondaine, a representation in keeping with Western iconographic symbolism which associates the animal with greed, gluttony, and lust (see, for example, Figure 6.15 and colour plate 18). In the left margin is a sketch of three men in top hats seated around a table playing cards, with smoke clouds leading towards and framing an image of the overground with two abject figures walking the street beneath. In the right margin are two tiny silhouettes, one of an encounter between a man and a policeman, the other of a man shooting another man. An elaborate tailpiece, meanwhile, coloured grey, of a lone cab and horse on a New York street with cats scurrying about, is the only image that accords with something described in the sketch. The illustrations thus fail to depict the more risqué aspects of the text, leaving much to the reader's imagination.

This omission, however, is remedied three issues later, in a drawing by Powers ("M'lle New York Is Awake"; see colour plate 19). The full-page image in four colours depicts M'lle New York as demi-mondaine, in bed, a man with tousled hair sleeping by her side. She is reading a letter that her maid, who casts a knowing glance backwards, has just delivered. The link between this picture and the prose sketch from the earlier issue is made through the caption, which cites its closing lines: "M'lle New York is awake. You have indulged in the innocent depravity of her morning kiss. Now ring the bell and bid your man bring you a tooth-brush and a glass of water." This link connecting a prose sketch appearing in an early August issue with a picture from late September might well be lost upon any but the most attentive armchair flâneur readers of the magazine, as might the "borrowings" of illustrations from French decadent periodicals. It suggests, however, that the magazine wanted its readers to be attentive flâneurs, noting the interplay between image and text within and across issues.

M'lle New York is clearly worlds away from the visual culture of *The Chap-Book* and *Bradley His Book*, magazines that offered a modern, but comparatively genteel, representation of fin-de-siècle artistic trends in publications aligned with high literature and bibliophilic culture.

The Chap-Book and *Bradley His Book* attracted a much larger readership. Bradley, for example, claimed to have upped his production from 10,000 to 25,000 copies between the first and second issues, a figure that is strikingly higher even than *The Chap-Book*'s 16,500 ("At the End of the Book"). Their readership most certainly reached beyond a literary, artistic, and media elite to encompass those described as "educated people of taste" in *Bradley His Book*'s promotional content (front matter), a description consonant with professional-managerial class identity in this period. *M'lle New York*, by contrast, was aligned with scandalous French satirical weeklies and framed its content seemingly to address, in an American context, a more restricted audience than I have been suggesting was the norm for these little magazines. Whereas many little magazines invited a female readership, *M'lle New York* was a decidedly masculine venue, a status reinforced by its construction of a male libertine reader and its advertisements for whisky, public baths for gentlemen, false teeth, a menswear shop, a wine dealer, and Au Chat Noir, a famed Fifth Avenue and Broadway hangout for New York bohemians. Indeed, evidence suggests that this little magazine was one that was directed to a coterie readership of like-minded souls, other little magazinists, for example, as well as male journalists across the country, men like Thompson, Huneker, Powers, and Fleming, who, as George Henry Payne commented, filled scrapbooks with bits from the magazine (qtd. in Hanighen 479). Unlike a number of other little magazines, *M'lle New York* was off the radar of broader culture, barely mentioned in mainstream newspapers or periodicals. *M'lle New York*, then, if not representative, in readership terms, of the little magazine of the period, is an important instance of a coterie publication, one with a strong avant-gardist and French influence, and one that more clearly serves as a precursor to modernist little magazines than others of this period.

Of *The Chap-Book*, *Bradley His Book*, and *M'lle New York*, then, the first two are most representative of the types and style of art found in little magazines with artistic content. Of these publications, *The Chap-Book* is most indicative of the manner in which such art was presented, as few little magazines were as invested as Bradley in making their publications a work of art in themselves to such a high degree of craftsmanship. The aesthetic influence of *The Chap-Book* is most strongly felt in magazines such as *Alkahest*, *Chips*, *The Clack Book*, *Les Jeunes*, *The Lotus*, *Miss Blue Stocking*, *Muse*, and the first numbers of *The Philosopher*. Some of these, however, opted for more elaborate details – often in the way of marginal illustrations for literary content. Others that, like *Bradley His Book* and *M'lle New York*, offered significant artistic content, including fuller text illustrations, are *John-a-Dreams, The Bachelor Book, Four O' Clock, The Rubric, Blue Sky, Twilight*, and *Quartier Latin*. Most of these featured distinctive poster-style covers as well as elaborately decorated poetic content, supplied by notable contributors. *John-a-Dreams*, for example, featured a cover design by John Sloan and illustrations by a young Booth Tarkington before he achieved fame as a writer. The Chicago-based *Four O'Clock, Blue Sky*, and *Rubric*, meanwhile, contained content by graphic designers, art teachers, and students who were involved with the Chicago Art Institute and/or the other numerous art schools, studios, and printing establishments in the local area, including Frederic Goudy, W.A. Dwiggins, J.C. Leyendecker, and Carl Werntz, while *Quartier Latin* was entirely the product of art students studying in Paris. Notable artistic content appeared also in little magazines devoted entirely or almost entirely to visual and/or graphic arts, such as *Brush and Pencil, Limner, The Echo, Modern Art, Pen and Ink Sketches, The Poster*, and *Poster Lore*.

Little magazines were thus an important medium for the development of graphic and visual arts in the period. They served as a publication venue for aspiring illustrators and artists, an alternative medium for experimentation for already established professionals, and a means by which a culturally aspirational middle and professional-managerial class could become attuned to developments in the arts. Little magazine art, in its efforts to capture modernity in various ways, reflected readers' senses of their own urbanity and sophistication. Little magazines did not have a monopoly on modern artistic trends. Posters, the art nouveau style, pen and ink sketches, etc. were trends exploited in mainstream media, too. They were, in many instances, however, more experimental in these modes and had an advantage as a form of cultural capital over the mainstream for their aspirational readership in terms of how they remediated modern art forms. Self-conscious in their privileging and promotion of these modern forms, selective in their exploitation of art, and designed as collectible and choice objects in their own right, little magazines gave greater cultural value and distinction to the art they represented.

Plate 1. One of a number of differently patterned wallpapers used for the production of the trapezoidal-shaped *Le Petit Journal des Refusées*. In possession of author.

Plate 2. A selection of American little magazines of the 1890s in chap-book format. In possession of author.

I

Wake! For the Sun behind yon Eastern height
Has chased the Session of the Stars from Night,
And, to the field of Heav'n ascending, strikes
The Sultán's Turret with a Shaft of Light.

II

Before the phantom of False morning died,
Methought a Voice within the Tavern cried,
"When all the Temple is prepared within,
"Why lags the drowsy Worshipper outside?"

III

And, as the Cock crew, those who stood before
The Tavern shouted—"Open then the Door!
"You know how little while we have to stay,
"And, once departed, may return no more."

IV

Now the New Year reviving old Desires,
The thoughtful Soul to Solitude retires,
Where the White Hand of Moses on the Bough
Puts out, and Jesus from the ground suspires.

V

Iram indeed is gone with all his Rose,
And Jamshýd's Sev'n-ring'd Cup where no one knows;
But still a Ruby gushes from the Vine,
And many a Garden by the Water blows.

Plate 3. Page from the Philosopher Press *Rubaiyat of Omar Khayaam* (1901), one of one hundred copies hand-printed and hand-illuminated by Helen Bruneau Van Vechten. Courtesy of Special Collections, University of Wisconsin-Milwaukee Libraries.

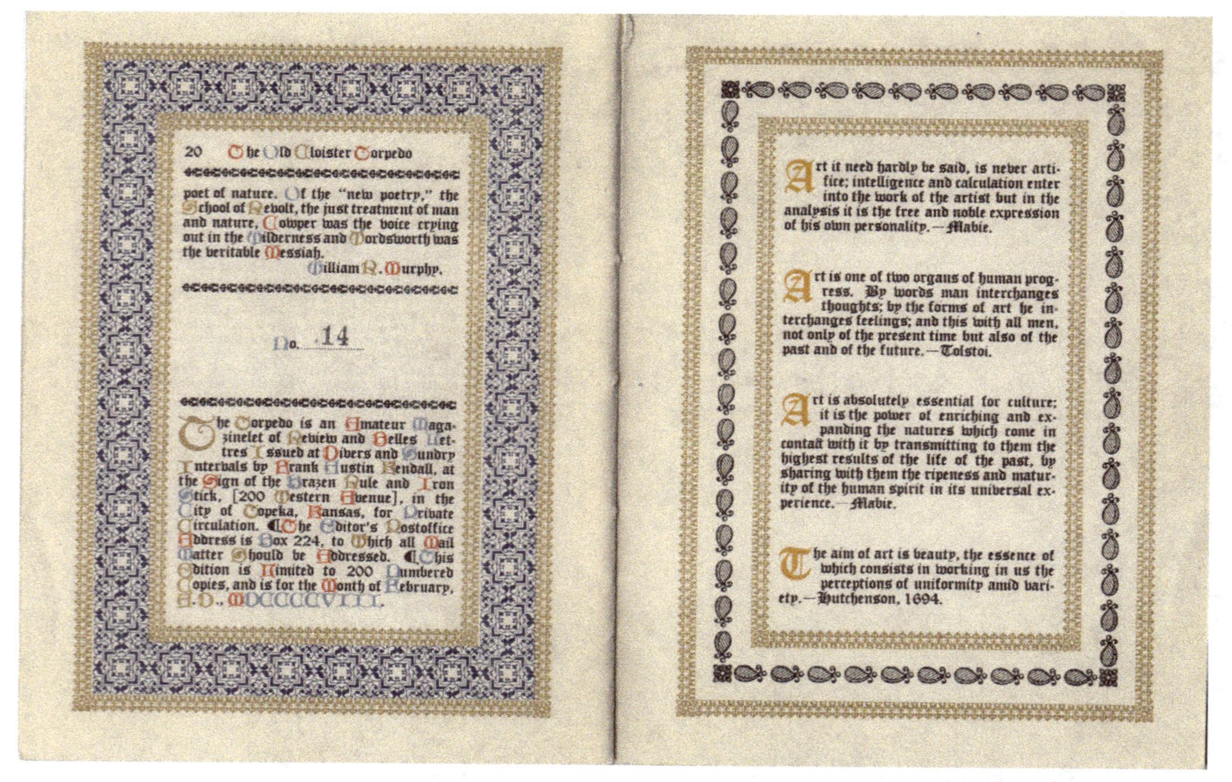

20 The Old Cloister Torpedo

poet of nature. Of the "new poetry," the School of Revolt, the just treatment of man and nature, Cowper was the voice crying out in the Wilderness and Wordsworth was the veritable Messiah.

William R. Murphy.

No. 14

The Torpedo is an Amateur Magazinelet of Review and Belles Lettres Issued at Divers and Sundry Intervals by Frank Austin Kendall, at the Sign of the Brazen Rule and Iron Stick, [200 Western Avenue], in the City of Topeka, Kansas, for Private Circulation. ¶The Editor's Postoffice Address is Box 224, to Which all Mail Matter Should be Addressed. ¶This Edition is Limited to 200 Numbered Copies, and is for the Month of February, A.D., MDCCCCVIII.

Art it need hardly be said, is never artifice; intelligence and calculation enter into the work of the artist but in the analysis it is the free and noble expression of his own personality.—Mabie.

Art is one of two organs of human progress. By words man interchanges thoughts; by the forms of art he interchanges feelings; and this with all men, not only of the present time but also of the past and of the future.—Tolstoi.

Art is absolutely essential for culture; it is the power of enriching and expanding the natures which come in contact with it by transmitting to them the highest results of the life of the past, by sharing with them the ripeness and maturity of the human spirit in its universal experience.—Mabie.

The aim of art is beauty, the essence of which consists in working in us the perceptions of uniformity amid variety.—Hutchenson, 1694.

Plate 4. Pages from the rubricated cloister edition of *The Torpedo* (February 1907). In possession of author.

Plate 5. *Clique*, May 1896. In possession of author.

Plate 6. Jules Chéret. "Papier à Cigarettes Job." Paris: Chaix, 1895. Lithograph in three colours. Art & Architecture Collection, Miriam and Ira D. Wallach Division of Art, Prints and Photographs, New York Public Library. New York Public Library Digital Collections.

Plate 7. Poster by leading American poster artist Edward Penfield. "*Harper's* June." New York: Harpers, 1899. Lithograph. Art & Architecture Collection, Miriam and Ira D. Wallach Division of Art, Prints and Photographs, New York Public Library. New York Public Library Digital Collections.

Plates 8–9. The poster-style cover of this issue of *The Echo* (plate 8) and an actual advertising poster for *The Clack Book* (plate 9) demonstrate the interrelationship between little magazines and art posters. Plate 8: *The Echo*, 15 May 1895. Cover by Will Bradley. In possession of author. Plate 9: Robert Leicester Wagner. "*The Clack Book*, July." [Lansing, MI: Wells and Hudson, 1896]. Colour lithograph. Courtesy of Library of Congress Prints and Photographs Division.

THE
CLACK BOOK
JULY

Plate 10. Quaker Oats poster-style advertisement in three colours in *The Clack Book*, December 1896. In possession of author.

Plate 11. *The Bibelot* in the various bindings offered by Mosher. From left to right: library binding; standard binding; levant leather bindings; and Japan vellum edition. Courtesy of the Bishop Collection of Thomas Bird Mosher & The Mosher Press.

Plate 12. A selection of poster-style little magazines that featured changing monthly covers. In possession of author.

Plate 13. Frank Hazenplug. "The Black Lady." Chicago: Stone and Kimball, 1896. Art & Architecture Collection, Miriam and Ira D. Wallach Division of Art, Prints and Photographs. New York Public Library, Astor, Lenox and Tilden Foundations.

Plate 14. Will Bradley. "May." Chicago: Stone and Kimball. Art & Architecture Collection, Miriam and Ira D. Wallach Division of Art, Prints and Photographs. New York Public Library. New York Public Library Digital Collections.

Plate 15. Will Bradley, "A Ballade of Baldness," advertisement for Ayer's Vigor in two colours. *Bradley His Book*, June 1896. Courtesy of The Harry Ransom Center, University of Texas at Austin.

Plate 16. *Le Rire*, 23 May 1896, with colour cover by Lucien Métivet. An example of the kinds of French satirical weeklies that inspired some American little magazinists. Courtesy of University of Minnesota Libraries, Twin Cities, Special Collections.

Plate 17. Thomas Powers cover for the first issue of *M'lle New York* (August 1895), setting the voyeuristic tone of the magazine. In possession of author.

Plate 18. Thomas Fleming poster for "*M'lle New York*: The New Fortnightly," featuring the recurring capitalist pig and demi-mondaine figures. In possession of author.

Plate 19. Thomas Powers, "M'lle New York is Awake," in *M'lle New York*, last fortnight in September, 1895. In possession of author.

CHAPTER 7

Literary Criticism and Editorials: "Every Dog Having His Day in Journalism"

The pontifical tone in criticism is only allowed to the small magazines of *les jeunes* and to Mr. G. Bernard Shaw.

– "Notes," *Chap-Book* 5, no. 3, 138 (1896)

The young editor [of *The Chap-Book*] kept his "Notes" restrained to narrow limits, and at first avoided that truculent cynicism which made these little publications as arrant fighters as so many bantam cocks, belaboring one another after a fashion which very soon grew tedious to the reader ... In literature people prefer to eliminate fault-finding. They are interested in what they like and wish to have their liking increased and intensified and made intelligent by the illumination of judicious criticism. They do not want to read about what they do not care for, and a penman must be mighty clever who can keep us amused by discussing subjects which are ridiculous or contemptible, however apt he finds them for whetting his wit. It is comparatively easy to be smart by way of being satirical, caustic or morose. It is easy to weep with them that weep. But it takes a real clever fellow to be good-natured and bright, just as to laugh with them that laugh requires true sympathy and good taste.

– *Boston Transcript* (1898)

While little magazines would become identified in the public mind with particular trends in fiction, poetry, and art, voice, alongside format and aesthetic appearance, was a crucial element of "little magazineness." Little magazines were associated with a particularly boisterous editorial and critical style. The two quotations above recall little magazinist

Kenneth Brown's concerns, discussed in chapter 2, about establishing editorial identity: his quandary over whether to adopt an "editorial We," "omniscient I," or "little i" style of discourse (14). Like Brown, the *Chap-Book* editor identifies the little magazine with a different kind of authoritative voice. What Brown describes as the "omniscient I," the editor of *The Chap-Book* deems "pontifical," a style that is clearly objectionable to the *Boston Transcript* commentator.

The dilemma registered by Brown, the *Chap-Book* editor, and the *Boston Transcript* journalist was a real one, not only for little magazinists, but in the broader periodical field as well, where, coinciding with the rise of the mass-market magazine, there was a drive to forge new styles of criticism and journalism. The competing ideas about editorial identity expressed here are linked to changes in literary, social, cultural, and political values and had repercussions for critical writing. This chapter and the next develop the topic of little magazine identity initiated in chapter 2, showing how the notions of individuality and personality suggested in these publications' materiality and paratextual elements were borne out in critical and editorial content. While this chapter focuses on the content and style of literary and belletristic criticism and commentary, and deals, as a consequence, primarily with aesthetic little magazines, the following explores social and political editorial writing with reference to periodicals of protest and hybrid magazines. As in the discussion of poetry, these chapters focus on the most representative and influential critical and editorial voices in little magazines.

It is hardly surprising that the personal note should become an important element of criticism at a time when the magazine field was undergoing such growth. In a large, competitive, mass-market milieu, individual magazines struggled for attention. Within this field, writing about literature and literary culture and the arts was more popular than ever before (Mott, *History* 122), appealing to a growing culturally aspirational readership, but one that was increasingly resistant to being dictated to by genteel editors. Generalist literary criticism in the way of biography, history, essays of appreciation, and book reviews appeared in magazines and newspapers of all kinds: general magazines, little magazines, and those devoted specifically to criticism and book reviews, including *The Literary World* (Boston), *The Dial* (Chicago), *The Critic* (New York), and *The Bookman* (New York City). Aesthetic and hybrid little magazines generally included at least one critical or occasional essay, a book review section, and editorial commentary on literature, the arts, the book world, periodicals and newspapers, etc. The interest in literary criticism was, on the one hand, an extension of the middle-class investment in cultural development that characterized the genteel Gilded Age and would carry on into the Progressive Era with an emerging professional-managerial class. On the other hand, it reflected newer emerging trends of literary gossip and the author as celebrity, trends exploited also by mass-market magazines.

As an organ for the development of literary criticism, appreciation, and opinion, aesthetic and hybrid little magazines reflected, as in other aspects of their makeup and content, the contradictory impulses of elitism and populism and of traditional and avant-garde or modern tastes. Some little magazines were quite conventional, locating value in a classical canon of literature. Others eschewed established tradition, looking to the past to uncover neglected figures as part of a new canon-making process. Some embraced the new, the modern, the avant-garde and, occasionally, more popular forms. Many steered a middle course. They participated in discussions about literary and cultural fads and created fads. As indicated previously, the little magazine world and mainstream magazines attracted considerable commentary in an industry prone to navel-gazing. Otherwise, topics of interest in critical writing were consistent with fictional and poetic content: decadence, symbolism, aestheticism, arts and crafts, art nouveau, the poster movement, realism, historical romance, dialect and regional literature, and the major European and American proponents of these trends. Book collecting, bibliophilia, and the fine press movement were also major topics of discussion in these magazines, notably those dedicated to the interests of booklovers, such as *Book Culture*, *Ex Libris*, *Book Lover*, and *Literary Collector*. In reviewing, there was attention to the range of new fiction and poetry, which included popular successes, but also to the books of small presses and literary publishers, many of which, of course, were themselves issuers of little magazines.

The state of America's literary culture, its traditions, legacy, and future in the development of fiction, poetry, and criticism, were widely discussed in little magazines, as they were in mainstream ones. To give one example, the potential legacies of Whitman and Poe to American literature were contested: both were largely underappreciated, though their fortunes would rise in this period.[1] Little magazines and the small presses played a role here. Much of the macabre fiction in aesthetic and hybrid magazines, for example, bears witness to the influence of

Poe, as does critical appreciation of him in these magazines, while *Chap-Book* publisher Stone and Kimball's issuing of a complete works of Poe (1894–5) garnered him further attention.[2] Meanwhile, Whitman – who was, as Michael Robertson insists, "a controversial figure through the 1890s" (278) – was celebrated by little magazinists, though more so, as previously discussed, for his symbolic value as an iconoclast than for his poetry. Features on Whitman appeared, for example, in *Little Journeys*, *Papyrus*, and *Alkahest*.[3] Positive commentary, more generally, is found in *The Chap-Book*, *M'lle New York*, *The Whim*, *Time and the Hour*, *Good Cheer*, *Papyrus*, *The Philistine*, *The Ishmaelite*, as well as in socialist and reform-oriented little magazines, most notably in Whitman acolyte Horace Traubel's *Conservator*, a hybrid little magazine devoted to bringing together Whitmanian ideas with his own radical socialist agenda.[4] In terms of leading lights of the new generation of American writers, Crane and Carman were notable, but controversial, as discussed in chapter 5.

Overall, there was much debate about what constituted America's literary culture. Did it, indeed, have one? Writing in *Les Jeunes*, Beeby-Collins thought not, declaring "America is without art" (8). How should it develop, then? By following British or other European models, or by developing a native tradition? While by no means unanimous in their views, little magazinists often favoured European-based models, though American Transcendentalists served as an important touchstone for some, while newer, native schools of literature, such as "local colour" or dialect writing, were more controversial. There were cultural divides in the little magazine world, and Eastern-based magazines often favoured traditional Anglo-American high culture, while regional ones, including *Alkahest*, a proudly Southern publication, and the Nebraskan *Kiote* were likely to endorse native models.

Another topic of interest was the state of critical writing itself, a debate linked to changing ideas about the role of the editor and his/her relationship to readers. Among the central transformations in non-fiction prose writing was the demise of the lengthy review article and the type of personal essay that had served as a staple of genteel magazines of the previous generation. Writers such as George William Curtis, Richard Henry Stoddard, Charles Eliot Norton, Oliver Wendell Holmes, and James Russell Lowell were central to this tradition, one that, as Stuckey-French argues, sought to "advance an aesthetic and an ideology that were conventional, sentimental, and didactic" (15). By the 1890s, however, the shorter, snappier, journalistic style of the mass-market monthlies was transforming these genres. These magazines were blamed for the homogenization of critical discourse and for the focus on authors as celebrities, while many book reviews were criticized as being mere advertisement (Wendy Schlereth 5; Mott, *History* 121–2). Little magazines were situated between these trends, participating in larger controversies about the state of the essay and critical writing in this period.

The Chap-Book provides an excellent example of oppositions between old and new forms of critical discourse in a discussion that played out in its pages at the end of 1896, and it is probably no coincidence that it occurred just prior to the magazine's transformation into a conventional literary journal in January 1897. The debate was initiated by a provocative new-style editor (likely to have been Herbert Stone and/or Harrison Garfield Rhodes). In the "Notes" column for September 1 (*Chap-Book* 5, no. 8), he responds to *Harper's* editor Charles Dudley Warner's claim, in his August "Editor's Study" column, that American critical writing is inferior to that of France (476–80). His remarks were followed up, in subsequent issues, by letters and essay contributions on the topic by Maurice Thompson (1844–1901), famed for his local colour and nature writing, who was widely published in the mainstream press; Hamilton Wright Mabie (1846–1916), a popular writer, critic, and lecturer, who served as associate editor for *Outlook*, a mainstream weekly family paper with a religious tone; Brander Matthews (1852–1929), an influential literary critic and professor of dramatic literature at Columbia, who had affiliations with an older New York bohemian literary set; noted little magazinist Walter Blackburn Harte; and the editor, who continued to weigh in on the topic.

As it played out, the debate underscored the central issues at stake in changing ideas about the role of the critic, while exemplifying styles of critical writing. In the main, there was a measured response to the quality of American criticism. None, initially, seemed ready to ascribe blame to writers. For the editor of *The Chap-Book*, if American criticism was not as good as French, it was at least not so bad as British ("Notes," *Chap-Book* 5, no. 8, 379).[5] For Harte, Thompson, and Mabie, meanwhile, the dearth of high quality work was attributed to the lack of a market and audience for it. Similarly, there was consensus about the characteristics of good critical writing in general terms, which were expressed in different ways but might be summarized as distinctive style, seriousness of approach, and intelligence of mind. On the issue of how such qualities manifested themselves, however, distinctions between the old guard and the new are apparent. Mabie's essay valorizes literature as one of "the greater resources of life[,] ... as one of the most vital and spiritual expressions of that life," and he insists on a critical tone worthy of this status (484). For Mabie, the ideal of critical writing is embodied in Matthew Arnold, who, in style and approach, "has touched things ... lightly," but with "toughness of fibre," "persistence of purpose," and "concentration of interest and thought," resulting in a "solid symmetry" (486). Mabie's idealized and spiritualized views and rhetorical style root him in the genteel tradition of essayists that, as Stuckey-French says, revered "art that reflected upper-middle-class values, Christian morality, the classical unity of truth and beauty, and a belief in the progress of (Anglo-American) civilization" (14).

The editor of *The Chap-Book*, by contrast, has a different understanding of what constitutes distinctive style, seriousness of approach, and intelligence of mind, and how that manifests itself in expression. He identifies bad criticism with "pedantic professors" and "ignorant journalists," and associates this work with two of the key venues for literary criticism of the day ("Notes" *Chap-Book* 5, no. 11, 526): the established and revered *Dial*, which he castigates for its "frozen scholarship and congealed criticism" that can never hope to "popularize literature," and the recently established New York *Bookman*, which he declares "commonplace," "conceited," and "vulgar" ("Notes," *Chap-Book* 6, no. 2, 88). His ideal finds a middle ground between these two modes, one that maintains the high critical standard of a genteel tradition but that aims to popularize high culture. The style of criticism that can achieve those ends, he says, will be "high but not too austere," "sane but spirited," "lively and entertaining" ("Notes," *Chap-Book* 6, no. 2, 94). The larger passage in which he identifies these traits is quoted more fully below to demonstrate how his prose style models the standard of criticism he calls for, one which aims to project personality and is reminiscent of Brown's "omniscient I" or, indeed, his own "pontifical tone":

> I do not write this out of any ill-feeling toward *The Bookman*. I criticise it merely as a journal which might do a great deal of good and is doing a great deal of harm. It might be as full of sense, and liveliness, and good English as it is of crudity and dullness and pedantry. American literature is still in the making, and a large literary public has yet to be born. It is of no use to criticise every new poet by the standard of Shelley, and damn every fresh novelist because he is not a Thackeray. That is too much the

> attitude of *The Dial*; a fine attitude and capitally preserved, but of very little use to America at present. Therefore I feel a special cordiality towards *The Bookman* which is working on the right line, but in the wrong way. When it at last emerges from its morass of platitudes and priggishness and takes on the tones of a man talking to men, it will be able to do a real service to our literature. Its standard ought to be high, but not too austere; its critiques ought to be sane and spirited – they are sometimes sane even now, but never spirited, and its tone should be lively and entertaining. It will then be a useful institution. ("Notes," *Chap-Book* 6, no. 2, 94)

While the editor demonstrates earnestness and a reformist impulse in his interest in the value of responsible criticism for the development of American literature in a way that chimes with Mabie and genteel values more broadly, he forgoes the spiritualized idealization of literature. Against what might be characterized as Mabie's rather austere, if sane, criticism, a criticism ironically heralded in the pages of *The Bookman*,[6] he presents his views in the forthright, spirited, lively, and plain-speaking terms he promotes, projecting personality in a striking, indeed "pontifical," manner associated with the magazines of "*les jeunes*." Importantly, however, this discourse is distinguished from that of *The Bookman*, a popular journal also aiming to establish a new personal and intimate style, but which, by the editor's account, fails.

Even while exemplifying a new kind of critical standard through the voice of the "Notes" columnist, *The Chap-Book*'s inclusion of essayist-critics like Mabie and Thompson attests to the persistence of genteel values and to the magazine's ambivalent position within the little magazine field. While Kramer claims that the inclusion of such critics served to ensure *The Chap-Book*'s respectability in the face of comments about its decadent tendencies (Kramer 49–50), there is no doubt that these established critical voices expressed ideals that were still valued, even by young little magazinists. Certainly, the more conventional style of essay-writing exemplified by Mabie and Thompson appeared in other little magazines, notably those styling themselves as literary journals, and it is worth considering, therefore, how a conservative critical voice such as Thompson's operated in this context. In addition to his numerous contributions to *The Chap-Book*, he featured in *The Clack Book* and *Ishmaelite*, and was highly praised as a critic in *The Alkahest*.[7] Thompson, a well-respected critic, poet, and fiction writer, with roots in the Midwest and the South, was a transitional figure in many respects, bringing together the genteel and the new.

So, while he has been described as "the locus classicus of the Genteel Tradition as it developed in the Midwest" by Otis B. Wheeler (138), he is also noted for the intense and dramatic quality of his writing. This style of writing, along with his willingness to treat subject matter popular with little magazinists – Verlaine, Sappho, Poe, Whitman, Villon, and the New Woman – made him a draw for some, even while his contributions usually critique modern tastes. So, for example, in "Nuts from Perigord," a celebration of Montaigne as exemplary essayist, a writer that many little magazinists looked to as a model for how to reinvigorate the essay, he criticizes the "fin de siècle" style of essayism, calling for a "return to nature" (478). Analogies to nature recur in Thompson's work, characteristic of his approach in "The Rustic Muse," "From the Critic's Point of View," "Literary Greens," and "The Conquering Provincial," for example. In these essays, Thompson repeatedly locates genius and sophistication in the rustic or country type, whether artist or reader, writing against the urban cosmopolitanism celebrated by aesthetes, decadents, and realists as a source for inspiration. Here is a representative example from "The Rustic Muse":

> The wholesome and natural artistic bent is found best developed in the rustic genius; and when this bent has a way opened for it to the light of literary or artistic education, we see it evolve into a Shakespearean force, the power of a Burns or the haunting lines and colors of a Millet. The Poes and Villons, the urban highest types of genius, to which belong the Verlaines and the Baudelaires, invariably voice a supremely artificial conception of life and its aspirations. Their flowers are flowers of evil; their trees bear Sodom apples; their birds sing dolorous songs, and the very air they breathe has a burden of sewer poison. (147)

Like his view of nature, his view of women is traditional. His exploration of New Women types in history, for example, in "Is the New Woman New?" downplays their threat, while in another *Chap-Book* contribution, "Return of the Girl," he praises the "girl," seeing the "dame" as a sign of "decadence" (404). Finally, Thompson reveals himself to be a hater of Whitman in his *Chap-Book* essay "Walt Whitman and the Critics," again, going against the grain of little magazinists.

Overall, Thompson is representative, rather than unique, as an example of a conservative critical voice in little magazines. His genteel ideals and ambivalence about modern developments in the arts are characteristic of a style of essay that was to be found in other little magazines also, in soberer commentaries on literature and the arts, and in shorter and more concise versions of the review article. This "man of letters" approach was often associated with the bibliophilic and book collecting magazines and their belletristic interests, though it could equally be found in other aesthetic and hybrid magazines. This type of commentary tended to be contributed by professors and older, established literary men whose names lent authority and respectability to the little magazines they wrote for, including *Alkahest*, *The Optimist*, *Symposium*, *Book Culture*, *Good Cheer*, *The Rubric*, and others.

Having considered the presence of more conventional modes of criticism in the little magazine, focus now turns to the little magazine's innovations in this area. The editorial voice of *The Chap-Book* is characteristic, more broadly, of a developing rhetorical style associated with little magazines. Little magazinists, in rethinking the nature of the literary essay, and of critical commentary more generally, sought to make a virtue of brevity – in line with the privileging of short forms in the medium – and to develop a modern personal voice, one characterized by individuality, self-referentiality, idiosyncrasy, cleverness, wit, urbanity, extravagance of style, and sophistication. While more radical little magazine essayists and critics shared similar ideals, their interests manifested themselves in a series of distinctive voices, of which the *Chap-Book* editor was but one. The most significant literary critical voices of the little magazines of this era were Vance Thompson (no relation to Maurice), Walter Blackburn Harte, Michael Monahan, Percival Pollard, and John Cowley-Brown. Though these critics are largely unknown today, most were recognized as formidable voices in their day and were part of a network that included William Marion Reedy, who remains known today.[8] These little magazinists were contemptuous of the likes of Mabie and Maurice Thompson, as comments by Monahan, for example, suggest:[9]

> Mabie wears the belt as the Champion Literary Introducer of America. He is the peerless Prefacer of the American era of Culture. He has written more introductions to authors who did not need to be introduced than any man now living. His favorite authors are all dead ones, for, unlike Mr. Howells, he has no hope of an American Literature, and he has never discovered or brought out any genius save his own. ("Side Talks by the Editor," *Papyrus* 2, no. 1, 8)

Monahan's style here, discussed in more detail later in the chapter, exceeds the forthrightness of the *Chap-Book* editor, casting judgment in a tone that accords with Kenneth Brown's conception of the "omniscient I" little magazinist.

With little inspiration from their immediate context, these critics looked to the past for traditional masters of the personal essay form, admiring the conversational and intimate style of Michel de Montaigne or Charles Lamb, the urbanity of Joseph Addison and Richard Steele, the spontaneity of Thoreau, and the idiosyncratic style of Thomas Browne.[10] They also looked to contemporary models. Walter Pater, for example, was influential as an exemplar of precious style, self-referentiality, and a new brand of creative criticism, what he called "aesthetic criticism" in *The Renaissance* (xxix). At the same time, these critics owed something to the contemporary sensationalist discourse of "yellow journalism" and its reform-minded offshoot, the muckraking movement. These forms of journalism, as famous muckraker Lincoln Steffens claimed, "were finding fault with 'things as they are'" (*Autobiography* 357),[11] and would become known as the "literature of exposure" (Fuller, *Muckrakers* 10; Weinberg and Weinberg xxii). Interestingly, the most distinctive little magazine commentary on the arts was framed in these terms – as exposing corruption in, or shams of, the establishment – what the *Boston Transcript* journalist dubbed, in language similar to Steffens's, "fault-finding." Further, the rhetoric of yellow journalism influenced the style and combative nature of discourse evidenced in little magazines. The new journalism of the 1890s valued plain speaking and "editors were often vigorous partisans, often eager to trade brickbats and insults, and not disinclined to urge or suggest the suppression of their rivals" (Campbell, *Yellow Journalism* 26). This style inflected criticism but also the competitive rivalries between little magazines that played out in editorials. Many little magazinists knew this journalistic world intimately through work in the mainstream industry. In effect, these writers brought together a style of preciosity and refinement adapted from European avant-garde literature with the more vernacular style and rhetorical effects of modern American journalism. Each, however, did it in a particular way. Indeed, this distinction is what the new breed of critics praised above all in criticism – "invention, individuality, and non-conformity" (Doyle 73).

The most prolific of this new breed in the little magazine context was Walter Blackburn Harte (1867–99), a British writer who settled in America in 1890 and the most vocal proponent of the American little magazine movement. As a critic and essayist, Harte exhibits a range of influences. Pollard would represent him as heroic martyr to the cause of incisive criticism in *Their Day in Court* (1909), identifying him with masters of the personal essay – Montaigne, Lamb, and Stevenson – and with the egoistic manner of George Bernard Shaw (322–30, 405–9), whom the *Chap-Book* editor regarded, also, as a model for little magazinist rhetoric ("Notes," *Chap-Book* 5, no. 3, 138). There are traces, too, of Paterean decadence and a modern journalistic style in Harte. Overall, his writing was characterized by a discursive and hyperbolic style that juxtaposed fierce denunciation of the type displayed by the editor of *The Chap-Book* with an earnest idealism reminiscent of Mabie. Harte served as editor of two little magazines, *The Fly Leaf* and *The Lotus*, and was involved in a brief partnership with Hubbard and *The Philistine*. In addition to editorial and critical contributions to these magazines, he wrote criticism, essays, and, occasionally, fiction for his own magazines and for *The Philosopher*, *The Ishmaelite*, *Time and the Hour*, *Moods*, *Poet-Lore*, *The Criterion*, *The Literary Review*, *Red Letter*, *The Knight Errant*, and the *Anti-Philistine*. Before becoming involved with little magazines, Harte worked in mainstream journalism, where he had served as assistant editor of two magazines. One of these, *New England*, was modelled after the genteel *Atlantic*. Harte had a regular column in this magazine, "About Books," later called "In a Corner at Dodsley's," in which he discoursed on a variety of subjects in an outspoken manner. As Doyle argues, "in the midst of the staid pages of a mass-circulation family magazine," Harte managed to establish "a counter-cultural periodical even more explicitly critical of the literary establishment than the relatively genteel *Mahogany Tree* and *Knight Errant*" (52). This column, however, appeared in the advertising pages, a section often overlooked and usually removed when magazines were bound in volume form.[12] Though he was able to express radical literary views in a mainstream periodical, his column's positioning gave it a lowly and ephemeral status. The little magazine, therefore, offered a better context for Harte's work. As with other literary and artistic content, the form and aesthetic of the little magazine played an important role in contextualizing critical content. In the little magazine, Harte's essays and editorials took pride of place, occupying up to half the content pages in some issues of *The Fly Leaf* and between five and ten pages, of a total of about thirty, in *The Lotus*.

Harte himself believed that the little magazine represented the best platform for his views and devoted himself almost exclusively to the form from 1895 until his untimely death in 1899. Commenting in 1895 on the growth of the genre in the wake of *The Chap-Book*, he said, "these things interest me more than ordinary magazines. They are breaking from some of the 20 year old 'traditions' of American literature and that is important from my point of view" (qtd. in Doyle 92). In his critical writing, he comments repeatedly on the dire state of American letters and journalism; the commercialization of the publishing and magazine industries; the need for a youthful and vibrant American literary culture; the perniciousness of American anglophilia in literary matters; and the necessity of the separation of art and morality. At the same time, he lauds neglected authors, such as Whitman and American decadent poet Francis Saltus, and rails against popular writers and books. He pays considerable attention to rival publications – notably *The Chap-Book* and *The Philistine* – and devotes space to promoting the little magazine movement.

Harte's gift as a critic was to mediate between seemingly incompatible positions within debates in a provocative way. In an essay for *The Philistine*, for example, he counters attacks that were launched against controversial dramatists such as Ibsen, Maeterlinck, and Hermann Sudermann, positing them as descendants of Shakespeare, as masters of a "true imaginative literature of insight, philosophy, poetry, and analysis of character" ("Shakespeare's Borrowings" 186). Similarly, he skirts the controversy over whether American literature should develop its own traditions or follow those of Europe, promoting a middle way. This topic finds him in one of his characteristic modes – a revolutionary and messianic "omniscient I" rhetorical style:

> After the decades of perfectly sapless and hollow, unreal literature, which have extinguished all original impulse in America, a new era is dawning. It comes partly from foreign influences – the French naturalists and realists, Ibsen and the Scandinavian and modern German school, and the English so-called "decadent school" – and partly from a stirring of audacity and rebellion on the ground here, which is an indication of a deepening sense of culture in the new generation, and a growing impatience with shoddy substitutes for the true spirit of literature. ("Résumé")

His description is apt, indeed, in terms of the aims and intentions of the literary and artistic output in little magazines as well as the criticism, all of which bring together European art trends with an American vernacular and rhetorical style.

Harte himself exhibits aspects of the contemporary foreign and native impulses he speaks of – the decadence of his home country and the "audacity and rebellion" of his adopted land. With respect to Harte's decadence, Doyle situates him within the euphuistic tradition of writing in the period, originating with Pater in Britain, and influencing Harte, Pollard, Ambrose Bierce, and others in America (71–4). In so doing, Doyle draws on Linda Dowling's work, which explores the revival of euphuism in fin-de-siècle British decadence, manifesting itself in an interest in the sound and rhythm of language, ornate style, and self-referentiality (Doyle 71; Dowling 121–5, 140–4). Though the writing voices of Harte, Pollard, and Bierce undoubtedly differ from the jeweled style of Pater, and, indeed, from each other, they share these qualities. In the case of Harte, this style is evident in an 1892 essay, "Rhapsody on Music," for *The Knight Errant*:

> [The musician] gives all who care to listen the freedom of that ancient Eastern city of dreams, which exists in the mind of almost every man, and far transcends in mystery and splendour the Orient men go out in ships to see. Looking into the stolid face of your neighbour you can scarcely think it conceivable that he is floating in a garlanded barge, lying on a bed of roses, with his head in the lap of Venus, stricken with the languor of love, drunk with the singing of the Bacchantes dancing at the prow, a King of love and life – floating idly beneath an amethyst sky, on a gently rocking purple sea, broken into wreaths of pearls by splashing nymphs. (38)

Harte's employment of this jeweled, image-rich style also characterizes his 1894 collection of essays, *Meditations in Motley*, which Doyle describes as an "extensive demonstration of the Euphuistic style," with complex and lengthy structuring of sentences, extensive use of subordinate clauses, parentheses, qualifications, refinements, and modifications (75, 76). Though Harte's euphuism is much in keeping with the rhetoric of many little magazinists, it is a style he largely abandons after 1894 when he turns to little magazine work full time and sets out to establish his own distinctive editorial voice (Doyle 80). His more characteristic mode during the bulk of his time as a little magazinist is in the forceful manner of his comments on American literature quoted above.

In developing his characteristic mode, Harte draws on the vernacular in a studied and purposeful manner. In his comments on American literature for example, his use of the terms "sapless" and "shoddy" are jarring, bringing the reader out of "polite" criticism and the idealizing strain he otherwise employs and into the realm of the sensationalizing yellow journalese that was undoubtedly a component of the "audacity and rebellion" that Harte identifies as American in style ("Résumé"). Occasionally, he uses slang to this effect, as when, in defending the little magazine movement, he writes: "This is the beginning of the modern era in English letters, and we hope to see Mrs. Grundy go bang, with her whole dirty-minded entourage of plug-uglies" ("Bubble and Squeak," *Lotus* 3, no. 2, 60). His deployment of the American slang term "plug-ugly" brilliantly reinforces the assault on Grundyism and, in more complex ways, on the genteel *English* literary tradition that Harte is often sceptical of in his calls for the development of a robust American literature. For Harte, the modern era in English letters is *American* and is embodied in its little magazine movement ("Bubble and Squeak," *Lotus* 3, no. 2, 57–66; "Résumé"). Doyle is critical of Harte's reliance on "hyperbolic praise" and "vehement denunciation" in his little magazine writing (111). It was these qualities, though, along with his spirited optimism, that gave him a characteristic voice, providing relief from much of the relentlessly "fault-finding" discourse in the medium that the *Boston Transcript* journalist identified as characteristic of the little magazine.

Of these negative voices, none was more idiosyncratic than that of Vance Thompson (1863–1925), editor of *M'lle New York*, whom Harte admired for his "sheer individual mastery of English style" ("Bubble and Squeak," *Lotus* 2, no. 7, 256). Like Harte, Thompson worked in the mainstream press, serving as critic for the *New York Commercial Advertiser*, one of a handful of newspapers appreciated by men like Harte for the high quality of its criticism ("Bubble and Squeak," *Lotus* 2, no. 7, 256). He was able, also, to exercise his style of criticism in the mainstream press, but the newspaper format and the limitations it placed on subject matter were not as conducive an outlet as the little magazine and, in addition to his work for *M'lle New York*, he contributed to *The Chap-Book*, *The Philistine*, and *The Criterion*. Thompson's literary criticism, like the magazine he edited, was among the most original of the period. The critical commentary in *M'lle New York* was ahead of its time, discussing the European symbolist and decadent writers that modernists would "discover" a generation later. While many aesthetic little magazines devoted critical attention to decadence and symbolism, *M'lle New York* was more singular in its focus. In addition, it ventured well beyond the narrow range of figures explored by other little magazines and was far less British-focused. It paid no mind, for example, to Wilde or Beardsley, who were widely discussed in other little magazines. While Thompson wrote about some writers who were well-represented in competing little magazines, including Verlaine, Rimbaud, Mallarmé, and Maeterlinck, he ventured beyond these familiar ones to discuss lesser-known European symbolists and decadents, including Charles Cros, Paul Fort, Eugenio de Castro, Knut Hamsun, Edvard Munch, and Stanislaw Przybyszewski.

Thompson's rhetorical style and critical preoccupations contrast tellingly with those of his genteel and little magazine counterparts. His rhetoric exudes personality – it is Kenneth Brown's "omniscient I" writ large, messianic, like Harte, but underwritten with a harsh misanthropy, rather than idealism. This misanthropy informed his views of art and culture. Unlike his namesake, Maurice Thompson, who posited a relationship between genius and the love and appreciation of nature and the natural world, Vance Thompson, in characteristically decadent mode, located genius in the *unnatural*: in outcasts, vagabonds, intellectual outlaws, anarchs, autolatrists, and individualists. In his criticism and editorial commentary he continually denounces democracy, patriotism, and bourgeois middle-class culture in favour of autolatry, individualism, and the aristocracy of intellect. His opening editorial for *M'lle New York*, for example, is a strident invective – in full decadent *épater la bourgeoisie* mode – against the "public," that "gross aggregation of foolish individuals [that] pretends to literary taste" ("Foreword"). His aim, then, unlike some of his more democratic and reform-minded counterparts, is not to appeal to a wide audience, but to separate the wheat from the chaff: "[*M'lle New York*'s] ambition," he writes, is "to disintegrate some small portion of the public into its original component parts – the aristocracies of birth, wit, learning and art and the joyously vulgar mob" ("Foreword"). His understanding of the "mob," as elaborated in this editorial, is an idealized, albeit patronizing, notion of the public, figured after that of the days of Shakespeare and Villon, an "instinct[ual]" and "ignorant" mob that, as he says, "attained a high state of intellectual receptivity and appreciation" ("Foreword"). Thompson's mode of address, then, is aimed at reaching an audience of like-minded souls and those instinctually receptive to the values and ideals he promotes.

His attacks on bourgeois taste inflect his decadent brand of criticism, as do juxtapositions of sham popular art with the heroic work of his beloved vagabonds, as in his essay "The Art and Artists of New York":

> in art matters the public is notoriously ignorant – the commercial canvases of the Morans, Chases, Dolphs, Cranes, Beckwiths and all the other shamelessly industrious tradesmen. What chance has an artist? How can a valid, vital, work of art make its way into these pawnshops of art? American artists? There are two of them, Whistler and Sargent. What the devil should they do in this gallery? ... They are exiles without honor in their own land, even as were those artists in verse, Poe and Whitman, exiled from among their contemporaries, unregarded in the country of their birth. Art in America to succeed must be the art of Church and Chase, Longfellow and Gilder – so smug, so shoppy, so inoffensive, so absolutely commonplace, so intolerably useless that it serves the picture-framers and the book-binders.

Unlike Harte, who often accentuates the positive, Thompson is pessimistic. The best artists are always, for him, unappreciated exiles. His invocation of Poe and Whitman in this context accords with the perspectives of other little magazinists and their interest in raising the status of these writers in the American literary tradition. Thompson participates in the process in a unique way, one that posits the relationship between American and European literature differently, for example, than Harte does. Where Harte sees promise in a generation of writers that is combining the "audacity and rebellion" of young America with new avant-garde trends of Europe, Thompson understands the direction of influence in the opposite manner, locating the origins of symbolism and decadence in American literature. He declares *vers libre* "American in genesis and development" – the invention of Whitman, carried on and developed by the young American poet Francis Vielé-Griffin before being taken up by the French. Poe, meanwhile, is represented as the father of French decadence:

> To him is due the vital principle in the work of Banville and the Parnassians, Leconte de Lisle, Goncourt, d'Aurevilly, Villiers de L'Isle Adam, Huysmans, and many other illustrious men from Baudelaire to Verlaine.
>
> He gave France an artistic concern.
>
> Himself a master of the short prose tale, he made possible that greater master, de Maupassant. ("Polite Letters")

The column in which this discussion appears, "Polite Letters," was an occasional feature and, in it, Thompson was anything but polite. His exploitation of this term is a deliberate mockery of a belles-lettres rhetorical tradition. His mode of address is, indeed, personal and conversational in tone, but not in the style of the familiar essay.

Thompson's critical mode is informed by various influences. Most strikingly, his sensationalized invective, centred on exposing sham and corruption in art, can be understood as a literary critical equivalent of the "literature of exposure" in newspaper journalism. He also, however, has a poetic mode of expression, one rooted in the aestheticism of Pater, the aphoristic quality of Nietzsche, and the positivism of Hippolyte Taine. Aspects of a Nietzschean style are apparent in his short, fragmented comments on Poe, for example, but he exhibits lyricism elsewhere, as in his discussion of Mallarmé's "Faune":

> A faun in the glow of an antique afternoon saw light nymphs, loving and joyous. They fled. And the faun is sad: it was a dream, gone forever. But he understands that all things seen are merely dreams of the soul. He summons again the mad and loving phantoms. He re-creates their forms. Their hot kisses stain his lips; he would fain clasp the fairest – and again the vision vanishes. But how vain would be regret! For, when he will, he may recall the riant nymphs, phantasies of the soul.
>
> This is at once Mallarmé's philosophy and mode.
>
> Poetry is an art as complex, as subtile [*sic*] and difficult, as the art of music. For a man unlearned in the art of music to admire Beethoven is an affectation and impertinence. Why should the uninstructed person pretend to judge the equally elaborate art of poetry? It is absurd. Mallarmé wrote for the savant in this beautiful art.
>
> Here and there a precise word, premeditated, logical, necessary for the development of the motif; for the rest, syllables purely musical. ("Technique")

Here, Thompson's style combines the mood of Pater's aesthetic criticism with a Nietzschean aphoristic style. In the manner of Pater's "aesthetic criticism" in *The Renaissance* (1873), Thompson sees Mallarmé's "Faune" as an embodiment of the poet's larger world view and approach. In contrast to Pater's euphuistic style, however, experimented with by Harte, Thompson opts for the declarative aphoristic quality of Nietzsche. At the same time, his essay aims to exemplify the kind of "scientific criticism" practiced by Hippolyte Taine. As Thompson himself described Taine's method, it was one which was "dialectic, passing from the work of art to the man who produced it, from the physical man to his soul, and then to the causes of his psychological state" ("Scalpel or Branding Iron?"). Thompson, too, in the first section of the passage quoted, tries to recapture Mallarmé's psychological moment of inspiration and composition.

In *M'lle New York*, then, decadent content went hand in hand with decadent form and style, giving Thompson one of the most distinctive critical voices in the field of little magazines. It was, by some accounts, a corrupting style, as a consideration of it in *The New Bohemian* suggests: "He manducates gall sweetly, and smacks his lips in your conscience ... He is a literary bandit, and social assassin, but you have to adore his virulent sparkle. He feeds on hell and sprays his breath into your helplessness. You execrate him for it, and want him to do it more" ("Between the Covers" 225). This writer has clearly caught the bug – his analysis of Thompson echoing the essayist's own style. By contrast, Harte, as already indicated, though an admirer of Thompson's style, did worry about the "intellectual influence of this astounding audacity on the tastes of readers and the enlarging moral freedom of writers in English" ("Bubble and Squeak," *Lotus* 2, no. 7, 256). Unlike Harte, Thompson did not temper his denunciations with idealistic rhetoric, and this troubled his contemporary: "if he will only moderate some of these Venusian frenzies, what a capful of fresh air and imagination he can bring to the craft of criticism" ("Bubble and Squeak," *Lotus* 2, no. 7, 257). Ultimately, though, Thompson had one of the strongest editorial personalities in the field, and he, like the magazine he edited, was ahead of the times. His style of discourse would not manifest itself in literary criticism until the next generation, for example in H.L. Mencken, who acknowledged the influence of *M'lle New York*, and in others too. Thus, it would not be much of a stretch to compare Ezra Pound's pyrotechnic style with Thompson's.

Pound, however, seems never to have claimed an indebtedness to, or indeed knowledge of, Thompson. He did, however, have something to say about Michael Monahan (1865–1933), a key critical voice in fin-de-siècle little magazines and editor of *Papyrus*, one of the longest-running publications of its type (1903–12). Pound praised Monahan's efforts in the magazine field in an endorsement that Monahan published in *Phoenix*, a successor to *Papyrus*:

> I detest the so-called "better magazines" of America ... "Too much womanism," males of seventy in skirts, etc., and 1876 as the date of the

> beginning and end of the world. I have always been glad that you made a break away from them and started your own purely and simply because it was your own.
>
> It is an excellent thing to confront the castrated world of American "literature" (saving the word) with the fact that Villon and Rabelais, and Fielding, and the Falstaff of Shakespeare, and Turgenev and Flaubert and certain other fine things have existed and are not exterminated. (Pound, untitled commentary)

Pound's view of Monahan was consistent with that of many who recognized him as a master of what was perceived to be a dying tradition. An article on Monahan in *Current Literature*, for example, described his *Papyrus* as "a permanent need with those who still love the art of the essay" ("Michael Monahan" 347).

Though he could be forthright in the modern manner of Harte or Vance Thompson, overall his style was more traditional and more intimate than that of his counterparts. Against Thompson's adoption of an aggressive and enigmatic persona, Monahan cultivated himself as a gentleman "amateur," in a particular sense popular in this period among members of the literary avant-garde trying to distinguish themselves from the emerging highly commercialized "professional" writer. As Ann Fabian argues, "some aspiring professional writers exploited vestiges of the eighteenth-century ideal of the gentleman writer, pretending to protect a pure (and amateur) literary tradition from the inroads of hacks who pandered to the market" (408). Certainly this attitude garnered one respect in the field and, though Monahan was largely unknown in a popular sense, he was respected within the intellectual and journalistic fields of his day, counting Jack London, William Marion Reedy, James Huneker, and Richard Le Gallienne among his admirers. Indeed, Monahan was largely regarded as a descendent of the great familiar essayists, including Montaigne, Lamb, Addison, Steele, and others. Le Gallienne, a British writer associated with the aesthetic and decadent movements, said of him:

> In an age of would-be literary dandies and superior persons, one is fathomlessly grateful for his gift of writing like a real human being, for his homely preferences, for his touch of old-world scholarship, for his quoting Horace, for his occasional tavern or "coffeehouse" manner, his air of telling us everything, his Rabelaisian tang, his gossipy chuckle, his ready tear, his quips, his snatches of song – and, above all, for that gift which

gathers up these and many other engaging characteristics, the gift of a natural style. (*Michael Monahan* 5–6)

While Harte's little magazine output included some social commentary, and Vance Thompson's writings often contained explicit social critique, their work was primarily focused on literature and the arts. Monahan, by contrast, practiced criticism and essay writing as belletristic literary genres in their broadest sense. Beyond literature, Monahan dwelt on personal and commonplace topics and social mores. The magazine was driven, as he claimed in the opening manifesto, by a "hatred of Sham and Fake under whatever forms they may appear" (back matter, *Papyrus*). For Monahan, the literary and the socio-political went hand in hand, and he regarded the "true literary character" as something "which has wrought so powerfully for truth and justice, for liberty and humanity in the world" ("Side Talks," *Papyrus* 1, no. 2, 11). His views chime with Harte's ideals with respect to the importance of art for social justice, but he has more freedom, in his one-man magazine, to pursue this relationship than Harte did. *The Papyrus* was thus a hybrid and one-man little magazine with almost equal parts of aesthetic and protest content. He is considered in this chapter, rather than the next, though, because of the more general character of his protest: he was not, ultimately, as explicitly political as his hybrid magazine and periodical of protest counterparts.

As a literary critic, Monahan, like Vance Thompson, championed underappreciated and neglected literary figures, sharing with him an enthusiasm for Whitman, Poe, and Maupassant. Where Thompson, however, steers clear of British decadence, Monahan defends artists like Wilde and Beardsley against charges of immorality. Other literary favourites are Heinrich Heine, Ernest Renan, and Charles Lamb. Monahan is also a key proponent of Irish writers and the Celtic Revival. While *Papyrus* stands out as a vehicle for his own voice, it featured notable outside contributors and reprint material that reflected his passions, including work by André Gide, Maxim Gorky, George Bernard Shaw, Jack London, Théophile Gautier, Alphonse Daudet, Anatole France, and Charles Baudelaire. While more conservative in its content than *M'lle New York*, *Papyrus* reflects well the tastes of the literary avant-garde in the first part of the twentieth century, as well as of those who regarded themselves as intellectuals. Monahan's readers, as indicated previously, included a range of high-profile professional men.

As a social critic, Monahan's favourite topics are America's obsession with European aristocracy, scandals involving prominent men and women, and the exploitation of the poor by the rich. Monahan is socialistic in this thinking and broad-minded in his religious views. On a personal level, Monahan provides glimpses into his life with commentary on his family, the places he lives in, his friends and acquaintances, and, much more so than other little magazines, his readers, featuring feedback from them and engagement with their views.

Though Harte and Vance Thompson had conversational aspects to their writing, Monahan exploits this style in more versatile ways. The criticism, familiar essays, and occasional poetry he contributes to his magazine range across literary, social, personal, and contemporary topics and represent a variety of moods – sometimes tender and sentimental, sometimes caustic, sometimes measured and critical – often occasioned or prompted by a personal anecdote or topical event. An overview of the first issue of the magazine is suggestive of his range. Monahan provides all but three items in this issue (poems by Edwin Markham and John Jerome Rooney and a Mr. Dooley sketch by F.P. Dunne). Most of it is taken up by his "Side Talks by the Editor" section, a normal occurrence in the magazine. In this issue, "Side Talks" includes ten short essays and a poem, content ranging in length from one to three pages. Other Monahan-authored content takes the form of a longer literary essay on Heine, a satirical fable in the style of humorist George Ade, and untitled miscellaneous literary notes, aphorisms, and snippets of commentary.

The first "Side Talk" is "A Modest Reason for Publishing," the kind of editorial piece that takes the reader into the little magazine world in the manner described in chapter 2. Monahan's tone here, unlike the more characteristic whimsical manner of other little magazinists, is heartfelt, sentimental, and highly intimate. He describes the magazine as "the darling first-born of my hope, which I now expose with fear and trembling to the cold world's charity," and he entreats the reader, whom he calls "kind reader," and "dear friend," in impassioned terms:

> Dear Friend, into your eyes I may never look, your bodily presence I may never feel, the sound of your voice I may never hear: yet I need you for the long way. And the day may come when some words of mine shall lighten the journey for you. Our most precious obligations, are they not to those whom we have never seen? Our dearest intimacies, are they not

of the mind? Our most loyal and helpful friends, are they not of the spirit? ("Side Talks" *Papyrus* 1, no. 1, 2)

In this address to the reader, Monahan invokes intimacy in a romantic sense, providing a highly personal glimpse into his character, one that emphasizes his vulnerability. Other pieces in the "Side Talks" for this issue reveal more about his life and character. "In the Country," for example, is a short reflective sketch celebrating his rural domestic life in Mount Vernon as an escape from the city. Its sentimental celebration of "Nature" as the "great worker and creator" and "Health" as the "first Muse" bears something in common with Maurice Thompson's views ("Side Talks" *Papyrus* 1, no. 1, 14–15). The piece immediately following, however, shifts tone, providing a humorous and sceptical perspective about the inhabitants of Mount Vernon and their obsession with clubs and societies. He abandons lyrical sentimentalism for plain-speaking colloquialisms, complaining, for example, about the "highfalutin' folderol" of club and society rituals (16). Further personal insight in a humorous vein is provided outside the "Side Talks" content. His "Patron of Arts and Letters," though framed as a fable about the hypocrisy of wealthy so-called patrons of the arts, invites the reader to regard it as autobiographical in its use of first-person narration and its focus on a man founding a little magazine (38).

The sceptical note of some of this personal content takes fuller force in other of the "Side Talks" in which Monahan engages in topical social commentary with a view to exposing sham, hypocrisy, corruption, and cultural decadence. "The Society of Reproach" begins with a variation on the proverb, "Whom the Gods would destroy, they first make mad," rendered as "What the gods wish to do away with they first make ridiculous" ("Side Talks," *Papyrus* 1, no. 1, 3). The short essay addresses one of his favourite topics – America's obsession with European aristocracy – launching a tirade against American women title-hunters. This tone carries forward into another attack, this time on New York café culture, in "The Café Bacillus," where his style resembles Vance Thompson's in its depiction of bacchic revelry: "Here the steams of incense arise to the twin divinities of Booze and the Flesh. Here the Belly-God is worshipped in all his glory. Here the riotous appetites are stimulated to their utmost, and flagging sensuality is coaxed by every kind of aphrodisiac" ("Side Talks," *Papyrus* 1, no. 1, 10). Another social topic is covered in "The Dependent Old," a plea that Andrew Carnegie take up a new form of philanthropy to help "the dependent old to help themselves" ("Side Talks," *Papyrus* 1, no. 1, 19). Though the tone of the piece is light and playful, its underlying critique is of an "industrial system" that treats the old as redundant. His approach to this topic is in keeping with his broader socialistic concerns about the exploitation and mistreatment of the weak by those in power. These interests are implicit in another "Side Talk" in the issue that treats the reception of Mark Twain's highly publicized attack on Christian Science and Mary Baker Eddy (17–18). Monahan takes a bemused view of the situation, using it as an opportunity to expose how the defence of Christian Science against Twain's attack by some critics is based on the fact that its adherents are prosperous and respectable. Such a defence serves, for him, as further proof America's thralldom to money and the moneyed classes.

Monahan's "Side Talks" in this issue also cover lighter content, addressing topics of currency in the literary world and periodical press. "The Passing Literary Show" castigates the literary marketplace (11–12), reminding readers of the ephemerality of much that is deemed immortal in this realm, while a poetic contribution to "Side Talks," "Ballade of Many Authors" (20–1), continues in this vein, advising writers not to waste their lives aspiring to elusive immortality. "As to Authors and Their Looks" (6–8), meanwhile, is equally irreverent about the celebrity culture around authorship, as Monahan comments on the general plainness of authors' appearances as evidenced in an illustrated catalogue of photographs. A more positive account of the current literary scene is represented outside the "Side Talks" material in "Edwin Markham: A Thumbnail Sketch." By Monahan's account, Markham serves as an exception to his general view of the "genus poetarum" as plain in appearance (27). Markham is a poet who "looks the part – the deep eye that denotes poetic power, the Jovian head, the godlike port" (28). Monahan has high praise for Markham, but is critical of his politicized poetry:

> Perhaps it is unfortunate that Mr. Markham should be so generally hailed as the laureate of the new socialism – I do not find it easy to imagine Apollo tuning his lyre to the praises of the trade-unions. There are truer, finer things in his poetry than the philippics which he hurls at the frowning brow of Capital. His minor strains – tender little songs of his heart and home – to my mind better attest [to] his poetical inspiration. (28)

His reservations about poetry's use for political purposes suggest that his conception of how literature serves truth, justice, liberty, and humanity was abstract and idealistic rather than pragmatic, as it would be for his more politicized fellow little magazinists.

If Monahan objects to making poetry political, he has high praise for the polemical journalism of William Cowper Brann, which, in his "Side Talk," "Note Upon Brann The Iconoclast," he claims was "something very like literature" (13). Brann, assassinated in 1898, and his magazine, *The Iconoclast*, were important models for little magazinists with interests in social protest and in exposing sham and fraud. Monahan's praise of Brann's style, therefore, is significant, a style he describes as "fantastical, exaggerative … grotesque … [like] a whip of scorpions" (13). His account of Brann as social outcast and martyr – "victim to a barbarous civilization" – recalls Vance Thompson's treatment of his iconoclastic heroes, while his encomiastic praise approaches Harte in its idealism: "there was no silken dalliance in his flagellation of sham and fraud, of crime and rascality. What we surely know is, that he was an honest man, with a heart aflame against every species of wrong and injustice; that he was a prophet of God, too, and sealed his mission with his blood; and that he died in the sacred cause of Truth, which has not in our day required a costlier sacrifice" (13, 14).

In another rhetorical mode, Monahan offers the longest literary piece in the issue, a fanciful creative essay, "Heine," an appreciation of the German writer that segues into a review of a recent translation of his works.[13] The essay takes the most intimate of forms, addressed as though to a lover, identified as "Madame." It moves from a personal account of the essayist's own feeble attempts at love poetry to praise Heine in Monahan's characteristic hyperbolic and reverential manner, before indulging in a reverie that takes the form of an allegorical fable about a worshipper of Love. Though Monahan continually positions himself as Heine's inferior, the essay's jeweled, intimate style serves as a form of seduction. Indeed, this is precisely the effect it would have on Alexander Harvey, editor of *The Bang*, a little magazine of the later modernist period. In a tribute to the essay published in 1916, Harvey argues that Monahan "conveys the perfect impression of being on his knees before" Madame (5). This image leads Harvey to his own reverie, of a jealous husband returning, ready to attack the lover, before succumbing himself, "charmed by the style of a master" (5). "Here is the kind of effect," he concludes, "over which [Monahan] triumphs like a witch riding a storm" (5). Harvey's comments indicate Monahan's success in conveying intimacy in his rhetorical style, while exemplifying what might be understood as the logical extension of Wilde's decadent conception of aesthetic criticism in "The Critic as Artist," that "the work of art is simply a suggestion" for the critic "for a new work of his own" (159). For Harvey, Monahan's aesthetic criticism has, in turn, engendered an imaginative critical response on the part of the reader.

Monahan, then, was one of the most versatile of critical voices in little magazines, covering literary and social topics while encompassing a range of rhetorical styles from "omniscient" to "small i." He was able to wax lyrical, sentimental, intimate in a friendly or romantic sense, hyperbolic, vehement, dogmatic, satirical, lightly humorous, and so on. While the editor of *The Chap-Book*, Harte, and Vance Thompson serve best to exemplify prominent and influential voices within the little magazine realm, Monahan is, in some respects, more representative. His versatility serves as an indication of the variety of voices and styles exhibited across a range of aesthetic periodicals, hybrid magazines, and periodicals of protest. His reach, however, would not come close to that of his one-time friend Elbert Hubbard, whose major influence on the development of social and political commentary in little magazines is the focus of the next chapter.

CHAPTER 8

Social and Political Commentary: "Finding Fault with Things as They Are"

The magazine of individual opinion seems to be born of impulse and becomes the sport of opportunity, and so they come and go almost in droves … Pamphleteering is the hope of literature to-day. If anything of the true spirit of literature shall be able to survive the period of the perfecting press, it will be because these scattered and wandering wayside knights preserve here and there some thoughts of the spirit.

– William Ellis, "The Book Corner" *Philosopher* 13, no. 5, 154 (1903)

If the exposure of corruption, hypocrisy, and sham was a considerable part of the literary and artistic discourse of little magazines, it was even more so in content that was focused on social and political reform. In this context, the influence of yellow journalism and muckraking was more explicit, as periodicals of protest and hybrid magazines covered the same topics that preoccupied the sensationalist and reformist press at the height of the muckraking period. This press was engaged in "finding fault," in Steffens's terms, "with 'things as they are'" (357), notably corruption within business, political, and religious spheres. While Monahan's preoccupations provide some sense of the kinds of social issues hybrid magazines and periodicals of protest took up, they are only the tip of the iceberg, as his magazine was less overtly political than many. In broader terms, the social and political topics engaged with in these magazines were trusts and monopolies; labour disputes and unionism; child labour; socialism and anarchism; charitable institutions; Cuba, the Philippines, and the Boer

War; the established church and its leaders; Mormonism; Christian Science; saloons; the food and drug industry; and the major politicians and robber barons of the day, including Theodore Roosevelt, William McKinley, Grover Cleveland, J.P. Morgan, Andrew Carnegie, John D. Rockefeller, and others.

The social and political interests of periodicals of protest and hybrid magazines also extended beyond such headline topics to the fringes of American cultural life of the period, exploring the byways of alternative religious and lifestyle movements and figures, either to expose them as shams or endorse them as a panacea for the ills of modern-day life. These included free thought; New Thought; Zionism; Christian socialism; atheism; Universalism; Theosophy; Kabbalah; arts and crafts colonies, communal living, cooperatives, and the single tax movement; dietetic practices such as Ralstonism and the Salisbury treatment; alternative medical therapies and treatments; etc. Finally, commentary might take a more general form, covering social morality and hypocrisy, personal ethics, and self-help themes. Social and political commentary in little magazines appeared in the way of editorials, personal and formal essays, journalistic articles, reviews of topical non-fiction books, and reports on or reprinting of speeches and sermons.

In this commentary, truth and honesty were often foregrounded in the discourse as much as exposure, and might be referenced in titles, subtitles, mottoes, and manifestos. Notions of truth, for example, are invoked in the titles of *Pro Cingulo Veritas* (For a Girdle, Truth), the Morrisian and Ruskinian arts and crafts journal; *Truth in Boston*, an early protest-style little magazine bent on exposing corruption in local affairs; and in the subtitle of *Lucifer's Lantern*, a "Parrhesian periodical," the mission of which was to expose the corruptions of Mormonism. Patrick Sweeney's *Chat*, meanwhile, called for "honesty in everything," its focus being personal communication, notably business sermons and practical talks. Horatio Dresser's New Thought magazine, *The Higher Law*, styled itself "a truth-seeker's periodical" ([Dresser], 64). A lens on the truth was offered, also, through the Kabbalah in Naphtali Herz Imber's *Uriel*. In the first issue of the magazine, which lays out its principles, the rhetoric, with its reference to frauds, revolution, humbug, and materialism, is as much socialist as spiritual in nature:

> In the present time, when the clouds of foggy frauds are dispersed by the stormy, restless, revolutionary mind of mankind, and the rays of shining

> Truth are beginning to pierce through the misty atmosphere of humbug – at the present last hour of night's parting, when humanity's position resembles that of the man who, after a hilarious time spent in music and amusement – after the ball – laden with headache and uncomfortable feelings sits reflecting, by the dim light of the lamp-post, upon his folly and the bitter remorse of such consequences, – in the same feeling the modern son of man sits now by the dawn of a better morning, reflecting and meditating upon the orgies he indulged in in the long night of materialism; regretting the way he degraded his dignity and manhood in the low mire of earthly things. (Publishers 2)

The magazine, with its kabbalistic teachings, is presented as a "message of true consolation" for "every class of people, without any distinction of denomination" (Publishers 2).

Other little magazinists were focused on more practical methods of piercing through the humbug, offering what they presented as sensible and non-partisan perspectives on the chaos of modern life. *A Stuffed Club for Everybody*, which sought to popularize medical knowledge, mediated between the extremes of the "drug therapeutist" and the "mental therapeutist," its motto declaring, "Truth lies between and requires a stuffed club to beat back the vandals." *The Gauntlet*, meanwhile, which styled itself "a magazine for the honest," set out "to favor the honest and pillory the dishonest" and professed to be "republican in principle but … serv[ing] neither the allied villainies of wealth nor the associated proletariate [*sic*] … [It] will favor no religion, but will oppose none; though [it] may challenge the acts of individuals offending in the name of religion" (Danziger 1–2).

The emphasis on truth had an influence on the major forms and styles of social and political commentary. At the same time, as in literary criticism, the personal and intimate were a key element of the discourse in I/i-centred editorials and personal essays. While this style evolved, in a literary critical context, in relation to genteel editorial traditions and to the new methods of mass-market magazines, its development in social and political commentary owes much to journalistic trends of the period. In this realm, too, the "personal" had resonance, notably in "personal journalism," "in which the editor's voice, experience, intellect and opinion infused the newspaper with singular character and personality" (Campbell, *Year* 23–4). This style of journalism, popularized in the mid-nineteenth century in America, was, according to W. Joseph Campbell, dying out in newspapers by the 1890s: "The intimacy of 'personal journalism' was untenable and even implausible as newspapers of the late nineteenth century inexorably grew into capital-intensive big businesses sustained increasingly by advertising revenues" (*Year* 24). Personal journalism was certainly not dead, however. Publications like Brann's *Iconoclast* (under Brann's editorship 1891, 1895–8), *Kate Field's Washington* (1890–5), *The Mirror* (under William Marion Reedy's editorship, 1893–1920), and John Gaylord Wilshire's *Challenge* and *Wilshire's* magazine, were all led by charismatic and outspoken figures and constitute notable examples of personal journalism of the 1890s. At the same time, various forms of yellow journalism and muckraking rejected neutrality, foregrounding the subjective and personal views of particular journalists. Their exposés often appeared, not in newspapers, but in the new mass-market monthlies that served as a vehicle for personal journalism as well as personal criticism. Personal journalism also found its place in little magazines.

While little magazines have not been considered within the history of yellow journalism and muckraking, the periodicals of protest and hybrid magazines within the genre are undoubtedly part of this development in their critique and exposure of corruption, their urging for reform, and their adoption of a personal, straightforward, plain-speaking style of rhetoric. Further, though little magazines did not generally break news, they did offer the perspectives of their outspoken editors and contributors on topical social and political issues and controversies. In this respect, these periodicals of protest functioned as "personal journalism," or what *Philosopher* editor William Ellis would call a "magazine of individual opinion," a form of "pamphleteering" by charismatic and idiosyncratic editors that flourished in the context of an emerging culture of personality ("Book Corner" 154). Little magazines in this period represented a new genre in which this kind of journalism thrived.

Social and political commentary and personal journalism manifested themselves in different ways across the range of little magazines that included such content. Magazines associated with reform, socialism, and Christian socialism contained general reportage and informational content, alongside various forms of personal journalism, including editorials, essays, and commentary providing personal and partisan perspectives on the news, current events, and on key political issues of the day at home and abroad. Magazines such as *Wilshire's*, *The Comrade*, and *The New Time* featured longer and more in-depth coverage of topics than was typical of most little magazines, and their larger and longer formats suited this purpose. Some even contained muckraking-style investigative journalism. *Wilshire's*, for example, serialized Jack London's study of East End London poverty in 1903, while *The New Time* undertook a series called "Suppressed News from Washington" in 1898. These magazines tended to rely less on the idiosyncratic and charismatic persona of a single editor (though, as in the case of *Wilshire's*, they may have had one) than to exploit a range of high-profile personalities to foster a sense of a collective enterprise for reform and change. And where, in more conventional periodicals of protest, emphasis was on idiosyncractic identity, reformist and socialist publications often foregrounded personality in the manner of mainstream magazines – personality as celebrity. The essays, commentaries, opinion pieces, and personal testimonials provided by these writers frequently exploited the discourse of exposure and/or truth in the interests of reform and were rendered personal in various ways. They were written in the first person, framed as letters or personal communiqués, drew on personal anecdotes, and were accompanied by photographs and/or autograph signatures of the author.

Examples from sample issues of *Wilshire's*, *The Comrade*, *Vanguard*, and *The New Time*, four of the most important reform and socialist-oriented publications, provide a sense of key figures in this realm and the topics they wanted to expose or promote. They include an impassioned attack on the Trusts, enlivened with personal anecdote by Wilshire ("Columbia's Race for Liberty"); an exposé-style report and call-to-action warning of the potential development of a grain trust written by a grain merchant and member of the Chicago Board of Trade (Greeley, "Does a Grain Trust Exist?"); a symposium representing a range of personal perspectives on the issue of direct legislation involving American and European university educators, accompanied by photographs ("Some Educators on Direct Legislation"); a perspective on the Trusts by B.O. Flower, an early figure in the muckraking movement ("Competition, Private Monopoly and Cooperation"); an account of recent Anarchist activity in Russia as communicated to the magazine by famed Russian revolutionary George Plechanoff, including photograph ("Russian Socialists and 'Terrorism'"); Julian Hawthorne's views, framed as a letter to Wilshire, on the topic of America as inherently socialist, including autograph signature and photograph ("The Soul of America"); Leo Tolstoy's discussion of modern forms of slavery ("Modern Slavery"); a propaganda piece by Wilshire promoting socialism to the working classes ("Why a Workingman Should

Be a Socialist"); Eugene Debs's Monahanesque reflection on America's thrall to royalty and wealth, prompted by a recent visit to America of Prince Henry ("Prince and Proletaire"); Edwin Markham's promotion of Christianity in socialist terms ("The Religion of Jesus"); a report on Christian socialist Herbert Bigelow's sermon on the theme of slavery as it operates in the white-collar world of business ("The Industrial Slave"); and a socialist version of the celebrity interview profile in Reverend T.H. Hagerty's contribution to *The Comrade* series, "How I Became a Socialist," including photograph and signature, "Fraternally yours."

The impassioned yet plain-speaking style of commentary represented in these periodicals, their preoccupations in terms of subject matter, and their exploitation of charismatic personalities to protest "things as they are" and to plead the causes of reform and socialism are qualities that manifest themselves in heightened form in the periodicals of protest and hybrid little magazines that are more representative of the little magazine genre – publications such as *The Ghourki*, *The Thistle*, *The Whim*, *The Philistine*, etc. In these magazines, the polyvocal nature of the reformist and socialist magazines, and the varied nature of the content, give way to the more intimate and focused setting of the one-man magazine in which one personality dominates. Journalistic and informational content is replaced by more personal genres – the editorial and the personal essay – and, while there is social and political critique, there is also a share of uplift sentiment that gives these publications a homely quality. Like the literary critics in aesthetic little magazines, commentators on social and political topics in one-man periodicals of protest were part of the move to substitute intimacy for impersonality. Readers did not go to these magazines for news: they went to them for individualized perspectives on the contemporary scene; not for journalism, but for *personal* journalism.

Of the dozens of such charismatic little magazinists, none was more influential than Elbert Hubbard. Hubbard, who, by Kenneth Brown's standards, qualifies as an "omniscient I" writ large, was certainly indebted to precursors like Brann and Field. Reedy, for example, noted the connection to Brann: "Brann was to the multitude what Elbert Hubbard afterwards became, a prophet of liberal thought; but Brann never went over to the enemy as Hubbard did, to some extent, in admiration and advocacy of the kind of success that was then hailed as representatively American" (qtd. in "New Books in Brief" 132). Hubbard was an innovator, however, in making the chap-book format a significant medium for personal journalism. This novelty, combined with his arts and crafts oriented productions in the way of books, furniture and decorative objects, helped him achieve a greater celebrity than those whose efforts preceded his own. As a consequence, it was Hubbard who inspired a host of imitators, notably, as I have argued, in the wake of the success of "A Message to Garcia," which prompted a rejuvenation of the little magazine movement, especially in the form of periodicals of protest and hybrid magazines.

The cornerstone of *The Philistine* was Hubbard's editorial column, "Heart to Heart Talks With Philistines by the Pastor of His Flock." Two terms in the title relevant to his personal style are "talks" and "pastor." We have already seen the term talk invoked by Monahan in his "Side Talks" editorial, a term borrowed, incidentally, from Hubbard, whose use of it predated Monahan's. Though a personal conversational style was key to literary criticism, the notion of "talk" is even more important to the social and political commentary in the personal journalism of Monahan, Hubbard, and others who cultivated a "talky," forthright, and plain-speaking style even more assiduously than their literary-minded peers. This talkiness relied, in particular, on mastering the informal oral quality of everyday speech. Hubbard achieves this by employing slang, vernacular expression, and, from 1898 to 1901, simplified spelling, to give his writing a folksy homespun feel. At the same time, and in a manner that distinguishes his talky quality from Monahan's, he employs a digressive style that is in keeping with the desultoriness of everyday talk. Hubbard was, indeed, a gifted orator and there was a connection between his magazine and talks he gave within the Roycroft community and, more importantly, nationally, as a major figure on the lecture circuit. Oral and written media, therefore, were of a piece for him and his talky writing style came easily. As one-time friend and rival Monahan noted, in Hubbard "the writing brain and the talking brain" worked in harmony, and his lectures (*Nemesis* 168), as one witness noted, were "in the same vein, the same style, and filled with the same sharp shafts that make the writings of 'Fra Elbertus' attractive" ("Hubbard Lectures" 2). His oratory, like his writing, was, by all accounts, unconventional, rejecting a traditional style in order to connect in a more intimate way with his audience. Reports of his lectures, for example, describe his delivery as "offhand, whimsical," "a decided relief from the average effort at oratory" ("Elbert Hubbard Lectured" 5), and praise his "conversational style" and ability to hold the attention of a "mammoth audience for two hours," with everyone in the room thinking "the speech was just for him" ("Carter

Lecture Course" 6). Though a number of witnesses found an added power in seeing the ideas that he expounded in his magazine animated by the charm of live delivery, for many, his written persona was quite as powerful and achieved similar effects. Monahan, for example, marks out for praise his ability to communicate: "The highest virtue of his style was, I think, his simple and always perfectly successful aim to share his thought with the reader" (*Nemesis* 157–8). He also lauds his controversial and forceful style:

> As a writer he permitted himself many freedoms which shocked and continue to shock the Dry-as-dust School of literary expression: but he never allowed himself to be dull ... Of his literary style he forged a perfect weapon that was now a whip of scorpions for his foes and the things he hated, and again for those who knew and understood him, a golden arrow tipped with love. (*Nemesis* 170)

Monahan, here, employs the same "whip of scorpions" analogy for Hubbard's style that he used for Brann. Tellingly, however, he alludes also to Hubbard's more multifaceted nature – his ability to write with a spirit of love also, an aspect that is often overshadowed by his reputation as a "knocker."

Monahan comments, too, in his memoir, on another feature of Hubbard's persona, the charismatic appeal, in a literal sense, that underwrote his appellation "pastor." Hubbard was not a clergyman; moreover, his agnosticism, outspoken attacks on the established church, and subject matter of his so-called pastor's talks, made his adoption of this title irreverent in the extreme, something he intended. Behind the audacity of his claim to the title of pastor, however, lies a truth about his persona and its effects. Monahan saw in Hubbard "something ... that smacked of the country parson," noting the "biblical accent of his speech and his writings" and his personal magnetism that drew both women and men to him (*Nemesis* 146, 153). Hubbard, then, was a kind of secular evangelist or, as Reedy claimed, "a prophet of liberal thought" for social, religious, and political issues of the day (qtd. in "New Books in Brief" 132). His writings in the *Philistine*, and elsewhere, often follow the structure of sermons as popularized in America in the nineteenth century, and, though Hubbard would use the secular term "talks" for his editorial section, in other writings, and for his lectures, he, and other little magazinists after him, might equally choose the term "preachment."[1] The sermon-like qualities of

Hubbard's talks include his use of an anecdote, illustration, analogy, or joke to launch into a more serious topic, one that is often intended to impart a lesson of some kind.

A sample issue of *The Philistine* at the height of its popularity and influence demonstrates the range of topics approached by Hubbard and his construction of a multifaceted editorial identity. In this April 1902 issue (14, no. 5), Hubbard's "Heart to Heart Talks with Philistines" comprise the entire content, apart from an opening doggerel quatrain. Hubbard's editorial pieces are more extended than Monahan's, digressive and seemingly desultory, though this casualness belies a clear underlying structure. The thirty-one pages of editorial content in this issue include five pieces, ranging from one page to twelve and a half pages, and half a page of sayings and aphorisms. Like Monahan, Hubbard had an interest in scandals and controversy relating to powerful figures and the two longest commentaries are in this vein. Another is representative of his religious stance, notably his opposition to creeds, while the remaining two concern social morality, one of them using a literary reference as its basis.

The lengthy leading commentary centres on John Alexander Dowie, a popular and charismatic evangelist faith healer of the day. Dowie claimed to be the third incarnation of the Biblical prophet Elijah and, like Christian Scientists, advocated for divine healing rather than the use of medicines. In 1896 Dowie established a cultish theocratic community north of Chicago called Zion City, which would become the subject of controversy in the popular press. Hubbard enters his subject in characteristic fashion – casually, indirectly, and by way of personal anecdote:

> There is a Frivolous Person on the Medill Pension Roll who occasionally refers to me and my hat in terms more or less complimentary. This Person is rude, ribald, occasionally rye-balled, often indelicate, and sometimes libelous.
>
> His latest offense is to call me the John Alex. Dowie of Erie County, New York.
>
> My attorneys are Clarence Darrow and Mary E. Miller, with A.S. Trade as Counsel. The case will come before Judge Hanecy next month. If Hanecy keeps his promises, there will be no more Line o' Type stockyards sweepings in the "Cook County Tribune"; and even if Hanecy should fail us, we have Judge Dunne in reserve. (129–30)

In this opening, Hubbard establishes intimacy through a playful style, but also through the gossipy nature of the material, which refers to an existing feud in "à clef" style. Like many other little magazinists, he draws readers into his personal world. For Hubbard, however, this peep into his life is not an end in itself but, rather, the frame for a larger, more digressive, narrative. Nevertheless, we see here how the personal journalism of Hubbard provides the same kind of challenge and mystique that Evans claims for aesthetic little magazines ("Ephemeral Bibelots" 136). These first few short paragraphs, for example, are replete with references that require a "knowing" reader, one attuned to the contemporary cultural and media scene. For a twenty-first century reader, these allusions are mostly obscure and need unpacking. Hubbard's references to Medill and the "Cook County Tribune" suggest the perpetrator of the libel might be a journalist for the *Chicago Tribune*, whose long-time editor and publisher, though deceased since 1899, was Joseph Medill. Hubbard's reference to "Line-o-Type stockyards" supports this interpretation and provides a further clue: "A Line-o-Type or Two" was the name of Bert Leston Taylor's popular *Tribune* column. Taylor had parodied *The Philistine* in his column the previous year and subsequently in little magazine format as *The Bilioustine* (see Figures 2.11 and 2.12). These clues would have been easy enough to decipher for "in-the-know" readers of the day. More familiar to the reader of today, though perhaps surprising in this context, is the reference to Clarence Darrow, who, at this point, though a successful labour lawyer and reformer, did not yet have the fame he would achieve in the twentieth century.[2] Hubbard's invocation of Darrow and Mary E. Miller, a prominent attorney and socialist, function obliquely to establish cultural authority, linking him with key figures of the progressive movement of the day.[3]

Hubbard draws the reader in, then, with an easy style and the promise of gossip and scandal. His play on "ribald" as "rye-balled" sees him skirting close to libel himself. "Rye-balled" points again, perhaps, to Taylor, who was famously anti-temperance, while Hubbard was a teetotaler. Hubbard's skillful wordplay at this point might lead the reader to expect him to launch on an evisceration of his libeller, or to defend himself against this comparison with a religious zealot; however, he takes a different tack. Certainly, for those unsympathetic to Hubbard, a comparison with Dowie might well have seemed apt. Both were charismatic leaders, preaching a gospel of one kind or another, presiding over communities that they had founded, and faring quite well financially in the bargain. Hubbard would have known this, and chooses not to engage. Instead, this anecdote serves to illustrate how the libelous comment roused his curiosity, prompting him to attend a Dowie event to see his counterpart in action.

Hubbard keeps his tongue well in cheek in this account, well enough that one unacquainted with his view of religion might be convinced that he is succumbing to the Prophet's influence. To those "in the know," however, the satire is clear:

> The psychology of it all – the lights, the music, the procession – all was perfect. I caught the feeling and let myself drift.
>
> It was like Judgment Day! There was Dowie on his throne, surrounded by his Prophets, and on the pyramid of seats behind him and on every side arose the white-robed chorus of singers – a great multitude! At a sign we bowed our heads in silence – many knelt, but we did not kneel to God, we knelt to Dowie. (133)

Even when he eventually launches into a critique of Dowie, it is restrained, not exhibiting the impulse to expose sham that is expected of Hubbard and of this mode of personal journalism more generally. For Hubbard, Dowie's creed is no worse than any other kind of organized religion in that, as he says, "it appeals to a certain type of temperament, and ministers to a certain type of man" (139). By the end of the piece, Hubbard comes back, fleetingly, to the association made by his libeller between him and Dowie: "No I am not jealous of Dowie … Neither of us encroaches on the other's preserve. Our grafts are different" (140). We see here not what Monahan calls Hubbard's "whip of scorpions," but, rather, a more subtle assertion of his power, one that manages to balance two seemingly irreconcilable identities – the "small i" and the "omniscient I." In keeping his whip of scorpions in check, in luring the reader in with his promise of scandal and gossip, in his employment of a homespun vernacular style, Hubbard exudes a folksy "small i" persona. The sly ending, however, as well as the overall premise that links Hubbard and Dowie are a reminder of his "omniscient I," his Pastor persona, and his own charismatic power, one which exists, as he insists, on quite a different plane to Dowie's.

Hubbard manages this balancing act again in his next commentary, which uses a literary anecdote about British author Walter Besant to impart a moral lesson. As Jonathan Clancy argues of Hubbard's engagement with literary culture, "his folksy patterns of speech … softened the literary references sprinkled throughout his texts, and made him seem more a man of the people than a self-referential, educated elitist" (180). This folksy style characterizes this piece, which is also presented in fairy tale mode, further subduing any hint of elitism accruing from the literary reference to Besant and his novel, *All Sorts and Conditions of Men*.

> In Lunnon, where live all sorts and conditions of men, once lived one Sir Walter Besant.
>
> Sir Walter often took a walk out through Hyde Park. At the entrance to the Park there used to crouch an old beggar woman, who held out a grimy hand and mumbled a woeful tale of a dead soldier husband and hungry mouths at home.
>
> Sir Walter always gave the woman a big copper penny as he passed.
>
> It grew into a habit. (140–1)

Hubbard's fairy tale, however, soon takes a more serious turn. More complex than a fable, his story imparts a twofold lesson as he moves into pastor mode after describing how the beggar woman turned on Besant with ingratitude. First, in the more predictable moral, he notes, "Your enemies are those you have helped the most" (143). The more important, and less obvious, lesson to be taken from the anecdote, however, follows on from this. "This sort of thing is what so often turns the milk of kindness to bonny-clabber. But if we are strong enough we would not resent it" (143). For Hubbard, it is most important not to lose the spirit of generosity, a message he ends on in a conventional preacherly mode: "God help those," he writes, "who through ignorance or folly push from them the generous hearts that might benefit and bless!" (143–4).

This style of sermonizing is quickly subverted in the next "heart to heart talk," which uses a recent changing of creeds in the Presbyterian church as a cue to attack his favourite targets, organized religion and creeds more generally: "To ask any living being to subscribe to a creed is a preposterous proposition" (145). Hubbard, instead, proposes an anti-creed, a series of "I do not believe" statements exposing hypocrisies he identifies in contemporary religious beliefs and practices. For example: "I do not believe that God ever listened to midgets and microbes who beseeched Him to take sides with them and help kill other midgets and microbes" (146–7). Though the net effect of this series of anti-creeds might seem to become sermonising and dogmatic, here, again, his vernacular mode helps to maintain a delicate balance between "small i" and "omniscient I," between man of the folk and oracular prophet. This ability was undoubtedly a key to his success, a popularity that far exceeded that of his little magazinist peers.

In the next short piece, he returns to his homelier mode, dishing out folk wisdom about the differences in character between those who have had an easy life and those who have struggled. Those who have struggled, he says, usually enter middle life gracious, serene, and uncomplaining, while those who have had it easy are bitter and fault-finding. Following this piece are a series of five Hubbardian mottoes, which precede a final long feature on Dr R.M. Bucke, a London, Ontario doctor and friend to Whitman, whose work reflected important and innovative reforms in the treatment of mental illness. This is Hubbard's most politicized piece in the issue, reformist in spirit, heralding Bucke as a hero of modern medicine. He uses the piece as a means to discuss the treatment of the mentally ill. He describes his visit to Bucke's asylum, some specific cases, and three ways in which the asylum is better than any in America. This commentary is followed by a reprint of Bucke's dedication to his deceased son from his book *Cosmic Consciousness* (1901), an account of his theory of higher mystical awareness. As well as providing, as Hubbard says, "a sort of spiritual index to [Bucke's] heart," this selection serves as evidence of Hubbard's openness to alternative spiritual ideas (156). An unforeseen addition to the piece follows, indicating that, just as the issue was going to press, Hubbard learned of Bucke's death. Hubbard eulogizes Bucke, quoting from a recent Roycroft talk in which he praises him for his "manliness," "intelligence," "honesty," "good cheer," "courage," "gentleness," "tenderness," and "sympathy" (159). This feature on Bucke demonstrates how, as Monahan says, his writing could be like a "golden arrow tipped with love" (*Nemesis* 170). The qualities Hubbard praises in Bucke are ones to which he returns repeatedly in his homages to figures he reveres. While Hubbard himself had a reputation for being the iconoclast, the anarch, or the outlaw, a type revered by Vance Thompson, among others, his own ideals for heroic types are more conventional. Despite his reputation, Hubbard himself carefully sought to construct a persona that embodied seemingly contradictory aspects – the whip of scorpions in one hand, the golden arrow tipped with love in the other; the folksy friend chatting intimately in one ear, the wise pastor sermonizing in the other.

Hubbard's complex editorial identity was designed to court controversy and he professed to welcome dissent and debate. He was proud that his magazine was "read by people who do not seem to share the editor's point of view … The magazine which makes the reader think is really doing a greater service than is the one that does the thinking for him" ("Side Talks With Philistines," *Philistine* 6, no. 4, 126). His magazine not only made people think. In its address to a middle-class fraction invested in the power of the word and an interest in self-expression through the medium of print, it provoked considerable response. The rhetorical style and content of his social and political commentary were hugely influential, as was his exploitation of the chap-book form as a venue for personal journalism. His topics served as cues for other little magazinists, who picked up on them and referenced Hubbard's views. His chatty, vernacular, and preachment styles were also imitated in protest and hybrid little magazines that emerged as part of the second wave of the little magazine phenomenon at the turn of the century. Often, these were headed by charismatic figures who styled themselves as cranks, freaks, or knockers. These included Monahan's *Papyrus*, Harold Llewellyn Swisher's *Ghourki*, Tim Thrift's *Lucky Dog*, Cresswell MacLaughlin's *Schoolmaster*, Mary D. Learned and Louise McPherson's *Pebble*, Lee Fairchild's *Thistle*, J.C. Worthington's *Homo*, Ralph Tallman's *Junk*, Ernest Crosby and Benedict Prieth's *Whim*, Albert Lane's *Erudite*, "Addison Steele's" (pseudonym of Leonard S. Levin) *Kit-Kats*, Charles Munn's *Ego*, G.A. Southworth's *The Leaven*, George Littlefield's *Ariel*, H.S. Kneedler's *Optimist*, William Ellis's *Philosopher* (in its post-1900 guise), Nixon Waterman's *Good Cheer*, Louis N. Megargee's *Seen and Heard by Megargee*; L.E. Rader's *Soundview*; and many others. Some of these little magazinists, like Hubbard, were professional orators of one kind or another. Monahan, for example, took to the lecture circuit with talks about, and readings of, authors such as Poe and Heine. Fairchild, meanwhile, gained fame as a stump speaker for Roosevelt, afterwards becoming known for his humorous lectures and dubbed the "Artemus Ward" of his day – "with the irresistible waggishness of that quaint philosopher" ("Personal" 77).

Comparisons between these magazines and *The Philistine* were legion. *The Papyrus*, for example, was declared to be "a little on *The Philistine* order, but different in that it cuts out the vulgarity" ("Side Issues" 4); *The Erudite* described by a reader as having "out-Hubbarded Elbert" ("Some Words of Goodness"); *The Leaven* "of a style somewhat like the everglorious and never too much commended Elbert Hubbard" ("Late Magazines" 24); and *Soundview* as "*The Philistine* of the Pacific" (*Soundview*, advertisement). Some of Hubbard's peers invoked the comparison themselves, including Albert Lane, who said, "I acknowledge frankly that *The Erudite* either would have been different or not at all had I grown to my present size without having seen *The Philistine*" ("Plain Tales" *Erudite* 1, no. 2, 62). Others tried to rebuff comparisons, such as Swisher of *The Ghourki*: "I have many times been accused of being an imitator of Elbert Hubbard but I am not. I admire Fra Elbertus, particularly his gall. I think he is a great man but not one-two-three compared with the Chief … He is Fra Elbertus and I am Chief of the Tribe of the Ghourki and don't have to imitate anybody" ("Harangues to the Ghourki," *Ghourki* 3, nos. 2–3, 7–8). Despite this denial, Swisher and many others clearly emulated Hubbard. His editorial column, "Harangues to the Ghourki by the Chief of the Tribe," is a humorous variation on Hubbard's "Heart to Heart Talks," while Tim Thrift's column in the *Lucky Dog*, "Heart Communion Talks," is an equally obvious borrowing.

Though Hubbard was an influence on these publications, there was ambivalence about him among his peers. His success showed what could be done in the way of personal journalism in the little magazine, and many entered the field with a view to countering or tempering his views. Most unpopular with the largely progressive-minded founders of these publications was his stance in "A Message to Garcia," a celebration of the worker who takes initiative, "works" as hard "when the boss is away" as "when he is at home," does not ask "idiotic questions, … never gets 'laid off' nor has to go on a strike for higher wages" ("Heart to Heart Talks With Grown Ups," *Philistine* 8, no. 4, 115). Hubbard's suggestion that this kind of worker was an exception, rather than the norm, riled many, especially in the context of the heated labour disputes of the period. Lane, of *The Erudite*, for example, otherwise an admirer of Hubbard, understood the essay in this way. Declaring himself one who has been "laborer and the laboree," "Jonesy and … Mr. Jones," "brother and … 'boss,'" Lane countered Hubbard's representation ("Plain Tales" *Erudite* 1, no. 3, 76). For Lane, Hubbard was writing for those "women and professional men who have no conception of business life," insofar as they have no experience of overseeing, or being overseen by others ("Plain Tales," *Erudite* 1, no. 3, 77). He sets about disabusing such readers of their notions about relations between bosses and workers. He addresses directly, also, the business owner: “Reader,” he writes,

> you sitting in your office – six clerks within call – do not lower yourself in your own estimation, and in the estimation of your trusted ones, by intimating that you find nothing but dolts, fishy-eyed dolts, to do the work you have laid out for them. Do not strain your eyes to find slipshod assistance, foolish inattention and dowdy indifference.
>
> It is much better to consider them parts of the great machine needed to run your business, and to tell them so. (“Plain Tales,” *Erudite* 1, no. 3, 83)

Hubbard’s “Garcia” would prompt a harsher and more politically charged response from Creswell McLaughlin of *The Schoolmaster*. McLaughlin’s critique, “The Thumbscrew,” puts the lie to Hubbard’s idealization of the obedient worker and criticizes the widespread practice of bosses distributing “Garcia” pamphlets to their workers in this period.[4] First, he imagines the case of a man in professional employ who loses everything when his company is merged with another and his position is abolished. The man who takes his place gives him a copy of “Garcia,” leaving the man to “lift his head, cr[y] aloud, then sink into oblivion with ‘A Message to Garcia’ clutched in his hand” (19). Second, he invokes a scenario featuring an underpaid blue collar worker – a train operator – whose stressful job with long hours means he has no time to spend with his family, let alone read “A Message to Garcia” if a copy were to be given to him. McLaughlin identifies in these men a potential “anarchist” and warns “beware of him when he is aroused. For his name is legion and the ballot is in his hand” (20).

The attention “Garcia” garnered here, and in other responses by little magazinists, aligns these publications with the interests and ideology of the middle classes – professional-managerial and business classes.[5] Indeed, Lane is attentive to distinctions among professional men, bosses, employers, and those who have had wide and varied experience in the working world. He sees professionals, for example, who have “no conception of business life,” independent as they are from the boss-worker dynamic, as particularly susceptible to Hubbard’s message. His concern here is indicative of the responsibility professionals were seen to bear in relations between capital and labour. It is as important for Lane to address this audience as it is the bosses whom he urges to take a different attitude towards employees.

McLaughlin's more politicized and graphic representation, meanwhile, raising as it does the spectre of anarchy, can be understood within the context of the considerable involvement of the professional-managerial class in reform and socialist politics of the era. The middle and professional-managerial class members of these political organizations positioned themselves to ease the considerable tensions in the labour disputes of the period, ones that, with the growth of the trusts, impacted the middle-class worker, like the one portrayed by McLaughlin, as much as the working-class one.

Hubbard's views on established religion were also controversial among his peers. William Ellis, of *The Philosopher*, objected to his treatment of the Church: "The Church has its faults, goodness knows," he quips, "but it hasn't got a butcher paper cover with a wrong quotation from scripture on it. Whatever its faults may be it can quote scripture right" ("In the Smoking Room," *Philosopher* 5, no. 6, 190). Others, quite simply, found Hubbard unpalatable, despising what they regarded as his self-promotional ways. Lee Fairchild was anxious to distinguish *The Thistle* from *The Philistine*, describing Hubbard as a pedlar of "vulgar," and "nasty" stuff to "liberal-minded folk who would rather have something rotten than something sound" (untitled 4, 5). Little magazinists like Lane, Fairchild, Ellis, Thrift of *The Lucky Dog*, and others believed that Hubbard went too far in his scathing critiques, breeding more cynicism than hope, and they responded with styles that, while still homespun and personal, were directed more towards uplift than "knock." A young Carl Sandburg characterized the difference between Hubbard and Fairchild in terms of their influence on him: "*The Thistle* inspires me toward purity, tenderness, and further good fellowship; *The Philistine* moves me to action" (17). Sandburg's admiration was shared by a core of followers in the little magazine community who, while recognizing Hubbard's flaws, credited him for his individualism. As Ernest Crosby of *The Whim* said, "he is himself and unlike anyone else and this is the greatest of virtues" ("Notes" 150). Indeed, it would be Hubbard, not any of his watered-down counterparts, who would be identified as one of six great editorial writers – those "most potent in the advocacy of human progress" – in an article by Frank Putnam in *The National* in 1906 (607). Hubbard's company in this field included Arthur Brisbane, the chief editorial writer for the Hearst newspapers and the only newspaperman in the selection; J.A. Wayland, of the socialist weekly *Appeal to Reason*; William Marion Reedy, editor of *Reedy's Mirror* and friend to many little magazinists, whom Putnam deems "the most brilliant living literary artist" (612); and Horace Traubel, long-time editor of the Whitmanophilic little magazine *The Conservator*, a "most uncompromising revolutionist" (612).

Hubbard's influence extended even to magazines with much narrower social and cultural interests that also addressed issues of relevance to an emerging professional-managerial class. By adopting the chap-book form and the quirky idiosyncratic discourse associated with Hubbard and other little magazinists, magazines that might otherwise have simply been trade, hobby, or special interest publications acquired the quality of "little magazineness," becoming aligned with the movement and with a broadly defined protest genre. Often, these more narrowly focused magazines were conducted by those who used the medium as an extension of their professional activities. While some of these types have been discussed already in chapter 1, it is worth offering a few more examples in the context of their relationship to the most characteristic styles of protest magazines.

J.H. Tilden's *Stuffed Club for Everybody*, for example, though confined primarily to medical topics, is styled so as to be positioned within the little magazine field. Tilden exploits the quirky titling associated with little magazines and labels his publication "*a magazine of protest* against superfluous surgery and use of drugs" (Stone 118), recalling Hubbard's subtitle, "a periodical of protest." He pitches his magazine to a lay audience and exploits the vernacular much in the manner of Hubbard. In the magazine, Tilden discourses, in Hubbardian fashion, on medical subjects but also on social phenomena from a medical perspective. The July 1900 issue, for example, contains an essay, "The Mob," which discusses criminality in relation to medical theories (101–15). Tilden occasionally includes poems in his magazine and he discusses other little magazinists – Hubbard and Ernest Crosby, for example.[6] Indeed, Tilden might be regarded as the doctor equivalent of Hubbard, himself an admirer of Tilden, of whom he said: "Tilden is a bigger man than he is a doctor. That is to say, he is a man first, and a physician afterward – a very human man, therefore a divine man. I would call him a Divine Healer, if the term had not been so abused, because the only hint in the universe we get of divinity is the glimpse of it we find in man and woman. To me a simple, safe, well-ballasted, healthy, direct and truthful person is divine" ("Heart to Heart Talks with Philistines," *Philistine* 25, no. 2, 60). This admiration for Tilden was shared by Frank Putnam, who, interestingly and perhaps idiosyncratically, featured him, alongside Hubbard, on his list of six great editorial writers (612).

Other examples of little magazines with narrowly focused agendas relevant to the interests of an emerging professional-managerial class include *Chat*, *Expression*, and *Corsair*. *Chat*, conducted by Patrick Sweeney, owner of the Manhattan Reporting Company, a stenography school, was dedicated loosely to business topics, addressing the aspirational interests of its readers. Modelled along Hubbardian principles, the magazine included "heart-to-heart" features, aphorisms, parables, homilies, practical advice for everyday life and work alongside poetry, quotations, and stories. S.S. Curry's *Expression*, the official organ of the School of Expression (Boston), was similarly engaged in a self-improvement agenda, along arts and crafts lines. With its focus on the spoken word, the magazine's interest was, quite literally, expression, more particularly the "reform[ation] and transform[ation]" of speaking as a means towards self-culture and universal education ([Curry] 7, 6). The little magazine influence extended, albeit in a more superficial manner, even to the realm of hobby-oriented publications, such as G.H. Walcott's *Corsair*, a chess magazine. While in substance no different from chess periodicals Walcott had previously edited and published, *The Corsair*'s pamphlet format and Walcott's framing of it with his motto – "the organ of Wally, giving him a chance to say what he has to say when there is something to be said"[7] – situate it within the realm of the little magazine by foregrounding individuality, idiosyncrasy, and self-expression. These examples, and numerous others that could be provided, demonstrate the broad influence that the little magazine as medium and concept would have for media amateurs using the form for their own professional or hobby interests.

There is much to gain in our understanding of the little magazines of this period by acknowledging these special interest protest periodicals as part of the broader movement – whether we consider them only tangentially related to the movement, or as full-fledged little magazines in their own right. Notably, we get a sense of the reach and flexibility of the genre and its importance as a signifier of difference and distinction for little magazinists and their audiences. The little magazine of this period was a genre amenable to a variety of uses across a range of professional and cultural fields of endeavour and interest. Key proponents of the genre, for example, touted its importance as "a means of personal expression" and a medium of "independent opinion and individual craftsmanship" (Burgess, *Bayside Bohemia* 19; Harte,

"Bubble and Squeak," *Lotus* 2, no. 8, 297), a factor that clearly attracted Walcott. The little magazine of this period, then, is a central form for the expression of individuality, a concept particularly important at a moment when mass culture seemed to threaten individual expression.

At the same time, this means of personal expression was capable of reaching outward. The relative cheapness of these productions and the ability to distribute them far afield was instrumental in forging networks of like-minded readers across the nation and, in some cases, beyond national borders. While mass-market magazines offered one way of imagining oneself as part of a larger class or national community, little magazines enabled various alternative and fringe movements to establish networks. It was this aspect of the little magazine that likely encouraged figures such as Tilden, Sweeney, Curry, and Walcott to experiment with the form.

While Hubbard occasionally griped about his imitators, he knew that controversy was good for his magazine, one that, with a circulation of over 100,000 by the early 1900s, was not likely to be threatened by newcomers. Moreover, this controversy, as his competitors also knew, was good for the "brand" – i.e., the periodical of protest – more broadly speaking. The dialogic aspect of little magazines, especially periodicals of protest, was central to their identity and to establishing a sense of a field, network, or community. It was as central, in many respects, as the notions of individuality and personality that constituted such an important element of "little magazineness." If little magazinists wielded the pen as sword against each other in a competitive literary field, they were united in an understanding that their publications were an antidote to the mainstream press and an important vehicle for free speech. In this spirit, William Ellis of *The Philosopher* spoke in support of "the booklet magazine," encouraging his readers to range across the field at large, even while acknowledging his disagreements with many of his competitors: "you never realize how smart you are yourself, until you get an opportunity to see how far wrong the other fellow is" ("Book Corner" 155). Talking about themselves and each other benefitted all, promoting the little magazine generally as an alternative media form. After all, as Hubbard himself would declare in one of his aphorisms, "Every knock is a boost!"[8]

CHAPTER 9

Sayings: The Short and Shorter of It

A version of the influence of Ruskin and Morris was spread by Hubbard and his followers with their crafts and their aphorisms.

– Henry May, *End of American Innocence*, 32 (1959)

In terms of how they function generally in magazines and newspapers, short forms, broadly falling under the category of "sayings," and including epigrams, aphorisms, proverbs, maxims, and quotations, are regarded as "filler." A more considered understanding of the ideological and cultural role that such forms might play for a magazine and its readers, however, belies this simplistic claim. Aphorisms, for example, have been considered, on the one hand, essays or sermons in miniature (Buechler 26–7), and, on the other, akin to poetry in their intensity (Gross viii). The same might be said of other types of sayings. In the genre of the little magazine, where smallness and concision were positive values, where short forms of all kinds were privileged, and where, it might be argued, nothing was superfluous, sayings functioned in important ways and were quintessential to the little magazine. For little magazinists such as Hubbard, brevity was indeed the soul of wit.

The small format and limited content of these publications meant that such material was not lost in a much larger sea of print as it was in the pages of newspapers and mass-market magazines. In these magazines, one or more of these short forms were often foregrounded in particular ways. Not simply filler, sayings were a key part of the front and back covers of little magazines, of editorial commentary, and were, at times, feature content in their own right. They served the broader ideological functions of little magazines, reflecting the themes, interests, and values represented in their longer content. At the same time, the use of these short forms in little magazines says much about their status, first, as self-styled oppositional publications, and, second, as representative of the values of an emerging professional-managerial class in Progressive-Era America. The different forms of sayings, then, performed cultural work in little magazines, serving as works of art in their own right and/or as prompts to readers to inquire further and reflect upon moral and ethical issues.

Scholars from a range of disciplines have been concerned with establishing clear distinctions between the various forms of sayings and with considering their social and cultural history. It is worth drawing attention to the most salient points of this critical context to frame the discussion of the function of short forms in little magazines.[1] In distinguishing between types of sayings, proverbs and maxims are understood to have a clarity and finality to them, an unarguable wisdom that establishes codes to live by. Epigrams and aphorisms, meanwhile, are complex, functioning as miniature forms of satire. In their greater complexity, these forms are identified with the educated elite, while proverbs are considered a folk form. With their didactic aims, proverbs, James Obelkevich argues, tend to be more popular at times when "earnestness and respectability" are core values, as in the Victorian era, while the epigram and aphorism are preferred modes in cultures dominated by aristocrats and/or the intellectual elite (60, 60–2). The authority of the proverb comes from its impersonality, which implies the consensus of community. Unlike proverbs, which, in their "anonymous, traditional, and authoritative" status take "no notice of what individuals in a situation may feel to be unique or personal about it" (Obelkevich 44), aphorisms and epigrams are individualistic in nature, tending to derive authority from identifiable authors. In keeping with the aphorism's association with the aristocratic, individualistic, and intellectual, it has also been characterized as a subversive genre by critics such as John Gross, J. Hillis Miller, and Gary Saul Morson.[2] As Gross argues, aphorisms are

> shafts aimed at the champions of an established viewpoint or a shallower morality. They tease and prod lazy assumptions … they warn us how insidiously our vices can pass themselves off as virtues; they harp shamelessly on the imperfections and contradictions which we would

> rather ignore. There are times when the very form of the aphorism seems to lend itself to a disenchanted view of human nature. (viii)

Those qualities that Obelkevich, Gross, Miller, and Morson identify in the aphorism – its aristocratic, individualistic, and subversive nature – can be applied equally to the prose epigram, the sophisticated and witty, though less philosophical, relation of the aphorism, a form that is best exemplified in this period by Wilde.

If proverbs regulate social behaviour and epigrams and aphorisms bring a critical perspective to received wisdom and social convention, quotations serve a more personal function. Obelkevich, who identifies the Victorian era as one of the high points in the popularity of the quotation, regards it as a middlebrow genre in this period in relation to the folk proverb and the aristocratic aphorism (61). It is, he suggests, an even more personalised form of wisdom than the aphorism, insofar as it serves as a means of "self-expression and self-realisation" for the person quoting (61, 62). To quote, he argues, is "to identify with the genius of the author and to lift oneself above the common herd" (62). Unlike the proverb, then, where authority resides in community, or the aphorism and epigram, which figure the author as authority, the quotation confers authority on both author and citer (Garber 2). Indeed, as Morson argues, the citer becomes a coauthor in the act of selection and presentation (*Words of Others* 93). These short forms, then, serve important social and cultural functions. Obelkevich's narrative of the social history of the proverb, for example, is one of decline, in which he tracks the "abandonment of the form by the educated classes" as, despite ebbs and flows in popularity, it faces challenges by short forms privileged by the elite – the epigram, the quotation, and the aphorism (45).

Though focused on the European context, Obelkevich's insights about the cultural status of aphorisms, quotations, and proverbs, alongside those of other key scholars, are suggestive for thinking about how sayings function in American little magazines of the 1890s. The social and artistic formation of little magazinists in genteel-era America shaped their understanding of the proverb, epigram, aphorism, and quotation. These genres were important to American Transcendentalists, who themselves served as inspirations for little magazinists. For Transcendentalists, aphorisms represented an "inspired" and "spontaneous" literary form (Buell, *American Transcendentalists* 422); epigrams turned the subjective voice into an oracular one, making truth out of the mood of a moment (Buell, "Transcendentalist Poets" 103); and proverbs were important as a "language of experience" (Mieder, *Proverbs Speak* 155). Quotation, too, was important to them, as their professional development involved creating a stockpile of references for use and inspiration. The Transcendentalists were, as the Zborays insist, "inveterate commonplace bookkeepers and quotation connoisseurs" ("Nineteenth Century Print Culture" 105). Quotation was more than a practical matter for Transcendentalists, though. Emerson, for example, gave careful consideration to the relationship between quotation, originality, and genius, insisting that there was an art to quotation: "We are as much informed of a writer's genius by what he selects as by what he originates. We read the quotation with his eyes, and find a new and fervent sense ... The profit of books is according to the sensibility of the reader. The profoundest thought or passion sleeps as in a mine until an equal mind and heart finds and publishes it" (102). The proverb, epigram, aphorism, and quotation, then, were tools for the "sage" writer in the American nineteenth century, a tradition that writers such as Hubbard, known sometimes as "the sage of East Aurora" (Kammen 211), and other protest magazinists saw themselves as part of.

Collecting quotations was common practice in Anglo-American culture and proliferated not only among writers who used them professionally, but also among ordinary people who recorded sayings of the good and great in commonplace books, journals, diaries, and scrapbooks as part of a middlebrow practice and form of self-culture and self-expression. The emergence of numerous anthologies of quotations in the nineteenth century commercialized this culture, while also making the process of finding them much easier. Significantly, it was in America that what has been called the first dictionary of quotations appeared, with the 1855 publication of *Bartlett's Familiar Quotations*, a book that achieved massive popularity and is still in existence.[3] At the same time, proverbs, aphorisms, and quotations had an even more material existence in American cultural life, making appearances as framed wall hangings, in decorative needlepoint work, carved into furniture or above mantelpieces and doorways in the homes of the middle class and professional people.

At the same time, aphorisms and epigrams had a more immediate, but equally influential, literary context. While proverbs had undergone a brief revival in the Anglo-American Victorian period, their popularity had declined considerably by the 1890s as the aphorism, epigram, and the "anti-proverb" (Mieder, *Proverbs: A Handbook* 28) or "perverted proverb" (Obelkevich 65) became fashionable. This form, representing a twisting, parodying, or fracturing of a proverb, arose, Obelkevich claims, as a consequence of the individualistic strain of modernism, its obsession with originality, and resistance to conventional and prescribed modes of behaviour and conduct (64–6). Characterized by a high degree of irony and cynicism, aphorisms, epigrams, and anti-proverbs were, indeed, central to the key avant-garde literary and artistic movements of the fin de siècle, notably aestheticism, decadence, and symbolism. They were exploited by Nietzsche, Baudelaire, Maeterlinck, Mallarmé, and Wilde, as well as by Stephen Crane, Vance Thompson, and other little magazinists. This style pertained, also, to the longer writings of Hubbard and of other periodical of protest and hybrid magazine editors. In short form, too, however, the epigram, aphorism, and anti-proverb functioned as a vehicle for the expression of revolt and protest in little magazines.

These forms, then, had both conventional and unconventional uses and contexts, all of which are reflected in the little magazines of the period. While aphoristic and epigrammatic elements are a feature of the longer content of aesthetic little magazines, however, they do not generally appear as privileged, independent short forms in these publications. Nor, indeed, do quotations. The showcasing of short forms is, by contrast, the norm in periodicals of protest and hybrid magazines. As an innovator of the periodical of protest form, Hubbard was a key influence on how these short forms were exploited in little magazines. He mastered these forms in their variety and, over the course of its twenty-year run, *The Philistine* was a treasure trove of quotation, epigram, and aphorism, one that would be mined for popular collections produced by the Roycroft Press.[4] Such was Hubbard's association with these forms that fellow little magazinist Thomas Wood Stevens, of *Blue Sky* fame, would refer to him as an "incarnate epigram" ("On Some American Bookmakers" 30).

Inspirational quotations of the great were central to these magazines and included bits of wisdom, short reflections, prose selections, as well as poetry and prayer. Unsurprisingly, quotations derived from figures who were also often topics of discussion in little magazines. The worthies drawn upon were sages, artists, and philosophers who were presented as central to the ethos of the magazine, and included Morris, Ruskin, Thoreau, Emerson, Carlyle, Longfellow, Whitman, Browning, Marcus Aurelius, Tennyson, Stevenson, Montaigne, Villon, Pascal, etc. These sages were popular across little magazines, generally, though some publications had particular favourites. Shakespeare and the Bible appeared frequently in *The Philistine*, for example, while *The Whim* distinguished itself through its interest in ancient Persian philosophers. The sayings of these greats frequently adorned covers and were sometimes interspersed in the pages of the magazine. As periodicals of protest generally did not adopt the changing monthly poster-style covers that their aesthetic counterparts did, changing quotations gave novelty to the issues month to month. Another way in which quotations were put to use in little magazines was as decorative content, especially in publications issued by small artistic presses. These magazines offered short poems, selections of prose, or wise sayings as supplements (see Figure 9.1) or decorative back covers (see Figures 9.2 and 9.3), employing the typographical designs and layouts of arts and crafts publications in order to showcase their presswork. This practice might be thought of as an equivalent, in the realm of the hybrid or protest magazine, of aesthetic little magazine poster art. Such periodicals rarely traded in posters, and were more likely to sell mottoes for framing. The selling of mottoes was particularly profitable for the Roycrofters, whose *Motto Book* catalogue demonstrates their range of offerings on everything from illuminated or plain paper to carvings on oak or ash half logs ([Fra Elbertus] 7, 11; see Figure 9.4).

Quotations performed ideological work for little magazines, conferring authority, for example, upon little magazines and their creators. Through quotation, little magazinists situated themselves within a tradition of their own shaping. The little magazine was an extension, in this respect, of the more private forms of commonplace book, journal, or scrapbook where quotations functioned as a means of self-realization and self-expression. The little magazine, though also a medium of self-expression, extended the self outward publicly, and, in turn, sought to shape the values of a like-minded community. Quotations helped little magazinists to express themselves in the words of others and served, for readers, as a highly individualized source of wisdom literature to draw upon in their aspirations to self-culture. Quotation, however, was not simply a means of self-authoring for an individual or a class fraction – it also functioned as a form of authoring in a more creative literary sense. While Morson considers how citers coauthor (*Words of Others* 93), they might also be said to *re-author*. Quotation, after all, is an act of remediation, where words and ideas are pulled out of one context, usually a longer work, and recontextualized, sometimes for different purposes. Little magazinists, in their remediation of

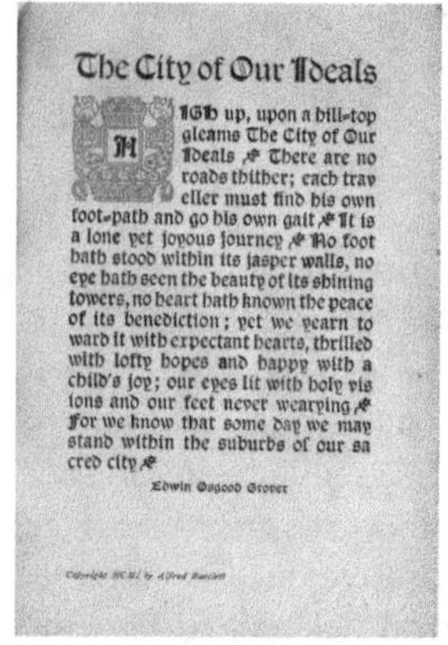

The City of Our Ideals

HIGH up, upon a hill-top gleams The City of Our Ideals ❧ There are no roads thither; each traveller must find his own foot-path and go his own gait ❧ It is a lone yet joyous journey ❧ No foot hath stood within its jasper walls, no eye hath seen the beauty of its shining towers, no heart hath known the peace of its benediction; yet we yearn toward it with expectant hearts, thrilled with lofty hopes and happy with a child's joy; our eyes lit with holy visions and our feet never wearying ❧ For we know that some day we may stand within the suburbs of our sacred city ❧

Edwin Osgood Grover

Copyright MCMI by Alfred Bartlett

Figure 9.1 Edwin Osgood Grover, "The City of Our Ideals." Cornhill Dodger, supplement to *The Cornhill Booklet*, August 1901, from a copy damaged in a fire in the Bartlett printshop. In possession of author.

Figure 9.2 Back cover mottoes in *The Philistine*, January 1900. In possession of author.

Figure 9.3 Back cover motto in *The Philistine* with Denslow cartoon, February 1906. In possession of author.

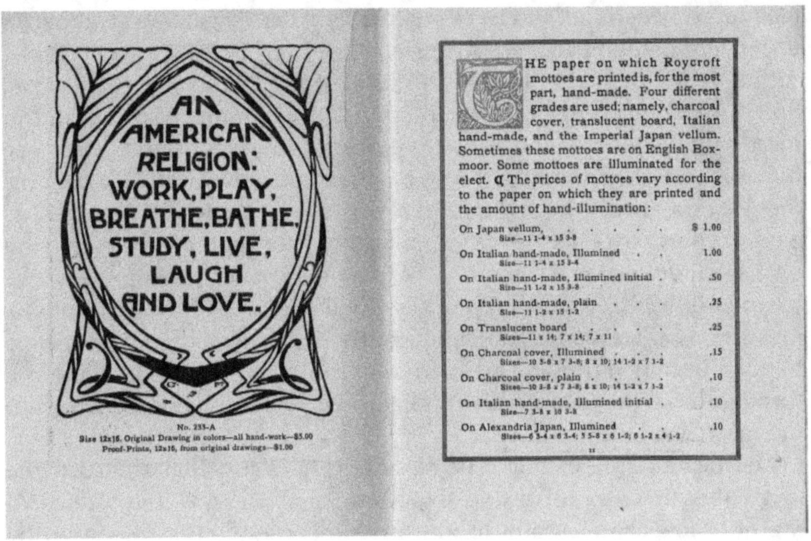

AN AMERICAN RELIGION: WORK, PLAY, BREATHE, BATHE, STUDY, LIVE, LAUGH AND LOVE.

No. 233-A

Size 12x16. Original Drawing in colors—all hand-work—$5.00

Proof-Prints, 12x16, from original drawings—$1.00

THE paper on which Roycroft mottoes are printed is, for the most part, hand-made. Four different grades are used; namely, charcoal cover, translucent board, Italian hand-made, and the Imperial Japan vellum. Sometimes these mottoes are on English Boxmoor. Some mottoes are illuminated for the elect. ¶ The prices of mottoes vary according to the paper on which they are printed and the amount of hand-illumination:

On Japan vellum, Size—11 1-4 x 15 3-8	$ 1.00
On Italian hand-made, Illumined Size—11 1-4 x 15 3-4	1.00
On Italian hand-made, Illumined initial Size—11 1-2 x 15 3-8	.50
On Italian hand-made, plain Size—11 1-2 x 15 1-2	.25
On Translucent board Sizes—11 x 14; 7 x 14; 7 x 11	.25
On Charcoal cover, Illumined Sizes—10 3-8 x 7 3-8; 8 x 10; 14 1-2 x 7 1-2	.15
On Charcoal cover, plain Sizes—10 3-8 x 7 3-8; 8 x 10; 14 1-2 x 7 1-2	.10
On Italian hand-made, Illumined initial Size—7 3-8 x 10 3-8	.10
On Alexandria Japan, Illumined Sizes—6 3-4 x 6 3-4; 5 5-8 x 8 1-2; 6 1-2 x 4 1-2	.10

11

Figure 9.4 Example of Roycroft motto as advertised in *The Motto Book* (left) and format options (right). *The Motto Book*. East Aurora: Roycrofters, 1909. In possession of author.

quotations, re-authored them in various ways. Sometimes quotations would go unattributed, for any number of reasons: perhaps a quotation was very well known, or the little magazinist thought it should be and needed no attribution; perhaps to pass as proverbial wisdom; to stand, possibly, as the thinking of the editor him- or herself; or because the little magazinist had not noted the source in collecting it. If authorship was indicated, the works from which quotations were taken were often not, making it difficult for readers to access the original source if they desired. At the same time, so-called quotations might, in fact, be paraphrases, rewordings, or abridgements, rather than direct quotations. Hubbard, meanwhile, was fond of the "kabojolism," a term he coined to mean the opposite of plagiarism, that is, attributing one's own ideas or writings to someone else ("Heart to Heart Talks with Philistines," *Philistine* 15, no. 4, 97–128). He, himself, was guilty of this with respect to Ruskin, Emerson, and Byron.[5]

The use of changing monthly quotations on covers represents an important way in which re-authoring occurred. Divorced from original contexts, the quotations that little magazinists chose took on new meanings, becoming, in effect, mottoes for the magazines. Hubbard's use of a quotation from the *Tempest*, "Here is everything advantageous to life," for the cover of the December 1899 *Philistine* is a case in point. A reference made by Antonio to the amenities of the island in the original context, its use in *The Philistine* invites the reader to see the magazine as providing "everything advantageous to life." Similarly, the use of a line by Wit from Congreve's *Way of the World* becomes, as a cover motto for October 1899, an apology for the magazine, playing on its controversial reputation: "Madame we have no animosity. We hit off a little wit now and then, but no animosity." In these instances, meaning has been changed significantly, with no change in wording. Extracting and reframing gives new meaning to the quoted phrase, turning the writings of great authors of the past into endorsements for the magazines they feature in.

Another notable example of re-authoring in a way that makes the original source an unwitting exponent of the ideals and values of the little magazine occurs in an intriguing way with a quotation by Theodore Roosevelt, adapted and designed as a motto to be displayed by two different little magazines in 1901. Roosevelt, who had just become president after the assassination of William McKinley, was a divisive figure among little magazinists. Some, for example, objected to his imperialistic and militaristic fervor, and, while he was in favour of trust-busting, a cause dear to many little magazinists, his approach was more moderate than some might have liked. Both *The Cornhill Booklet*, a bibliophilic small press aesthetic little magazine that issued "literary leaflets" called "Cornhill Dodgers," and *The Junk*, a hybrid magazine, created mottoes on the theme of "strife" drawing from an 1899 speech of Roosevelt's. His original wording was: "The law of worthy national life, like the law of worthy individual life is, after all, fundamentally, the law of strife. It may be strife military, it may be strife civic; but certain it is that only through strife, through labor and painful effort, by grim energy and by resolute courage, we move on to better things" ("Response" 266). In the mottoes produced by the little magazines, however, the phrasing becomes poetical and loses the militaristic and patriotic sentiments of the original quotation, which itself comes from a longer speech defending America's position with respect to the Philippines. Neither magazine references the longer source of the quotation or its broader context, other than identifying Roosevelt. Further, while *The Cornhill Booklet* acknowledges, though not quite accurately, alterations to the original through the use of ellipses, *The Junk* does not:

> The law of worthy life … is fundamentally the law of strife … It is only through labor and painful effort, by grim energy and resolute courage that we move on to better things. (Roosevelt, "Strife," *Cornhill Booklet*)

> The Law of worthy life is fundamentally the law of Strife. It is only through labor and painful EFFORT, by grim ENERGY and resolute COURAGE that we move on to Better Things. (Roosevelt, "Strife," *The Junk*)

Abridged and stripped of its original context, Roosevelt's words align neatly with the interests of little magazinists and their readership in self-help, especially in *The Junk* version with its full-word capitalisation of "effort," "energy," and "courage." Without much of a stretch, Roosevelt's ethos might be said to chime with the arts and crafts philosophy of Ruskin and Morris. Take, for example, one of the inclusions in a feature on Ruskin quotations that appeared in *The Craftsman* in the same month as *The Cornhill Booklet*'s Roosevelt motto: "It is only by labor that thought can be made healthy, and only by thought that labor can be made happy" (Ruskin, "Chosen from the Words of John Ruskin"). Here, Ruskin, in a phrase taken from *Stones of Venice* (source uncredited in the magazine), preaches, like Roosevelt, the virtues of labour, the two becoming unlikely allies in a common cause.

While little magazinists could, in Emerson's sense, express their genius through their selections of quotations and give them new meanings in new contexts, they were also prodigious producers of original epigrams, aphorisms, and maxims. These also appeared on the front and back covers of the magazines, interspersed with other kinds of commentary in the long editorial sections, or collected and presented as a feature content section under titles such as "Random Shots," "Philosophical Observations," "Thoughts," "Philosophisings," "Aphorisms," and so on. Like the quotations of the greats, these might be in the service of uplift or inspiration. In this respect, they were part of the larger investment of periodicals of protest and hybrid magazines in progressive and reformist causes as well as the emerging discourse of self-help. Speaking particularly of the inspirational motto both in terms of its message and as a decorative print object, Handel Zanque, of *The Junk*, reflects on its talismanic power: "Give it a place where it can be oft-times read and thereby bring to your mind how, perhaps, a bit of kindness and thoughtfulness might lift a cloud of despair and anxiety, and contribute to the surroundings that are to bring success and happiness to some good and worthy person" (5).[6] Though Zanque provides a sentimentalized account of the form, often this wisdom literature was presented in a manner more in keeping with the plain-speaking vernacular style of critical writing in these magazines. Indeed, maxims, epigrams, and aphorisms often appeared as part of the long editorial-style sections, such as Hubbard's "Heart to Heart Talks," that characterized periodicals of protest and hybrid magazines. Some examples of this frank approach include maxims appearing on the January 1901 (2, no. 4) cover of Albert Lane's *Erudite* – "To Be Good, just Do Good – Simple, Easy Work. Start at It" (front cover) – and in the pages of *The Lucky Dog* – "When you have nothing to say, for heaven's sake, say nothing!" (Thrift 31).

This kind of folksy wisdom, underpinned by reformist aims, was less common in these magazines than more subversive forms that might be expected in publications that self-identified as periodicals of protest, revolt, and rebellion. These forms served to identify and attack the same kinds of behaviours and qualities that little magazinists went after in their topical commentary. Short forms, however, enabled them to make generalizable, universal, and pithy statements about the greed, hypocrisy, and stupidity they witnessed more generally in everyday American cultural life, and to promote values that might define the emerging professional middle-class in the Progressive Era. These sayings might be highly topical, reflecting cynical and satirical views about current business and political issues, such as these following three aphorisms from *Homo*, *The Ghourki*, and *The Philosopher*:

> The motto of THE Trust: Oil well, thy ways. ("Some Thoughts of a Wise Dog" 176)

> There is a place in business for the Golden Rule but generally it is an unfilled want. ("Philosophical Observations" 5)

> As long as the Public Treasury holds out there will always be those who are satisfied with things as they are. ("The Philosophers" 64)

Most, however, were more abstract and generalizable critiques of human conduct, with an emphasis on greed, corruption, prudery, ignorance, and social and religious hypocrisy – lessons for how and how not to behave, geared towards the conditions of modern-day life and expressed, often, in plain-speaking or vernacular style, as in the following that appeared in *The Philistine*, *The Philosopher*, *The Ghourki*, and *The Erudite*:

> Profanity does not consist in saying damn. Profanity consists in writing it d – n. (front cover, *Philistine*)

> The life of graft is too good to let go of easy. ("Philosophers" 64)

> It takes people who don't know that they don't know a long time to find out. ("Philosophical Observations" 5)

> The world is not improved to any great extent, by those who do no wrong. Such do precious little of real Good. (front cover, *Erudite* 1, no. 6)

Sometimes the aphorisms and epigrams could take on a dark, even Nietzschean tone. Notable here is a semi-regular feature in *The Junk* called "Cold Tongue" (sometimes "Bits of Cold Tongue"), a series of original, unsigned epigrams, maxims, and aphorisms, the title of which gestures towards the telling of harsh truths. Among its cynical observations are:

> Annihilation is best after all, then there will be no danger of meeting unpleasant persons. ("Cold Tongue" 128)

> Write your name on the sand; it will be easier to obliterate when you wish to be forgotten. ("Few Bits of Cold Tongue" *Junk* 2, no. 2, 43)

> If mirrors reflected our thoughts, how many persons would dare look in the glass? ("Few Bits of Cold Tongue," *Junk* 2, no. 3, 71)

> Selfishness has never received its just praise. It is the royal road to success. ("Few Bits of Cold Tongue," *Junk* 2, no. 3, 71)

This section, with its nihilistic and disenchanted view of the world, represents a telling contrast to the usual inspirational and aspirational nature of the magazine's mottoes and the more positive reformist style of Zanque's editorial section, "A Junklet of Thoughts and Things." The noticeably darker tone of the speaking voice in "Cold Tongue" functions as an alter ego to the main editorial voice.

Other little magazinists also employed an alter ego to make particular kinds of critiques and observations. More embodied forms of alter ego were usefully employed to enable little magazinists to say things that they might not say in their own voice. These alter egos were generally located outside mainstream bourgeois culture and include Hubbard's Ali Baba and Harold Llewellyn Swisher's Moocha Saba. Though problematic in terms of their classist and racist underpinnings, these representations enabled kinds of satire and critique unavailable to, or less effective in, the mouths of their white middle-class creators. Hubbard's alter ego, Ali Baba, was an aged, drinking, tobacco-smoking, plain-speaking country bumpkin – a source of humorous stories, homespun wit, and comic cartoon images. Ali Baba was based on a real Roycroft member, handyman Anson Blackman, who became apocryphal under Hubbard's treatment and one of the star attractions for visitors to the Roycroft community. Through Ali Baba, as Marie Via argues, Hubbard was able to express "crust[ier]" and more ribald wisdom, such as "Art is largely a matter of a haircut" and "Two in the bush are the root of all evil" (MV [Marie Via] 129). Given Hubbard's own self-consciously stylized bohemian appearance, the former quip would not work as well coming from his persona. It garners humour and effectiveness through being spoken by a naive outside observer of bohemian literary culture. The latter is an example of the anti-proverb created by combining two proverbs ("a bird in the hand is worth two in the bush" and "the love of money is the root of all evil"). The result of this combination is sexually suggestive, perhaps too much so for Hubbard to lay claim to in his own voice, but is safe, and more effective, in coming from the mouth of the naive and ignorant Ali Baba, who might be presumed to be oblivious to his error or to any untoward meaning.

Howard Llewellyn Swisher of *The Ghourki*, who styled himself Chief of the Tribe of Ghourki in a similar spirit to Hubbard's pose as Fra Elbertus, had an alter ego in Moocha Saba, one of his followers, who "sets the totem-poles and lights the pine cone fire" ("Harangues to the Ghourki," *Ghourki* 2, no. 5, 447). Like Ali Baba, Moocha Saba's sayings were a source of humour, though more sacrilegious, satirical, and pointed in sentiment than Ali Baba's:

> I would rather go to church than to go to hell, but I don't have to go to either place. ("Harangues to the Ghourki," *Ghourki* 2, no. 5, 447)

> An honest man is the noblest work of God but the Lord is too busy to make many of them. ("Harangues to the Ghourki," *Ghourki* 2, no. 12 – 3, no. 1, 5)

> There are some people who say that money is the root of all evil. Usually their fortune has not sprouted yet. ("Harangues to the Ghourki," *Ghourki* 2, no. 12 – 3, no. 1, 5)

Moocha Saba's targets in these sayings are religion and religious people, and the first two, especially, are sacrilegious in nature. Some of Moocha Saba's sayings also, like Ali Baba's, are a form of anti-proverb, reflecting the disenchanted and cynical spirit of the fin de siècle. Instead of mixing proverbs, however, these anti-proverbs function differently, invoking popular wisdom only to immediately subvert it. Mieder calls this type of anti-proverb a proverbial aphorism (*Proverbs Are Never Out of Season* 36). The second, for example, begins with a famous epigram from Pope's *Essay on Man* ("An honest man's the noblest work of God"), proverbial by this period, only to cynically subvert it with an aphoristic turn in the second part. The third is, likewise, an example of a proverbial aphorism with Biblical origins. The opening, "There are some people who say," subtly casts doubt on the proverb, becoming a more explicit subversion in the aphoristic second sentence, where the envious and self-righteous are revealed as those who use the Bible as a shield for their own hypocrisy.

The proverbial aphorism was not the sole province of alter egos. It is a significant short form that little magazinists employ in their own voices, too, appearing across a range of protest and hybrid magazines. Its potency and relevancy for these magazines is clear if understood with respect to Mieder's identification of it as a particularly modern form in which

> the old and familiar proverb is consciously manipulated in innovative fashion to create ... expressions that might fit certain aspects of modern life more precisely ... These alterations ... might be mere humorous wordplay, but more often than not such anti-proverbs represent a critical reaction to the worldview expressed in seemingly antiquated proverbs. It is important to notice that proverbs are no longer sacrosanct bits of wisdom laying out a course of action that must be adhered to blindly. Instead proverbs are considered as questionable and as at best apparent truths that are called on if the shoe (proverb) happens to fit. When that is not the case, they are freely changed to express opposite points of view. The juxtaposition of the traditional proverb text with an innovative variation forces the reader into a more critical thought process. Where the old

> proverbs acted as preconceived rules, the modern anti-proverbs are intended to activate us into overcoming the naïve acceptance of traditional wisdom. (Mieder, *Proverbs Are Never Out of Season* 90)

The proverbial aphorism, then, was highly suited to the aims of little magazinists and their readers who were questioning received wisdom and the conventions of their contemporary moment as they strove to promote new values and ideals for an emerging progressive America. At the same time, the hybrid form of the proverbial aphorism is the logical product of such a view. In its invocation and subsequent aphoristic subversion of the proverb, it is a conscious formal embodiment of the modernist rejection of conventional wisdom in an individualistic and intellectualized form.

Sayings, then, though easy to disregard, prove, upon closer consideration, integral to the cultural meaning and value of little magazines. As with other content, the types of sayings that prevailed, the manner in which they were used, and the values and ideals expressed in them, root these magazines firmly in the professional-managerial class context. They were a means through which their makers could realize their ideals of self-culture and self-expression and demonstrate their cultural distinction and idiosyncratic personae. Whether the saying was a careful selection and mediation of the words of another, a creative invention, or a witty subversion, little magazines, with their privileging of all things short, strove to be the last word in the shortest of short forms.

Afterword
Little Magazines, Not So Little After All?

As all fads do, the little magazine phenomenon of the 1890s died out – or so Faxon declared in his 1903 bibliography. Faxon's comments, however, apply to the little magazine *phenomenon* rather than the *genre*, and to a *collecting fad* rather than a *new* media form, the *novelty* of which, it is true, had begun to wear out. Some magazines that started out little became more mainstream in orientation as they "grew up," changing format, morphing into other magazine types, or becoming more mainstream. The *What to Eat* of 1908, for example, soon to become *The National Food Magazine*, bore little relation to its 1896 incarnation – a poster-style magazine with aesthetic little magazine type content. The more commercial story magazines that Faxon included in his bibliographies began to stand apart as a distinctive genre of their own, and to breed a new form, the pulp magazine. Little magazines, however, did continue to be issued after 1903 in fits and starts; they just garnered less attention, until the form was exploited as a key vehicle for the modernist movement. Though little magazines of the 1890s were, for the most part, ephemeral, they were culturally important as a medium of expression for a newly emerging elite professional-managerial class. But what of their broader importance beyond the historical moment? What of their legacy? If they were largely forgotten by even 1903, how can they be said to have had a significant influence?

By Hoffman, Allen, and Ulrich's terms, of course, they have not. Unlike the magazines they document, those of the 1890s cannot be said to have published 80 per cent of the most important critics, novelists, poets, and storytellers of the period (1), even while writers like Kate Chopin, Henry James, Jack London, Stephen Crane, H.L. Mencken, and notable British and French authors of the period published in them. And this, of course, is to say nothing of the importance of these magazines in the domain of illustration, graphic design, and the visual arts. If there is not enough of a critical mass here to argue for the importance of these magazines to conventional literary history with its top-down approach, there is substantial material, however, for the bottom-up approach that, following recent trends in historical studies, is increasingly being taken up by literary scholars. Magazines of all stripes provide excellent fodder for constructing a "people's literary history," one that is important for recuperating figures and contexts, but also for revisioning canonical artists and texts.

Another way of accounting for the legacy of the American little magazines of the 1890s is to look for evidence of influence on modernist little magazines. This is an area of inquiry that needs further exploration and is beyond the scope of this book, but here are a few pertinent points. In the moment when modernist little magazines emerged in the 1910s, there were still figures from the earlier period carrying on their magazine work. Even if we discount Hubbard, whose *Philistine*, with its substantial circulation, could probably no longer be called a "little" magazine, there was Mosher, whose *Bibelot* ceased publication only in 1915; there was Monahan, whose hybrid magazine the *Papyrus* ran up to 1912 and was replaced by the short-lived *Phoenix* from 1914 to 1916; and, there was Harriet Monroe, a contributor to 1890s little magazines, whose Modernist-era publication, *Poetry*, founded in 1912, was one of the most influential magazines of this period. *Poetry*'s Morrisian visual aesthetic, in fact, owes much to the publications of the 1890s. Other notable figures of the modernist moment who were involved with little magazines in both periods include Carl Sandburg, H.L. Mencken, Bliss Carman, Arthur Symons, and Yone Noguchi. Symons and Noguchi were a significant influence on modernist writers: Symons for his *Symbolist Movement in Literature* (1898; updated 1919), Noguchi for his ideas that shaped Pound's formulation of Imagism. Mencken, meanwhile, is important for linking the emerging aesthetic sensibilities of the proto-modernist 1890s with those of the 1910s and 1920s. In his memoir, *Newspaper Days*, he recalls having been inspired by the little magazines of the 1890s, especially Vance Thompson and James Huneker's *M'lle New York* (61). Mencken's acerbic, witty style was largely based on that developed by Huneker, Hubbard, and other notable little magazinists of the previous era.

In thinking about the relationship between the two little magazine movements, we might also expand the field of inquiry beyond the small core of elite modernist little magazines that tend to attract most attention: *The Dial*, *Poetry*, *The Little Review*, *Broom*, and *The Masses*. There was, after all, a body of other magazines emerging in this period that are more clearly aligned with the little magazine tradition that goes back to the 1890s, some of which are included, some not, in Hoffman, Allen, and Ulrich and Moss. Publications such as Walter Storey's *Vision: A Quarterly Journal of Aesthetic Appreciation of Life* and George Wolfe Plank's *Butterfly Quarterly*, for example, owe much to the aesthetic and literary spirit of magazines that emerged from small presses of the 1890s, while *Philopolis* and *The Arroyo Craftsman* continued the tradition of arts and crafts publications. In addition, Ben Hecht and Max Bodenheim's *Chicago Literary Times* and Guido Bruno's numerous Greenwich Village-based publications of the 1910s and 1920s self-consciously evoke 1890s decadence and are undeniably reminiscent of Thompson and Huneker's New York publication *M'lle New York*. There are, no doubt, many more examples, yet to be discovered, of synergies between the little magazines of the 1890s and those of the 1910s and 1920s.[1]

I want to suggest, however, that the legacy of these magazines may become more substantial when considered in less specific terms. These magazines exerted their power in diffuse and subtle ways that are best understood not through the individual articles, stories, poems or the magazines themselves. The concept of mediamorphosis, for example, with its fluid understanding of relations between and developments of media forms, suggests thinking about the genealogy of the little magazine in broader terms, looking beyond its most obvious descendant – the modernist little magazine. How did the little magazine of the 1890s morph into other media forms of the twentieth and twenty-first century? From a media history perspective, the little magazine of the 1890s, specifically the story magazine accounted as part of the genre in the period, is linked also, as has been suggested, to the pulp magazines of the twentieth century. In its more characteristic mode as a democratic vehicle of personal expression, however, the little magazine bears thinking about more fully in the context of "personal media." Zines, for example, may well have more in common with the American little magazines of the 1890s than modernist magazines do in terms of contexts and conditions of production. Stephen Duncombe's characterization of twentieth-century zines is much in keeping with this book's account of 1890s little magazines. They are produced, he says, by "the sons and daughters of the American middle class" who are "trained to be individuals" and "prepared to make *their* mark on the world," in ways figured as oppositional to dominant society (179–80). The more recent digital media context is relevant, too, in this respect. The little magazines of the 1890s and, indeed, zines, might well be considered analogue forms of the digital social media of today that Katie Day Good describes as a means for people to "interact with media texts to express themselves socially, ... to document their lives," or to engage in creative practices (559). As cultural practices, zining, facebooking, blogging, and little magazining testify powerfully to the possibility that highly individualized and personalized forms of media can exist within, and be enabled by, a mass media context that is understood as commercial and impersonal. Indeed, the emphasis on individuality and self-expression that is central to these forms is rooted in the middle-class identity that emerges at the turn of the twentieth century and that asserts itself powerfully in the little magazine of this period. Little magazinist Wally (George Walcott), in his pronouncement that *The Corsair* represented "a chance to say what he has to say when there is something to be said," might well have been speaking of Facebook, his blog, or his Twitter account if he were alive today.

Another more abstract way of thinking about the legacy of the little magazines is in socio-cultural terms. This takes us back to where I began their story – with their makers – the little magazinists, looking not to their cultural formation but to their development AFTER the peak of the little magazine movement. These magazines, as I have shown, touch on an extremely broad range of social and cultural movements, many of them rooted in the progressivism of this period. Though many of these were fringe interests, they were the fringe interests of a powerful class. The little magazines were often only one – and a minor one – of the venues in which the professional-managerial class makers of these magazines exerted their cultural power. The legacy of these magazines, then, lies not so much in the magazines themselves, but in the opportunities they represented, and the outcomes they realized, in the way of their makers' contributions to American cultural life more broadly during, and more especially after, their involvement with these magazines.[2] With their access to education and culture, their possession of inborn gifts and talents, and their positions within well-connected networks of friends and acquaintances, little magazinists were often renaissance types, professional polymaths who had a number of careers. These included related careers in media, but also other kinds of artistic, intellectual, and professional work.

More obviously, little magazines involved those who would contribute to the mediamorphosis of the period that saw a massive expansion of media and an accompanying growth of media professionals. Little magazines were, after all, often stepping stones for their editors and contributors to important and influential careers in print media and its related industries – mainstream magazines, advertising, publishing, printing, and the graphic arts – and this is where many of them ended up in the twentieth century. In addition to their little magazine work, little magazinists were, or would become, publishers and editors of, or writers and artists for, mainstream magazines, pulps, trade, and specialty publications; book publishers; printers; typographers; newspaper columnists, journalists and reporters; writers of occasional prose and verse volumes; book and magazine illustrators; artists and art directors for book and magazine publishers; children's writers; platform lecturers; advertising writers and artists; film directors, publicists, and scriptwriters; playwrights and theatre producers; radio broadcasters, etc. Will Bradley's little magazine work, for example, represented a small fraction of a broad and varied career, mostly in the mainstream media. He also designed typefaces and typographical layouts; designed and printed books; worked in advertising; created designs for Royal Doulton; did a series of interior, furniture, and house designs for *Ladies' Home Journal*; served as art editor of *Colliers*, *Century*, *Good Housekeeping*, *Metropolitan*, *National Weekly*, *Pearson's*, and *Success*; became art director for Hearst publications and motion pictures; and even wrote and directed his own films. Like Bradley, Rob Wagner, who served as art editor and artist for *The Clack Book* and was a contributor to *The Criterion* and *The Chap-Book*, found his way to Hollywood, where he was a screenwriter, director, and eventually editor of a left-leaning literary magazine called *Script*.

There were other artist little magazinists who were even more successful than Bradley and Wagner, including Maxfield Parrish, a prominent magazine illustrator in the 1910s and 1920s; J.C. Leyendecker, commercial illustrator, most famous for his creation of the iconic "Arrow Collar Man"; Arthur Wesley Dow, an influential artist and arts educator, teacher of Georgia O'Keeffe; and John Sloan, who would go on to become a major figure in the Ashcan school of realist artists of the early twentieth century. The little magazines were also a training ground for those who would transform book, magazine, advertising, and typographic design in the twentieth century, notably Bruce Rogers, considered the first professional book designer, who would design over four hundred books, and William Addison Dwiggins, who revolutionized book design in the 1920s and 1930s and who coined the term "graphic designer" in 1922 to refer to the myriad activities involved in the kinds of work he did.

Sometimes the cultural reach of little magazinists was broader. Ralph Adams Cram, of the *Chap-Book* set, would become a noted American architect of churches and university campus buildings all over America. He would continue to publish throughout his life and was an important public intellectual, making the cover of *Time* magazine in 1926. Tudor Jenks, who wrote for *Bradley His Book*, *Chips*, *The Philistine*, and *The Criterion*, wavered between a writing career and a law career, finally settling on law, but never giving up his writing. He was a prolific magazine contributor and well-known writer of juvenile fiction. Herman Schneider, who was one of the editors of *The Hour Book*, had an equally rich and varied involvement with American cultural life. He was an architect, bridge builder, award-winning storywriter, essayist, educator, researcher, labour mediator, wartime administrator, art collector, university president, and is widely regarded as the founder of the cooperative education movement.

Others who participated in the little magazine movement in the 1890s and early 1900s would go on to contribute to America's cultural life in significant ways: Clarence Darrow, part of Chicago's bohemian set and contributor to *The Rubric* and *The Goose-Quill*, who was, in the little magazine period, already a successful free speech and labour activist, would go on to achieve greater fame with the Leopold and Loeb murder case and the Scopes Monkey trial; Irving Morrow, associate editor and art editor of *The Muse*, would become one of the architects of the Golden Gate Bridge and choose its controversial burnt red-orange colour; William Dallam Armes, a *Muse* contributor, English professor at Berkeley, and one of the founding members of the Sierra Club; *Blue Sky* editor Thomas Wood Stevens, founder of the first degree-granting theatre program in the United States; Charles Howard Shinn, *Muse* contributor, would become a leading California environmentalist and first superintendent of Yosemite Park; Ora Eddleman, editor of *Twin Territories* and the first Native American radio talk show host; Sydney Prentice, *Lotus* and *Goose-Quill* contributor, became an internationally renowned scientific illustrator, especially in paleontology; Charles Edward Russell, contributor to *The Conservator*, *The Socialist Spirit*, and *The Literary Collector*, and later one of the founders of the National Association for the Advancement of Colored People; Theodore Schroeder, editor of the anti-Mormon *Lucifer's Lantern*, would found the Free Speech League, precursor to the American Civil Liberties Union; J.C. Johansen, editor of *Rubric*, an artist who would be commissioned to document the Versailles Treaty and to paint official White House portraits. The roster of little magazinists is replete with these kinds of figures and many more examples could be given.

Thus, while little magazines of the 1890s cannot lay claim to hosting 80 per cent of the most important writers or artists of the period, they do, nevertheless, constitute a repository for fascinating and important figures in American cultural life across a range of fields. If little magazines were at the centre of the fin-de-siècle mediamorphosis, the futures of their makers and contributors suggest that they also represent an important documentation of what might be called the "sociomorphosis" of the period that saw the transformation of American middle-class life with the rise of the professional-managerial class. The little magazine was central to the sociomorphosis of the period for a class that, broadly speaking, had a keen interest in expressing itself in print. It was a medium of expression and self-realization for individuals and for a class fraction that shaped, in really influential ways, the cultural life of America's twentieth century. "Little" they might have been, but these magazines are a "big" part of America's cultural history in the twentieth century.

Appendix
Updated Bibliography of American Little Magazines of the 1890s

This updated bibliography of little magazines amalgamates Faxon's three bibliographies that identify a total of 268 North American titles.[1] It adds sixty-six additional entries derived from other sources, amounting to a total of 334 entries. Though I have not made a systematic effort of seeking out titles that Faxon may have missed and, like him, make no claim to comprehensiveness, a sufficient number have come to my attention such that I feel it worth expanding the bibliography. Clearly, however, more work can be done in developing the field. Drawing on Donnelly's account of amateur publications that took little magazine form, I have added twenty titles that do not appear in Faxon. Moss's bibliography of little magazines, contributes a further eighteen, and I have added twenty-eight on the basis of information from various sources.

While the rationale for inclusion of Donnelly's titles is self-explanatory, a few words about other additions is in order. Moss's titles cover a number of categories and represent some important additions to the list. Most notable are four important socialist titles: *Comrade*, *Wilshire's*, *Ariel*, and *The Conservator*. These are not out of place as additions to Faxon, given his inclusions of single-tax and reform-oriented publications, and have been important to my arguments about periodicals of protest and the social and political function of little magazines. Moss also considers little magazines to include a few general monthly or weekly magazines (general, literary, or story) with a more progressive bent – *Pearson's Magazine* (New York edition), *Golden Gate*, *Reedy's Mirror*, *The Raven*, *Saxby's*, and *Smart Set*. Again, while some might quibble about the extent to which these are little magazines, they are not out of line with some of Faxon's own inclusions and there are certainly connections and overlaps between the editors of and contributors to these publications and the little magazine community. Moss's bibliography also contributes titles to the bibliophilic realm of the aesthetic little magazine in *Poet Lore* and *Book Lover*, and to the amateur arm of the movement with *The Hobo*. *Camera Work*, meanwhile, a title also considered by Hoffman, Allen, and Ulrich in their "supplementary list," might well have been a title that escaped Faxon's notice in 1903, the year *Camera Work* was first issued, and is in line with some of the photography-oriented titles he does include. Moss also considers the early academic-style intellectual journals *Sewanee Review* (in Hoffman, Allen, and Ulrich's supplementary list) and *South Atlantic Quarterly* to be little magazines. I include them here, as I have all Moss's titles from the appropriate date range, though they are not quite in keeping with the more characteristic university-based little magazine publications of the 1890s. Finally, another Moss title is *The Writer*, again, not a little magazine per se, but, as a trade journal for aspiring writers of the day, it is an invaluable resource for information about these publications.

Like Moss's, my own additions are various. They are based on references within the little magazines of the period themselves, on the participation of little magazinists in them, or on secondary source references. Certainly many more could have been added if I had made that a priority. To the category of aesthetic little magazines, I have added arts and crafts titles (*The Artsman*, *The Craftsman*); graphic-arts oriented titles (*Lotos*, *The Sketch Book*, *Brush and Pencil*, *The Bill Poster* [Chicago]); bibliophilic titles (*The Literary Collector*, *The Literary Review and Book-Plate Collector*); aesthetic little magazines after the manner of *The Chap-Book* (*Gil Blas*, *Moods*, *Morningside*); an amateur publication (*Cypher*); a general style literary weekly that included the work of many little magazinists (*Criterion*); and two unknown types – likely aesthetic (*The Monthly Visitor* and *The Optimist* [Detroit]). I have also added titles to the protest category, mainly in the way of socialist publications (*Challenge*, the precursor to *Wilshire's*; *The New Time*, the follow-up to *New Occasions*, a title included in Faxon 1897; *The Social Crusader*, *Socialist Spirit*, and *Vanguard*). Other additions include *The Basis*, a race reform periodical; two medical-literary journals to accompany Faxon's *Stuffed Club – Doctor's Magazine and How to Live* and *Moody's Magazine of Medicine*; *Ithuriel*, an early manifestation of the protest style that Hubbard would popularize in *The*

Philistine. Four Canadian titles are added (derived from Irvine's article on Canadian little magazines), on the basis that Faxon himself listed some Canadian titles: these are *Tarot* and *The Lamp*, occultist periodicals; *Arcadia*, an aesthetic little magazine; and *Neith*, an Africadian little magazine.

In terms of the content and format of the bibliography, I have added additional information, when it has been possible to find any, and where lacking from Faxon, Moss, and Donnelly. I have also silently corrected some errors in the earlier bibliographies. The entries include as much of the following information as possible: title; location; publisher; run information, with volume and number, where known; notable editors for the period in question (though not necessarily all the editors); mottoes or additional information as provided by the consulted bibliographies, catalogue entries from holding libraries as identified on OCLC Worldcat, or the magazines themselves; the genre and subgenre of the periodical; any additional relevant notes. The category "reference" indicates the key source of information for the entry, whether Faxon, Moss, Donnelly, or, if it has not been included in earlier bibliographies, MacLeod. In the case of Faxon's two 1903 bibliographies, Faxon 1903a refers to his *Bulletin of Bibliography* list ("Ephemeral Bibelots"), 1903b to the pamphlet version (*"Ephemeral Bibelots"*). If the magazines are digitized with fully searchable issues available on HathiTrust, I indicate so with an asterisk (more titles may, of course, become available in the future). Other locations of digitized versions appear in the notes, though researchers should be aware that there are often problems with digital copies (missing pages, misordering of pages, inaccurate cataloguing, etc.). A number of these titles do not appear in OCLC Worldcat, which is, nevertheless, an excellent resource for identifying locations to view physical copies of these magazines. Princeton, Yale, and the New York Public Library have significant holdings of these publications. It should be noted that the library cataloguing of these ephemeral publications is haphazard. In many cases, it is very difficult to arrive at reliably full information, especially about run lengths.

The Acorn
Berkeley, CA: Acorn Press
December 1901–April 1903
Editor: Thomas Frederick Folger

Type: Aesthetic (amateur)
Reference: Donnelly

The Alkahest*
Atlanta, GA: Franklin Printing and Publishing Company
Monthly. Illustrated. Vol. 1, no. 1, May 1896–[1903?]
Note: "The leading literary gossip book of America"
Type: Aesthetic
Reference: Faxon 1897, 1903ab

The Amateur Printer-Journalist
Type: Aesthetic (amateur)
Reference: Donnelly

American Cooperative News*
Cambridge, MA: Cooperative Union
Monthly. Illustrated. Vol. 1, no. 1, July 1896–February 1899
Note: "Devoted to the Rochdale plan of cooperation"
Type: Protest (co-op movement)
Reference: Faxon 1897

Angel Food*
Los Angeles, CA: Angelus Publishing Company
Weekly; bi-weekly; monthly. Vol. 1, no. 1, 21 August 1901–Vol. 1, no. 2, September 1901
Editor: John Humphrey Burke
Note: "A Compound of Froth and Air. Mostly for Men – and foolish angels"
Note: Succeeded by *Monologue*. Catalogued as *Monologue* on HathiTrust
Type: Protest (satire)
Reference: Faxon 1903ab (mistitled as *Angel's Food*)

The Anti-Philistine
London, UK: John and Horace Cowley
Monthly. Vol. 1, no. 1, 15 June 1897–Vol. 1, no. 4, 15 September 1897
Note: "A monthly magazine and review of belles-lettres, also a periodical of protest"

Note: Published in London, but contained mostly American material. A response to Elbert Hubbard's *Philistine*
Type: Aesthetic
Reference: Faxon 1903ab

Arcadia
Montreal, QC: J. Gould
Semi-monthly. Vol. 1, no. 1, 2 May 1892–vol. 1, no. 21, 1 March 1893
Editor: Joseph Gould
Note: "Devoted to music, art and literature"
Type: Aesthetic
Reference: MacLeod

The Ariel
Westwood, MA: George E. Littlefield
Monthly. [1902?]–1911
Editor: George Littlefield
Note: "Liberal religion, new thought, socialism and co-operation"
Type: Protest (socialist)
Reference: Moss

The Artsman*
Philadelphia, PA: Rose Valley Press
Monthly; bimonthly. Illustrated. Vol. 1, no. 1, October 1903–Vol. 4, April 1907
Editor: H.L. Traubel
Type: Protest (Arts and Crafts)
Reference: MacLeod

Atmos
San Francisco, CA: Society for Human Endeavor (Orlow Institute)
Monthly. Vol. 1, no. 1, September 1902–[1905?]
Editor: O.N. Orlow
Note: "New light upon old truths"
Note: Digitized issues at International Association for the Preservation of Spiritualist and Occult Periodicals (www.iapsop.com)
Type: Protest (metaphysical)
Reference: Faxon 1903ab

Autocrat
Chicago, IL
Monthly [only one issued?]. Illustrated. Vol. 1, no. 1, April 1895
Note: "Devoted to the social interests of young men"
Type: Unknown
Reference: Faxon 1903b

The Bachelor Book*
Chicago, IL: Marion Thornton Egbert and Page Waller Sampson
Monthly. Illustrated. Vol. 1, no. 1, March 1900–Vol. 2, no. 2, November 1900
Editor: Marion Thornton Egbert and Page Waller Sampson (Chicago); William Ellis (Wausau)
Note: William Ellis served as editor for Vol. 2, no. 2
Type: Aesthetic
Reference: Faxon 1903ab; Moss

The Bachelor of Arts*
New York, NY: The Bachelor of Arts Company
Monthly. Vol. 1, no. 1, May 1895–Vol. 5, no. 1, July 1898
Editor: John Seymour Wood
Note: "A monthly magazine devoted to University interests and general literature"
Type: Aesthetic (general literary)
Reference: Faxon 1897

The Basis
Buffalo, NY: S. McGerald & Sons for the Citizens' Publishing Company
Weekly; monthly. March 1895–April 1896
Editor: Albion Tourgée
Note: "A Journal of Citizenship"
Type: Hybrid
Reference: MacLeod

The Baton
Kansas City, MO: Baton Publishing Company
Monthly. Illustrated. Vol. 1, no. 1, April 1895–Vol. 4, no. 4, November 1897

Editor: Robert Wiziarde
Note: "A monthly journal devoted to Western music matters"
Type: Aesthetic (music and literary)
Reference: Faxon 1897, 1903ab

The Bauble
Washington, DC: Willard Holcomb, Will A. Page, H.C. Bursley
Monthly. Illustrated. Vol. 1, no. 1, July 1895–Vol. 3, no. 5, February 1897
Editor: Willard Holcomb, Will A. Page, H.C. Bursley
Note: "There is no slander in an allowed fool"
Type: Aesthetic (humour)
Reference: Faxon 1897, 1903ab

Beforehand*
Buffalo, NY: Peter Paul Book Company
Bi-monthly [only one issued]. Illustrated. Vol. 1, no. 1, October 1896
Note: "A literary journal"
Type: Aesthetic (bibliophile)
Reference: Faxon 1903ab

The Bibelot*
Portland, ME: Thomas B. Mosher
Monthly. Vol. 1, no. 1, January 1895–Vol. 20, December 1914
Editor: Thomas B. Mosher
Note: "A reprint of poetry and prose for book lovers, chosen in part from scarce editions and sources not generally known"
Type: Aesthetic
Reference: Faxon 1897, 1903ab; Moss

The Bilioustine*
Evanston, IL: William S. Lord
No. 1, May 1901–No. 2, October 1901
Editor: Bert Leston Taylor
Note: A periodical of knock"
Type: Aesthetic (humour)
Reference: Faxon 1903ab

The Bill Poster
Chicago, IL: Associated Bill Posters' Association
Monthly. Vol. 1, no. 1, February 1896–Vol. 2, 1898
Note: William Denslow cover, poster, and column
Type: Aesthetic (printing, advertising)
Reference: MacLeod

The Bill Poster
Toronto, ON
Monthly. Illustrated. Vol. 1, no. 1, March 1896–Vol. 1, no. 8, December 1896
Note: "A monthly journal devoted to the art of poster and other outdoor advertising"
Type: Aesthetic (advertising)
Reference: Faxon 1897

Birds*
Chicago, IL: Nature Study Publishing Company
Monthly. Illustrated. Vol. 1, no. 1, January 1897–Vol. 3, no. 6, June 1898
Note: "A monthly serial designed to promote knowledge of bird-life"
Note: "Illustrated by color photography"
Note: Succeeded by *Birds and All Nature*
Type: Miscellaneous (hobby)
Reference: Faxon 1897

The Blackboard
St Paul, MN: Blackboard Company
Monthly. Vol. 1, no. 1 July 1902–February 1903[?]
Note: "A monthly containing five short stories"
Type: Aesthetic (story)
Reference: Faxon 1903ab

The Black Book*
New York, NY: Black Book Publishing Company
Quarterly [only one issued]. Illustrated. Vol. 1, no. 1, October 1895
Editor: P. Maxwell and E.P. Upjohn
Note: "An illustrated quarterly magazine of art and affairs"

Type: Aesthetic (art)
Reference: Faxon 1897, 1903ab

The Black Cat*
Boston, MA: Shortstory Publishing Company
Monthly. Vol. 1, no. 1, October 1895–[February 1922?]
Note: “A monthly magazine of original short stories”
Type: Aesthetic (story)
Reference: Faxon 1897, 1903ab

The Blue Book
Cincinnati, OH
Weekly. Illustrated. Vol. 1, no. 1, 31 October 1895–Vol. 1, no. 2, 9 November 1895
Note: “A weekly record of events that interest people of the earth earthy”
Type: Miscellaneous (society gossip)
Reference: Faxon 1903ab

The Blue Sky*
Chicago, IL: Blue Sky Press
Monthly; bi-monthly. Illustrated. Vol. 1, no. 1, August 1899–Vol. 5, no. 1, April 1902
Editor: Thomas Wood Stevens
Note: “Happy is the man who sees ever the blue sky”
Note: Absorbed by *The Rubric*
Type: Aesthetic
Reference: Faxon 1903ab; Moss

The Bohemian*
Boston, MA: Bohemian Publishing Company (1900–3). Deposit, NY: Outing Press (1903–9)
Monthly. Illustrated. Vol. 1, no. 1, December 1900–1909
Note: “A monthly magazine of unique stories”
Note: Preceded by *The Future*
Type: Aesthetic (story)
Reference: Faxon 1903ab; Moss

The Bohemian
Philadelphia, PA
Monthly. Vol. 1, no. 1, November 1897–Vol. 2, no. 2, February 1898
Type: Aesthetic
Reference: Faxon 1903ab

The Book Booster*
Evanston, IL: William S. Lord
Single issue. Vol. 1, no. 1, December 1901
Editor: Bert Leston Taylor
Note: "A periodical of puff"
Type: Aesthetic (humour)
Reference: Faxon 1903ab

Book Culture*
Boston, MA: E.B. Hall
Monthly. Vol. 1, no. 1, January 1899–Vol. 1, no. 7, September 1899
Editor: Nathan Haskell Dole
Type: Aesthetic (bibliophile)
Reference: Faxon 1903ab

The Book-Lover*
San Francisco, CA (1899–1901); New York, NY (1901–4): Book-Lover Press
Quarterly; monthly; bi-monthly. Vol. 1, no. 1, Autumn 1899–Vol. 5, June 1904
Editor: W.E. Price
Note: "A magazine of book lore"
Note: Preceded by *Home Magazine*
Note: Succeeded by *Appleton's Booklovers Magazine*
Type: Aesthetic (bibliophile)
Reference: Moss

The Book of the Month
Yonkers, NY: J.B. Sullivan
Monthly. Vol. 1, no. 1, April 1903–[?]
Type: Miscellaneous (astrology)
Reference: Faxon 1903ab

Bradley His Book
Springfield, MA: Wayside Press
Monthly. Illustrated. Vol. 1, no. 1, May 1896–Vol. 2, no. 3, January 1897
Note: "Devoted to art, literature, and fine printing, with especial attention to illuminated advertisements"
Note: Digitized issues at JSTOR (www.jstor.org) and Internet Archive (www.archive.org)
Type: Aesthetic
Reference: Faxon 1897, 1903ab; Moss

Brush and Pencil*
Chicago, IL: Phillips and Company; Brush and Pencil Publishing Company
Monthly. Illustrated. Vol. 1, no. 1, September 1897–Vol. 19, no. 5, May 1907
Editor: Charles Francis Browne; Frederick W. Morton
Note: "An illustrated magazine of the arts today"
Type: Aesthetic (Art; Arts and Crafts)
Reference: MacLeod

Buzz Saw
New York, NY: Lord No Zoo
Illustrated. No. 1–No. 2 [1897].
Note: "Perkin Warbeck's literary and pictorial newspaper and magazine of useful and ornamental facts"
Type: Miscellaneous (humour)
Reference: Faxon 1897, 1903ab

By the Way
Editor: Alfred Victor Peterson
Type: Aesthetic (amateur)
Reference: Donnelly

Cambridge Magazine*
Cambridge, MA: Cambridge Magazine Company
Monthly. Illustrated. Vol. 1, no. 1, February 1896–Vol. 1, no. 2, June 1896
Note: "Devoted to education, cooperation, and brotherhood"

Note: Incorporated with *American Cooperative News*
Type: Protest (co-op movement)
Reference: Faxon 1897, 1903ab

Camera Work
New York, NY: Alfred Stieglitz
Quarterly. Illustrated. No. 1, January 1903–No. 49–50, June 1917
Editor: Alfred Stieglitz
Note: "An illustrated quarterly magazine devoted to photography"
Note: Digitized issues at Modernist Journals Project (www.modjourn.org/)
Type: Aesthetic (photography)
Reference: Moss

The Challenge*
Los Angeles, CA: Gaylord Wilshire
Weekly. Vol. 1, no. 1, December 1900–No. 40, October 1901
Editor: Gaylord Wilshire
Note: "Let the nation own the trusts"
Note: Succeeded by *Wilshire's Magazine*
Type: Protest (socialist)
Reference: MacLeod

C.H. and D. Chap Book
Cincinnati, OH: Cincinnati, Hamilton, and Dayton Railroad Company
Monthly. Illustrated. No. 1, December 1894
Note: Printed on hand-finished paper, ragged edges, two colours, "abounds in odd conceits"
Note: Succeeded by *Chandee Works*
Type: Aesthetic (story)
Reference: Faxon 1903a

Chandee Works
Cincinnati, OH: Cincinnati, Hamilton, and Dayton Railroad Company
Monthly. Illustrated. No. 2, January 1895
Note: Preceded by *C.H. and D. Chapbook*
Type: Aesthetic (story)
Reference: Faxon 1903a

The Chap-Book*
Cambridge, MA; Chicago: Stone and Kimball
Semi-monthly. Illustrated. Vol. 1, no. 1, 15 May 1894–Vol. 9, no. 4, 1 July 1898
Note: "A miscellany and review of belles-lettres"
Note: Absorbed by *The Dial*
Type: Aesthetic
Reference: Faxon 1897, 1903ab; Moss

Chapters
Manlius, NY
Monthly. Vol. 2, no. 1, November 1896–Vol. 2, no. 4, March 1897
Note: "A journal of education and literature"
Note: Preceded by *Little Chap*
Type: Aesthetic
Reference: Faxon 1903ab

Chat
New York, NY: Manhattan Reporting Company
Monthly. Vol. 1, no. 1, March 1901–December 1903[?]
Editor: Patrick J. Sweeney
Note: "A magazine of business sermons and practical talks"
Note: "Honesty in everything"
Type: Protest (business)
Reference: Faxon 1903ab

Chips
New York, NY: Chips Publishing Company
Monthly; weekly. Illustrated. Vol. 1, no. 1, March 1895–Vol. 4, no. 2, June 1896
Editor: Will M. Clemens
Note: "from literary workshops"
Type: Aesthetic
Reference: Faxon 1897, 1903ab

The Chop-Book
New York, NY
Single issue. 1896
Note: "Semi-humorous"

Type: Aesthetic (humour)
Reference: Faxon 1897, 1903ab

The Clack Book
Lansing, MI: Wells and Hudson
Monthly. Illustrated. Vol. 1, no. 1, April 1896–Vol. 3, no. 3, June 1897
Note: "A burlesque on the popular little magazines of the day"
Type: Aesthetic
Reference: Faxon 1897, 1903ab

The Clipping Collector
New York, NY: F[rank]. A. Burrelle
Monthly. Vol. 1, no. 1, January 1896–Vol. 1, no. 8, October 1896
Note: "A monthly magazine devoted to the collecting of newspaper clippings for pleasure or profit"
Type: Miscellaneous (collecting)
Reference: Faxon 1897

Clips
New York, NY: Clips Publishing Company
Weekly. Illustrated. Vol. 1, no. 1, 21 November 1895–Vol. 3, no. 59, 2 January 1897
Editor: H.B. Eddy
Note: "zest of the best; wit of the world"
Type: Miscellaneous (reprint and some original)
Reference: Faxon 1897, 1903ab

The Clique*
Maywood, IL: Clique Publishing Company
Monthly [only one issued]. Illustrated. Vol. 1, no. 1, May 1896
Type: Aesthetic (amateur)
Reference: Faxon 1897, 1903ab

The Comrade*
New York, NY: Comrade Publishing Company
Monthly. Illustrated. Vol. 1, no. 1, October 1901–Vol. 4, no. 4, April 1905
Editor: John Spargo
Note: "An illustrated socialist monthly"

Type: Protest
Reference: Moss

The Conservator*
Philadelphia, PA: H.L. Traubel
Monthly. Vol. 1, no. 1, March 1890–30th year, no. 4, June 1919
Editor: H.L. Traubel
Type: Protest
Reference: Moss

The Cornhill Booklet*
Boston, MA: Alfred Bartlett
Monthly; quarterly. Illustrated. Vol. 1, no. 1, July 1900–Vol. 4, no. 3, December 1914. Suspended 1906–13
Editor: Alfred Bartlett
Type: Aesthetic (bibliophile)
Reference: Faxon 1903ab

The Cornucopia
New York, NY: Cornucopia Company
Monthly [only one issued?]. Illustrated. Vol. 1, no. 1, January 1897
Note: "A magazine for the million; art and literature; short stories"
Type: Aesthetic (story)
Reference: Faxon 1897

The Corsair*
Roxbury, MA; Boston, MA: New England Chess Company
Weekly. 1902–11
Editor: George H. Walcott
Type: Miscellaneous (chess)
Reference: Faxon 1903ab

Country Time and Tide
Montague, MA: Edward P. Pressey
Monthly; quarterly. Vol. 1, no. 1, January 1902–Vol. 11, no. 3, Winter 1909
Note: "A magazine of more profitable and interesting country life"
Type: Protest (Arts and Crafts)
Reference: Faxon 1903ab

Courrier Innocent
Scituate, MA; Giverny, France: Salt Marsh Press
Irregular. Illustrated. No. 1, 1891–No. 7, Spring 1897
Type: Aesthetic
Reference: Faxon 1897, 1903ab

The Craftsman*
Eastwood, NY: United Crafts
Monthly. Illustrated. Vol. 1, no. 1, October 1901–Vol. 31, no. 3, December 1916
Editor: Gustav Stickley
Note: "The lyf so short, the craft so long to lerne"
Note: "An illustrated monthly magazine in the interest of better art, better work, and a better and more reasonable way of living"
Type: Protest (Arts and Crafts)
Reference: MacLeod

Cranbrook Papers
Detroit, MI: Cranbrook Press
Monthly. Illustrated. Book 1, June 1900–February 1901
Editor: George Gough Booth
Type: Aesthetic (Arts and Crafts; bibliophile)
Reference: Faxon 1903ab

The Crier*
Toledo, OH: Cromelithe Press
Monthly [only one issued]. Illustrated. Vol. 1, sec. 1, September 1900
Editor: A.H. Merrill
Note: "A little journal for discerning people"
Type: Hybrid
Reference: Faxon 1903a

The Criterion
St Louis, MO (1896–7); New York, NY (1897–1905): G[race]. L. Davidson
Weekly; monthly. Illustrated. 1896–Vol. 6, no. 2, May 1905
Editor: Henry Dumay; Joseph I.C. Clarke
Note: Preceded by *Life* (St Louis, MO)
Type: Hybrid
Reference: MacLeod

Cupid
Washington, DC
Vol. 1, no. 1, December 1901
Type: Unknown
Reference: Faxon 1903a

Current Thought
New York, NY: Continental Publishing Company
Monthly. Vol. 1, no. 1, February 1897–Vol. 1, no. 2, March 1897[?]
Note: “A magazine of individual opinion, research, scientific, educational, sociological”
Type: Protest
Reference: Faxon 1897

The Cypher
Chicago, IL: Warren Dean
Weekly. Vol. 1, no.1, February 15–[?]
Type: Aesthetic
Reference: MacLeod

The Daily Tatler
New York, NY: Stone and Kimball
Daily. No. 1, 7 November 1896–No. 13, 21 November 1896
Type: Aesthetic
Reference: Faxon 1903ab

The Debutante
Chicago, IL
Note: Advertised to appear in April 1895
Type: Unknown
Reference: Faxon 1903b

The Dee Tees
1901–[?]
Note: “You can have ’em for ten cents”
Type: Unknown
Reference: Faxon 1903a

The Dilettante
Issued from various locations, including Indianapolis, IN; Alameda, CA; Denver, CO: Samuel J. Steinberg
Monthly. 1890–1902
Editor: Samuel J. Steinberg
Type: Aesthetic (amateur)
Reference: Donnelly

The Dilettante
Seattle, WA
Monthly. Illustrated. Vol. 1, no. 1, April 1898–Vol. 5, no. 1, July 1901
Editor: Joe Smith
Note: "A monthly literary magazine"
Type: Aesthetic
Reference: Faxon 1903ab

Doctor's Magazine and How to Live
Alma, MI: George F. Butler Publishing Company
Monthly. Illustrated. Vol. 2, no. 4, 15 September 1900–March 1903
Editor: George F. Butler
Note: "The best magazine of health and literature in America"
Note: Preceded by *Doctor's Magazine*
Note: Succeeded by *How to Live*
Type: Protest (health)
Reference: MacLeod

Dorothy Maddox Magazette
Philadelphia, PA: Dorothy Maddox Company
Bi-weekly. Vol. 1, no. 1, June 1901–December 1901[?]
Note: "Red outside and read all through"
Note: "Written for women but men will read it"
Type: Hybrid
Reference: Faxon 1903a

The Dreamer
Milwaukee, WI: Julius O. Roehl
Vol. 1, no. 1, 1903–[?]
Type: Aesthetic (amateur)
Reference: Faxon 1903ab; Donnelly

Drift
Portland, OR
Monthly. Vol. 1, no. 1, August 1898
Note: Preceded by *Pacific Empire*
Note: Succeeded by *Pacific Monthly*
Type: Aesthetic
Reference: Faxon 1903ab

Duo Lambda
Brooklyn, NY: L.E. Bisch
Vol. 2, no. 1, October 1902–[?]
Editor: Louis Edward Bisch and Louis Charles Wills
Type: Aesthetic (amateur)
Reference: Donnelly

The Dwarf
Morton Park, IL
Monthly. Vol. 1, no. 1, April 1901–Vol. 1, no. 2, May 1901
Note: "A monthly publication for the home"
Type: Aesthetic
Reference: Faxon 1903ab

The Dwarf Magazine
New York, NY
Monthly. Vol. 1, no. 1, May 1896–Vol. 1, no. 4, Sept 1896
Type: Unknown
Reference: Faxon 1897 (as *Dwarf*), 1903ab

The Easy Chair
Macon, GA: Press of the J.W. Burke Company
Monthly [only one issued?]. Vol. 1, no. 1, October 1895
Editor: Carl W. Stead
Note: "A monthly journal for the home"
Type: Aesthetic
Reference: Faxon 1897

Ebell
Los Angeles, CA: Ebell Club of Los Angeles
Monthly. Illustrated. Vol. 1, no. 1, January 1898–Vol. 3, no. 7, November 1899

Editor: Grace Atherton Dennen
Note: "A monthly journal of literature and current events"
Note: Digitized issues at Internet Archive (www.archive.org)
Type: Aesthetic
Reference: Faxon 1903ab

The Echo
Chicago, IL
Semi-monthly. Illustrated. Vol. 1, no. 1, 1 May 1895–Vol. 4, no. 3, 1 February 1897
Editor: Percival Pollard
Note: "A humorous and artistic publication"
Type: Aesthetic
Reference: Faxon 1897, 1903ab

Editorial
Dowagiac, MI
Monthly. Vol. 1, no. 1, August 1901–[?]
Editor: Roy Marshall and Thomas J. Brosnan
Type: Aesthetic (amateur)
Reference: Donnelly

The Ego
Carbondale, PA
Monthly. Vol. 1, no. 1, March 1902–Vol. 1, no. 6, August 1902[?]
Editor: Charles Munn
Note: "A periodical for the expression of all kinds of thoughts, published . . . for anybody that wants it, and especially for those who don't"
Type: Protest
Reference: Faxon 1903ab

The Empire
New York, NY: E.S. Hine and Co.
Monthly. Illustrated. Vol. 1, no. 1, January 1897–Vol. 1, no. 5, June 1897[?]
Type: Aesthetic (story)
Reference: Faxon 1897

The Enfant Terrible
New York, NY: R.H. Russell
Quarterly [only one issued]. Illustrated. No. 1, April 1898
Editor: Gelett Burgess
Type: Aesthetic (humour)
Reference: Faxon 1903ab

Epi-lark*
San Francisco, CA: William Doxey
Illustrated. May 1897
Note: Final number of *The Lark*
Editor: Gelett Burgess
Type: Aesthetic (humour)
Reference: Faxon 1897, 1903ab

The Erudite*
Worcester, MA; Concord, MA: Erudite Publishing Company
Monthly. Vol. 1, no. 1, April 1900–Vol. 5, no. 2, February 1903
Editor: Albert Lane
Note: "A magazine of utt'rances"
Type: Protest
Reference: Faxon 1903ab

The Essene
Denver, CO: Reed Publishing Company
Monthly. Vol. 1, no. 1, June 1902–1917. Suspended for long periods.
Editor: Grace Mann Brown and James Arthur Edgerton
Note: "A magazine of construction"
Note: Digitized issues at International Association for the Preservation of Spiritualist and Occult Periodicals (www.iapsop.com/)
Type: Protest (spiritual)
Reference: Faxon 1903ab

Events
Wheeling, West VA
Monthly. Vol. 1, no. 1, September 1897–Vol. 1, no. 6, February 1898
Type: Unknown
Reference: Faxon 1903ab

Ex Libris
Washington, DC: American Bookplate Society; Washington Ex Libris Society
Quarterly. Illustrated. Vol. 1, no. 1, July 1896–Vol 1, no. 4, April 1897
Type: Aesthetic (bibliophile)
Reference: Faxon 1897

Expression*
Boston, MA: School of Expression
Quarterly; annually. Vol. 1, no. 1, June 1895–[?]
Note: "Art, literature, the spoken word"
Type: Protest (elocution, vocal and dramatic)
Reference: Faxon 1897

The Fad
Indianapolis, IN
Weekly. Illustrated. Vol. 1, no. 1, 6 March 1897–[?]
Note: "Up to date in all things"
Type: Unknown
Reference: Faxon 1897

The Fad
San Antonio, TX: Kypfer and Seng
Weekly. Vol. 1, no. 1, 18 January 1896–Vol. 2, no. 3, 16 January 1897
Editor: Sara Hartmann
Note: "Age cannot wither nor custom stale her infinite variety"
Type: Miscellaneous (society gossip)
Reference: Faxon 1903ab

Fisic for Folks
Leominster, MA
Monthly. January [1899]–March/April [1899]
Note: "Printed sometimes by the society for the dispersion of common ignorance"
Type: Protest
Reference: Faxon 1903ab

The Fly Leaf
Boston, MA: Fly Leaf Publishing Company

Monthly. Vol. 1, no. 1, December 1895–Vol. 1, no. 5, April 1896
Editor: Walter Blackburn Harte
Note: "A Pamphlet periodical of the new – the new man, the new woman, new ideas, whimsies and things."
Type: Aesthetic
Reference: Faxon 1897, 1903ab; Moss

Footlights
Philadelphia, PA
Weekly. Illustrated. Vol. 1, no. 1[?] –Vol. 4, no. 10, 14 November 1896
Editor: Charles Bloomingdale Jr. and E. St Elmo Lewis
Note: "A Weekly journal for the theatre-goer"
Type: Aesthetic (theatre)
Reference: Faxon 1897

Forms and Fantasies
Chicago, IL: Forms and Fantasies Publishing Company
Monthly. Illustrated. Vol. 1, no. 1, May 1898–Vol. 2, no. 2, June 1899
Note: "An illustrated monthly magazine of decorative art"
Type: Aesthetic (Arts and Crafts; Decorative Arts)
Reference: Faxon 1903ab

Four O'Clock
Chicago, IL: A.L. Swift and Company
Monthly. Illustrated. No. 1, February 1897–No. 71, December 1902
Note: "A monthly magazine of original writings. Sincerity, beauty, ease, cleverness"
Note: Absorbed by *Philharmonic*
Type: Aesthetic (story)
Reference: Faxon 1897, 1903ab

The Freak
Sharon, MA, Boston, MA: Freak Publishing Company
Monthly. Illustrated. Vol. 1, no. 1, 21 January 1902–May 1906
Editor: Edmund R. Brown
Note: "The youngest editor in America"
Note: "At first typewritten with a circulation of three copies. First printed number was vol. 1, no. 9 Sept. 1902"

Type: Aesthetic (amateur)
Reference: Faxon 1903ab

The Future
Taunton, MA
Monthly. Vol. 1, no. 1[?], 1899–Vol. 2, no. 4, July 1900
Editor: F. Ernest Hofman
Note: "A few pages of bizarre bookishness, published now and then when the spirit moves"
Note: Succeeded by *The Bohemian* (Boston)
Type: Aesthetic
Reference: Faxon 1903ab

The Gauntlet
Chicago, IL: Adolphe Danziger
Monthly [only one issued?]. Vol. 1, no. 1, March 1903
Note: "A magazine for the honest"
Type: Hybrid
Reference: Faxon 1903ab

Gems of American Patriotism
Washington, DC: Patriotic Publishing Company
Quarterly. Vol. 1, no. 1, April 1898–Vol. 1, no. 3, October 1898
Type: Miscellaneous (history)
Reference: Faxon 1903ab

The Ghourki*
Morgantown, WV: The Chief's Print Shop
Monthly. Irregular. Vol. 1, no. 1, July[?] 1901–Vol. 6, no. 2, April 1909
Editor: Harold Llewellyn Swisher
Note: "Face to the front and keep going"
Note: Digitized issues at International Association for the Preservation of Spiritualist and Occult Periodicals (www.iapsop.com/)
Type: Protest
Reference: Faxon 1903ab

Gil Blas
Philadelphia, PA: Gil Blas Company

Weekly. No. 1, 2 November 1895–[?]
Editor: John Sloan
Type: Aesthetic
Reference: MacLeod

Girldom
Washington, DC: E. Jean Connell
Vol. 1, no. 1, January 1901–[?]
Editor: E. Jean Connell
Note: "Conducted entirely by young ladies in the interests of good literature and amateur journalism"
Type: Aesthetic (amateur)
Reference: Donnelly

Golden Gate
Oakland, CA: Twentieth Century Printing and Publishing Company
Monthly. Illustrated. Vol. 1, no. 1, May 1902–Vol. 1, no. 9, December 1902
Editor: Edward Beal
Note: "A monthly magazine of the West"
Type: Aesthetic (general literary)
Reference: Moss

Good Cheer
Boston, MA: Forbes and Company
Monthly. Vol. 1, no. 1, November 1900–Vol. 2, no. 3, July 1901
Editor: Nixon Waterman
Note: "A monthly magazine for cheerful thinkers"
Note: Succeeded by *National Magazine*
Type: Hybrid
Reference: Faxon 1903ab

The Goose-Quill
Chicago, IL
Monthly; bimonthly. Irregular. Illustrated. No. 1, February 1900–No. 3, 15 May 1900. New series, Vol. 1, no. 1, 1 November 1901–Vol. 3, no. 3, March 1904.
Editor: John Stapleton Cowley-Brown
Note: "An Anglo-American magazine"

Type: Hybrid
Reference: Faxon 1903ab; Moss

The Grasshopper
Newport, RI
Semi-monthly; monthly. Illustrated. Vol. 1, no. 1, 15 May 1897–Vol. 2, no. 10, September 1898
Editor: Mollie Brownell
Type: Aesthetic (humour)
Reference: Faxon 1903ab

The Gray Goose
Cincinnati, OH (1897–1902); Franklin, OH (1903–4); Deposit, NY (1904–9)
Monthly. Vol. 2, no. 5, May 1897–Vol. 22, no. 6, June 1909
Editor: James Knapp Reeve
Note: "A monthly magazine of original short stories"
Note: Preceded by *American Home Magazine*
Type: Aesthetic (story)
Reference: Faxon 1897, 1903ab

The Great Round World*
New York, NY: W.B. Harrison
Weekly. Illustrated. Vol. 1, no. 1, December 1896–Vol. 21, no. 340, 16 May 1903
Note: "The Great round world and what is going on in it"
Note: "A weekly newspaper for boys and girls"
Note: Name change to *Week's Progress* in 1903
Type: Miscellaneous (news)
Reference: Faxon 1897, 1903ab

Handicraft
Boston, MA: Society of Arts and Crafts
Monthly. Illustrated. Vol. 1, no. 1, April 1902–12. Suspended 1904–10.
Note: "Representing the arts and crafts movement"
Type: Aesthetic (Arts and Crafts)
Reference: Faxon 1903ab; Moss

Hart's Yarns
New York, NY: Bibelot Brothers.
Monthly. [Vol 1, no. 1], November 1901–Vol. 2, no. 4, August 1902
Note: Percy William Edward Hart
Note: "A monthly magazine for you"
Type: Unknown
Reference: Faxon 1903ab

The Hatchet
Leavenworth, KS
Monthly. Illustrated. Vol. 4, no. 1, November 1896–[8th no.] June 1897
Note: "A little journal of literature, edited at odd spells and published at Leavenworth, Kansas"
Note: Vols. 1–3 issued as a paper by the High School students
Type: Aesthetic
Reference: Faxon 1903ab

Hesperides
New York, NY
Vol. 1, no. 1, 1902–[?]
Editor: John Leary Peltret
Type: Aesthetic (amateur)
Reference: Donnelly

The Higher Law
Boston, MA: H.W. and J.P. Dresser
Monthly. Vol. 1, no. 1, December 1899–Vol. 6, nos. 1–2, August–September 1902
Editor: H.W. Dresser
Note: "A monthly periodical of advanced ideals"
Note: Absorbed by *Country Time and Tide*
Note: Digitized issues at International Association for the Preservation of Spiritualist and Occult Periodicals (www.iapsop.com/)
Type: Protest (New Thought)
Reference: Faxon 1903ab

The Hobby
Baltimore, MD: American Press Company

Quarterly. Illustrated. Vol. 1, no. 1 Autumn 1902–Vol. 1, no. 3, Winter 1903–4
Note: “An illustrated magazine of entertaining polite literature”
Note: “An illustrated magazine for book lovers and collectors”
Type: Aesthetic
Reference: Faxon 1903ab

The Hobo
Cleveland, OH
1902
Editor: Samuel Loveman
Type: Aesthetic (amateur)
Reference: Moss

Home Craft
Chicago, IL: Home Craft Institute
Monthly. Illustrated. Vol.1, no. 1, November[?] 1899–Vol. 2, no. 6, October 1900
Note: “Published every new moon or thereabouts”
Type: Unknown
Reference: Faxon 1903ab

Homo
Beverly, NJ
Monthly. Vol. 1, no. 1, June 1901–Vol. 3, no. 5, October 1902
Editor: J.C. Worthington
Note: “A periodical for men and the women who look over their shoulders”
Type: Protest
Reference: Faxon 1903ab

The Honey Jar
Columbus, OH: Champlin Press
Monthly. Illustrated. Vol. 1, no. 1, [November] 1898–Vol. 4, no. 6, 15 October 1900
Editor: D.C. Sapp
Note: “A receptacle for literary preserves”
Type: Aesthetic
Reference: Faxon 1903ab; Moss

The Hoppergrass
Ashland, VA; Richmond, VA
Monthly. Illustrated. Vol. 1, no. 1, January 1899–Vol. 7, 1905
Editor: Mildred Bryce, Virginia Bryce, Clarence Archibald Bryce, and Jeanette Bryce Staton
Note: "Published monthly by the little Bryces"
Note: Type composed and set by the editors. Illustrated by Mildred Bryce
Type: Aesthetic (amateur)
Reference: Faxon 1903ab

The Horn Book*
New York, NY
Bi-monthly [only one issued?]. Vol. 1, no. 1, August 1895
Note: "of periodical literature"
Type: Aesthetic
Reference: Faxon 1903ab

The Hour Book
Cumberland, MD: Hour Book Publishing Company
Monthly. Illustrated. Vol. 1, no. 1, October 1895–Vol. 1, no. 8, May 1896
Editor: John G. Wilson, Herman Schneider, and John Edwards
Type: Aesthetic
Reference: Faxon 1897, 1903ab

The House Beautiful*
Chicago, IL: Herbert S. Stone and Company
Monthly. Illustrated. Vol. 1, no. 1, December 1896–ongoing
Editor: Herbert Stone
Note: "A monthly magazine of art and artisanship"
Type: Aesthetic (Arts and Crafts; Decorative Arts)
Reference: Faxon 1897

The Hub Club Quill
Type: Aesthetic (amateur)
Reference: Donnelly

Humanity
Kansas City, MO: Cooperative Reform Publishing Company

Monthly. Illustrated. Vol. 1, no. 1, April 1896–March 1897[?]
Note: "Equal Opportunity"
Note: "A monthly magazine of social ethics"
Type: Protest
Reference: Faxon 1897

The Idol
San Francisco, CA: Idol Publishing Company
Monthly. Vol. 1, no. 1, June 1901–Vol. 1, no. 6, December 1901[?]
Note: "A monthly magazine of bright short stories"
Type: Aesthetic (story)
Reference: Faxon 1903ab

The Impressionist
New York, NY
Monthly. Illustrated. Vol. 1, no. 1, November 1899–Vol. 1, no. 12, October 1900
Note: "A magazine of originality"
Type: Unknown
Reference: Faxon 1903ab

The Impressionist
St Louis, MO: American Music Syndicate
Monthly. Illustrated. Vol. 1, no. 1, July 1902–[?]
Editor: John Arthur Nelson
Note: "A periodical of soliloquies for the sophisticated as sparkling as champagne, as harmless as soda"
Type: Aesthetic
Reference: Faxon 1903ab

Impressions
San Francisco, CA: D.P. Elder and M. Shepard
Monthly; quarterly. Illustrated. Vol. 1, no. 7, September 1900–Vol. 3, March 1902–Vol. 6, December 1905
Editor: Paul Elder and Morgan Shepard (1900–2); Paul Elder (1903–5)
Note: Preceded by *Personal Impressions*
Note: Title change to *Impressions Quarterly* in March 1902
Type: Aesthetic (bibliophile)
Reference: Faxon 1903ab

In Lantern Land
Hartford, CT: C.D. Allen.
Monthly. Vol. 1, no. 1, 3 December 1898–Vol. 1, no. 6, 6 May 1899
Editor: Charles Dexter Allen and William Newnham Carlton
Type: Hybrid
Reference: Faxon 1903ab

In Many Keys
Muskegon, MI: D. Malloch
Monthly. Vol. 1, no. 1, March 1900–Vol. 4, no. 1, March 1902
Editor: Douglas Malloch
Note: "A little magazine made up entirely of the writings of Douglas Malloch"
Type: Aesthetic
Reference: Faxon 1903ab

The Interpolitan
Omaha, NE: Jessen Bros.
Monthly.
Type: Aesthetic (amateur)
Reference: Donnelly

Ishmaelite*
Indianapolis, IN: Mount Nebo Press
Monthly. Vol. 1, no. 1, December 1896–Vol. 5, no. 6, May 1899
Editor: Hewitt H. Howland
Type: Hybrid
Reference: Faxon 1897, 1903ab

Items
Chicago, IL
Weekly [only one issued?]. Vol. 1, no. 1, 17 March 1902
Note: "The 20th Century pocket journal"
Type: Unknown
Reference: Faxon 1903ab

Ithuriel
Des Moines, IA
Monthly. Vol. 1, no. 1, February 1895–[?]

Editor: Ed. A. Janeway
Type: Protest
Reference: MacLeod

Jabs
Chicago, IL
Monthly. Illustrated. Vol. 1, no. 1, November 1901–Vol. 2, no. 7, May 1903[?]
Note: "The same being hypodermic injections of gall and ginger administered with a quill"
Type: Protest
Reference: Faxon 1903ab

The Jester*
Chicago, IL: Jester Publishing Company
Monthly [only one issued?]. Vol. 1, no. 1, January 1901
Note: "His thoughts thinkfully thunk, respectfully rendered. Timely topics tunefully tendered"
Type: Protest
Reference: Faxon 1903ab

Les Jeunes*
New York, NY
Monthly [only one issued]. Illustrated. Vol. 1, no. 1, March 1900
Editor: Helen Woljeska
Type: Aesthetic
Reference: Faxon 1903ab

John-a-Dreams
New York, NY: Corell Press and the Press of the Classical School
Monthly. Illustrated. Vol. 1, no. 1, July 1896–Vol. 2, no. 6, June 1897
Editor: John Corell
Note: "A magazine for the conservative iconoclast and the practical dreamer; devoted to mere literature and classical typography"
Type: Aesthetic
Reference: Faxon 1897, 1903ab

The Junk
Ogdensburg, NY: Junk Workers

Monthly. Vol. 1, no. 1, April 1901–Vol. 3, no. 1, April 1902[?]
Note: Published by Ralph Tallman
Type: Hybrid
Reference: Faxon 1903ab

The Kansas Knocker
Topeka, KS: J.F. Jarrell and Myron A. Waterman
Quarterly. Illustrated. Vol. 1, no. 1, April 1900–Vol. 1, no. 4, January 1901
Note: "A journal for cranks"
Type: Protest
Reference: Faxon 1903ab

The Kiote*
Lincoln, NB: Schuyler W. Miller and Harry G. Shedd
Monthly. Illustrated. Vol. 1, no. 1, February 1898–Vol. 4, no. 6, 1901
Note: "A New Venture by a New Folk in a New Field: Being a Literary Monthly Dedicated to the Prairie Yelper"
Type: Aesthetic
Reference: Faxon 1903ab

A Kipling Note Book
New York, NY: M.F. Mansfield and A. Wessels
Monthly. Illustrated. No. 1, February 1899–No. 12, January 1900
Type: Aesthetic (Kipling-oriented)
Reference: Faxon 1903ab

The Kit-Bag
Fredericton, NB: Bodkin, Winslow, and Roberts
Monthly. Illustrated. Vol. 1, no. 1, 26 November 1902–Vol. 1, no. 2 (no. 34) 24 December 1902
Note: "a chap-book"
Type: Aesthetic
Reference: Faxon 1903ab

Kit-Kat
Philadelphia, PA: Keighton Brothers.
Weekly. Vol. 1, no. 1, 23 May 1896–Vol. 2, no. 8, 9 January 1897

Note: "A Weekly magazine for the home"
Note: One-cent weekly
Type: Aesthetic
Reference: Faxon 1903ab

Kit-Kats
Pittsburg, PA
Monthly. Vol. 1, no. 1, December 1900–Vol. 2, no. 3, September 1901
Editor: Addison Steele [pseudonym of Leonard S. Levin]
Note: "A monthly periodical of independent thought"
Type: Hybrid
Reference: Faxon 1903ab

Kleon
Scranton, PA
Monthly. Vol. 1, no. 1, August 1900–Vol. 2, no. 6, July 1901
Note: "A Scranton monthly journal"
Type: Aesthetic
Reference: Faxon 1903ab

Klondike Grubstakes
Seattle, WA. Grubstakes Publishing Company
Monthly. Vol. 1, no. 1, October 1897–Vol. 1, no. 4, February 1898
Note: "Where to get them, what to take"
Note: "Practical information for Yukoners and others"
Type: Miscellaneous (Gold mining)
Reference: Faxon 1903ab

The Knight-Errant
Boston, MA: Francis Watts Lee. Printed for the Proprietors at the Elzevir Press
Quarterly. Illustrated. Vol. 1, no. 1, April 1892–Vol. 1, no. 4, January 1893
Note: "A quarter yearly review of the liberal arts, being a magazine of appreciation"
Note: Digitized issues at at Internet Archive (www.archive.org)
Type: Aesthetic
Reference: Faxon 1903ab; Moss

The Knocker
Blair, NE: Will A. Campbell
Monthly. Vol. 1, no. 1, January 1902–Vol. 4, no. 1, August 1903[?]
Note: “A journal for cranks”
Type: Protest
Reference: Faxon 1903ab

The Knocker
Philadelphia, PA: Knocker Company
Monthly. Vol. 1, no. 1, May 1901–Vol. 1, no. 6, October 1901
Note: “Here’s a knocking indeed”
Type: Protest
Reference: Faxon 1903ab

Knots
Type: Miscellaneous (puzzles)
Reference: Faxon 1903ab

The Lamp
Toronto, ON
Monthly. Illustrated. Vol. 1, no. 1, August 1894–Vol. 4, no. 7, September 1900
Editor: Albert E.S. Smythe
Note: “A theosophical monthly”
Note: Digitized issues at International Association for the Preservation of Spiritualist and Occult Periodicals (www.iapsop.com/)
Type: Hybrid (Theosophy)
Reference: MacLeod

The Lark*
San Francisco, CA: William Doxey
Monthly. Illustrated. Vol. 1, no. 1, May 1895–Vol. 2, no. 24, April 1897
Note: “By les jeunes”
Type: Aesthetic (humour)
Reference: Faxon 1897, 1903ab; Moss

The Leaven
Northfield, MN
Monthly. Vol. 1, no. 1, March 1900–Vol. 2, no. 5, January 1901

Editor: G.A. Southworth
Note: "Practical people's pungent periodic protest"
Type: Protest
Reference: Faxon 1903ab

The Limner
New York, NY: Art Students' League
Monthly. Vol. 1, no. 1, February 1895–Vol. 1, no. 6, July 1895
Type: Aesthetic
Reference: Faxon 1903ab

The Lincoln House Review
Boston, MA
Bi-monthly; quarterly; monthly. Vol. 1, no. 1, November 1895–October 1898
Note: "To record the work of social organizations about Boston, especially of the Lincoln House"
Editor: William Anthony Clark
Type: Protest (settlement house movement)
Reference: Faxon 1897

The Lion's Mouth
Cincinnati, OH: Partridge Press
Monthly. Illustrated. Vol. 1, no. 1, November 1900–Vol. 1, no. 4, March 1901
Note: "Society of Those Who Do Not Need Diagrams"
Type: Aesthetic (humour)
Reference: Faxon 1903ab

The Literary Collector*
New York, NY: G.D. Smith. Greenwich, CT; Literary Collector Company
Monthly. Vol. 1, no. 1, 1900–Vol. 10, 1905
Note: "A monthly magazine of booklore and bibliography"
Type: Aesthetic (bibliophile)
Reference: MacLeod

The Literary Dot
New York, NY
Monthly. Vol. 1, no. 1, November 1899–Vol. 1, no. 6, April 1900[?]

Editor: Rev. John J. Mallon
Type: Aesthetic
Reference: Faxon 1903ab

The Literary Messenger
Cambridge, MA
Monthly [only one issued?]. Vol. 1, no. 1, February 1897
Note: "Published in the interests of the Cambridge Literary Society"
Type: Aesthetic (bibliophile)
Reference: Faxon 1897

The Literary Review
Boston, MA
Monthly. Vol. 1, no. 1, 15 January 1897–Vol. 4, no. 7, July 1900
Editor: Richard Gorham Badger
Note: "A monthly news journal of belles-lettres"
Note: "A book's a book although there's nothing in it"
Note: Followed by *New Literary Review*
Type: Aesthetic (bibliophile)
Reference: Faxon 1897, 1903ab

The Literary Review and Book-Plate Collector
Boston, MA: Charles E. Peabody
Monthly [only one issued]. Vol. 1, no. 1, November 1902
Editor: C.E. Peabody, A.E. Churchill, G.H. Westley, W.P. Truesdell
Type: Aesthetic (bibliophile)
Reference: MacLeod

The Little Chap*
Manlius, NY
Monthly, Vol. 1, no. 1, April 1896–Vol. 1, no. 5, October 1896
Note: "Issued by the cadets of the St John's School, Manlius, NY"
Note: Continued as *Chapters*
Type: Aesthetic
Reference: Faxon 1903ab

The Little Cyclist
Chicago, IL
[March 1896; possibly never issued]

Type: Miscellaneous (hobby)
Reference: Faxon 1903b

Little Journeys*
New York, NY; London, UK: G.P. Putnam's Sons (1894–1900). East Aurora, NY: Roycroft (1900–9)
Monthly. Illustrated. Vol. 1, no. 1, December 1894–Vol. 25, 1909
Note: "Each year covers a different subject. e.g. to the homes of good men and great, of American authors, of famous women, of American statesmen, of eminent painters, of famous poets, of great musicians, of eminent artists, of eminent orators"
Type: Aesthetic
Reference: Faxon 1897, 1903ab

The Little Monthly
New York, NY
Monthly. Illustrated. Vol. 1, no. 1, April 1893–Vol. 4, no. 1, January 1894
Note: "To amuse, to instruct, to reward"
Type: Unknown
Reference: Faxon 1903ab

The Little Smoker
Chicago, IL: Phillips
Monthly [only one issued]. Illustrated. Vol. 1, no. 1, January 1896
Note: "Published monthly for all true lovers of the weed"
Type: Miscellaneous (smoking)
Reference: Faxon 1903ab

A Little Spasm*
Easthampton, MA: Clifford Richmond
1901 [only one issued]. Illustrated
Note: "At the home of Wolfgang Mozart"
Type: Aesthetic (humour)
Reference: Faxon 1903ab

The Lotos
New York, NY: Cycle Publishing Company
Monthly. Illustrated. Vol. 9, no. 8, February 1896-[?]

Note: "A high class monthly of Art and Letters"
Note: Arthur Dow cover and poster
Note: Preceded by *New Cycle*
Type: Aesthetic
Reference: MacLeod

The Lotus*
Kansas City, MO: Intercollegiate Publishing Company
Semi-monthly; monthly. Illustrated. Vol. 1, no. 1, 1 November 1895–Vol. 3, no. 11, November 1897
Editor: Walter Blackburn Harte
Type: Aesthetic
Reference: Faxon 1897, 1903ab; Moss

Lucifer's Lantern*
Salt Lake City, UT
Irregular. No. 1, June 1898–No. 9, 1901
Editor: A.T. Schroeder
Note: "Issued whenever the spirit moves"
Type: Protest (Anti-Mormon)
Reference: Faxon 1903ab

The Lucky Dog
Springfield, OH: T.B. Thrift
Bi-monthly. Irregular.Vol. 1, no. 1, April 1900–Vol. 6, 1906[?]; 1908–10; 1940–3[?]. Suspended 1906–8; None published 1910–39.
Editor: Timothy Burr Thrift
Type: Hybrid
Reference: Faxon 1903ab

The Machete
Keene, NH
Monthly. Vol. 1, no. 1, January 1900–Vol. 2, no. 6, December 1900
Editor: George L. Thompson
Type: Protest
Reference: Faxon 1903a

Magazine of Poetry
New York, NY

Monthly. Vol. 1, no. 1, May 1900–Vol. 1, no. 2, June 1900
Editor: Daniel Mallett
Note: Louis J. Rhead cover for first number
Type: Aesthetic
Reference: Faxon 1903ab

The Magpie*
Charlottesville, VA
Monthly. Vol. 1, no. 1, June 1896–Vol. 1, no. 5, October 1896
Editor: Kenneth Brown
Note: "One of the ephemerals"
Type: Aesthetic
Reference: Faxon 1897, 1903ab

The Mahogany Tree
Boston, MA: Mahogany Tree Company
Weekly. Vol. 1, no. 1, 2 January 1892–Vol. 2, no. 14, 10 December 1892
Type: Aesthetic
Reference: Faxon 1903ab

Ye Manual
Providence RI
Quarterly. Illustrated. Vol. 1, no. 1, December 1902–Vol. 1, no. 2, January 1903[?]
Note: "Published in the interests of ye Manual Training High School, Providence, RI"
Type: Unknown
Reference: Faxon 1903ab

The Manuscript
New York, NY: Manuscript Press
Monthly. Vol. 1, no. 1, April 1901–Vol. 1, no. 6, December 1901
Note: "Issued every month in the interests of book buyers"
Editor: Marion Miller
Type: Aesthetic (bibliophile)
Reference: Faxon 1903ab

McC's Monthly
Detroit, MI: Fred H. McClure Company

Monthly. Illustrated. Vol. 1, no. 1, December 1897–Vol. 1, no. 5, April 1898
Note: "short stories"
Type: Aesthetic (story)
Reference: Faxon 1903ab

Medical Tractates
Mount Hope, MA; Boston, MA
Monthly. Faggot 1 [September 1902]–Faggot 4 [December 1902]
Note: Leon Noel [pseudonym of Charles Everett Warren]
Note: "A faggot of facts and fancies picked up and tied together by Leon Noel"
Type: Protest (health)
Reference: Faxon 1903ab

The Mermaid
Chicago, IL
[March or May 1896; possibly never issued]
Type: Unknown
Reference: Faxon 1903b

Mirror
St Louis, MO
Weekly. 1891–1920.
Editor: William Marion Reedy
Note: "A Weekly dealing in politics and literature"
Note: "A journal of comment on anything of human interest"
Note: Issued under the following titles: *Sunday Mirror* (1891–5); *Mirror* (1895–6); *Reedy's Paper* (1896–1913); *Reedy's Mirror* (1913–20)
Type: Hybrid
Reference: Moss

Miss Blue Stocking
Boston, MA: Miss Blue Stocking Publishing Company
Semi-monthly; monthly. Illustrated. Vol. 1, no. 1, 1 January 1896–Vol. 2, no. 1, April 1896
Editor: Richard Gorham Badger
Note: "And she is fair, and fairer than that word of wondrous virtues"

Type: Aesthetic
Reference: Faxon 1897, 1903ab

M'lle New York*
New York, NY: M'lle New York Publishing Company
Bi-weekly. Illustrated. Vol. 1, no. 1, 1 August 1895–Vol. 1, no. 11, January 1896; new series: Vol. 2, no. 1, November 1898–Vol. 2, no. 4, January 1899
Editor: Vance Thompson and James Huneker
Type: Aesthetic
Reference: Faxon 1897, 1903ab; Moss

Modern Art
Indianapolis, IN; Boston, MA: L. Prang and Company
Quarterly. Illustrated. Vol. 1, no. 1, January 1893–Vol. 5, no. 1, January 1897
Editor: J.M. Bowles
Note: Designs by Bruce Rogers
Type: Aesthetic
Reference: Faxon 1897, 1903ab

Modern Ideas
Joliet, IL
Monthly [only one issued?]. Vol. 1, no. 1, August 1898
Note: "An up-to-date monthly"
Type: Unknown
Reference: Faxon 1903ab

Monologue*
Los Angeles, CA
Monthly. Vol. 1, no. 3, October 1901–Vol. 1, no. 4, November 1901
Note: Preceded by *Angel Food*
Type: Aesthetic (humour)
Reference: Faxon 1903ab

Monthly Visitor
Indiana, IN[?]
July 1895–[?]
Editor: Rev. Klingel

Type: Unknown
Reference: MacLeod

Moods*
Philadelphia, PA: Jenson Press
Irregular (2 numbers). Illustrated. 1894–5
Note: John Sloan, art ed.
Note: "A journal intime"
Type: Aesthetic
Reference: MacLeod

Moody's Magazine of Medicine
Atlanta, GA
Monthly. Illustrated. Vol. 1, no. 1, August 1896–[?]
Note: "Medico-surgical literary journal"
Editor: Ralcy H. Bell
Note: Absorbed by *The Raven*
Type: Hybrid (health; literary)
Reference: MacLeod

The Morningside*
New York, NY: Columbia University
Every third Tuesday. Illustrated. Vol. 1, no. 1, [January 1896]–[?]
Type: Aesthetic
Reference: MacLeod

The Muse*
Oakland, CA: Lotos Club
Quarterly. Illustrated. No. 1, June 1900–Vol. 2, no. 2, September 1902
Editor: Adam Hull Shirk
Note: "A little book of art and letters"
Type: Aesthetic
Reference: Faxon 1903ab

Neith
St John, NB
Monthly. Illustrated. Vol. 1, no. 1, 1903–Vol. 1, no. 5, 1904
Editor: A.B. Walker

Note: "A magazine of Literature, Science, Art, Jurisprudence, Criticism, History, Reform, Economics"
Type: Protest (African-Canadian)
Reference: MacLeod

The New Bohemian*
Cincinnati, OH: Bohemian Publishing Company
Monthly. Illustrated. Vol. 1, no. 1, October 1895–Vol. 3, no. 2, August 1896
Note: "A modern monthly"
Type: Aesthetic
Reference: Faxon 1897, 1903ab

The New Literary Review
Boston, MA
Monthly. New series. Vol. 1, no. 1, March 1901–Vol. 1, no. 2, April 1901
Note: Preceded by *Literary Review*
Note: Followed by *New Review*
Type: Aesthetic (bibliophile)
Reference: Faxon 1903ab

New Occasions*
Chicago, IL: Charles H. Kerr and Company
Monthly. Vol. 1, no. 1, June 1893–May 1897
Note: Absorbed by *New Time*
Note: Catalogued on HathiTrust as *New Time*
Type: Protest (reform)
Reference: Faxon 1897

The New Race
Kansas City, MO
Monthly. Illustrated. Vol. 1, no. 1, December 1896–Vol. 3, 1898
Editor: David H. Reeder
Note: "A monthly magazine of interest to everyone"
Type: Protest (physical culture movement)
Reference: Faxon 1897

The New Review
Boston, MA

Bi-monthly. New series. Vol. 1, no. 1, August 1902–Vol. 1, no. 3, December 1902
Editor: Richard Gorham Badger
Note: A new series of *New Literary Review*
Note: "A news journal of belles-lettres"
Type: Aesthetic (bibliophile)
Reference: Faxon 1903ab

The New Time*
Chicago, IL: Charles H. Kerr and Company
Monthly. Illustrated. Vol. 1, no. 1, July 1897–Vol. 3, no. 5, November 1898
Editor: B.O. Flower
Note: "A magazine of social progress"
Note: "For people who think"
Type: Protest (reform, socialism)
Reference: MacLeod

The Nickell Magazine
Boston, MA; New York, NY (Fiction Publishing Company); Buffalo, NY
Monthly. Illustrated. Vol. 4, no. 1, July 1895–Vol. 23, no. 5, November 1905
Editor: J.C. Clark
Note: Preceded by *The Whole Family*
Type: Miscellaneous (aesthetic)
Reference: Faxon 1897, 1903ab

The Night-Cap
Chicago, IL
[March or May 1896; possibly never issued]
Type: Unknown
Reference: Faxon 1903b

Noon*
Evanston, IL: W.S. Lord
Monthly. Vol. 1, no. 1, October 1900–Vol. 2, no. 12, October 1902
Type: Aesthetic
Reference: Faxon 1903ab

North Carolina Booklet*
Raleigh, NC
Monthly. Vol. 1, no. 1, May 1901–Vol. 20, 1920
Note: "Great events in North Carolina history"
Note: North Carolina Society of the Daughters of the Revolution
Type: Miscellaneous (history)
Reference: Faxon 1903ab

The North Star
Westfield, MA: North Star Publishing Company
Monthly. Vol. 1, no. 1, February 1895–December 1897
Editor: Joseph Duport
Note: "Published in the interests of Westfield, Mass., and surrounding country"
Type: Unknown
Reference: Faxon 1897

The Occasional One
Dunkirk, NY: A. Walton Damon
Monthly. Illustrated. Lot 1, first occasion, 15 November 1901–[?]
Note: "Devoted to no particular creed or party"
Note: "Published in the interests of astrology and a few other things"
Note: "A Monthly Magazine belonging to the Fraternity of Little Magazines"
Type: Protest (astrology)
Reference: Faxon 1903ab

The Olio
Perkasie, PA
Monthly. December 1895–June 1896
Note: aka *Literary Olio*
Type: Aesthetic
Reference: Faxon 1903ab

The Onlooker
New York, NY
Weekly. Vol. 1, no. 1, 21 May 1902–Vol. 8, no. 3, 17 December 1902
Type: Aesthetic (story)
Reference: Faxon 1903ab

The Opera Glass*
Boston, MA: Opera Glass Publishing Company
Monthly. Illustrated. Vol. 1, no. 1, 17 February 1894–Vol. 5, 1898
Note: "A musical and dramatic magazine"
Type: Aesthetic (music, drama)
Reference: Faxon 1897

The Optimist
Boone, IA: Nevernod Press
Monthly. Vol. 1, no. 1, September 1900–Vol. 2, no. 3, May 1901
Editor: H.S. Kneedler
Note: "A little journal of criticism, review, and inspiration"
Type: Hybrid
Reference: Faxon 1903ab

The Optimist
Detroit, MI
Editor: Thad Stevens Varnum
Type: Unknown
Reference: MacLeod

The Optimist
Orlean, NY
Monthly. Vol. 1, no. 1, April 1899–Vol. 1, no. 3, June 1899
Note: "This pamphlet will come once a month to the moderately well-to-do and those who labour"
Type: Unknown
Reference: Faxon 1903ab

Our Country
New York, NY: Patriotic League of America
Monthly. Vol. 1, no. 1, February 1895–1898[?]
Note: "Monthly textbook and magazine of the Patriotic League"
Type: Protest (educational)
Reference: Faxon 1903ab

The Owl
Boston, MA; New York, NY: Owl Publishing Company

Monthly. Illustrated. Vol. 1, no. 1, July 1896–Vol. 8, no. 2, February 1900
Note: "A monthly magazine of original short stories"
Type: Aesthetic (story)
Reference: Faxon 1897, 1903ab

The Owl
Lowell, MA
Monthly. Vol. 1, no. 1–Vol. 1, no. 2, April–May 1896
Note: "A monthly magazine of fact, fiction, and fantasy"
Type: Aesthetic
Reference: Faxon 1903ab

The Papyrus
Newburgh, NY
Spring 1896
Type: Unknown
Reference: Faxon 1903ab

The Papyrus*
Mount Vernon, NY; Westchester County, NY
Monthly. Vol. 1, no. 1, July 1903–3rd. series, Vol. 4, no. 1, May 1912. No numbers issued April–May 1904. Suspended September 1906–June 1907, May 1910–October 1910
Editor: Michael Monahan
Note: Succeeded by *The Phoenix*
Note: Absorbed *The Whim*
Type: Hybrid
Reference: Faxon 1903a; Moss

Paragraphs
Boston, MA: W.D. Forest
Monthly. Vol. 1., no. 1, February 1896–Vol. 2, no. 5, December 1896
Note: "of appreciation and depreciation"
Type: Protest
Reference: Faxon 1897, 1903ab

The Parisian*
New York, NY: M.L. Dexter

Monthly. Illustrated. Vol. 1, no. 1, February 1896–April 1901
Note: "Devoted to the reproduction in English of articles from the leading French and other continental periodicals"
Type: Aesthetic (general literary)
Reference: Faxon 1897

The Passing Show
Kansas City, MO
Weekly. Illustrated. Vol. 1, no. 1, 1 August 1896–Vol. 1, no. 3, 15 August 1896
Type: Unknown
Reference: Faxon 1897

Pearl Magazine
Boston, MA: Beacon Ethical Union
Monthly [only one issued?]. Vol. 1, no. 1, May 1901
Note: "A monthly publication of short stories"
Type: Aesthetic (story)
Reference: Faxon 1903ab

Pearson's Magazine*
New York, NY: Pearson Publishing Company
Monthly. Illustrated. Vol. 1, no. 1, March 1899–1925
Editor: Frank Harris
Note: Partial reprint of the London edition
Type: Aesthetic (general literary)
Reference: Moss

The Pebble*
Omaha, NB: Mary D. Learned and Louise McPherson
Monthly. Vol. 1, part 1, March 1900–Vol. 3, part 1, April 1901
Editor: Mary D. Learned and Louise McPherson
Note: "A little work, a little play to keep us going and so good day"
Type: Hybrid
Reference: Faxon 1903ab

Pen and Ink Sketches
New York, NY
Monthly [only one issued]. Illustrated. Vol. 1, no. 1, July 1895

Type: Aesthetic
Reference: Faxon 1903ab

Penny Fiction*
New York, NY: Cornucopia Company
Monthly. Illustrated. Vol. 1, no. 1, January 1897–8[?]
Note: "A magazine for the million"
Type: Aesthetic (story)
Reference: Faxon 1897

Penny Magazine
New York, NY: Penny Publishing Company
Monthly. Illustrated. Vol. 1, no. 1, March 1896–Vol. 9, no. 4, October 1900
Editor: Thomas Charles Quinn
Note: Succeeded by *Unique Monthly*
Type: Aesthetic (story)
Reference: Faxon 1897, 1903ab

Penny Magazine
Philadelphia, PA: Penny Magazine Company
Monthly. Vol. 1, no. 1, April 1896–Vol. 2, no. 3, December 1896
Type: Aesthetic (story)
Reference: Faxon 1897, 1903ab

Personal Impressions
San Francisco, CA: D.P. Elder and M. Shepard
Monthly. No. 1 (vol. 1), March 1900–No. 6 (vol. 1), August 1900
Note: "A magazine of literature and art"
Note: Succeeded by *Impressions*
Type: Aesthetic (bibliophile)
Reference: Faxon 1903ab

Petit Journal des Refusées
San Francisco, CA: James Marrion [Gelett Burgess]
Quarterly [only one issued]. Illustrated. Vol. 1, no. 1, 1 July 1896
Editor: Gelett Burgess
Type: Aesthetic (humour)

Note: Digitized issue at Modernist Journals Project (www.modjourn.org/)
Reference: Faxon 1897, 1903ab; Moss

The Philistine*
East Aurora, NY: Society of the Philistines
Monthly. Vol. 1, no. 1, June 1895–Vol. 41, no. 2, July 1915
Editor: Elbert Hubbard
Note: "A periodical of protest"
Type: Protest
Reference: Faxon 1897, 1903ab; Moss

The Philosopher*
Wausau, WI: Van Vechten and Ellis
Monthly. Vol. 1, no. 1, January 1897–1906[?]. Vol. 10, nos. 1–2 never issued; suspended October 1904–March 1905
Note: "Thoughtful but not too thoughtful"
Type: Hybrid
Reference: Faxon 1897, 1903ab; Moss

The Phoenician
Type: Aesthetic (amateur)
Reference: Donnelly

Phonogram
New York, NY: H. Shattuck
Monthly. Illustrated. No. 1, May 1900–Vol. 6, no. 2 (32nd no.), December 1902
Note: "Printed monthly for those interested in phones, graphs, grams & scopes. Devoted to the arts of recording and reproducing sound"
Type: Miscellaneous (technology)
Reference: Faxon 1903ab

Phyllida
San Francisco, CA: [Gelett Burgess and Porter Garnett]
Bi-weekly. Vol. 1, no. 1, 1 January 1897–Vol. 1, no. 2, 15 January 1897
Editor: Gelett Burgess
Note: "Phyllida, or the milkmaid. A review devoted to literary topiks, and reflections upon the doings of the town"

Type: Aesthetic
Reference: Faxon 1897, 1903ab

Pickwick
Chicago, IL: Pickwick Publishing Company
Monthly. Illustrated. Vol. 1, no. 1, May 1898–Vol. 1, no. 4, September 1898
Editor: Arthur N. Hosking
Note: "Inspiring everybody with his looks of gladness and delight"
Type: Aesthetic
Reference: Faxon 1903ab

Pierrot
Kansas City, MO
Illustrated. Vol. 1, no. 1, March 1896–vol. 1, no. 2, May 1896
Note: "Published occasionally, perhaps not that often"
Note: "a fin de siècle effort, a printer-ink freak"
Type: Aesthetic
Reference: Faxon 1897, 1903ab

The Pilgrim
Milwaukee, WI: Chicago, Milwaukee, and St Paul Railway Company
Semi-annually. Vol. 1, no. 1, December 1895–Vol. 1, no. 3, December 1896
Editor: Helen M. Boynton
Type: Aesthetic (story)
Reference: Faxon 1897, 1903ab

The Pirate
Evanston, IL
1898–[?]
Editor: Theo B. Thiele
Type: Aesthetic (amateur)
Reference: Donnelly

The Pocket Magazine*
New York, NY: Frederick A. Stokes Company
Monthly; bi-monthly. Vol. 1, no. 1, November 1895–Vol. 9, no. 5, December 1901

Editor: Irving Bacheller
Note: "Short stories by well-known authors"
Note: "*Pocket Magazine Quarterly* was formed by binding up three monthly numbers of this as a single number"
Type: Aesthetic (story)
Reference: Faxon 1897, 1903ab

Poet Lore*
Philadelphia, PA; Boston, MA: The Poet Lore Company
Semi-annual; quarterly. Vol. 1, no. 1, 1889–ongoing
Editor: Richard Gorham Badger
Type: Aesthetic
Reference: Moss

Poker Chips
New York, NY: F. Tousey
Monthly. No. 1, June 1896–No. 6, November 1896
Note: "A monthly magazine devoted to original stories of the great game"
Note: Succeeded by *White Elephant*
Type: Aesthetic (story)
Reference: Faxon 1897, 1903ab

The Porcupine
Boston, MA
Weekly. Vol. 1, no. 1, 23 August 1902–Vol. 1, no. 10, 24 December 1902
Note: "Man so loves wit that he gives it a soul"
Type: Unknown
Reference: Faxon 1903ab

The Poster
New York, NY: Will M. Clemens
Monthly. Illustrated. Vol. 1, no. 1, 1896–Vol. 1, no. 5, May 1896
Note: Absorbed by *Red Letter*
Type: Aesthetic
Reference: Faxon 1897, 1903ab

Poster Lore
Kansas City, MO: Frederic Thoreau Singleton

Bi-monthly. Irregular. Illustrated. Vol. 1, no. 1, 15 January 1896–Vol. 2, no. 1, September 1896
Editor: Frederic Thoreau Singleton
Note: “A journal of enthusiasm, devoted to the appreciation of modern posters”
Type: Aesthetic
Reference: Faxon 1897, 1903ab

Pot-Pourri
Boston, MA
Bi-weekly. Illustrated. Vol. 1, no. 1, 15 January 1896–Vol 1, no. 2, 29 January 1896
Note: “An illustrated vagary of paper and ink, conducted by a freak”
Type: Aesthetic (humour)
Reference: Faxon 1897, 1903ab

Pot-Pourri
Fremont, OH
Monthly. Illustrated. Vol. 1, no. 1, May 1898–Vol. 1, no. 12, April 1899
Editor: Lucy Elliott Keeler
Type: Aesthetic (general literary)
Reference: Faxon 1903ab

The Powder Magazine
Detroit, MI: Jefferson Press
Weekly. Vol. 1, no. 1, 28 March 1901–Vol. 1, no. 5, 25 April 1901
Note: “Cleversome wolverine weekly. A little off the top for folk who are up to snuff”
Type: Unknown
Reference: Faxon 1903ab

The Prairie Dog
Topeka, KS
Type: Aesthetic
Reference: Faxon 1903ab

The Princess
Chicago, IL

Monthly. Illustrated. Vol. 1, no. 1, April 1901–Vol. 2, no. 8, December 1902[?]
Note: Giselle D'Unger, publisher
Note: "An illustrated magazine for all"
Type: Aesthetic (general literary)
Reference: Faxon 1903ab

Pro Cingulo Veritas*
Concord, MA: Frederick Parsons
Quarterly. Illustrated. Vol. 1, no. 1, April 1903–January 1904
Editor: Frederick Parsons
Note: "for a girdle, truth"
Note: "For Craftsmen and Christian Socialists"
Type: Protest (Arts and Crafts)
Reference: Faxon 1903ab

Ye Quaint Magazine
Boston, MA: Quaint Publishing Company
Bimonthly; monthly. Illustrated. Vol. 1, no. 1, February 1901–8[?]
Note: "for the collection of old, queer and curious sayings"
Note: Digitized issues at International Association for the Preservation of Spiritualist and Occult Periodicals (http://www.iapsop.com/)
Type: Miscellaneous (humour; oddities; astrology)
Reference: Faxon 1903ab

The Quartier Latin
Paris, France; London, UK; New York, NY: American Art Association of Paris
Monthly. Illustrated. Vol. 1, no. 1, July 1896–Vol. 5, no. 30, March 1899
Editor: Trist Wood and A.A. Anderson
Note: "Compiled monthly in Paris and published in London"
Note: "A little book devoted to the arts"
Note: Digitized issues at Internet Archive (www.archive.org)
Type: Aesthetic
Reference: Faxon 1897, 1903ab

The Quest
Birmingham, UK: Press of the Birmingham Guild of Handicraft. Boston, MA: Daniel Berkeley Updike

Quarterly. Illustrated. Vol. 1, no. 1, November 1894–Vol. 2, no. 6, September 1896
Type: Aesthetic
Reference: Faxon 1897, 1903ab

The Quiet Observer
Pittsburgh, PA
Weekly. Vol. 1, no. 1, 3 May 1900–Vol. 2, no. [?], November 1901
Editor: Erasmus Wilson
Note: "It is different"
Type: Hybrid
Reference: Faxon 1903ab

Quips and Snips
Mt. Hope, Boston, MA
Vol. 1, no. 1, March 1902 [only one issued]
Editor: Charles Everett Warren
Note: "and twisted proverbs"
Type: Unknown
Reference: Faxon 1903ab

Quivera Legends
Roca, NB: E.E. Blackman
Monthly. Vol. 1, no. 1, 17 December 1898–Vol. 2, no. 6, November 1900
Editor: E[lmer] E[llsworth] Blackman
Type: Miscellaneous (folklore)
Reference: Faxon 1903ab

The Raven*
Oakland, CA: California Publishing Company
Monthly. Irregular. Vol. 1, no. 1, December 1899–Vol. 7, 1906[?]
Editor: Mary Lambert; Theodore Lowe
Type: Aesthetic (story)
Reference: Moss

Realization
Washington, DC
Bi-monthly. Vol. 1, no. 1, November 1900–Vol. 3, no. 2, March–April 1903[?]

Type: Unknown
Reference: Faxon 1903ab

The Rebel
Lincoln, NE
Monthly. Vol. 1, no. 1, September 1900–Vol. 1, no. 7, March 1901
Note: "An advocate of social progress"
Type: Protest
Reference: Faxon 1903ab

The Rebel
Philadelphia, PA: Rebel Publishing Company
Monthly. Vol. 1, no. 1, March 1901–Vol. 1, no. 5, July 1901
Editor: Melville Philips
Note: "The hypocrite reign not lest the people be ensnared"
Type: Hybrid
Reference: Faxon 1903ab

The Red Letter
Boston, MA
Monthly. Illustrated. Vol. 1, no. 1, August 1896–Vol. 2, no. 2, April 1897
Editor: Richard Gorham Badger
Note: "An illustrated monthly"
Note: Absorbed *The Poster*
Type: Aesthetic
Reference: Faxon 1897, 1903ab

The Reverie
Newton Center, MA
1902–[?]
Editor: Frank S. Norton
Type: Aesthetic (amateur)
Reference: Donnelly

The Rhymester
Hedrich, IA: Clyde A. Henry
Monthly. Vol. 1, no. 1, January 1901–Vol. 1, no. 5, May 1901
Note: "A little journal for good verses"

Type: Aesthetic
Reference: Faxon 1903ab

Robinson Crusoe
Type: Unknown
Reference: Faxon 1903ab

The Rough Rider
Butte, MT
Monthly. Vol. 3, no. 1, July 1901–Vol. 3, no. 5, November 1901
Note: "A monthly magazine of clever, fascinating, high-grade stories"
Type: Aesthetic (story)
Reference: Faxon 1903ab

Roycroft Quarterly
East Aurora, NY: Roycroft
Quarterly. Vol. 1, no. 1, May 1896–Vol. 1, no. 3, November 1896
Note: "Being a goodly collection of literary curiosities from references not easily accessible to the average truth lover"
Type: Aesthetic
Reference: Faxon 1897, 1903ab

The Rubric
Chicago, IL: Rubric Studios
Bi-monthly. Illustrated. Vol. 1, no. 1, October 1901–Vol. 2, no. 2, December 1902
Note: "A magazine deluxe"
Note: Absorbed *Blue Sky*
Note: Absorbed by *Philosopher*
Type: Aesthetic
Reference: Faxon 1903ab; Moss

The Sage Leaf
Boston, MA
Monthly. Vol. 1, no. 1, March 1901–Vol. 1, no. 5, September 1901
Note: "A monthly magazine of criticism and commendation"
Type: Aesthetic
Reference: Faxon 1903ab

Saxby's Magazine
Cincinnati, OH
Monthly. 1893–1924.
Editor: Howard Saxby
Note: "A monthly"
Type: Aesthetic (general literary)
Reference: Moss

The Schoolmaster
Cornwall-on-Hudson, NY
Monthly. Illustrated. Vol. 1, no. 1, March 1900–Vol. 11, 1906[?]
Editor: Creswell McLaughlin
Note: "This is the tune of our catch, played by the picture of nobody"
Type: Protest
Reference: Faxon 1903ab

The Scribbler
Type: Aesthetic (amateur)
Reference: Donnelly

The Scroll
Montreal, QC: J. Macaulay
Monthly. Vol. 1, no. 1, December 1900–Vol. 2, no. 1, June 1901
Note: "Being a publication of literary selections from masters past and present"
Type: Aesthetic (bibliophile)
Reference: Faxon 1903ab

Seen and Heard by Megargee*
Philadelphia, PA: L.N. Megargee
Weekly. Vol. 1, no. 1, 9 January 1901–[?]
Editor: Louis N. Megargee; James Hoyt
Type: Protest
Reference: Faxon 1903ab

Sewanee Review*
Sewanee, TN
Quarterly. Vol. 1, no. 1, November 1892–ongoing
Editor: William P. Trent

Type: Aesthetic (general literary)
Reference: Moss

The Shadow*
Cambridge, MA: Printed at the University Press
Monthly. Vol. 1, no. 1, February 1896–Vol. 1, no. 4, June 1896
Note: "The best in this kind are but shadows"
Type: Aesthetic
Reference: Faxon 1897, 1903ab

Silver Lining
Philadelphia, PA: Frederick S. Gore
Vol. 1, no. 1, March 1902–[?]
Type: Protest (Success)
Reference: Faxon 1903a

The Skeptic
Boston, MA: The Everett Press
Monthly. Vol. 1, no. 1, December 1896–Vol. 1, no. 3, February 1897
Editor: Wilson Davis
Type: Protest
Reference: Faxon 1897, 1903ab

The Sketch Book*
Chicago, IL: Art Institute of Chicago; Sketch Book Publishing Company
Monthly. Illustrated. Vol. 1, no. 1, February 1902–1907
Editor: Elizabeth Colwell
Type: Aesthetic
Reference: MacLeod

Smart Set*
New York, NY: Ess Ess Publishing Company
Monthly. Vol. 1, no. 1, March 1900–1930
Type: Aesthetic (story)
Reference: Moss

Snap Shots Magazine
New York, NY
Monthly. Illustrated. Vol. 1, no. 1, February 1901–[?]

Editor: Roland Burke Hennessy
Type: Miscellaneous (photography; humour; actresses)
Reference: Faxon 1903ab

Social Crusader*
Chicago, IL
Monthly. Illustrated. Vol. 1, no. 1, September 1898–Vol. 3, no. 8, August 1901
Note: Succeeded by *Socialist Spirit*
Type: Protest (Christian socialist)
Reference: MacLeod

Socialist Spirit*
Chicago, IL: F.H. Wentworth
Monthly. Vol. 1, no. 1, September 1901–Vol. 2, no. 6, February 1903
Note: Preceded by *Social Crusader*
Type: Protest (Christian socialism)
Reference: MacLeod

Sothoron's Magazine
Philadelphia, PA: Sothoron's Magazine Company
Monthly. Illustrated. Vol. 1, no. 1, May 1896–Vol. 2, no. 5, May 1897
Type: Aesthetic (Literary)
Reference: Faxon 1897, 1903ab

Soundview
Olalla, WA: Soundview Company; The Evergreens
Monthly. Vol. 1, no. 1, October 1902–Vol. 10, September 1908
Editor: L.E. Rader and Frank T. Reid
Note: "A magazinelet devoted to the obstetrics of thought and the philosophy of existence"
Note: "Exponent of the Society of Evergreens"
Note: Digitized issues at International Association for the Preservation of Spiritualist and Occult Periodicals (www.iapsop.com/)
Type: Protest
Reference: Faxon 1903a

Sound View, Jr
Olalla, WA

Quarterly [only one issued]. Vol. 1, no. 1, 1st quarter 1903
Type: Protest
Reference: Faxon 1903a

South Atlantic Quarterly
Durham, NC
Quarterly. 1902–ongoing
Editor: John Spencer Bassett
Type: Aesthetic (general literary)
Reference: Moss

The Stiletto
New York, NY: Stiletto Publishing Company
Monthly. Vol. 1, no. 1, August 1900–Vol. 1, no. 6., February 1901
Editor: Estelle L. Matteson
Note: "A magazine with no fads"
Type: Aesthetic
Reference: Faxon 1903ab

The Story-teller
Terre Haute, IN: Moore and Langen Printing Company
Monthly, except July and August. Illustrated. Vol. 1, no. 1, January 1900–[?]
Editor: Walter W. Storms
Note: "Tales true and otherwise, for children of all ages from 3 to 70"
Type: Aesthetic (story)
Reference: Faxon 1903ab

A Stuffed Club for Everybody
Denver, CO
Monthly. Vol. 1, no. 1, May 1900–Vol. 7, no. 12, April 1907
Editor: J.H. Tilden
Note: "There is a happy mean between the extreme drug therapeutist and the mental therapeutist. Truth lies between and requires a stuffed club to beat back the vandals"
Note: Continues as *A Stuffed Club*, 1907–15
Type: Protest (health)
Reference: Faxon 1903ab

The Stylus
Landsdowne, PA: F. Gilroy
[1900?–?]
Editor: Foster Gilroy
Type: Aesthetic (amateur)
Reference: Donnelly

The Symposium*
Northampton, MA
Monthly. Vol. 1, no. 1, October 1896–Vol. 1, no. 3, December 1896
Editor: George W. Cable
Note: "A monthly literary magazine"
Type: Aesthetic
Reference: Faxon 1897, 1903ab

Tabasco
Lapeer, MI: Tabasco Publishing Company
Monthly. Vol. 1, no. 1, October 1902–Vol. 1, no. 3, December 1902
Note: "The magazine of realism"
Type: Aesthetic (story)
Reference: Faxon 1903ab

Tarot
Toronto, ON
Monthly. Illustrated. Vol. 1, no. 1, February 1896–Vol. 1, no. 2, March 1896
Editors: Harriet Ford, George Reid, Carl Ahens
Note: "A bohemian literat [*sic*]"
Type: Hybrid (occult)
Reference: MacLeod

The Tattler Magazine
Boston, MA
Monthly. Vol. 1, no. 1, [December 1897]–Vol. 1, no. 2, February 1898
Type: Unknown
Reference: Faxon 1903ab

10 Story Book
Chicago, IL: Daily Story Publishing Company

Monthly. Illustrated. Vol. 1, no. 1, June 1900–[?]
Type: Aesthetic (story)
Reference: Faxon 1903ab

The Thistle*
New Rochelle, NY: Croscup and Sterling Company
Monthly. Vol. 1, no. 1, March 1902–Vol. 1, no. 11, January 1903
Editor: Lee Fairchild
Note: "A journal of opinion, aggressive and digressive"
Type: Hybrid
Reference: Faxon 1903ab

The Thomas Cat
Waterbury, CT: Jackson Quick Print
Yowl 1 May 1902–Yowl 5 November 1903[?]
Type: Aesthetic (amateur)
Reference: Faxon 1903a; Donnelly

Time and the Hour*
Boston, MA: Time and the Hour
Vol. 1, no. 1, 14 March 1896–Vol. 11, no. 13, 3 March 1900
Note: "Taverner helped by a book-taster, a playgoer, a reformer, a gossip, a dilettante, and a story-teller"
Type: Aesthetic
Reference: Faxon 1897, 1903ab

The Torpedo
Prairie du Sac, WI; Topeka, KS
December 1900–[?]
Editor: Frank A. Kendall
Type: Aesthetic (amateur)
Reference: Donnelly

Truth in Boston
Boston, MA: Truth Association
Weekly. No. 1, 21 December 1895–No. 22, 16 May 1896
Note: "Tell truth and shame the devil"
Type: Protest
Reference: Faxon 1897, 1903ab

Twilight
San Francisco, CA
Monthly. Illustrated. No. 1, May 1898–No. 2, June 1898
Editor: Yone Noguchi, M. Takahashi
Type: Aesthetic
Reference: Faxon 1903ab

Two-cent Monthly
New York, NY: Cornucopia Company
Monthly [only one issued?]. Illustrated. Vol. 1, no. 1, December 1896
Note: "A magazine for the million"
Type: Aesthetic (story)
Reference: Faxon 1897

Two Penny Classics
Chicago, IL
Quarterly. Vol. 1, no. 1, April 1901–[?]
Type: Aesthetic (story)
Reference: Faxon 1903ab

Uriel*
Boston, MA: The Cabbalistic Publishing Company
Monthly. Vol. 1, no. 1, August 1895–Vol. 1, no. 2, September 1895
Editor: Naphtali Herz Imber
Note: "A monthly magazine devoted to cabalistic science"
Note: Digitized issues at International Association for the Preservation of Spiritualist and Occult Periodicals (www.iapsop.com)
Type: Protest (spiritual)
Reference: Faxon 1897, 1903ab

The Valley Magazine
St Louis, MO: William Marion Reedy
Monthly. Illustrated. 1902–3
Editor: William Marion Reedy
Type: Aesthetic
Reference: Moss

The Vandal
Pittsburgh, PA

Vol. 1, no. 1[?]–Vol. 1, no. 2, April 1900[?]
Note: "A monthly journal of criticism inflicted once a month in the interests of the publishers"
Type: Protest
Reference: Faxon 1903ab

Vanguard
Green Bay, WI
Monthly. Vol. 1, no. 1, November 1902–Vol. 6, no. 12, October 1908
Note: Digitized issue at International Association for the Preservation of Spiritualist and Occult Periodicals (www.iapsop.com)
Type: Protest (socialism; Christian socialism)
Reference: MacLeod

Vanity Fair: A Whim
Note: E.J. Hulse, printer and ed.
Type: Aesthetic (amateur)
Reference: Donnelly

The Varied Year
Note: Edith Miniter, printer and ed.
Type: Aesthetic (amateur)
Reference: Donnelly

Villa de Laura Times
Chicago, IL and other locations
Irregular. 1898?–[?]
Editor: Linden D. Dey
Note: "A magazinelet of literary and opinional originality by Linden D. Dey of Chicago, Illinois"
Type: Aesthetic (amateur)
Reference: Donnelly

The Washingtonian
Washington, DC
Monthly. Illustrated. Vol. 1, no. 1, June 1897–1899[?]
Note: "An illustrated monthly magazine"
Type: Aesthetic (general literary)
Reference: Faxon 1903ab

Wayside Tales
Detroit, MI: M-S Company
Monthly. Illustrated. Vol. 1, no. 1, August 1901–[?]
Note: "short stories of interest, ranging from three to five thousand words"
Note: Preceded by *Detroit Monthly* (1899–1901)
Type: Aesthetic (general literary)
Reference: Faxon 1903ab

Westminster Chap Book
Franklin, IN: Westminster Press
Monthly. Illustrated. Book 1, part 1, June 1902–Book 1, part 2, August 1902
Note: "A miscellany for bookish people and others artistic"
Type: Aesthetic
Reference: Faxon 1903ab

The Wet Dog
Boston, MA: Wet Dog Publishing Company
Weekly. No. 1, 15 February 1896–No. 5, 14 March 1896
Note: "A paper for people with money to burn. Boston's brightest, best, and biggest circulated weekly"
Type: Unknown
Reference: Faxon 1897, 1903ab

What to Eat
Minneapolis, MN: Pierce and Pierce
Monthly. Illustrated. Book 1, no. 1, August 1896–Vol. 25, 1908
Note: "An authority upon foods, cooking, serving, table decoration and furnishings"
Note: Succeeded by *National Food Magazine*
Type: Hybrid
Reference: Faxon 1897, 1903ab

What's the Use?
East Aurora, NY: Society for the Propagation of Decency
Monthly. Vol. 1, no. 1, June 1901–Vol. 1, no. 6, November 1901; Vol. 2, no. 1, March 1903–[?]

Note: "Printed occasionally for the society for the propagation of decency"
Type: Protest
Reference: Faxon 1903ab

The Whim*
Newark, NJ: Grand Order of Whimsical Folk
Monthly. Vol. 1, no. 1, February 1901–Vol. 8, January 1905
Editor: Ernest H. Crosby and Benedict Prieth
Note: "A periodical without a tendency, published ever and anon, or say once a month"
Note: Absorbed by *Papyrus*
Type: Hybrid
Reference: Faxon 1903ab; Moss

Whims
New York, NY: The Whims Company
Monthly. Illustrated. Vol. 1, no. 1, January 1896–Vol. 2, no. 3, September 1896
Type: Aesthetic
Reference: Faxon 1897, 1903ab

The Whisper
East Aurora, NY: L.H. Kinder
Monthly. Vol. 1, no. 1, June 1901–Vol. 1, no. 11, April 1902
Editor: L.H. Kinder
Note: "A magazine of brief practical suggestions for bookbinders"
Type: Aesthetic (book binding)
Reference: Faxon 1903ab

The White Elephant
New York, NY: F. Tousey
Monthly. No. 7, December 1896–No. 16, September 1897
Note: Preceded by *Poker Chips*
Note: "A monthly magazine of original stories"
Type: Aesthetic (story)
Reference: Faxon 1897, 1903ab

The White Owl
Philadelphia, PA
Monthly. Vol. 1, no. 1, December 1901–Vol. 1, no. 7, June 1902
Note: "A magazine of tip-top tales"
Type: Aesthetic (story)
Reference: Faxon 1903ab

The White Rabbit
Oberlin, OH; Norwalk, OH: White Rabbit Publishing Company
Monthly. Vol. 1, no. 1, March 1897–Vol. 1, no. 4, July 1897
Note: "A monthly magazine of short stories by known authors"
Type: Aesthetic (story)
Reference: Faxon 1897, 1903ab

Why?
Cedar Rapids, IA: F. Vierth
Monthly. Vol. 1, no. 1, March 1898–Vol. 6, no. 2, February 1903[?]
Note: "A single-tax periodical"
Type: Protest (single-tax)
Reference: Faxon 1903ab

Wilshire's Magazine*
New York, NY; Toronto, ON
Monthly. Vol. 1, December 1900–Vol. 17, February 1915
Editor: Gaylord Wilshire
Note: Preceded by *The Challenge*
Type: Protest (socialist)
Reference: Moss

Wiziarde's Annual (Baton Quarterly)
Kansas City, MO
Annual [only one issued?]. Illustrated. Vol. 1, no. 1, December 1898
Editor: Robert Wiziarde
Note: "title under which the *Baton Quarterly* is published"
Type: Aesthetic (music and literary)
Reference: Faxon 1903ab

Woman Cyclist
Chicago, IL

Monthly [only one issued?]. Illustrated. Vol. 1, no. 1, May 1896
Note: "her book"
Note: "Devoted to the lady of the wheel and kindred sports"
Type: Miscellaneous (cycling)
Reference: Faxon 1897

The World
Type: Aesthetic (amateur)
Reference: Donnelly

The Writer
Boston, MA: Writer Publishing Company
Monthly. Vol. 1, no. 1, April 1887–ongoing
Note: "A monthly magazine for literary workers"
Type: Miscellaneous (authorship)
Reference: Moss

The Yahoo
St Louis, MO: The Society for the Vivisection of Yahoos and the Spiritual Uplifting of the Human Species
Monthly. Vol. 1, no. 1, August 1903–Vol. 1, no. 4, November 1903
Note: "A journal of vast potentialities"
Type: Protest
Reference: Faxon 1903a

The Yellow Book
New York, NY: Howard, Ainslee, and Company
Monthly. Illustrated. Vol. 1, no. 10, August 1897–No. 15 (Vol. 2, no. 1), January 1898
Note: Preceded by *The Yellow Kid*
Note: Succeeded by *Ainslee's Magazine*
Type: Aesthetic (story)
Reference: Faxon 1903ab

The Yellow Dog
Chicago, IL: Yellow Dog Publishing Company
Monthly [only one issued?]. Vol. 1, no. 1, April 1901
Note: "Look at Me! Well?"
Note: "A monthly short story"

Type: Aesthetic (story)
Reference: Faxon 1903ab

The Yellow Kid
New York, NY: Howard, Ainslee, and Company
Semi-monthly and monthly. Illustrated. Vol. 1, no. 1, 20 March 1897–Vol. 1, no. 9, July 1897
Note: "A semi-monthly of wit, fiction and illustration"
Type: Aesthetic (story)
Reference: Faxon 1897, 1903ab

Young Folks' World
Denver, CO: Chapin Publishing Company
Monthly. Illustrated. Vol. 1, no. 1, November 1896–1897[?]
Type: Miscellaneous (Juvenile news)
Reference: Faxon 1897

Notes

Introduction

1 The four pre-1905 titles are *The Mirror* (St Louis), a weekly edited from 1893 by William Marion Reedy; *The Chap-Book*; *M'lle New York*; and *The Papyrus*. All titles but Reedy's *Mirror* are in Faxon.

2 These magazines, for example, are often not included in special collections of little magazines. In some research institutions they are shelved in the open stacks, rather than special collections or an offsite facility. Princeton is an exception here and most of the Faxon titles they hold are part of an identified little magazine collection.

3 I have consulted both physical copies in institutional and private collections as well as digital copies available in online databases, including HathiTrust and the Internet Archive. Some of the titles are so obscure that I have been unable to locate any copies in libraries or with booksellers.

4 Bersanti affirms that the origin of the term little magazine to characterize "a historically specific category" is unclear (464). As in the 1890s, a number of terms were used to discuss such publications in the 1910s and 1920s. The bibliographies of Moss and Hoffman, Allen, and Ulrich were undoubtedly instrumental in establishing the term "little magazine."

5 While Freedman establishes this social context for the little magazines of the 1890s, he does not fully consider the role of non-professionals in the movement, as I do in chapter 1. Johanna Drucker, whose work in this field has focused on one of these magazines, *Le Petit Journal des Refusées*, also considers the genre a "bourgeois" and "middlebrow" one ("Bohemian by Design"; "*Le Petit Journal des Refusées*").

6 Evidence suggesting that Hoffman, Allen, and Ulrich knew of these magazines exists in correspondence between Hoffman and Ulrich in Box 1, folder 14 of the Frederick John Hoffman Papers at University of Wisconsin-Milwaukee. Early in the collaboration, Ulrich, in particular, is hopeful that the volume will be as "complete and many-sided [a] study" as possible and asks Hoffman how "inclusive" they shall be (Ulrich to Hoffman, Thursday night; Ulrich to Hoffman, 25 January 1943). Within a few months, however, the correspondence suggests that the collaborators have agreed to focus on the 1912–43 period (Ulrich to Hoffman, 7 April 1943), and that they are discarding from consideration those from or with the flavour of "the period of the 90s" (Ulrich to Hoffman, 1 December 1943).

7 The most notable of these digital resources for modernist magazines are the *Modernist Journals Project* (http://modjourn.org/) and the *Modernist Magazines Project* (http://www.modernistmagazines.com/). The best sources, however, for digitized versions of some of the American little magazines of the 1890s are the non-specialist digital libraries HathiTrust (www.hathitrust.org) and Internet Archive (www.archive.org).

8 Sean Latham, for example, in a 2013 MLA session entitled "What Is a Journal? Toward a Theory of Periodical Studies," called for thinking about the modern magazine as a "new media technology" (4). Latham's paper and the others on this panel have been influential, prompting, for example, the "Magazines and/as Media" symposium held at the University of Alberta in August 2014. The symposium, and special issues of *English Studies in Canada* and the *Journal of Modern Periodical Studies* that developed from it, consider the magazine's relationship to other media and how digital technologies provide new methodological frameworks for studying the form. See Hammill et al. eds., "Magazines and/as Media: Periodical Studies and the Question of Disciplinarity" and "Magazines and/as Media: The Politics and Aesthetics of Periodical Form."

9 This influence is evident, for example, in the work of contributors to Brooker and Thacker's ambitious three-volume *Oxford Critical and Cultural History of Modernist Magazines*.

10 Brooker and Thacker address the difficulties of defining littleness and the little magazine in volume 1 of their collection ("General Introduction" 11–17), as do Churchill and McKible in their introduction to an earlier groundbreaking revisionist volume of essays on modernist little magazines (2–4).

11 *The Chap-Book* has garnered most critical attention, including a monograph by Wendy Schlereth that provides an understanding of

its production and its relationship to the key literary trends of the era. Bergel, meanwhile, brings a book history and materialist approach to this publication as he considers its ambiguous positioning between elite and popular culture. This interest also informs Brinkman's and my own previous work on *The Chap-Book*. Where Brinkman argues that *The Chap-Book* deliberately "enact[s] a dialectic of the old and the new, the ephemeral and the permanent, the elite and the popular" (195), I have understood this tension as part of the magazine's participation in debates about the development of America's literary culture in the period ("Art for America's Sake"). Weir has also written about *The Chap-Book* and other notable proto-modernist little magazines, *M'lle New York* and *The Lark*, as part of a wide-ranging study of the appropriation, adaptation, and popularisation of decadence in America between 1890 and 1926. It is precisely *The Lark*'s proto-modernist status that concerns Evans in his insistence on the counter-cultural and deliberately ephemeral nature of this magazine and of its bibelot counterparts of the era ("*Vogue* and Ephemera"; "Ephemeral Bibelots"). He argues that these magazines promoted a new way of being artistic, one that was predicated on esoteric and obscure allusions and circulation networks for their aesthetic effect ("Ephemeral Bibelots"; "What Travels?"). Like Evans, Melinda Knight considers these publications in the context of modernism, locating in them a tension between progressivism and conservatism, socialism and fascism, feminism and misogyny. In contrast to Evans and Knight, who regard 1890s American little magazines as a counter-cultural, elitist, and anti-bourgeois phenomenon, Drucker provocatively argues for their bourgeois nature ("Bohemian by Design"; "*Le Petit Journal*"). Focusing on *Le Petit Journal des Refusées*, a magazine that Evans sees as "the first aesthetic salvo of the modernist movement" (Review of *Le Petit Journal des Refusées*, 231), she argues that "it is situated within a middle-brow world, far from radical ideals except those of humor but wonderfully self-conscious about the scene on which it depends" ("*Le Petit Journal*" 137).

Some broader considerations of the phenomenon have also been undertaken. Doyle's monograph on Walter Blackburn Harte, one of the key proponents of the little magazine movement, is insightful about the larger movement and its figures, while Evans's essay on the movement expands the terrain of artistic little magazines of the period, accounting well for their aesthetic particularities as proto-modernist publications ("Ephemeral Bibelots"; "What Travels?"). My own earlier work has drawn attention to these little magazines as notable phenomena within the literary, print, and media culture of the period, raising issues that are developed in greater detail in this book ("Fine Art"; *American Little Magazines*; "American Little Magazines"). Irvine's "'Little Magazines' in English Canada" is worth consulting, too. While its historical scope is broader and its focus is on the Canadian context, it includes cogent commentary on and analysis of little magazines of the 1890s, Canadian ones as well as American ones with Canadian connections.

12 While Faxon clearly informs Mott's section on "Ephemeral Bibelots" (*History* 387–91), some of his titles are discussed by Mott in portions dealing with "five-cent" and "all-fiction" magazines (*History* 47–51, 114–17). It should be noted that Mott also includes feature sections on some of the more important little magazines of the 1890s: *The Chap-Book*, *The Philistine*, *The Bibelot*, Reedy's *Mirror*, and *The Sewanee Review*.

13 For Cohen "forgotten literature" encompasses once-famous, now forgotten, texts and works disregarded even in their own time. It can also, however, include widely known texts if their significance undergoes a substantial shift when reframed within "a horizon of expectation that has been erased" (62).

14 Cohen articulates distant reading as a response to close reading and symptomatic reading, neither of which, in her view, accounts adequately for forgotten literature. Close reading is too time-consuming to deal with large archives of unfamiliar material and, in some cases, this material is not amenable to this kind of reading (59). Symptomatic reading, meanwhile, she argues, cannot accommodate texts that fall outside of the modernist and/or realist mode and require an understanding of generic expectations in a historicized context (57–8). While Cohen acknowledges the influence of Franco Moretti, an acclaimed proponent of distant reading based on quantitative methods, she argues for the continued importance of "perceptive reading" (59).

15 Though Casey Blake acknowledges that the journal of opinion owes its origins to the late nineteenth century, he, like many modernist scholars in their treatment of little magazines, mentions them only cursorily. He provides no examples from this period and identifies only twentieth-century publications as exemplars.

1. The Social and Cultural Formation of the Little Magazinist

1 The Ehrenreichs were the first to theorize the professional-managerial class. There has been debate as to whether to see the professional-managerial class as a distinct class, class faction, or as a contradictory position between labour and capital. In the context of this book, I treat

it as a faction whose values and ideals become dominant in the broader middle-class context around the turn of the century, while attending, at relevant moments, to its positioning between labour and capital. My understanding of the professional-managerial class in this sense coincides with that of other scholars who have been instrumental to my work on little magazines. First, Ohmann, whose understanding of mass-market magazines as central to the class formation and identity of the professional-managerial class corresponds closely with my view of the role of little magazines (*Selling Culture*). Second, Levin, whose consideration of how bohemianism functioned as a means of class positioning and formation for a professional-managerial class in late-nineteenth century America has helped shape my thinking about bourgeois engagements with bohemianism and the avant-garde.

2 Detailed information about "life membership in Philistia" appeared in advertising inserts that appeared in the magazine in 1904. An extant example of this advertising appears between pages 80 and 81 of the February 1904 issue digitized for HathiTrust by the University of California.

3 See, for example, comments from his subscribers included in "Side Talks By the Editor," *Papyrus* 3, no. 6, 2–6.

4 For more on Eddleman and her magazine work, see Parins (240–5). Evidence of her efforts to circulate the magazine to a white audience is found in correspondence with popular mid-West writer Hamlin Garland, whose work appeared in *The Chap-Book* (Garland, *Selected Letters*, 184–5), and with little magazinist Howard Llewellyn Swisher, founder and editor of *The Ghourki* ("Tucheta").

5 *The Basis* does not appear in Faxon's list, nor does it have the characteristic format and appearance of a typical little magazine. It does, however, combine a protest mission with a literary one, as many of the little magazines do, and is jibed at by Harry P. Taber in *The Philistine* ("Side Talks" 66). It is included in the updated bibliography.

6 See, also, Levine for a discussion of how many of the philanthropic cultural projects of the nineteenth century carefully controlled access to and defined the terms of engagement with culture in ways that were exclusionary (83–169).

7 For a consideration of the connection between self-help and new religious movements in America, see Anker.

8 Whitman's importance as an influence on the reform and socialist movements of the period is suggested, for example, by the inclusion of the first two stanzas of this poem under the title "Personality" (attributed to "Old Walt"), in the Christian Socialist little magazine *Socialist Spirit*

in May 1902. For a detailed analysis of Whitman's interest in personality, celebrity, and publicity, see David Haven Blake.

9 For more information about such colonies, see Timothy Miller; Boris, *Art and Labor*; Fogarty; and Lears.

10 Notable accounts of the arts and crafts movement in America include Kaplan, ed; Boris, *Art and Labor*; Johnson; and Lears (59–96). On aestheticism in the American context, see Blanchard; Mendelssohn; and Freedman.

11 For a detailed account of amateur uses of the small press, see Elizabeth M. Harris. For a history of the amateur press movement, see Spencer. The Fossils website and journal (both at http://www.thefossils.org) are further sources of information about the history of amateur journalism, as are publications by the National Amateur Press Association (http://www.amateurpress.org/).

12 Notable studies of scrapbooking include Helfland's general history, Tucker, Ott, and Buckler's edited collection, and Garvey's account of the period from the mid-nineteenth to early twentieth century.

13 The records of local archives and museums, as well as newspaper databases and genealogical websites, have been valuable for collecting information about little magazinists. While I am focusing on some of the more notable figures in the movement, the profiles I am documenting are common across the hundreds of little magazinists that I have traced.

14 While there are a number of biographical works on Hubbard, many are flawed and there is no critically authoritative one. These include Shay's hagiography; Balch, which relies much on Shay; Champney's more measured but error-riddled *Art and Glory*; Roycrofters Dirlam and Simmons's *Sinners, this Is East Aurora*, and Charles Franklin Hamilton's *As Bees in Honey Drown*, the best consideration yet. Albert Lane, though an apologist for Hubbard, is of interest for offering the perspective of a fellow little magazinist and contemporary.

15 The Virginia Historical Society holds the Bryce family papers as well as a run of the magazine. Advertisements and commentary in the magazines identify C.A. Bryce as a doctor, printer, and editor/publisher. See, for example, back matter, *Hoppergrass*.

16 For a full account of London's involvement with these magazines and this Bay Area coterie, see MacLeod, "First Appearance."

17 More information about the literary scene in and around Harvard in this period is found in Shand-Tucci, *The Crimson Letter*; Parrish; Fanning, *Through an Uncommon Lens* and "Francis Watts Lee"; and Weir 50–85.

18 The Harvard connections of these little magazinists are documented in the Harvard Secretary Reports for particular years that are available on HathiTrust.

19 There is virtually no scholarship on Edgerly, a fascinating but forgotten figure, who wrote over a hundred books of the self-help type, pseudo-scientific and spiritual, mail-order publications that he circulated through the Ralston Health Club. He claimed there were a million adherents to Ralstonism and he aspired to found a Ralston community in New Jersey. The Ralston-Purina company, led, in the day, by a proponent of Edgerly, took Ralston into its name after the success of a wheat cereal it produced that Edgerly had endorsed as "Dr. Ralston."

20 Imber did achieve fame in another sense, writing the poem that served as the basis for what would become the Israeli national anthem. He lived a bohemian and peripatetic life, dying penniless.

21 On his deathbed in 1924, Orlow would claim that he was the missing, presumed dead, Archduke of Austria, Johann Salvatore.

22 There is a large body of scholarship on these political movements. In terms of understanding their connections to the print culture of the period, the most useful works are by Quint; Ruff; and Szefel.

23 For more on Rose Valley and New Clairvaux, see Timothy Miller (50–5).

2. Print Revolutions and the Making of the Little Magazine

1 In the context of print, for example, there are debates as to whether it is more accurate to account for some of the major transformations as revolutions or evolutions. At the same time, there is a divide between those scholars who grant agency to technology as a revolutionary force and those who emphasize the importance of human agency for mobilizing the power of print. Most famously, this debate has been played out between Elizabeth Eisenstein and Adrian Johns, with Eisenstein focused on the technology and Johns interested in the role of users within print communities. See, for example, their articles on the subject in *American Historical Review*.

2 Frank Luther Mott was among the first scholars to characterize the rise of the mass-market magazine in the 1890s as a revolution because of its importance to social developments at the turn of the century ("Magazine Revolution"). This conceptualization of the phenomenon persists in more recent work on these magazines by Ohmann (*Selling Culture*) and Schneirov. Susan Otis Thompson, meanwhile, has discussed the rise

of the small and private press movement in America as a revolutionary counterpart to the British revival of fine printing of the same period. Though less explicitly theorized, the transatlantic poster movement has also been dubbed a revolution by some critics. See, for example, Meggs and George.

3 I am informed here by Genette's conceptualization of paratext, though adapting it to a book historical/textual critical frame to suggest that there are ways in which the linguistic coding of paratexts can be material insofar as they play a role in setting a tone.

4 Given the date of Mosher's comments to Stedman, it is likely he was provoked by *The Chap-Book*'s critique.

5 Susan Otis Thompson provides information about Blue Sky Press (105–7) and the Philosopher Press (199–200). On the Philosopher Press, see, also, Wallin.

6 In her analysis of early graphic design periodicals in America, Thomson notes the emphasis in trade journals of the 1880s and 1890s on printing as "art" ("Early Graphic Design"). Benton, meanwhile, discusses the professionalization of printing in the fine press movement of the modernist period. The origins of the transformation she describes, however, can be traced to the 1890s, when artists and art students, architects, and the university-educated took up printing and publishing. Indeed, a number of the figures she discusses were involved, in various ways, in the earlier movement, including Porter Garnett, T.M. Cleland, William Berkeley Updike, William A. Dwiggins, and Bruce Rogers.

7 There was a huge vogue for the *Rubâiyât* in this period (see Hart, *Popular Book* 138–9) and numerous translations, imitations, parodies of and commentary on it. Among the small press/little magazine publishers that issued such works were Elder and Shepard, Thomas Mosher, Doxey's, Roycroft, Philosopher Press, Blue Sky Press, M.F. Mansfield, the Wayside Press, and Nevernod Press. Little magazinists Gelett Burgess and Carolyn Wells did a number of parodies of the *Rubâiyât*.

8 Donnelly's claim is based on his examination of about six hundred titles from this period in the collection of Louis B. Gardner. Donnelly identifies twenty-two titles from this collection that he says reflect the influence of the fine press movement. These have been added to the updated bibliography of little magazines (Appendix). Gardner's collection is now held at the American Antiquarian Society (pre-1900 titles) and at the University of Iowa, Special Collections (post-1900 titles).

9 See "He 'Kicks' the Press Himself," for a detailed feature, including a picture of Kendall at his press.

10 Sources on the poster movement in America include Margolin; Johnson (163–213); Brandt; and Kiehl.
11 That there was enthusiasm for the poster movement among small presses is evidenced in the image of the Philosopher Press print shop (see Figure 2.6), the walls of which feature magazine posters identifiable as the work of Edward Penfield, Will Bradley, Frank Hazenplug, and others.
12 Unless otherwise indicated, the information in this and the following paragraph come from Mott, *History*, chapter 1.
13 Circulation figures for little magazines are not as readily available as they are for mainstream magazines. Only sometimes do the publications themselves provide circulation information (and these figures may not be entirely reliable). *Ayer and Sons Newspaper Annuals* for relevant years provide figures for some, but the Ayer annual is not necessarily reliable for little magazines, as its focus was on identifying suitable publications for advertisers. Little magazines were of little interest for this market.
14 Other little magazinists who divulged cost-related information include W.E. Price of *The Book-Lover*, and Willard Holcomb, Will A. Page, and Harry Chipman Bursley editors of *The Bauble*. Price claimed that the increase in the cost of paper between 1899 and 1900 had upped the cost of production of his 13,000 copies by $390 – though he does not say what the total cost is. Meanwhile, the much smaller-scale, amateur-produced *Bauble* advertised in October 1896 that a second edition of five hundred copies of any of its issues could be produced at a cost of $30 prepaid (front matter).
15 For more on the bicycle craze of the 1890s, see Hammond.
16 Ohmann offers an extensive analysis of the 1890s Quaker Oats magazine ad ("History and Literary History" 26–34).
17 That *Alkahest*'s projection of 50,000 was rather unlikely is indicated by the fact that in November 1897 they are claiming 5,000 subscribers and are aiming for 10,000 (back matter).
18 Other publications notable for their attention to the comings and goings of little magazines are *Alkahest*, *Clack Book*, *Bauble*, *Chap-Book*, *New Bohemian*, *Lotus*, *Philistine*, *Whims*, *Goose-Quill*, and *Muse*.
19 See, for example, Thomas Wood Stevens's article on *The Bachelor Book*, "The Story of a Book," and his comments on *The Philosopher* in "Stray Clouds," *Blue Sky* 5, no. 1, 72–3. *The Pebble* editors discuss *Blue Sky* in "From the Sanctum" columns for August 1900 (1, no. 5, 160–1) and March 1901 (2, no. 6, 191–2). Members of the *Blue Sky* and *Philosopher* coterie, meanwhile, published in *The Bachelor Book*, which would be taken over by William Ellis of *The Philosopher* before folding.

20 Evans makes this claim about little magazines, focusing particularly on *The Lark*, which, he argues, "advertises itself as the epitome of all we will ever not know" ("*Vogue* and Ephemera 25).
21 Evans develops these ideas about the importance of citation and citation practices as a form of circulation in the transatlantic bibelot movement in "What Travels?" Because of its publication date, I have been unable to make fuller use of Evans's work here.

3. The Big Little Magazines and the Evolution of the Genre

1 Though no editors were listed in the magazine, Cram and Carman were identified as such by *The Independent* (New York), when the magazine was issued (Doyle 41). More recently, Shand-Tucci has ascribed editorship to Cram, Goodhue, Day, and Lee (*Ralph Adams Cram* 355).
2 For more on Chicago and its little magazines, see Fleming.
3 Stetz and Samuels Lasner and Brake detail *The Yellow Book*'s implication in the commercial magazine marketplace.
4 Sources providing a fuller consideration of *The Chap-Book*'s relationship to decadence include Brinkman; Weir (101–10); and MacLeod, "Art for America's Sake." Wendy Schlereth's monograph, meanwhile, provides broad coverage of the literary content of the magazine, focusing on its engagement with romanticism, realism, and symbolism.
5 The little magazine *Modern Art*, for example, was critical of *The Chap-Book*'s inclusion of advertising. See [Bowles].
6 In the "Notes" column for 15 March 1896, the editor, in Wildean mode, dismisses the notion that he should treat "live issues," "political matters," and "questions of social reform," declaring them "too important to be vital" (*Chap-Book* 4, no. 9, 445).
7 Mosher's publications are accounted for in detail by Bishop.
8 Ironically, Mosher refused to publish Pound's poems in 1905 because, as he told the young poet, he found them "too old world," not "modern" (qtd. in Moody 42). Michael Monahan, editor of *Papyrus* (and later *The Phoenix*), felt similarly. Responding to Pound's query as to whether he "care[d] for any literature since the nineties," his riposte was "of course I should like to have his published poems" ("Side Talks By the Editor," *Phoenix* 3, nos. 2–3, 62).
9 Bruce A. White (24–30) offers a detailed discussion of the conflicting accounts of the early days of *The Philistine*.
10 Circulation figures are derived from Bruce A. White 22; Champney 58; and McKenna 64.

11 See Bruce A. White (130–3) for a discussion of Hubbard's importance as advertising innovator.

12 See, for example, the most recent biography of Crane by Paul Sorrentino (178–81).

13 For information about Denslow's work for Hubbard, see Koch, "Elbert Hubbard's Roycrofters." For more on Denslow generally, see Greene, "W.W. Denslow" and "W.W. Denslow, Illustrator."

14 The feud between Harte and Hubbard was widely reported in various little magazines.

15 His antagonisms towards certain of those mentioned in the manifesto cannot necessarily be taken at face value. Though Hubbard, a difficult man, did fall out with many people, he also staged antagonisms and feuds, recognizing their publicity value. This might have been at the heart of his relationship with Crane, as it certainly was with William Marion Reedy. Their "running feud," as Bruce A. White notes, "was designed for publicity and entertainment" (115). This kind of staged antagonism is utilized in "Manifesto," too, as Hubbard's relations with many of those named were not severed at this point.

16 "A Message to Garcia" is credited with being one of the top-selling works of all time and continues to be exploited as a motivational piece in business and the military. On its influence in these spheres see, for example Razeghi 188–9 and Challans 160–1.

17 *Moods: A Journal Intime* may be said to hold a prior claim. There were only two numbers of this subscription-only quarterly magazine, however, issued in 1894 and 1895. Both had poster-style covers and were in hardcover format.

4. Fiction: "Literature Staggering Blindfold"

1 See, for example, Richard Fusco's full-length study of this phenomenon.

2 The magazine and issues sampled are as follows: *Alkahest* 1, no. 1 (May 1896); *American Cooperative News* 1, no. 4 (October 1896); *Angel Food* 1, no. 2 (September 1901); *Bachelor Book* 1, no. 3 (May 1900); *Bauble* 2, no. 4 (May 1896); *Bibelot* 2, no. 5 (May 1896); *Black Book* 1 (October 1895); *Black Cat* 1, no. 8 (May 1896); *Blue Sky* 2, no. 4 (May 1900); *Bohemian* [Boston] 1, no. 4 (March 1901); *Book Booster* 1, no. 1 (1901); *Bradley His Book* 1, no. 1 (May 1896); *Chap-Book* 4, no. 12 (May 1, 1896); *Chips* 3, no. 4 (April 1896); *Clack Book* 1, no. 2 (May 1896); *Clique* 1, no. 1 (May 1896); *Comrade* 2, no. 1 (October 1902); *Conservator* 13, no. 1 (March 1902); *Cornhill Booklet* 1, no. 11 (May

1901); *Crier* 1, no. 1 (September 1900); *Criterion*, 8 April 1899; *Dilettante* [Seattle] 3, no. 4 (December 1900); *Doctor's Magazine and How to Live* 6, no. 4 (March 1902); *Fly Leaf* 1, no. 5 (April 1896); *Four O'Clock* 6 (July 1897); *Gauntlet* 1, no. 1 (March 1903) *Ghourki* 1, no. 10 (May 1902); *Goose-Quill* 2, no, 1 (May 1902); *Gray Goose* 4, no. 2 (February 1898); *Ishmaelite* 1, no. 6 (January 1897); *Les Jeunes* 1, no. 1 (March 1900); *John-a-Dreams* 1, no. 1 (July 1896); *Kiote* 3, no. 3 (March 1900); *Kit-Kats* 1, no. 1 (December 1900); *Lark* 13 (May 1896); *Little Chap* 1, no. 2 (May 1896); *Lotus* 1, no. 12 (May 15, 1896); *Magpie* 1, no.1 (June 1896); *Miss Blue Stocking* 2, no. 1 (April 1896); *M'lle New York* 1, no. 1 (August 1895); *Moods* 1 (1894); *Moody's Magazine of Medicine* 1, no. 1 (August 1896); *Morningside* 2, no. 1 (2 February 1897); *Muse* 1, no. 1 (June 1900); *New Bohemian* 2, no. 5 (June 1896); *Optimist* 2, no. 3 (May 1901); *Papyrus* 1, no. 1 (July 1903); *Pebble* 1, no. 2 (May 1900); *Petit Journal des Refusées* 1 (June 1896); *Philistine* 2, no. 6 (May 1896); *Personal Impressions* 1, no. 1 (March 1900); *Philosopher* 1, no. 4 (May 1897); *Pocket Magazine* 2, no. 1 (May 1896); *Ye Quaint Magazine* 2, no. 2 (April 1902); *Quartier Latin* 1, no. 1 (July 1896); *Rubric*, 1, no. 3 (April 1902); *Shadow* 1, no. 3 (May 1896); *Smart Set* 1, no. 3 (May 1900); *Symposium* 1, no. 1 (October 1896); *Thistle* 1, no. 2 (April 1902); *Time and the Hour* 2, no. 2 (June 20, 1896); *What to Eat* 1, no. 1 (August 1896); *Whim* 1, no. 4 (May 1901); *Whims* 1, no. 4 (May 1896); *Wilshire's* 45 (April 1902).

3 Ohmann employs a similar methodology in his analysis of mass-market magazine fiction in *Selling Culture*. His analysis is also based on a sampling of two hundred stories, though these are from longer runs of issues from 1895–7 and 1902–3 across just three mass-market magazines (*Munsey's*, *Cosmopolitan*, and *McClure's*). These dates conveniently cover the same period as I do and I am indebted to his observations as a basis for comparison with little magazine fiction content.

4 Levin offers an extended analysis of this magazine's complex positioning in relation to the oppositional poles of bourgeois/bohemian, popular/avant-garde, old/new, East/Mid-West, region/nation and its affiliation with professional-managerial class values (266–75).

5 Hoffman, Allen, and Ulrich include *Smart Set* in a "supplementary list" of titles that, as they say, "do not answer strictly to the definition of the little magazine; however their interests and histories are similar to those of the advance guard periodicals" (376). They limit their consideration of its status in this guise, however, to its post-1912 period. Earle (17–69) and Sharon Hamilton (226–39), while generally focusing on *The Smart*

Set's later period under the editorship of H.L. Mencken and George G. Nathan, both discuss its ambiguous positioning between little and mass magazine.

6 Though the British writer May Sinclair published in her early days under the name Julian Sinclair, this story is unlikely to be her work. The table of contents identifies the writer as being from New York.

7 See Richard and Henriette Hovey for further elaboration on the relationship between symbolism and allegory.

8 Townsend's approach to immigrant culture in his *M'lle New York* story may be uncharacteristic. By Laura Hapke's account, Townsend, a popular writer of New York slum fiction, did, in other contexts, exhibit a sentimentalizing and moralistic gaze upon the slums (49). Perhaps the radical venue gave him more scope for experimentation.

9 Other critics have explored the postcolonial aspects of this fictional genre. Amy Kaplan, for example, understands it as a "cognitive and libidinal map of U.S. geopolitics during the shift from continental conquest to overseas empire" that "refigure[s] the relation between masculinity and empire" (221).

5. Poetry: "Literature on 'a Drunken Spree'"

1 Recent scholarship has drawn attention to this aspect of the history of poetry in America. See Rubin and Paula Bernat Bennett.

2 The magazines included in this sampling are: *Alkahest* 1, no. 1 (May 1896); *American Cooperative News* 1, no. 5 (November 1896); *Angel Food* 1, no. 2 (September 1901); *Atmos* 1, no. 1 (September 1902); *Bachelor Book* 1, no. 3 (May 1900); *Bauble* 2, no. 4 (May 1896); *Beforehand* 1, no. 1 (October 1896); *Black Book* 1, no. 1 (October 1895); *Blue Sky* 2, no. 4 (May 1900); *Bohemian* [Boston] 1, no. 4 (March 1901); *Book Booster* 1, no. 1 (1901); *Bradley His Book* 1, no. 1 (May 1896); *Chap-Book* 4, no. 12 (1 May 1896); *Chips* 3, no. 4 (April 1896); *Clack Book* 1, no. 2 (May 1896); *Clique* 1, no. 1 (May 1896); *Comrade* 2, no. 1 (October 1902); *Conservator* 13, no. 1 (March 1902); *Crier* 1, no. 1 (September 1900); *Criterion* April 8, 1899; *Dilettante* [Seattle] 3, no. 4 (December 1900); *Doctor's Magazine and How to Live* 6, no. 4 (March 1902); *Expression* 1, no. 2 (September 1895); *Fly Leaf* 1, no. 5 (April 1896); *Four O'Clock* 6 (July 1897); *Gauntlet* 1, no. 1 (March 1903); *Good Cheer* 2, no. 1 (May 1901); *Goose-Quill* 2, no. 1 (May 1902); *Gray Goose* 4, no. 2 (February 1898); *In Lantern Land* 1, no. 5 (April 1899); *Ishmaelite* 1, no. 6 (January 1897); *Ithuriel* 1, no. 1 (February 1895); *Jester* 1 (January

1901); *Les Jeunes* 1, no. 1 (March 1900); *John-A-Dreams* 1, no. 1 (July 1896); *Junk* 1, no. 6 (September 1901); *Kansas Knocker* 1, no. 2 (July 1900); *Kiote* 3, no. 3 (March 1900); *Kit-Kats* 1, no. 1 (December 1900); *Knight Errant* 1, no. 1(April 1892); *Lark* 13 (May 1896); *Literary Collector* 1, no. 1 (October 1900); *Little Chap* 1, no. 2 (May 1896); *Lotus* 1, no. 12 (15 May 1896); *Lucky Dog* 3, no. 1 (December 1901); *Magpie* 1, no. 1 (June 1896); *Miss Blue Stocking* 2, no. 1 (April 1896); *M'lle New York* 1, no. 1 (August 1895); *Moods* 1 (1894); *Moody's Magazine of Medicine* 1, no. 1 (August 1896); *Morningside* 2, no. 1 (February 1897); *Muse* 1, no. 1 (June 1900); *New Bohemian* 2. No. 5 (June 1896); *New Time* 3, no. 1 (July 1898); *Noon* 1, no. 1 (October 1900); *Optimist* 2, no. 3 (May 1901); *Papyrus* 1, no. 1 (July 1903); *Pebble* 1, no. 2 (May 1900); *Petit Journal des Refusées* 1 (June 1896); *Philistine* 2, no. 6 (May 1896); *Philosopher* 12, no. 1 (July 1902); *Pro Cingulo Veritas* 1, no. 1 (April 1903); *Quartier Latin* 1, no. 1 (July 1896); *Ye Quaint Magazine* 2, no. 2 (May 1902); *Rubric* 1, no. 3 (April 1902); *Schoolmaster* 1, no. 1 (March 1900); *Seen and Heard by Megargee* 2, no. 78 (2 July 1902); *Shadow* 1, no. 3 (May 1896); *Smart Set* 1, no. 3 (May 1900); *Social Crusader* 3, no. 1 (January 1901); *Socialist Spirit* 1, no. 3 (June 1902); *Symposium* 1, no. 1 (October 1896); *Thistle* 1, no. 2 (April 1902); *Time and the Hour* 2, no. 2 (20 June 1896); *Truth in Boston* 2 (28 December 1895); *Uriel* 1, no. 1 (August 1895); *Vanguard* 1, no. 8 (June 1903); *What to Eat* 1, no. 1 (August 1896); *Whim* 1, no. 4 (May 1900); *Whims* 1, no. 4 (May 1896); *Wilshire's* 45 (April 1902).

3 A consideration of Crane's writing in relation to the poster movement is a fruitful area for research. It has been overlooked in Crane scholarship, even by Bill Brown, whose *Material Unconscious: American Amusement, Stephen Crane and the Economics of Play*, offers a rich consideration of Crane in relation to mass culture of the period.

4 The untitled poem beginning with the lines "In the Night," was published as "Verses" in *The Chap-Book*. The fifteen publications in the *Philistine* are documented by Bruce A. White, *Elbert Hubbard's The Philistine*, 63.

5 See also Penn, "New Mysticism."

6 The 15 October 1895 issue of *The Chap-Book* (3, no. 11) contains a brief reference to her in the "Notes" section (446). Meanwhile, *Noon* 1, no. 6 (March 1901) included "Constant" in its "Poems of Friendship" issue (137). For more on Dickinson's status in the 1890s, see Buckingham. John D. Barry documented Dickinson's influence on Crane as early as 1899. See his commentary in Monteiro (202).

7 Joe Pellegrino says that Scollard's title for a never-published autobiography was "Adventures of a Minor Poet" (379).
8 Scollard also engaged with this theme. His "Invitation of the Road" was reprinted in *The Philosopher* in one of the editorial columns ("Matter of Opinion" 19).
9 Brown does not name her, but cites the preface to *Poems of Passion*. Brown writes an extended critique of the "Poetess of Passion," as he identifies her, in his volume of essays *Critical Confessions* (171–200).
10 As recently as 1992, this poem was included Martin Gardner's *Best Remembered Poems*. In his introduction to the poem, Gardner says, "Framed printings of the poem may still hang on the walls of thousands of American homes" (32).
11 For a discussion of his immensely popular "Man with the Hoe," see Szefel (67–78) and Cary Nelson (15–22). Szefel's chapter on Markham is one of the few scholarly considerations of this largely neglected poet. Fuller's biography is a rich source of information also (*Unknown Edwin Markham*).
12 Outside of the sampling, other sympathetic tributes to McKinley appeared in *The Erudite*: a poem by British author Richard Le Gallienne, "McKinley Dead" (140–1), and editorial commentary by Albert Lane in "Plain Tales" (3, no. 4, 155–60).
13 Beyond the sampling, this poem was also reprinted in *Wilshire's Magazine* in August 1902.

6. Visual Art: "Art Running Amuck through Posterdom"

1 Bogart documents, for example, how the rise of the commercial, advertising-based mass-market magazine was tied to a shift in understanding about the status of magazine illustration as art (20–6). Neil Harris, by contrast, details the controversy from the literary point of view, discussing the various objections to illustrated fiction (*Cultural Excursions* 337–48).
2 On celebrity and authorship in this era, see Glass.
3 The *Times-Picayune* commented on the trend in early 1896: "A striking thing about the all-pervading poster … is the important part that woman plays in its makeup … No matter what the poster commemorates or calls attention to … it is sure to be a woman who is chosen to set it forth and impersonate it" ("The Poster Girl" 3).
4 Henry G. Fangel seems to have had Hazenplug's poster in mind when he designed the cover for the December 1897 issue of *Quartier Latin*,

an image that reverses the menace by having Pierrot set upon by women (see colour plate 12, top left).

5 Richardson's contributions and those of Raymond Crosby, Bragdon, and Hazenplug, discussed later, are identified in Wendy Schlereth and in the indices to *The Chap-Book*. These artists may have done other work for the magazine, as the art is not always attributed. For more on Richardson, see Procopio. Though Procopio does not treat Richardson's *Chap-Book* connection, it does provide a document of the newspaper and book work of this otherwise neglected artist.

6 For more on this topic, see William S. Peterson 292 and McGann, *Black Riders* 75.

7 Cate and Wick provide a detailed consideration of developments in colour printing processes in this period, noting that the photomechanical process *gillotage*, a method for applying a mechanical tint to a line drawing, "revolutionized illustration for ... magazines of humor" (81).

8 For further analysis of *M'lle New York*'s role in a broader literary context of decadent constructions of the fin de siècle and modernist New York landscape, see Murray 168–71.

9 Vance Thompson compared Fleming to Jossot with respect to his mastery of line ("Newspaper Illustrators" 546). Jossot's work, like Fleming's, does incline to representations of the grotesque, though in a bolder mode.

10 Other magazines, including, most obviously, *The Black Cat* (see colour plate 12, bottom right), exploited the decadent symbolic function of the cat. For more on the symbolic aspects of the black cat, see Schiau-Botea who notes that in French avant-garde and cabaret culture, the cat had both "mystical and sexual connotations" and "convey[ed] a hedonistic philosophy of life" (44). Evans tracks the dissemination of this iconography to the American context in "*Vogue* and Ephemera."

7. Literary Criticism and Editorials: "Every Dog Having His Day in Journalism"

1 On Whitman's reputation, see Brodhead, who notes that the poet had a lesser status in this period than Oliver Wendell Holmes, James Russell Lowell, Henry W. Longfellow, Nathaniel Hawthorne, John Greenleaf Whittier, and Ralph Waldo Emerson. For Poe's reputation in this period, see Hutcherson.

2 A notable example of Poe appreciation in little magazines includes Michael Monahan's dedication of his "Side Talks" column to him in November 1904 (*Papyrus* 3, no. 5, 7–25), a topic he also offered as

a talk on the lecture circuit. Other Poe appreciation is found in Maurice Thompson, "Poe and His Art"; Henley Abbott, "Poe Versus Doyle"; and in reprints of unsigned essays from *Graham's Magazine* (1851) that appeared in *The Philosopher*: "The Genius and Characteristics of the Late Edgar Allan Poe," and "The Critical Characteristics of Edgar Allan Poe."

3 The theme for Hubbard's *Little Journeys* volume of 1896 was "Homes of American Authors" and Whitman featured in the June number (vol. 2, no. 6). See also Michael Monahan's "Side Talks," *Papyrus* 3, no. 1, for a discussion of "Whitmanites" (1–4), and Ella M. Powell, "Walt Whitman and His Friends," in *Alkahest*.

4 Robertson deals extensively with Traubel's position as a Whitmanite (232–76).

5 The editor offers a contradictory view of British criticism in "Notes" for 15 October 1896 (*Chap-Book* 5, no. 11), praising the "trenchant liveliness" of *The Saturday Review* and the "benign dignity" of *The Athenaeum* and *Academy* (526). This contradiction may indicate that there was more than one writer of the column or, rather, an interest in deliberately provoking controversy.

6 A feature on Mabie as critic by James MacArthur appeared in a "Living Critics" series in *The Bookman* that contained all the trappings of the author as celebrity that were anathema to little magazinists, notably stylized photographs of the author, his fireplace, and his library. Mabie was also a contributor to *The Bookman*.

7 See Laing's review of Thompson's novel *Alice of Old Vincennes* in *Alkahest* 7, no. 12.

8 Early recognition of these critical voices of the 1890s came from H.L. Mencken (*Prejudices* 129). Gorham B. Munson also identified these critics as formidable (251–2).

9 For Pollard's barbed digs at Mabie, see *Their Day in Court* 257, 259, 390, 391.

10 Some aesthetic little magazines, such as *The Rubric*, and reprint magazines, including *Noon* and *The Bibelot*, published the work of these masters of the genre, while the editor of *Kit-Kats* took the name "Addison Steele" as a pseudonym.

11 Steffens was, in fact, published in a little magazine. Under the name J.L. Steffens, he published two stories in *The Chap-Book* about immigrant experiences in America: "Schloma: The Daughter of Schmuhl," about Jewish life, and "Yalan Mohamadac," about a Syrian immigrant. These works are a reminder that fiction of this period could function as a form of social and political protest and, indeed, that muckraking could take fictional

form. While hybrid periodicals, however, were keen to exploit literature for social and political purposes, aesthetic periodicals, most of which promoted an art-for-art's sake agenda, tended to be more wary of such trends.

12 Because libraries generally remove advertising content in magazines for binding, Harte's columns are extremely difficult to come by.

13 This essay was previously published in *The Philistine* in December 1898.

8. Social and Political Commentary: "Finding Fault with Things as They Are"

1 Hubbard described his "Message to Garcia" as a "preachment" in advertisements. Other little magazinists who exploited the term included Frederick Benjamin in *The Whim*, William Ellis in *The Philosopher*, and Mae Lawson in *The Ghourki*. Robert Horton, meanwhile, wrote "Preachings" for Albert Lane's *Erudite*, while Traubel had a regular feature in *The Conservator* called "Collect," a liturgical term for a type of Christian prayer.

2 The Roycroft Press published Darrow's first book, *A Persian Pearl and Other Essays* (1899), which included literary essays on the *Rubáiyát*, Walt Whitman, Robert Burns, realism in art and literature, and death.

3 The comparison to Dowie does not occur in Taylor's parody and may have appeared in another context, which I have been unable to trace. Hubbard does not seem to have been all that bothered by the parody, at any rate, as he includes an advertisement for it in his own magazine over several months (see, for example, *The Bilioustine*, advertisement). Though Taylor seems the most likely candidate, there is a complicating factor. Three months later, in July 1902, Hubbard would attribute the libelous phrase to Opie Read and the *Chicago American* (front matter, *Philistine*). Read was a popular writer and journalist of the period and the *Chicago American* was Hearst-controlled rather than connected to Medill or the "Line-O'-Type or Two" column. Perhaps Taylor borrowed from Read and Hubbard later discovered that it originated with Read rather than Taylor? Judges Hanecy and Dunne, however, mentioned by Hubbard, had been involved in a controversial libel case involving the *Chicago American* a few months earlier in December 1901. I have found no trace of Hubbard being involved in a libel case connected to this issue.

4 George H. Daniels, of the New York Central railroad, established this trend when he ordered 100,000 copies of the pamphlet to be printed for

distribution to railway employees. The practice was soon taken up by other business and military leaders.

5 Another notable response was that of George Heafford, a man who held the same position as Daniels, but for the Chicago, Milwaukee and St Paul Railway Company. He objected to Hubbard's pamphlet and to having been sent 1,000 copies by Daniels to distribute to his employees, and penned an objection, "An Open Letter," to George H. Daniels (printed as a pamphlet). This letter was reprinted in *The Philosopher* in July 1899 and its editor offered to issue copies from his press to any interested parties, touting it as "A Message to Daniels" (Ellis, "In the Smoking Room," *Philosopher* 6, no. 1, 27–9). Apparently, Heafford's message did not get through. Four months later, Heafford resigned from his position to go into the insurance business, and "A Message to Garcia" would be issued in millions of copies in the twentieth- and twenty-first century.

6 Lists of the table of contents for the first two issues of the magazine in the third number for July 1900 include the following articles as having appeared in June 1900: "The World Is Growing Healthier: the Great Burlington R.R. and Elbert Hubbard Are Given as Proofs" and "Mr. Ernest H. Crosby's Conception of Love" (front matter, *Stuffed Club*).

7 This motto is taken from the cover of *Corsair* 6, no. 85 (13 June 1907), the earliest number I have been able to view.

8 This aphorism, and an accompanying cartoon, adorn the back cover of *Philistine* 22, no 3 (February 1906).

9. Sayings: The Short and Shorter of It

1 Along with Buechler and Gross, the following sources inform the discussion throughout this chapter: Obelkevich; Mieder, *Proverbs Are Never Out of Season* and *"Proverbs Speak Louder than Words"*; Morson, *Words of Others* and "The Aphorism"; Garber.

2 Gross is speaking more generally of the aphorism as a form in his introduction to *The Oxford Book of Aphorisms* (vii). J. Hillis Miller and Morson, by contrast, offer case studies. Miller considers Nietzsche's use of the aphorism in detail, arguing that it serves as central to his desire to bring about, in his readers, the revaluation of all values (70). Morson, meanwhile, is concerned with defining the opposition between the Dionysian impulse of the aphorism and the Apollonian nature of the dictate ("Aphorism" 409–29).

3 Morson takes exception to this widely made claim, noting that anthologies of quotations have a long history, which he charts (*Words of Others* 28–34).
4 These collections included *The Motto Book* (1909, 1914), *A Thousand and One Epigrams* (1911), *The Roycroft Dictionary* (1914), *Elbert Hubbard's Scrap Book* (1923), and *The Note Book of Elbert Hubbard* (1927).
5 For Hubbard's Emerson and Ruskin kabojolisms, see Bruce A. White 101–4; on Byron, see Balch 235–7.
6 I can find no record of a person called Handel Zanque, which may be the pen name of Ralph Tallman, editor of *The Junk*.

Afterword

1 Apart from Guido Bruno's publications, there is scant scholarship on these other publications. On Bruno, see Stephen Rogers.
2 The following findings about the afterlives of 1890s little magazinists constitute a small, but representative portion, of the information that I have derived through Internet searches that have taken me to local history museums and archives sites, genealogical sites, published book sources, and the humble Wikipedia. I omit documentation here, as this information can be taken to be standard general knowledge about these figures.

Appendix

1 Faxon's initial 1897 bibliography includes ninety-eight titles. Of these, ninety-four are North American, four British. Of the North American titles, one is Canadian (*The Bill Poster* of Toronto) and one is an American-produced publication compiled by Americans in Paris. One of the British titles in this list was published simultaneously in Birmingham and Boston (*The Quest*) and, because of this American connection, is included in the list. Faxon's 1903 bibliographies, meanwhile, compiled after the second wave of the movement, are substantially larger. The version published in the *Bulletin of Bibliography* includes a total of 246 titles, 236 of which are North American or transatlantic publications, including two Canadian (*The Kit-Bag*, of Fredericton, New Brunswick, and *The Scroll*, of Montreal) and ten British. Of these North American titles, 218 appear as main entries, thirteen as addenda, and five are mentioned in the introduction as heard of but not seen. Another 1903 bibliography, based on this one, contains 238 titles, 228 of which are North American,

ten British. This bibliography differs from the other 1903 one in various inclusions and exclusions. It includes one additional entry – *The Autocrat*, a Chicago magazine – and mentions four different titles in its introduction that Faxon identifies as announced publications that were probably never issued (*"Ephemeral Bibelots"* 6). It excludes the addenda of the *Bulletin of Bibliography* version and the five titles mentioned in that introduction.

Bibliography

Abbott, Henley. “Poe Versus Doyle.” *Alkahest* 7, no. 7 (January 1901): 28–32.

Aberdeen, Ishbel. Introduction to “Beyond the Marshes,” by Ralph Connor. *Cornhill Booklet* 1, no. 11 (May 1901): 330.

“Additional Locals.” *Lincoln Evening News* (NB). 5 October 1898. no pag.

“Advertisements.” *New Bohemian* 1, no. 1 (October 1895): ii–viii.

“Advertisements.” *Philistine* 1, no. 2 (July 1895): 72.

Alden, Henry Mills. “Editor’s Study.” *Harper’s Monthly Magazine* 104 (December 1901): 167–70.

“The American Fraternity of Writers.” *Editor* 5, no. 3 (March 1897): 87–9.

American Medical Association. “The Home Health Club.” In *Some Quasi-Medical Institutions*, 17–24. Chicago: American Medical Association, 1916.

American Newspaper Directory. New York: Geo. P. Rowell, 1897.

Anker, Roy M. *Self-Help and Popular Religion in Modern American Culture: An Interpretive Guide*. Westport, CT: Greenwood Press, 1999.

“Announcement.” *Four O’Clock* (July 1897): no pag.

“Announcement.” *Quartier Latin* 1, no. 1 (July 1896): 1–3.

“Announcements.” *Chap-Book* 6, no. 3 (15 December 1896): xxi.

Applegate, Edd. *Muckrakers: A Biographical Dictionary of Writers and Editors*. Plymouth, UK: Scarecrow Press, 2008.

Arnold, Olga. “Parilee’s Dream.” *Fly Leaf* 1, no. 5 (April 1896): 14–16.

Ashton, John. “Chap-books.” *Chap-Book* 3, no. 1 (15 May 1895): 3–13.

“At the End of the Book: The Character of Some Future Numbers Together with Notes of General Interest.” *Bradley His Book* 1, no. 1 (May 1896): no pag.

Atherton, Gertrude. “One of the Problems.” *Goose-Quill* 2, no. 1 (May 1900): 6–21.

Back matter. *Alkahest* 3, no. 3 (November 1897): no pag.

Back matter. *Bradley His Book* 1, no. 3 (1896): no pag.
Back matter. *Chips* 2, no. 13 (23 November 1895): no pag.
Back matter. *Hoppergrass* 1, no. 1 (January 1899): 16.
Back matter. *Lotus* 1, no. 1 (November 1895): no pag.
Back matter. *Papyrus* 1, no. 1 (July 1903): no pag.
Back matter. *Philistine* 14, no. 5 (April 1902): no pag.
Badger, Richard Gorham. "The Slight Forgetfulness of the Knight of the Four Oaks." *Miss Blue Stocking* 2, no. 1 (April 1896): 2–8.
[–] "Notes." *Miss Blue Stocking* 2, no. 1 (April 1896): 23–7.
Baker Printing Co. Advertisement. *Muse* 1, no. 1 (Summer 1900): no pag.
Balch, David Arnold. *Elbert Hubbard: Genius of Roycroft*. New York: Frederick Stokes Company, 1940.
"A Ballade of Baldness." *Bradley His Book* 1, no. 2 (June 1896): no pag.
"Barcans, Slim" [Carman, Bliss]. "To a Portrait of a Western Poet." *Chap-Book* 2, no. 7 (15 February 1895): 320–1.
Bardeen, Frances H. "Romance in Fiction." *Philosopher* 1, no. 4 (May 1897): 110–13.
"Barman, Cliss" [Bliss Carman]. "A Lyric of Grief." *Bauble* 1, no. 2 (August 1895): 17.
Bates, Charles Austin. Untitled editorial matter. *Charles Austin Bates Criticisms* 2, no. 2 (August 1897): 114–19.
Beardsley, Aubrey. "After Himself." *Chap-Book* 1, no. 1 (15 May 1894): 17.
– "A Design by Aubrey Beardsley in Illustration of Poe's Tale, 'The Masque of the Red Death.'" *Chap-Book* 1, no. 7 (15 August 1894): 156.
– "A Drawing." *Chap-Book* 1, no. 5 (15 July 1894): 108.
Beck, Leonora. "Two Women." *New Bohemian* 2, no. 5 (May 1896): 213.
Beeby-Collins. "American Art." *Les Jeunes* 1, no. 1 (March 1900): 7–8.
Beegan, Gerry. *The Mass Image: A Social History of Photomechanical Reproduction in Victorian London*. Basingstoke: Palgrave Macmillan, 2008.
Beerbohm, Max. "*Chap-Book* Caricatures." *Chap-Book* 5 nos. 8–12 (1 September 1896–1 November 1896).
Belin, H.E. "What Is Poetry?" *Optimist* 2, no. 3 (May 1901): 140–5.
Bennett, Frederic C. "An Etching." *Little Chap* 1, no. 2 (May 1896): 27.
Bennett, Paula Bernat. *Poets in the Public Sphere: The Emancipatory Project of American Women's Poetry, 1800–1900*. Princeton: Princeton University Press, 2003.
Benton, Megan L. *Beauty and the Book: Fine Editions and Cultural Distinction in America*. New Haven: Yale University Press, 2000.
Bergel, Giles. "The Chap-Book." In Brooker and Thacker, *Oxford Critical and Cultural History*, vol. 2, 154–75.

Bersanti, Michael. “Little Magazines.” In *Oxford Encyclopedia of American Literature*, edited by Jay Parini, 462–8. Oxford: Oxford University Press, 2004.

Berthon, Paul. “Drawing for a Poster.” *Chap-Book* 4, no. 5 (15 January 1896): 350.

– “Portrait of M. Andhré des Gachons.” *Chap-Book* 4, no. 7 (15 February 1896): 347.

“Between the Covers.” *New Bohemian* 2, no. 5 (May 1896): 223–6.

Bieze, Michael. “Ruskin in the Black Belt: Booker T. Washington, Arts and Crafts, and the New Negro.” *Notes in the History of Art* 24, no. 4 (Summer 2005): 24–34.

Bigelow, Herbert E. “The Industrial Slave.” *Vanguard* 1, no. 8 (June 1903): 18–20.

The Bilioustine. Advertisement. *Philistine* 13, no. 1 (June 1901): no pag.

“Biography of Elia Wilkinson Peattie, 1862-1935.” *Elia Peattie: An Uncommon Woman, an Uncommon Writer*. Accessed 15 August 2015. http://plainshumanities.unl.edu/peattie/index.html.

Bishop, Philip R. *Thomas Bird Mosher: Pirate Prince of Publishers*. New Castle, DE: Oak Knoll, 1998.

Blake, Casey. “Journals of Opinion.” In *A Companion to American Thought*, edited by Richard Wightman Fox and James T. Kloppenborg, 355–8. London: Blackwell, 1998.

Blake, David Haven. *Walt Whitman and the Culture of American Celebrity*. New Haven: Yale University Press, 2005.

Blanchard, Mary Warner. *Oscar Wilde's America: Counterculture in the Gilded Age*. New Haven: Yale University Press, 1998.

Bledstein, Burton J. *The Culture of Professionalism: The Middle Class and the Development of Higher Education in America*. New York: Norton, 1976.

Blumenthal, Joseph. *The Printed Book in America*. Boston: David R. Godine, 1977.

Bogart, Michèle. *Artists, Advertising, and the Borders of Art*. Chicago: University of Chicago Press, 1995.

Bok, Edward. *The Americanization of Edward Bok*. New York: Charles Scribner's Sons, 1921.

Bolter, Jay David, and Richard Grusin. *Remediation: Understanding New Media*. Cambridge, MA: MIT Press, 1998.

“Book Reviews.” *Atlanta Medical and Surgical Journal* 13, no. 7 (September 1896): 501–4.

“Borders of Bohemia.” *New Bohemian* 2, no. 6 (June 1896): 282–4.

Boris, Eileen. *Art and Labor: Ruskin, Morris, and the Craftsman Ideal in America*. Philadelphia: Temple University Press, 1986.

– "'Dreams of Brotherhood and Beauty:' The Social Ideas of the Arts and Crafts Movement." In Wendy Kaplan, *"Art That Is Life,"* 208–22.

Bornstein, George. *Material Modernism: The Politics of the Page.* Cambridge: Cambridge University Press, 2001.

Boston Transcript, 27 July 1898. Francis Browne files, Midwest MS Browne (Box 7, folder 360). Newberry Library, Chicago.

Bourdieu, Pierre. *Distinction: A Social Critique of the Judgement of Taste.* Translated by Richard Nice. London: Routledge, 2010.

Bourne, May Ethelyn. "A Black Cat." *Gray Goose* 4, no. 2 (February 1898): 20–2.

[Bowles, J.M.]. "Echoes." *Modern Art* 3, no. 1 (Winter 1895): no pag.

"*Bradley His Book*: Prospectus." 1896. no pag.

Bradley, Will. Designs for "Night-Blooming Cereus," by Harriet Monroe. *Bradley His Book* 1, no. 1 (May 1896): no pag.

– Designs for "Island Queen," by Tudor Jenks. *Bradley His Book* 1, no. 2 (June 1896): 14–25.

– "May." Stone and Kimball, May 1895. Lithograph. New York Public Library Digital Collections. Accessed 10 July 2015. http://digitalcollections.nypl.org/items/510d47e2-9135-a3d9-e040-e00a18064a99.

– "The Poet and His Lady." Stone and Kimball, January 1895. Lithograph. New York Public Library Digital Collections. Accessed 10 July 2015. http://digitalcollections.nypl.org/items/510d47e2-9135-a3d9-e040-e00a18064a99.

– *Will Bradley, His Chap Book*. New York: The Typophiles, 1955.

Bradley, William Aspenwall. "Dagonet." *Morningside* 2, no. 1 (2 February 1897): 6–10.

Bragdon, Claude F. "Drawing." *Chap-Book* 5, no. 2 (1 June 1896): 57.

– *The Secret Springs: An Autobiography*. London: Dakers, 1938.

Brake, Laurel. "Aestheticism and Decadence: *The Yellow Book* (1894–7), *The Chameleon* (1894), and *The Savoy* (1896)." In Brooker and Thacker, *Oxford Critical and Cultural History*, vol. 1, 76–100.

Brandt, Frederick R. *Designed to Sell: Turn-of-the-Century American Posters.* Exhibition Catalogue. Richmond: University of Washington Press, with Virginia Museum of Fine Arts, 1995.

Brinkman, Bartholomew. "A 'Tea-Pot Tempest:' *The Chap-Book*, 'Ephemeral Bibelots,' and the Making of the Modern Little Magazine." *Journal of Modern Periodical Studies* 1, no. 2 (2010): 193–215.

Brodhead, Richard. "American Literary Field: 1860–1890." In *Cambridge History of American Literature.* Vol. 3, *Prose Writing, 1860–1920*, edited by Sacvan Berkovitch, 11–62. New York: Cambridge University Press, 2005.

Brooker, Peter, and Andrew Thacker. "General Introduction." In Brooker and Thacker, *Oxford Critical and Cultural History*, vol. 1, 1–27.

– eds. *Oxford Critical and Cultural History of Modernist Magazines*. Vol. 1, *Britain and Ireland 1880–1955*. Oxford: Oxford University Press, 2009.

– *Oxford Critical and Cultural History of Modernist Magazines*. Vol. 2, *North America 1894–1960*. Oxford: Oxford University Press, 2012.

– *Oxford Critical and Cultural History of Modernist Magazines*. Vol. 3, *Europe 1880–1940*. Oxford: Oxford University Press, 2013.

Brown, Bill. *Material Unconscious: American Amusement, Stephen Crane and the Economics of Play*. Cambridge: Harvard University Press, 1997.

Brown, Kenneth. "Little Things." *Magpie* 1, no. 1 (June 1896): 14–19.

Brown, Neal. "Advice to a Philosopher." *Philosopher* 1, no. 1 (January 1897): 14–19.

– *Critical Confessions*. Wausau, WI: Philosopher Press, 1899.

[Browne, Francis F.] "American Periodicals." *Dial* 13 (1 October 1892): 203–4.

"Bruce Porter (Designer)." Pacific Coast Architecture Database, 2005–15. Accessed 15 August 2015. http://pcad.lib.washington.edu/.

Bryant, Edward W. "The Stirrup Cup." *John-a-Dreams* 1, no. 1 (July 1896): no pag.

Buckingham, Willis J. *Emily Dickinson's Reception in the 1890s: A Documentary History*. Pittsburgh: University of Pittsburgh Press, 1989.

Buechler, Ralph W. "Aphorism." In *The Encyclopedia of the Essay*, edited by Tracy Chevalier, 26–7. Chicago: Fitzroy Dearborn, 1997.

Buell, Lawrence. "The Transcendentalist Poets." In *Columbia History of American Poetry*, edited by Jay Parini, 97–120. New York: Columbia University Press, 1993.

– ed. *The American Transcendentalists: Essential Writings*. New York: Random House, 2006.

Bulson, Eric. "Little Magazine, World Form." In *The Oxford Handbook of Global Modernisms*, edited by Mark Wollaeger and Matt Eatough, 267–87. Oxford: Oxford University Press, 2012.

Burgess, Gelett. "The Avocations of Vivette." *Lark* 15 (July 1896): no pag.

– *Bayside Bohemia: Fin de siècle San Francisco and Its Little Magazines*. San Francisco: Book Club of California, 1954.

– "*Petit Journal des Refusées*." *Lark* 6 (October 1895): no pag.

Burgess, Gelett, and Bruce Porter. "Memoir." *Epi-Lark* 25 (May 1897): no pag.

Byron, Lord [George Gordon Byron]. "Hispanoila [*sic*] (From *Childe Harold*)," *New Time* 3, no. 1 (July 1898): 26.

Cady, Ethel Smith. *A History of Union Congregational Church, 1836–1955*. Green Bay: The Church, 1955.

Campbell, W. Joseph. *The Year That Defined American Journalism: 1897 and the Clash of Paradigms*. New York: Routledge, 2006.

– *Yellow Journalism: Puncturing the Myths, Defining the Legacies*. Westport, CT: Greenwood Publishing Co., 2001.

Carman, Bliss. "Along the Trail." *Bibelot* 10, no. 9 (September 1904): 275.

– "Ballad of Saint Kavin." *Chap-Book* 4, no. 12 (1 May 1896): 559–60.

– "In Philistia." *Philistine* 3, no. 4 (February 1897): 65–6.

– *Letters of Bliss Carman*. Edited by H. Pearson Gundy. Montreal: McGill-Queen's University Press, 1981.

– "Little Lyrics of Joy – IV." *Chap-Book* 2, no. 11 (15 April 1895): 435.

– "Mr. Gilbert Parker." *Chap-Book* 1, no. 12 (1 November 1894): 339–43.

– "Night Washers." *Chap-Book* 2, no. 2 (1 December 1894): 62–4.

– "The Paupers." *Lotus* 2, no. 2 (October 1896): 189.

– "To P.V." *Chap-Book* 5, no. 10 (1 October 1896): 479–80.

Carter, John. *English Private Presses 1757–1961*. London: Times Bookshop, 1961.

"Carter Lecture Course." *Wichita Daily Eagle*, 24 September 1903, 6.

"Cartman, Joy." "Little Delirics of Bliss." *Philistine* 1, no. 1 (June 1895): 22.

Casper, Scott E. "The Census, the Post Office, and Governmental Publishing." In Casper et al., *History of the Book in America*, 178–93.

Casper, Scott E., et al., eds. *The History of the Book in America*. Vol. 3, *The Industrial Book, 1840–1880*. Chapel Hill: University of North Carolina Press, 2007.

Cate, Phillip Dennis, and Peter A. Wick. "Printing in France 1850–1900: The Artist and New Technologies," *Gazette of the Grolier Club*, new series, 28–9 (June/December 1978): 57–82.

Cave, Roderick. *The Private Press*. London: Faber and Faber, 1971.

Cazals, F.-A. "Portrait of P.V. by F.-A. Cazals from *Epigrammes*." *Chap-Book* 2, no. 9 (15 March 1895): 373.

Challans, Timothy L. *Awakening Warrior: Revolution in the Ethics of Warfare*. Albany: State University of New York, 2007.

Champney, Freeman. *Art and Glory: The Story of Elbert Hubbard*. New York: Crown Publishers, 1968.

Chan, Winnie. *The Economy of the Short Story in British Periodicals of the 1890s*. New York: Routledge, 2007.

Chatfield-Taylor, H.C. "If at First You Don't Succeed." *Smart Set* 1, no. 3 (May 1900): 97–105.

Chesnutt, Charles W. Letter to Albion W. Tourgée, 3 September 1895. Albion Winegar Tourgée Collection, New York Heritage Digital Collections.

Accessed 6 July 2015. https://www.nyheritage.org/collections/albion-winegar-tourgee-collection.

Chesterton, G.K. *Charles Dickens*. New York: Dodd and Mead, 1906.

The Chief's Print Shop (Acme Publishing Co.). Advertisement. *Ghourki* 3, nos. 2–3 (September–October 1903): no pag.

"Chips for 1896." *Chips* 2, no. 16 (21 December 1895): inside back cover.

"The Church of the Living Christ." *Essene* 1, no. 1 (July 1902): 30–4.

Churchill, Suzanne, and Adam McKible. Introduction to *Little Magazines and Modernism: New Approaches*, edited by Suzanne Churchill and Adam McKible, 3–18. Burlington, VT: Ashgate, 2007.

"Clacks." *Clack Book* 1, no. 3 (June 1896): 82–5.

– *Clack Book* 1, no. 4 (July 1896): 122–4.

– *Clack Book* 2, nos. 2–3 (December 1896): 110–17.

Clancy, Jonathan. "Transcendentalism and the Crisis of Self in American Art and Culture 1830–1930." PhD diss., City University of New York, 2008. Proquest (AAT 3306980). Accessed 17 July 2015. http://search.proquest.com/.

Clegg, Blanche Cox. "Myrtle Reed." In *American National Biography Online*. February 2000. Accessed 3 July 2015. http://anb.org.

[Clemens, Will M.] Untitled commentary. *The Poster* 1, no. 1 (January 1896).

Cohen, Margaret. "Narratology in the Archive of Literature." *Representations* 108, no. 1 (Fall 2009): 51–75.

"Cold Tongue." *Junk* 1, no. 6 (September 1901): 128.

"Comment." *Lotus* 1, no. 3 (December 1, 1895): 90–1.

"Condemned Contemporaries." *Bauble* 2, no. 4 (May 1896): 53–7.

Connor, Ralph. "Beyond the Marshes." *Cornhill Booklet* 1, no. 1 (May 1901): 331–41.

Cram, Ralph Adams. *My Life in Architecture*. Boston: Little Brown and Company, 1936.

Crane, Stephen. *Correspondence of Stephen Crane*. Edited by Stanley Wertheim and Paul Sorrentino. New York: Columbia University Press, 1988.

– "A Grey Sleeve." *Pocket Magazine* 2, no. 1 (May 1896): 69–103.

– "Lantern Song." *Philistine* 1, no. 4 (September 1895): 124.

– *Stephen Crane: Letters*. Edited by R.W. Stallman and Lillian Gilkes. New York: New York University Press, 1960.

– "Verses." *Chap-Book* 4, no. 8 (1 March 1896): 372.

Crane, Walter. "Of Aesthetic Pessimism and the New Hope." *Knight Errant* 1, no. 2 (July 1892): 40–3.

"The Critical Characteristics of Edgar Allan Poe." *Philosopher* 14, no. 4 (October 1903): 104–18.

Crosby, Ernest. "The Great Joy." *Social Crusader* 3, no. 1 (January 1901): 24.
– "The New Creation." *Social Crusader* 3, no. 1 (January 1901): 17.
[–] "Notes." *Whim* 4, no. 5 (December 1902): 145–53.
– "A Vision of Art." *Whim* 1, no. 4 (May 1901): 97.
Crosby, Raymond. "A Drawing." *Chap-Book* 5, no. 10 (1 October 1896): 451.
[Curry, S.S.] "Development of the Artistic Nature." *Expression* 1, no. 1 (June 1895): 1–7.
Daniels, E.D. *A Twentieth Century History and Biographical Record of Laporte County*. Chicago: Lewis Publishing Co., 1904.
Danziger, Adolphe. Untitled editorial matter. *Gauntlet* 1, no. 1 (March 1903): 1–2.
Davis, Richard Harding. "At the Opera." *Bradley His Book* 1, no. 1 (May 1896): no pag.
Dawe, Carlton. "A Silken Cord." *Smart Set* 1, no. 3 (May 1900): 127–34.
"Dawe, Carlton." In *Oxford Companion to Edwardian Fiction*, edited by Sandra Kemp, Charlotte Mitchell, and David Trotter, 91. Oxford: Oxford University Press, 1995.
Dawson, Polly. "Into the Deeps." *Conservator* 13, no. 1 (March 1902): 5.
Debs, Eugene. "Prince and Proletaire." *Wilshire's* 45 (April 1902): 65–7.
Deland, Margaret. "A Study for a Picture." *Pocket Magazine* 2, no. 1 (May 1896): 148–59.
Des Gachons, Andhré. "Supplement for no. 7." *Chap-Book* 4, no. 6 (1 February 1896): no pag.
– "Illustration for a Poem by Jean Lorrain." *Chap-Book* 4, no. 7 (15 February 1896): 350.
Dickinson, Emily. "Constant." *Noon* 1, no. 6 (March 1901): 137.
Diebel, Anne. "'The Dreary Duty:' Henry James, *The Yellow Book* and Literary Personality." *Henry James Review* 32, no. 1 (2011): 45–59.
Dirlam, H. Kenneth, and Ernest Simmons. *Sinners, This Is East Aurora: The Story of Elbert Hubbard and the Roycrofters*. New York: Vantage, 1964.
Dix, Dorothy. "The Bear Who Found Nothing in Economy." *Wilshire's* 45 (April 1902): 44.
Doctor's Magazine and How to Live. Advertisement. *Erudite* 3, no. 4 (December 1901): no pag.
Dolmetsch, Carl R. *The Smart Set: A History and Anthology*. New York: Dial Press, 1966.
Donnelly, Sean. "An Ajay Time Capsule." *Fossil* 101, no. 4 (July 2005): 8–9.
Dowling, Linda. *Language and Decadence in the Victorian Fin de Siècle*. Princeton: Princeton University Press, 1986.

Doyle, James. *The Fin de Siècle Spirit: Walter Blackburn Harte and the American/Canadian Literary Milieu of the 1890s*. Toronto: ECW Press, 1995.

[Dresser, Horatio W.]. "Editor's Study." *Higher Law* 5, no. 2 (March 1902): 63–4.

Drucker, Johanna. "Bohemian by Design: Gelett Burgess and *Le Petit Journal des Refusées*." OpenStax cnx. 2009. http://cnx.org/contents/77d466ec-6cf6-4e81-ab4d-18cb3c0527be@1.

– "*Le Petit Journal des Refusées*: A Graphical Reading." *Victorian Poetry* 48, no. 1 (Spring 2010): 137–69.

Duncombe, Stephen. *Notes From Underground: Zines and the Politics of Alternative Culture*. Bloomington, IN: Microcosm, 2008.

Dunsmore, Cora T. "Percival Pollard: The Iowa Connection." *Books at Iowa* 23 (1975): 34–45.

Dwiggins, William A. "D.B. Updike and the Merrymount Press." *Fleuron* 3 (1924): 1–8.

Earl, Sophie. "A Prophecy." *Bohemian* [Boston] 1, no. 4 (March 1901): 10–13.

Earle, David. *Recovering Modernism: Pulps, Paperbacks and the Prejudice of Form*. Burlington, VT: Ashgate, 2009.

East Aurora School of Philosophy. "Side Talks With the Philistines: Being Sundry Bits of Wisdom Which Have Been Heretofore Secreted, and Are Now Set Forth in Print." *Philistine* 1, no. 1 (June 1895): 17–29.

Eble, Eugene. "A Game of Chess." *Whims* 1, no. 4 (May 1896): 119–31.

"Economics." *Atmos* 1, no. 1 (September 1902): 30–1.

Edelheim, Carl. "The Kelmscott Press." *Modern Art* 4, no. 2 (Spring 1896): 36–9.

"Editorial." *Southern Medical Record* 26, no. 10 (October 1896): 519–23.

The Editors. "By Way of Epilogue." *Knight Errant* 1, no. 4 (January 1893): no pag.

– "The Quest: Being an Apology for the Existence of the Review Called *The Knight Errant*." *Knight Errant* 1, no. 1 (April 1892): 1–2.

Edwards, Louise Betts. "Mary the Prig." *Criterion* (8 April 1899): 7–9.

Edwards, Rebecca. *New Spirits: Americans in the Gilded Age, 1865–1905*. New York: Oxford University Press, 2006.

"Egbert Divorce Case Reopened." *Chicago Daily Tribune*, 24 April 1906, 5.

Ehrenreich, John, and Barbara Ehrenreich. "The Professional Managerial Class." In *Between Labor and Capital*, edited by Pat Walker, 5–45. Boston: South End Press, 1979.

Eisenstein, Elizabeth L. "An Unacknowledged Revolution Revisited." *American Historical Review* 107 (2002): 87–105.

"Elbert Hubbard Lectured at the Grand Last Night." *Atlanta Constitution*, 26 November 1901, 5.

Ellis, William. "The Book Corner. Some Bypaths in Reading." *Philosopher* 13, no. 5 (May 1903): 154–60.

– "In the Smoking Room." *Philosopher* 1, no. 1 (January 1897): 22–32.

– "In the Smoking Room." *Philosopher* 4, no. 1 (July 1898): 22–32.

– "In the Smoking Room." *Philosopher* 5, no. 6 (June 1899): 85–92.

– "In the Smoking Room." *Philosopher* 6, no. 1 (July 1899): 27–32.

– "In the Smoking Room." *Philosopher* 6, no. 4 (October 1899): 121–8.

Ellyson, John Regnault. "Habelais." *Smart Set* 1, no. 3 (May 1900): 119–24.

Emerson, Ralph Waldo. "Quotation and Originality." *Collected Works of Ralph Waldo Emerson*. Vol. 8, *Letters and Social Aims*, edited by Glen M. Johnson and Joel Myerson, 93–107. Cambridge, MA: Harvard University Press, 2010.

Emery, Brainerd Prescott. "In the Shadow of the Sphinx." *Clique* 1, no. 1 (May 1896): no pag.

Emery, Edwin, and Michael Emery. *The Press in America*. 5th ed. Englewood Cliffs, NJ: Prentice Hall, 1984.

"Emma Carleton Is Dead at New Albany." *Indianapolis News* (Indianapolis, IN), 31 December 1924, 20.

"End of the Book: Some Kindly Comments of the Press and Public." *Bradley His Book* 1, no. 3 (July 1896): 110–13.

Engs, Ruth Clifford. *Clean Living Movements: American Cycles of Health Reform*. Westport, CT: Greenwood Press, 2000.

Espey, John. "The Inheritance of Tò Kalón." In *New Approaches to Ezra Pound*, edited by Eva Hesse, 319–30. Berkeley: University of California Press, 1969.

"The Essenes." *The Essene* 1, no. 1 (July 1902): 3–5.

Evans, Brad. "Ephemeral Bibelots in the 1890s." In Brooker and Thacker, *Oxford Critical and Cultural History*, vol. 2, 132–53.

– Review of *Le Petit Journal des Refusées* (facsimile edition), edited by Johanna Drucker. *Journal of Modern Periodical Studies* 1, no. 2 (2010): 229–41.

– "*Vogue* and Ephemera: The Little Magazines of the 1890s." *Modernist Journals Project* (n.d): 37 pp. http://library.brown.edu/cds/mjp/pdf/vogueandephemera.pdf.

– "What Travels? The Movement of Movements; or, Ephemeral Bibelots from Paris to Lansing, with Love." In *Print Culture Histories beyond the Metropolis*, edited by James J. Connolly et al. Toronto: University of Toronto Press, 2016.

Fabian, Ann. "Amateur Authorship." In Casper et al., *History of the Book in America*, 407–15.

"Fad Periodicals." *Critic*, 2 January 1897, 12.

Fairbanks, Henry George. *Louise Imogen Guiney: Laureate of the Lost.* Albany: Magi Books, 1972.

Fairchild, Lee. "Friendship's Shame." *Thistle* 1, no. 2 (April 1902): 10.

[–] Untitled editorial matter. *Thistle* 1, no. 7 (September 1902): 4–5.

Fanning, Patricia J. "Francis Watts Lee: A Reintroduction." *History of Photography* 36, no. 1 (2012): 15–32.

– *Through an Uncommon Lens: The Life and Photography of F. Holland Day.* Amherst: University of Massachusetts Press, 2008.

Faxon, Frederick Winthrop. "A Bibliography of Ephemeral Bibelots." *Bulletin of Bibliography and Magazine Notes* 1 (1897): 21–3.

– "Ephemeral Bibelots." *Bulletin of Bibliography and Magazine Notes* 3 (1903–4): 72–4, 92, 106–7, 124–6.

– *"Ephemeral Bibelots:" A Bibliography of the Modern Chap-books and Their Imitators.* Boston: Boston Book Company, 1903.

"Features of July Number." *Bradley His Book* 1, no. 2 (June 1896): no pag.

Ferns, John. "Eden Phillpotts." *Dictionary of Literary Biography.* Vol. 135, *British Short Fiction Writers 1880–1914: The Realist Tradition*, edited by William Thessing, 269–75. Detroit: Gale, 1994.

"A Few Bits of Cold Tongue." *Junk* 2, no. 2 (November 1901): 43.

"A Few Bits of Cold Tongue." *Junk* 2, no. 3 (December 1901): 71.

Fidler, Roger. *Mediamorphosis: Understanding New Media.* Thousand Oaks: Pine Forge Press, 1997.

Field, Richard S. "The Woodcut Revival in Context." In *The Artistic Revival of the Woodcut in France 1850–1900.* Exhibition Catalogue. Edited by Richard S. Field and Jacquelynn Baas, 22–9. Ann Arbor: University of Michigan Museum of Art, 1994.

Finlay, Nancy. "American Posters and Publishing in the 1890s." In Kiehl, *American Art Posters of the 1890s*, 45–55.

Fleming, Herbert E. "Magazines of a Market-Metropolis: Being a History of the Literary Periodicals and Literary Interests of Chicago." PhD diss., University of Chicago, 1906. Accessed 1 August 2015. https://archive.org/details/magazinesamarke00flemgoog.

Flower, B.O. "Competition, Private Monopoly and Cooperation." *New Time* 3, no. 1 (July 1898): 11–13.

Fogarty, Robert S. *All Things New: Communes and Utopian Movements, 1860–1914.* Lanham, MD: Lexington Books, 2003.

Ford, Sewell. “The Freak Magazine.” *Waterloo Daily Courier* (IA), 2 April 1896, 4.

Foss, Sam Walter. “I Shall Not Pass This Way Again.” *Good Cheer* 1, no. 4 (February 1901): 103.

– “Talking Horse and Talking God.” *Socialist Spirit* 2, no. 1 (September 1902): 22.

– “To a Poet.” *Lotus* 2, no. 6 (October 1896): 197.

– “The Wail of the Hack Writer.” *Fly Leaf* 1, no. 2 (January 1896): 10.

– “Walk Right Up and Say ‘Hullo.’” *Ghourki* 4, no. 12 (1905): 25.

Fra Elbertus [pseudonym of Elbert Hubbard]. *The Motto Book: Being a Catalogue of Epigrams.* East Aurora: Roycrofters, 1909.

Fredeman, William. “Thomas Bird Mosher and the Literature of Rapture: A Chapter in the History of American Publishing.” In Bishop, *Thomas Bird Mosher*, 5–33.

Frederick, Peter J. *Knights of the Golden Rule: The Intellectual Christian Reformer in the 1890s.* Lexington, KY: University Press of Kentucky, 1976.

Freedman, Jonathan. *Professions of Taste: Henry James, British Aestheticism and Commodity Culture.* Stanford: Stanford University Press, 1990.

Front cover. *Erudite* 1, no. 6 (September 1900).

Front cover. *Erudite* 2, no. 4 (January1901).

Front cover. *Philistine* 8, no. 4 (1899).

Front matter. *Alkahest* 1, no. 2 (Autumn 1896), no pag.

Front matter. *Alkahest* 4, no. 1 (March 1898), no pag.

Front matter. *Atmos* 1, no. 1 (September 1902): no pag.

Front matter. *Bauble* 3, no. 1 (October 1896): no pag.

Front matter. *Bohemian* [Boston] 1, no. 1 (December 1900): no pag.

Front matter. *Bradley His Book* 1, no. 3 (July 1896): no pag.

Front matter. *Chips* 1, no. 1 (March 1895): no pag.

Front matter. *Clique* 1, no. 1 (May 1896), [2].

Front matter. *Dilettante* 3, no. 4 (December 1900): no pag.

Front matter. *Ghourki* 1, no. 1 (July? 1901): no pag.

Front matter. *Higher Law* 5, no. 2 (March 1902): no pag.

Front matter. *Personal Impressions* 1, no. 1 (March 1900): 1.

Front matter. *Philistine* 15, no. 2 (July 1902): no pag.

Front matter. *A Stuffed Club for Everybody* 1, no. 3 (July 1900): no pag.

Fuller, Louis. *The Muckrakers.* University Park: Pennsylvania State University Press, 1976.

– *Unknown Edwin Markham: His Mystery and Its Significance.* Yellow Springs, OH: Antioch, 1966.

Fusco, Richard. *Maupassant and the American Short Story: The Influence of Form at the Turn of the Century*. University Park, PA: Pennsylvania State University Press, 1994.

Gale, Robert L. "Gelett Burgess." In *American National Biography Online*. February 2000. Accessed 3 July 2015. https://anb.org

Gandal, Keith. *The Virtues of the Vicious: Jacob Riis, Stephen Crane and the Spectacle of the Slum*. Oxford: Oxford University Press, 1997.

Garber, Marjorie. *Quotation Marks*. New York: Routledge, 2003.

Gardner, Martin. *Best Remembered Poems*. Mineola, NY: Dover, 1992.

Garland, Hamlin. "Battle Hymn of the Wronged." *New Time* 3, no. 1 (July 1898): 53.

– "Battle Hymn of the Wronged." *Wilshire's Magazine* 49 (August 1902): 72.

– *Crumbling Idols*. Chicago: Stone and Kimball, 1894.

– *Selected Letters of Hamlin Garland*. Edited by Keith Newlin and Joseph B. McCullogh. Lincoln: University of Nebraska Press, 1998.

Garrique, Philemon. "Proem." *Lotus* 1, no. 12 (May 1896): no pag.

Garrison, J.H. "What We Stand For." *Vanguard* 1, no. 8 (June 1903): 9.

Garvey, Ellen Gruber. *Writing with Scissors: American Scrapbooks from the Civil War to the Harlem Renaissance*. Oxford: Oxford University Press, 2012.

G.E.B. and B.G.G. [Bertram Grosvenor Goodhue]. "Concerning Recent Books and Bookmaking." *Knight Errant* 1, no. 4 (January 1893): 123–8.

Genette, Gérard. *Paratexts: Thresholds of Interpretation*. Translated by Jane E. Lewin. Cambridge: Cambridge University Press, 1997.

"The Genius and Characteristics of the Late Edgar Allan Poe." *Philosopher* 14, no. 3 (September 1903): 72–88.

George, Hardy. *Paris 1900*. Oklahoma City: Oklahoma City Museum of Art, 2007.

Gitelman, Lisa. *Always Already New: Media, History and the Data of Culture*. Cambridge: MIT Press, 2006.

Glass, Loren Daniel. *Authors Inc: Literary Celebrity in the Modern United States, 1880–1980*. New York: New York University Press, 2004.

Glazener, Nancy. *Reading for Realism: The History of a US Literary Institution, 1850–1910*. Durham, NC: Duke University Press, 1997.

Gnichtel, A. Lawrence. "From a Hall Window." *Bohemian* [Boston] 1, no. 4 (March 1901): 7–9.

Good, Katie Day. "From Scrapbook to Facebook: A History of Personal Media Assemblages and Archives." *New Media and Society* 15, no. 4 (2012): 557–73.

Goudy, Frederic W. *A Half Century of Type Design and Typography, 1895–1945*. New York: Typophiles, 1946.

Graff, Gerald. *Professing Literature: An Institutional History*. Chicago: University of Chicago Press, 1988.

Greeley, S.H. "Does a Grain Trust Exist?" *New Time* 3, no. 1 (July 1898): 3–6.

Greene, Douglas G. "W.W. Denslow (1856–1915)." *Dictionary of Literary Biography*. Vol. 188, *American Book and Magazine Illustrators to 1920*, edited by Steven E. Smith, Catherine A. Hastedt, and Donald H. Dyal, 68–73. Detroit, MI: Gale 1998.

– "W.W. Denslow, Illustrator." *Journal of Popular Culture* 7, no. 1 (Summer 1973): 86–96.

"Greetings." *Comrade* 1, no. 1 (October 1901): 12.

Grooms, Harry M. "The Old Dinner Pail." *Wilshire's* 45 (April 1902): 57–8.

Gross, John. Introduction to *Oxford Book of Aphorisms*, edited by John Gross, vii–x. Oxford: Oxford University Press, 1983.

Hagerty, Rev. T.H. "How I Became a Socialist." *Comrade* 2, no. 1 (October 1902): 6–7.

Haley, Andrew P. *Turning the Tables: The Aristocratic Restaurant and the Rise of the American Middle Class 1880–1920*. Chapel Hill: University of North Carolina Press, 2011.

Hallowell, G.H. "A Titlepage Design" [for *Lincoln's Grave*, by Maurice Thompson]. *Chap-Book* 1, no. 6 (1 August 1894): 128.

Hamilton, Charles Franklin. *As Bees in Honey Drown: Elbert Hubbard and the Roycrofters*. South Brunswick, NJ: Barnes, 1973.

Hamilton, Kristie. *America's Sketchbook: The Cultural Life of a Nineteenth-Century Literary Genre*. Athens: Ohio University Press, 1998.

Hamilton, Sharon. "American Manners: *Smart Set* (1900–1929), *American Parade* (1926)." In Brooker and Thacker, *Oxford Critical and Cultural History*, 224–48.

Hammill, Faye, Paul Hjartarson, and Hannah McGregor. "Magazines and/as Media: Periodical Studies and the Question of Disciplinarity." Special issue of *Journal of Modern Periodical Studies* 6, no. 2 (2015): iii–xiii.

– "Magazines and/as Media: The Politics and Aesthetics of Periodical Form." Special issue of *English Studies in Canada* 41, no. 1 (2015): 1–18.

Hammond, Richard. "Progress and Flight: An Interpretation of the American Cycle Craze of the 1890s." *Journal of Social History* 5, no. 2 (1971–2): 235–57.

Hanighen, Frank C. "Vance Thompson and *M'lle New York*." *Bookman* 75 (September 1932): 472–81.

Hapke, Laura. *Girls Who Went Wrong: Prostitutes in American Fiction 1885–1917*. Bowling Green, OH: Bowling Green State University Popular Press, 1989.

Harlan, Robert D. *At the Sign of the Lark*. San Francisco: Book Club of California, 1983.

Harris, Elizabeth M. *Personal Impressions: The Small Printing Press in Nineteenth-Century America*. Boston: David R. Godine, 2004.

Harris, Julian. "A Double Deception." *Alkahest* 1, no. 1 (May 1896): 13–15.

Harris, Neil. "American Poster Collecting: A Fitful History." *American Art* 12, no. 1 (1998): 10–39.

– *Cultural Excursions: Marketing Appetites and Cultural Tastes in Modern America*. Chicago: University of Chicago Press, 1990.

Hart, James D. Introduction to *Bayside Bohemia*, by Gelett Burgess, v–viii. San Francisco: Book Club of San Francisco, 1954.

– *The Popular Book: A History of America's Literary Taste*. Berkeley: University of California Press, 1963.

[Harte, Walter Blackburn]. "Bubble and Squeak." *Fly Leaf* 1, no. 1 (December 1895): 26–31.

[–] "Bubble and Squeak." *Fly Leaf* 1, no. 2 (January 1896): 25–32.

[–] "Bubble and Squeak." *Lotus* 2, no. 7 (November 1896): 253–8.

[–] "Bubble and Squeak." *Lotus* 2, no. 8 (December 1896): 295–300.

[–] "Bubble and Squeak." *Lotus* 3, no. 2 (February 1897): 57–66.

[–] "A Résumé and a Prophecy." *Lotus* 2, no. 8 (December 1896): no pag.

– "A Little Revolt in American Literature." *Philosopher* 3, no. 3 (March 1898): 102–8.

– "A Rhapsody on Music." *Knight Errant* 1, no. 2 (1892): 34–9.

– "Shakespeare's Borrowings." *Philistine* 2, no. 6 (May 1896): 184–7.

Harvey, Alexander. Untitled editorial commentary. *Bang* 9, no. 22 (21 February 1916).

Hawthorne, Julian. "The Soul of America." *Wilshire's* 45 (April 1902): 14–20.

Hazenplug, Frank. "The Black Lady." Stone and Kimball, April 1896. Lithograph. New York Public Library Digital Collections. Accessed 13 August 2015. http://digitalcollections.nypl.org/items/510d47df-fcc3-a3d9-e040-e00a18064a99.

– "The Blind." *Chap-Book* 3, no. 2 (1 June 1895): 73.

– Designs for "Ballad of an Artist's Wife," by John Davidson. *Chap-Book* 3, no. 11 (15 October 1895): 423–9.

– "Drawing." *Chap-Book* 3, no. 7 (15 September 1895): 305.

– "Drawing." *Chap-Book* 4, no. 9 (15 March 1896): 405.

– "A Drawing (with apologies to Mr. Beardsley)." *Chap-Book* 2, no. 5 (15 January 1895): 215.

– "The Envious Black Hair'd Queen." *Chap-Book* 5, no. 5 (15 July 1896): 200.

– "The Red Lady." Stone and Kimball, November 1895. Lithograph. New York Public Library Digital Collections. Accessed 10 August 2015. http://digitalcollections.nypl.org/items/510d47df-fcc4-a3d9-e040-e00a18064a99.

Heafford, George. "An Open Letter." *Philosopher* 6, no. 1 (July 1899): 23–6.

Helfland, Jessica. *Scrapbooks: An American History*. New Haven: Yale University Press, 2008.

"He 'Kicks' the Press Himself." *Topeka Daily Capital*, 11 November 1906, 20.

Herron, George D. "In Bruges Town." *Comrade* 2, no. 1 (October 1902): 2.

Herwegh, George. "Comrades' Song." Translated by Hebe. *Comrade* 2, no. 1 (October 1902): 9.

Herzel [pseudonym of Naphthali Herz Imber]. "Madame Blavatsky Unveiled." *Uriel* 1, no. 1 (August 1895): 57–62.

Hewlett, Maurice. "Quattrocentisteria." *Bibelot* 2, no. 5 (May 1896): 115–48.

Hill, Bill. "The Quat'z' Arts Ball." *Quartier Latin* 1, no. 1 (July 1896): 18–24.

Hoadley, Francis A. "A Triangular Irony." *Miss Blue Stocking* 2, no. 1 (April 1896): 9–12.

Hoffman, Frederick, Charles Allen, and Carolyn Ulrich. *The Little Magazine: A History and Bibliography*. Princeton: Princeton University Press, 1946.

Holmes, Florence L. "The Woman Who Understood." *Gray Goose* 4, no. 2 (February 1898): 8–12.

Hovey, Richard. "Modern Symbolism and Maurice Maeterlinck." In *The Plays of Maurice Maeterlinck*, by Maurice Maeterlinck, 3–11. Translated by Richard Hovey. Chicago: Stone and Kimball, 1894.

Hovey, Richard, and Henriette Hovey. "New York Tattle." *Time and the Hour* 4, no. 12 (27 February 1897), 7–8.

Howells, W.D. "The Man of Letters as a Man of Business." *Scribner's* 14, no. 4 (October 1893): 429–45.

– "The Prose-Poem." Introduction to *Pastels in Prose*, v–viii, translated by Stuart Merrill. New York: Harper and Brothers, 1890.

"How to Live." *Medical Era* 14, no. 7 (March 1905): 231–3.

[Hubbard, Elbert]. "Heart to Heart Talks with Grown-Ups by the Pastor of His Flock." *Philistine* 8, no. 3 (February 1899): 66–96.

[–] "Heart to Heart Talks with Grown-Ups by the Pastor of His Flock." *Philistine* 8, no. 4 (March 1899): 97–128.

[–] "Heart to Heart Talks with Philistines by the Pastor of His Flock." *Philistine* 14, no. 2 (January 1902): 33–64.

[–] "Heart to Heart Talks with Philistines By the Pastor of His Flock." *Philistine* 14, no. 5 (April 1902): 129–61.
[–] "Heart to Heart Talks with Philistines by the Pastor of His Flock." *Philistine* 15, no. 4 (September 1902): 97–128.
[–] "Heart to Heart Talks with Philistines by the Pastor of His Flock." *Philistine* 25, no. 2 (July 1907): 52–64.
– "An Interesting Personality: Elbert Hubbard." *Cosmopolitan* 32 (January 1902): 309–20.
– "Joseph Addison." *Little Journeys*. Vol. 7, *To The Homes of English Authors*, no. 3 (September 1900): 57–84.
[–] "Side Talks With the Philistines: Conducted by the East Aurora School of Philosophy." *Philistine* 6, no. 4 (March 1898): 119–28.
– "Thomas Arnold." *Little Journeys*. Vol. 23, *To the Homes of Great Teachers*, no. 2 (August 1908): 29–49.
– "Walt Whitman." *Little Journeys*. Vol. 2, *To the Homes of American Authors*, no. 6 (June 1896): 167–96.
"Hubbard Lectures at Grand." *Atlanta Constitution*, 30 April 1904, 2.
Huneker, James Gibbons. *Steeplejack*. 2 vols. New York: Scribner's, 1921.
Hunter, Dard. "Elbert Hubbard and 'A Message to Garcia.'" *New Colophon* 1 (1948): 27–35.
Huss, Boaz. "Forward, to the East: Naphthali Herz Imber's Perception of Kabbalah." *Journal of Modern Jewish Studies* 12, no. 3 (November 2013): 398–418.
Hutcherson, Dudley R. "Poe's Reputation in England and America, 1850–1909." *American Literature* 14, no. 3 (1942): 211–33.
Hyman, Max R., ed. *Hyman's Handbook of Indianapolis: An Outline History and Description of the Capitol of Indiana*. Indianapolis: M.R. Hyman Company, 1898.
"The Influence of Intimate Surroundings." *Overland Monthly* 44 (September 1904): 387–90.
Irvine, Dean. "Little Magazines in English Canada." In Brooker and Thacker, *Oxford Critical and Cultural History*, vol. 2, 602–28.
Isbell, Minnette. "The Mountain." *Optimist* 2, no. 3 (May 1901): 145–7.
Iskin, Ruth E. *The Poster: Art, Advertising, Design, and Collecting, 1860s–1900s*. Hanover, NH: Dartmouth College Press, 2014.
James, Henry. "The Way It Came." *Chap-Book* 4, no. 12 (1 May 1896): 562–93.
J.C.W. "The Mountain Climbers." *Ghourki* 1, no. 10 (May 1902): 312–13.
Jenson Press. "To Authors, Publishers, and Bibliophiles." Advertisement. *Moods* 2 (1895): no pag.

Jerrold, Laurence. "The Literary Pilgrimage and the Youth's Progress." *Chap-Book* 7, no. 1 (15 May 1897): 8–11.

J.L.S. "*M'lle New York*." *Record-Union* (Sacramento), 14 August 1895, 4.

John-a-Dreams. "*John-a-Dreams*, His Ad." Advertisement. *John-a-Dreams* 1, no. 1 (July 1896): no pag.

Johns, Adrian. "How to Acknowledge a Revolution." *American Historical Review* 107 (2002): 106–25.

Johnson, Diane Chalmers. *American Art Nouveau*. New York: Abrams, 1979.

"Journalistic Notes." *Publisher's Weekly* 55, 18 March 1899, 518.

Jungen, Frank J. "Ralstonism – In General." *What to Eat* 1, no. 1 (August 1896): 6–7.

Kammen, Michael. "'A Little Journey:' Elbert Hubbard and the Roycroft Community at East Aurora, New York." In *American Places: Encounters With History*, edited by William Leuchtenberg, 201–18. Oxford: Oxford University Press, 2000.

Kaplan, Amy. "Romancing the Empire: The Embodiment of American Masculinity in the Popular Historical Novel of the 1890s." In *Postcolonial Theory and the United States: Race, Ethnicity, and Literature*, edited by Amritjit Singh and Peter Schmidt, 220–43. Jackson, MS: University of Mississippi Press, 2000.

Kaplan, Wendy. "Spreading the Crafts: The Role of the Schools." In Wendy Kaplan, *Art that Is Life*, 298–307.

– ed. *"The Art that Is Life:" The Arts and Crafts Movement in America, 1875–1920*. Boston: Museum of Fine Arts, with Little Brown and Company, 1982.

Karsner, David. *Horace Traubel: His Life and Work*. New York: Egmont Arens, 1919.

"Katharine Lee Bates." *American National Biography Online*. February 2000. Accessed on 18 August 2015. https://anb.org.

Keating, Peter. *The Haunted Study: A Social History of the English Novel 1875–1914*. London: Secker and Warburg, 1989.

Kiehl, David, ed. *American Art Posters of the 1890s*. Exhibition Catalogue. New York: Metropolitan Museum of Art, with Harry N. Abrams, 1987.

Kinmarck, Michael [pseudonym of Thomas Wood Stevens]. "What Did She Do With Her Left Hand?" *Blue Sky* 2, no. 4 (May 1900): 105–14.

Knapp, Margaret L. "A Moment Musical." *Chips* 3, no. 4 (April 1896): 119–21.

Knight, Frank R. "Henry Brevoort Eddy, Artist." *Bradley His Book* 1, no. 3 (July 1896): 87–93.

Knight, Melinda. "Little Magazines and the Emergence of Modernism in the *Fin de Siècle*." *American Periodicals* 6 (1996): 29–45.

Koch, Robert. “Elbert Hubbard’s Roycrofters as Artist-Craftsmen.” *Winterthur Portfolio* 3 (1967): 67–82.

– *Will H. Bradley: American Artist in Print. A Collector’s Guide*. New York: Hudson Hills Press, 2002.

Kramer, Sidney. *A History of Stone and Kimball and Herbert S. Stone and Company 1893–1905*. Chicago: Norman W. Forgue, 1940.

“Krayne, Bliss.” “A Karmenokranian Idyl.” *Clack Book* 2, no. 5 (March 1897): 158–9.

Laing, Olive. Review of *Alice of Old Vincennes*, by Maurice Thompson. *Alkahest* 7, no. 12 (June 1901): 49–50.

Lane, Albert. *Elbert Hubbard and His Work*. Worcester, MA: Blanchard Press, 1901.

[–] “Plain Tales from the Hills with Something of Criticism.” *Erudite* 1, no. 2 (May 1900): 49–64.

[–] “Plain Tales from the Hills with Something of Criticism.” *Erudite* 1, no. 3 (June 1900): 76–96.

[–] “Plain Tales from the Hills.” *Erudite* 3, no. 4 (September 1901): 142–60.

“The Late Magazines.” *Times Picayune* (New Orleans), 23 December 1900, 24.

Latham, Sean. “Affordance and Emergence: Magazine as New Media.” Presented at the Modern Language Association Convention 2013, Special Session 384, Boston, MA, 2013. Accessed 11 February 2017. https://seeeps.princeton.edu/wp-content/uploads/sites/243/2015/03/mla2013_latham.pdf.

Laurie, Bruce. “Labor and Labor Organization.” In Casper et al., *History of the Book in America*, 7–89.

[Learned, Mary D., and Louise McPherson]. “From the Sanctum.” *Pebble* 1, no. 5 (August 1900): 159–61.

[–] “From the Sanctum.” *Pebble* 2, no. 6 (March 1901): 186–92.

Lears, T.J. Jackson. *No Place of Grace: Antimodernism and the Transformation of American Culture, 1880–1920*. New York: Pantheon, 1981.

Le Gallienne, Richard. “McKinley Dead.” *Erudite* 3, no. 4 (September 1904): 140–1.

– *Michael Monahan: An Appreciation*. South Norwalk, CT: Phoenix Press, 1914.

Lehmann-Haupt, Hellmut, Lawrence C. Wroth, and Rollo G. Silver. *The Book in America: A History of the Making and Selling of Books in the United States*, 2nd ed. New York: Bowker, 1951.

Levin, Joanna. *Bohemia in America 1858–1920*. Stanford: Stanford University Press, 2010.

Levine, Lawrence W. *Highbrow/Lowbrow: The Emergence of Cultural Hierarchy in America*. Cambridge, MA: Harvard University Press, 1988.

Levy, Andrew. *The Culture and Commerce of the American Short Story*. Cambridge: Cambridge University Press, 1993.

Lewis, E. St Elmo. "Life's Quest." *Moods* 1 (1894): no pag.

Linthicum, Richard. "The American Flag." *New Time* 3, no. 1 (July 1898): 31.

"The Little Magazines." *The Times* (Philadelphia), 26 January 1896, 7.

The Lotus. Advertisement. *Philistine* 2, no. 6 (May 1896): no pag.

Lupfer, Eric. "The Business of American Magazines." In Casper et al., *History of the Book in America*, 248–57.

Mabie, Hamilton Wright. "Curiosity and Concentration." *Chap-Book* 5, no. 11 (15 October 1896): 482–6.

MacArthur, James. "Living Critics: Hamilton Wright Mabie." *Bookman* 2, no. 4 (December 1895): 298–305.

MacKendrick, Louis K. "Grues and Gaunts: Carman's Gothic." In *Bliss Carman: A Reappraisal*, edited by Gerald Lynch, 129–40. Ottawa: University of Ottawa Press, 1990.

Mackenzie, Janet. *The Editor's Companion*. Cambridge: Cambridge University Press, 2004.

MacLeod, Kirsten. "American Little Magazines of the 1890s and the Rise of the Professional-Managerial Class." *English Studies in Canada* 41, no. 1 (2015): 41–68.

– *American Little Magazines of the 1890s: A Revolution in Print*. Exhibition Catalogue. Sunderland: Bibelot Press with the Grolier Club, 2013.

– "Art for America's Sake: Decadence and the Making of American Literary Culture in the Little Magazines of the 1890s." *Prospects: An Annual of American Cultural Studies* 31 (2006): 309–39.

– *Fictions of British Decadence: High Art, Popular Writing, and the fin de siècle*. Basingstoke: Palgrave, 2006.

– "The Fine Art of Cheap Print: Turn-of-the-Century American Little Magazines." In *Transatlantic Print Culture 1880–1940: Emerging Media, Emerging Modernisms*, edited by Ann Ardis and Patrick Collier, 182–98. Houndmills, UK: Palgrave, 2008.

– "The First Appearance of Jack London's 'Bald Face' (1900)." *Papers of the Bibliographical Society of America* 104, no. 3 (2010): 347–52.

"The Magazines." *Reading Times* (Reading, PA), 29 May 1901, 6.

Margolin, Victor. *American Poster Renaissance*. New York: Castle Books, 1975.

Markham, Edwin. "The Religion of Jesus." *Vanguard* 1, no. 8 (June 1903): 12–13.

Martinot, Sadie. "Dream of the Ideal." *Smart Set* 1, no. 3 (May 1900): 107–9.

Mathieson, J.F. "To Columbia." *Junk* 1, no. 6 (September 1901): 134–5.

"A Matter of Opinion: Set Down for What It May Be Worth." *Philosopher* 12, no. 1 (July 1902): 14–22.

May, Henry. *The End of American Innocence: A Study of the First Years of Our Own Time, 1912–1917*. New York: Knopf, 1959.

Maynard, Frederick. "Revenge of Izzedin." *Rubric* 1, no. 3 (April 1902): 72–3.

MBS [Marjorie B. Searle]. "Hubbard and Chautauqua." In Via and Searle, *Head, Heart and Hand*, 45.

M'Causland, Austin Arnold. "As Told by the Persian." *Lotus* 1, no. 12 (May 15, 1896): 331–6.

M'Connell, Marion Daniel. "Bliss Carman." *Alkahest* 7, no. 11 (May 1901): 5–10.

McCune, Eva Mary. "What's in a Name?" *Kiote* 3, no. 3 (March 1900): 49–57.

McGann, Jerome. *Black Riders: The Visible Language of Modernism*. Princeton: Princeton University Press, 1995.

– *The Textual Condition*. Princeton: Princeton University Press, 1991.

McIntire, Warren. "An Inconsistent Philosopher." *Bachelor Book* 1, no. 3 (May 1900): 4–7.

McIntosh, William. "The Literary Sweat Shop." *Philistine* 5, no. 3 (October 1896): 129–32.

McKenna, Paul. *A History and Bibliography of the Roycroft Printing Shop*. North Tonawanda, NY: Tona Press, 1986.

McLaughlin, Cresswell. "The Thumbscrew." *Schoolmaster* 1, no. 1 (March 1900): 16–20.

Meggs, Philip B. "Turn-of-the-Century American Art Posters: Art + Technology = Graphic Design." In Brandt, *Designed to Sell*, 33–45.

Memorandum of Agreement Between Smith and Sale and Thomas B. Mosher. [1897]. Gleeson Library, University of San Francisco.

Mencken, H.L. *Newspaper Days: Mencken's Autobiography 1899–1906*. Baltimore, MD: Johns Hopkins University Press, 2006.

– *Prejudices: First Series*. New York: Knopf, 1919.

Mendelssohn, Michèle. *Henry James, Oscar Wilde, and Aesthetic Culture*. Edinburgh: Edinburgh University Press, 2007.

Meteyard, Thomas B. "Titlepage Designed for *The Ebb Tide*." *Chap-Book* 1, no. 1 (15 May 1894): 4.

"Michael Monahan: The Survivor of a Disappearing Art." *Current Literature* 52, no. 3 (March 1912): 347–9.

Mieder, Wolfgang. *Proverbs: A Handbook*. Westport: Greenwood Press, 2004.

– *Proverbs Are Never Out of Season*. Oxford: Oxford University Press, 1993.

– *"Proverbs Speak Louder than Words:" Folk Wisdom in Art, Culture, Folklore, History, Literature and Mass Media*. New York: Peter Lang, 2008.

Miller, George McA. "Uncle Ike on the War." *New Time* 3, no. 1 (July 1898): 14.

Miller, J. Hillis. "Aphorism as Instrument of Political Action in Nietzsche." *Parallax* 10, no. 3 (2004): 70–82.

Miller, Muriel. *Bliss Carman: Quest and Revolt.* St John's, NL: Jesperson Press, 1985.

Miller, Timothy. *The Quest for Utopia in Twentieth-Century America.* Vol. 1, *1900–1960.* Syracuse: Syracuse University Press, 1998.

"M'lle New York." *M'lle New York* 1, no. 1 (August 1895): no pag.

[Michael Monahan]. "Edwin Markham (A Thumbnail Sketch)," *Papyrus* 1, no. 1 (July 1903): 27–9.

– "Heine." *Papyrus* 1, no. 1 (July 1903): 29–36.

– "Heine." *Philistine* 8, no. 1 (December 1898): 5–13.

– *Nemesis.* New York: Frank-Maurice, 1926.

[–] "A Patron of Arts and Letters: With Apologies to George Ade." *Papyrus* 1, no. 1 (July 1903): 38–9.

[–] Untitled announcement. *Papyrus* 2, no. 2 (February 1904): 10.

– "Side Talks by the Editor." *Papyrus* 1, no. 1 (July 1903): 1–21.

– "Side Talks by the Editor." *Papyrus* 1, no. 2 (August 1903): 1–15.

– "Side Talks by the Editor." *Papyrus* 2, no. 1 (January 1904): 1–12.

– "Side Talks by the Editor." *Papyrus* 3, no. 1 (July 1904): 1–15.

– "Side Talks by the Editor." *Papyrus* 3, no. 5 (November 1904): 7–25.

– "Side Talks by the Editor." *Papyrus* 3, no. 6 (December 1904): 1–18.

– "Side Talks by the Editor." *Phoenix* 3, nos. 2–3 (August 1915): 52–64.

"Monahan, Michael." In *National Cyclopedia of American Biography*, 415–16. New York: James T. White, 1930.

Monsman, Gerald Cornelius. *Walter Pater.* New York: G.K. Hall and Co, 1977.

Monteiro, George, ed., *Stephen Crane: The Contemporary Reviews.* Cambridge: Cambridge University Press, 2009.

Moody, A. David. *Ezra Pound: Poet.* Vol. 1, *The Young Genius.* Oxford: Oxford University Press, 2007.

Moorehead, Helen G. "A Wood Engraving." *New Bohemian* 2, no. 5 (May 1896): 214.

Morris, Lewis. "The New Time." *Vanguard* 1, no. 8 (June 1903): 17.

Morris, Mary Lenox. "My Heart and I: A Mosaic." *Optimist* 2, no. 3 (May 1901): 149–50.

Morris, William. Installment of *News From Nowhere. Comrade* 2, no. 1 (October 1902): 12–16.

– "When the World Grows Fair." *Vanguard* 1, no. 8 (June 1903): 17.

Morrisson, Mark S. *The Public Face of Modernism: Little Magazines, Audiences, and Reception 1905–1920.* Madison: University of Wisconsin Press, 2001.

Morson, Gary Saul. "The Aphorism: Fragments from the Breakdown of Reason." *New Literary History* 34, no. 3 (2003): 409–29.

– *The Words of Others: From Quotations to Culture*. New Haven: Yale University Press, 2011.

Mosher, Thomas Bird. "*The Bibelot*." *Bibelot* 1, no. 1 (January 1895): no pag.

– Foreword to *The Bibelot: General Index*, xi–xiv. Portland, ME: Thomas Bird Mosher, [1915].

Moskowitz, Eva L. *In Therapy We Trust: America's Obsession With Self-fulfillment*. Baltimore: Johns Hopkins University Press, 2001.

Moss, David. "A Bibliography of the Little Magazine Published in America Since 1900." *Contact* 1–3 (1932): 91–109, 134–9, 111–24.

Mott, Frank Luther. *A History of American Magazines*. Vol. 4, *1885–1905*. Cambridge, MA: Harvard University Press, 1938.

– "The Magazine Revolution and Popular Ideas in the Nineties." *Proceedings of the American Antiquarian Society* 64 (1954): 195–214.

Mount, Nick. *When Canadian Literature Moved to New York*. Toronto: University of Toronto Press, 2005.

"Mrs. Myron D. Learned." In *Blue Book of Nebraska Women*, edited by Winona Reeves, 204. Mexico, MO: Missouri Printing and Publishing Company, 1916.

[Munsey, Frank]. "To the Readers of *Munsey's Magazine*." *Munsey's Magazine* 37 (July 1907): 433–6.

Munson, Gorham B. "The Limbo in American Literature." *Broom* 2, no. 3 (June 1922): 250–60.

Murdock, Charles. *A Backward Glance at Eighty*. Privately printed, 1921.

Murray, Alex. *Landscapes of Decadence: Literature and Place at the Fin de Siècle*. Cambridge: Cambridge University Press, 2016.

MV [Marie Via]. "Ali Baba." In Via and Searle, *Head, Heart and Hand*, 129.

Nathan, Ray Trum. "Renunciation." *Bohemian* [Boston] 1, no. 4 (March 1901): 18–19.

Nelson, Cary. *Revolutionary Memory: Recovering the Poetry of the American Left*. New York: Routledge, 2011.

Nelson, James G. *A View From the Bodley Head*. Cambridge, MA: Harvard University Press, 1971.

"New Books in Brief." *Current Opinion* 69, no. 1 (July 1920): 132.

Newell, Lyman C. "The Teacher's Problem." *Higher Law* 5, no. 2 (March 1902): 45–50.

Newton, A.E. *This Book Collecting Game*. Boston: Little Brown, 1928.

Nicholson, Meredith. "Cuba." *Ishmaelite* 1, no. 2 (January 1897): 1–2.

"A Night in Bohemia." *New Bohemian* 1, no. 1 (October 1895): 19.

Nobel, Charles. "The Doctor's Argument." *Miss Blue Stocking* 2, no. 1 (April 1896): 16–21.

Norton, Charles Eliot. "A Portion of an Address Given in MDCCCLXXXVIII." *Knight Errant* 1, no. 1 (April 1892): 4–6.

"Notes." *Chap-Book* 1, no. 7 (15 August 1894): 172–4.

– *Chap-Book* 2, no. 11 (15 April 1895): 445–52.

– *Chap-Book* 3, no. 3 (15 June 1895): 109–12.

– *Chap-Book* 3, no. 10 (1 October 1895): 399–403.

– *Chap-Book* 3, no. 11 (15 October 1895): 443–52.

– *Chap-Book* 3, no. 12 (1 November 1895): 507–9.

– *Chap-Book* 4, no. 9 (15 March 1896): 442–8.

– *Chap-Book* 5, no. 1 (15 May 1896): 29–48.

– *Chap-Book* 5, no. 3 (15 June 1896): 134–44.

– *Chap-Book* 5, no. 8 (1 September 1896): 375–84.

– *Chap-Book* 5, no. 11 (15 October 1896): 521–8.

– *Chap-Book* 6, no. 2 (1 December 1896): 88–96.

"Notes of Periodicals." *Editor* 4, no. 1 (July 1896): 18–22.

"Notes on the Artists." In Kiehl, *American Art Posters*, 184–93.

N.W. Ayer and Sons American Newspaper Annual. Philadelphia: N.W. Ayer and Son, 1897.

Obelkevich, James. "Proverbs and Social History." In *The Social History of Language*, edited by Peter Burke and Roy Porter, 43–72. Cambridge: Cambridge University Press, 1987.

O'Donnell, Thomas F. "Oneida County: Literary Highlights." In *Upstate Literature: Essays in Memory of Thomas F. O'Donnell*, edited by Frank Bergmann, 39–70. Syracuse: Syracuse University Press, 1985.

Ohmann, Richard. "History and Literary History: The Case of Mass Culture." In *Modernity and Mass Culture*, edited by James Naremore and Patrick Brantlinger, 24–41. Bloomington: Indiana University Press, 1991.

– *Selling Culture: Magazines, Markets, and Class at the Turn of the Century.* London: Verso, 1996.

Old Walt [Walt Whitman]. "Personality." *Socialist Spirit* 1, no. 9 (May 1902): 18.

Ottolengui, Rodrigues. "For Fame, Money, or Love?" *Black Cat* 1, no. 8 (May 1896): 1–12.

"Our Clubbing List." *Petit Journal des Refusées* 1 (Summer 1896): no pag.

Parins, James W. *Literacy and Intellectual Life in the Cherokee Nation, 1820–1906.* Norman: University of Oklahoma Press, 2013.

Parker, Gilbert. "Across the Jumping Sand-hills." *Pocket Magazine* 2, no. 1 (May 1896): 126–45.

– Introduction to *Romany of the Snows*, by Gilbert Parker, viii–ix. London: Macmillan and Co., 1913.

Parrish, Stephen Maxfield. *Currents of the Nineties in Boston: Fred Holland Day, Louise Imogen Guiney, and Their Circle*. New York: Garland, 1987.

Parry, Albert. *Garretts and Pretenders: A History of Bohemianism in America*. New York: Cosimo Classics, 2005.

The Pastor [Elbert Hubbard]. "A Manifesto!" *Philistine* 8, no. 2 (January 1899): 33–9.

Pater, Walter. *The Renaissance*. Oxford: Oxford University Press, 1986.

"Paul Verlaine from a Photograph in the Possession of Henry Copley Greene." *Chap-Book* 1, no. 4 (1 July 1894): 80.

Peattie, Elia W. *Star Wagon*. Edited by Joan Stevenson Falcone. Accessed 15 March 2015. http://plainshumanities.unl.edu/peattie/ep.starwagon.html.

Pellegrino, Joe. "Clinton Scollard." In *Encyclopedia of American Poetry: The Nineteenth Century*, edited by Eric L. Haralson and John Hollander, 379–80. Chicago: Fitzroy Dearborn, 1998.

Pemberton, Jno. P. "The Pack-Rat." *Quartier Latin* 1, no. 1 (July 1896): 26.

Penn, Jonathan. "A Little Study of Stephen Crane." *Lotus* 2, no. 6 (October 1896): 208–11.

– "The New Mysticism." *Fly Leaf* 1, no. 1 (December 1895): 5–10.

Perkins, David. *A History of Modern Poetry: From the 1890s to the High Modernist Mode*. Cambridge, MA: Belknap Press, 1976.

"Personal." *The Scroll of Phi Delta Theta* 31, no. 1 (October 1906): 77.

Peterson, Theodore. *Magazines in the Twentieth Century*. 2nd ed. Urbana: University of Illinois Press, 1964.

Peterson, William S. *The Kelmscott Press: A History of William Morris's Typographical Adventure*. Oakland, CA: University of California Press, 1991.

Philistine. Advertisement. *Philistine* 14, no. 1 (December 1901): no pag.

Philistine. Advertisement. *Philistine* 18, no. 3 (February 1904): no pag.

Phillpotts, Eden. "In the King's Chamber." *Smart Set* 1, no. 3 (May 1900): 87–94.

"The Philosophers: Observations Concerning the Elect." *Philosopher* 14, no. 2 (August 1903): 59–64.

"Philosophical Observations by a Ghourkite." *Ghourki* 2, no. 11 (June 1903): 5–6.

Picaroon. "F. Frankfort Moore." *Chap-Book* 5, no. 6 (August 1, 1896): 259–66.

Pierce, Gilbert. "The Salisbury Treatment." *What to Eat* 1, no. 1 (August 1896): 21–2.

[Pierce, Paul]. "Our Magazine and Its Mission." *What to Eat* 1, no. 1 (August 1896): 18.

Pingree, Geoffrey B. and Lisa Gitelman. "Introduction: What's New About New Media?" In *New Media 1740–1915*, edited by Geoffrey B. Pingree and Lisa Gitelman, xi–xxii. Cambridge: MIT Press, 2003.

Pissarro, Georges. "In the Garden." *Chap-Book* 3, no. 9 (15 September 1895): 350.

"Poeta Pants." "The Stovepipe of Navarre." *Book Booster* (1900): 6–10.

Pollard, Percival. "In Eighteen Ninety-Five." *Echo* 1, no. 8 (August 1895): 172–3.

– *Their Day in Court.* New York: Neale, 1909.

Poole, F.H.R. "Boston Notes." *Editor* 4, no. 6 (December 1896): 245.

"The Poster Girl." *Times-Picayune* (New Orleans), 18 February 1896, 3.

"Poster Girls in Life." *Pittsburgh Daily Post*, 1 November 1896, 18.

Pound, Arthur. *The Only Thing Worth Finding: The Life and Legacies of George Gough Booth.* Detroit: Wayne State University Press, 1964.

Pound, Ezra. Untitled commentary. *Phoenix* 3, no. 4 (September 1915): no pag.

– "Lionel Johnson." In *Literary Essays of Ezra Pound*, edited by T.S. Eliot, 361–70. New York: New Directions, 1981.

– *Ezra Pound's Letters to William Watt*, edited by William Watt. Marquette: Northern Michigan University Press, 2001.

Powell Clarke G. "The Art Workers' Society of Omaha." *Pebble* 1, no. 2 (May 1900): 48–52.

Powell, Ella M. "Walt Whitman and His Friends." *Alkahest* 7, no. 9 (March 1901): 14–17.

Powers, Thomas. "M'lle New York Is Awake." *M'lle New York* 1, no. 4 (Last fortnight in September 1895): no pag.

Price, W.E. "Ego Notes." *Book-Lover* 4 (Summer 1900): B.

"Prizes for Stories." *Oakland Tribune*, 17 November 1899, 4.

Procopio, Joseph V. *The Lost Art of Frederick Richardson.* Silver Spring, MD: Lost Art Books, 2010.

The Publishers. "Presentation." *Uriel* 1, no. 1 (August 1895): 2–13.

Putnam, Frank. "Six Great Editorial Writers." *National Magazine* 24 (September 1906): 607–12.

Quint, Howard H. "*The Challenge, Wilshire's Magazine.*" In *The American Radical Press*, vol. 1, edited by Joseph Robert Conlin, 72–82. Westport, CT: Greenwood Press, 1974.

– "*Social Crusader, Socialist Spirit.*" In *The American Radical Press*, vol. 1, edited by Joseph Robert Conlin, 43–6. Westport, CT: Greenwood Press, 1974.

Rader, L.E., and Frank T. Reid. "We." *Soundview* 1, no. 1 (October 1902): 1–3.

"Ralston Health Followers." *Piqua Daily Call* (Ohio), 20 April 1897, 9.

Ransom, Will. *Private Presses and Their Books.* New York: Duchness, 1963.

Razeghi, Andrew. *Hope: How Triumphant Leaders Create the Future.* San Francisco: Jossey-Bass, 2006.

Reedy, William Marion. "The Ending of *The Bibelot*." In *The Bibelot: General Index*, 187–91. Portland, ME, Thomas Bird Mosher, [1915].

– "A Little Journey to East Aurora." In *The Feather Duster or, Is He Sincere?* by William Marion Reedy, Benjamin de Casseres, Harold Bolce, and Brainard Leroy Bates, 11–55. East Aurora, NY: Roycrofters, 1912.

Review of *The Isle of Content and Other Waifs of Thought* (unsigned), by George F. Butler M.D. *Medical Standard* 25, no. 12 (December 1902): 685–6.

Rhodes, Harrison Garfield. "A Little Boy Among the New Masters." *Chap-Book* 4, no. 9 (15 March 1896): 412–18.

Richardson, Fred. "Joaquin Miller at Home." *Chap-Book* 2, no. 12 (1 May 1895): 472.

– "Mr. Hope." *Chap-Book* 3, no. 9 (15 September 1895): 357.

– "Mr. Zangwill." *Chap-Book* 3, no. 9 (15 September 1895): 347.

– "Portrait of Ralph Adams Cram." *Chap-Book* 4, no. 1 (1 April 1896): 457.

[Rittenhouse, Jessie]. "A Year's Harvest in American Poetry." *New York Times Book Review*, 28 November 1915, 464–5.

Robertson, Michael. *Worshipping Walt: The Whitman Disciples*. Princeton: Princeton University Press, 2008.

Robinson, Harold C. "The Third Lesson: A Story of the Multi-billion Trust." *Comrade* 2, no. 1 (October 1902): 19–20.

Rogers, Bruce. "An Address." In *The Work of Bruce Rogers: Jack of All Trades, Master of One*. Exhibition Catalogue. American Institute of Graphic Arts and Grolier Club, xxvii–liv. New York: Grolier Club, with Oxford University Press, 1939.

Rogers, Stephen. "Bruno's Bohemia." In Brooker and Thacker, *Oxford Critical and Cultural History*, vol. 2, 445–64.

Roosevelt, Theodore. Response to the Toast "The State of New York," Lincoln Club Dinner, New York, 13 February 1899. In *Public Papers of Theodore Roosevelt, Governor* (Albany: Brandow, 1899), 262–8.

– "Strife." *Cornhill Booklet* 2, no. 5 (November 1901): no pag.

– "Strife." *Junk* 2, no. 3 (December 1901): 72.

Rubin, Joan Shelley. *Songs of Ourselves: The Uses of Poetry in America*. Cambridge, MA: Belknap Press, 2007.

Ruff, Allen. *We Called Each Other Comrade: Charles H. Kerr and Company, Radical Publishers*. Urbana: University of Illinois Press, 1997.

Ruskin, John. "Chosen from the Words of John Ruskin." *Craftsman* 1, no. 2 (November 1901): no pag.

Russell, Charles E. [Untitled excerpt from *Picardy*]. *Conservator* 13, no. 1 (March 1902): 1.

Russell, G. Frederic. “A Change of Thought.” *Moods* 1 (1894): no pag.
“Russian Socialists and ‘Terrorism.’” *Comrade* 2, no. 1 (October 1902): 18.
Rust, Robert Charles, and Kitty Turgeon. *Roycroft Campus*. Charleston, SC: Arcadia Publishing, 2013.
Sandburg, Carl. Letter to Lee Fairchild. *Thistle* 1, no. 9 (November 1902): 17.
Schade, Benjamin A. “The Artistic Standpoint II.” *John-a-Dreams* 1, no. 4 (December 1896): 118–24.
Schiau-Botea, Diana. “Performing Writing.” In Brooker and Thacker, *Oxford Critical and Cultural History*, vol. 3, 38–59.
Schlereth, Thomas J. *Victorian America: Transformations in Everyday Life 1876–1915*. New York: Harper Collins, 1991.
Schlereth, Wendy. *The Chap-Book: A Journal of American Intellectual Life in the 1890s*. Ann Arbor, MI: UMI Research Press, 1982.
Schneirov, Matthew. *Dream of a New Social Order: Popular Magazines in America, 1893–1914*. New York: Columbia University Press, 1993.
Scholes, Robert. “Small Magazines, Large Ones, and Those In-Between.” In *Little Magazines and Modernism: New Approaches*, edited by Suzanne W. Churchill and Adam McKible, 217–25. Burlington, VT: Ashgate, 2007.
Schwab, Arnold T. *James Gibbons Huneker: Critic of the Seven Arts*. Stanford: Stanford University Press, 1963.
Scollard, Clinton. “Autumn Twilight.” *Chap-Book* 3, no. 9 (15 September 1895): 331.
– “Ballade of Dead Poets.” *Chips* 1, no. 2 (April 1895): no pag.
– “Ballade of Mid-Summer.” *Chips* 1, no. 6 (August 1895): no pag.
– “Chant of Prester John.” *Chap-Book* 6, no. 2 (1 December 1896): 56–7.
– “Dancing of Suleima.” *Smart Set* 4, no. 1 (May 1901): 55–6.
– “Dark Day.” *Chips* 2, no. 14 (7 December 1895): no pag.
– “Fog in the City.” *Smart Set* 2, no. 4 (October–November 1900): 76.
– “A Grain Field.” *Clack Book* 3, no. 3 (June 1897): 13.
– “Henry Timrod.” *Chips* 1, no. 1 (March 1895): no pag.
– “Homesick.” *Chap-Book* 8, no. 2 (December 1, 1897): 76.
– “In an Egyptian Garden.” *Smart Set* 3, no. 3 (March 1901): 114.
– “Invitation to the Open Road.” *Philosopher* 12, no. 1 (July 1902): 19.
– “Moods.” *Philistine* 2, no. 5 (April 1896): 141.
– “Night in the Desert.” *Smart Set* 4, no. 2 (June 1901): 115.
– “Roses.” *Smart Set* 4, no. 4 (August 1901): 138.
– “Turning of the Tide.” *Lotus* 2, no. 5 (September 1896): 149.
– “Upon the Birth of a Babe.” *Chips* 1, no. 4 (June 1895): no pag.
– “The Walk.” *Chap-Book* 1, no. 8 (1 September 1894): 183.

Sedgwick, Ellery. "Magazines and the Profession of Authorship in the United States, 1840–1900." *Papers of the Bibliographical Society of America* 94, no. 3 (2000): 399–425.

Senior, Nicholas. "In the Print Shop." *John-a-Dreams* 2, no. 4 (April 1897): 179–83.

Séon, Alexandre. "Douleur de la Chimère." *Chap-Book* 2, no. 9 (15 March 1895): 384.

Shaddy, Robert Alan. *Books and Book Collecting in America, 1890–1930.* Lewiston, NY: Edwin Mellen Press, 2000.

Shand-Tucci, Douglass. *Boston Bohemia, 1881–1900: Ralph Adams Cram: Life and Architecture.* Amherst: University of Massachusetts Press, 1995.

– *The Crimson Letter: Harvard, Homosexuality and the Shaping of American Culture.* New York: St Martin's Press, 2004.

– *Ralph Adams Cram: An Architect's Four Quests–Medieval, Modernist, American, Ecumenical.* Amherst: University of Massachusetts Press, 2005.

Shaw, Paul. "Tradition and Innovation: The Design Work of William Addison Dwiggins." In *Design History: An Anthology*, edited by Dennis P. Doordan, 28–42. Cambridge, MA: MIT Press, 2000.

Shaw, Valerie. *The Short Story: A Critical Introduction.* New York: Routledge, 2013.

Shay, Felix. *Elbert Hubbard of East Aurora.* New York: W.H. Wise, 1926.

Shirk, A.H. "In a Studio." *Muse* 1, no. 1 (June 1900): 20.

[Shirk, A. Hull]. "Musings." *Muse* 1, no. 1 (June 1900): 27–8.

"Short Stories of Topeka's Happenings." *Topeka Daily Capital* (Topeka, KS), 18 December 1907, 6.

Shumway, David R. *Modern Love: Romance, Intimacy, and the Marriage Crisis.* New York: New York University Press, 2003.

Sicherman, Barbara. "Ideologies and Practices of Reading." In Casper et al., *History of the Book in America*, 279–303.

"Side Issues." *Post-Standard* (Syracuse, NY), 12 December 1904, 4.

Simmons, James R., Jr. "Stanley J. Weyman." *Dictionary of Literary Biography.* Vol. 156, *British Short Fiction Writers, 1880–1914: The Romantic Tradition*, edited by William F. Naufftus, 397–403. Detroit: Gale, 1995.

Sinclair, Julian. "Rhapsody in Red." *Les Jeunes* 1, no. 1 (March 1900): 6.

Singleton, Frederic Thoreau. "In This Dusk: Being an Imitation of a Man Commenting Upon Things Degenerative and Otherwise." *Poster Lore* 1, no. 1 (15 January 1896): 23–8.

Sloan, Helen Farr. *The Poster Period of John Sloan.* Privately published, 1967.

Smith, Katharine J. "The Month of Mary." *Bohemian* [Boston] 1, no. 4 (March 1901): 1–5.

Smith, Susan Harris, and Melanie Dawson. Introduction to *American 1890s: A Cultural Reader*, edited by Susan Harris Smith and Melanie Dawson, 1–14. Durham: Duke University Press, 2000.

Smith, W.A. "The Man Without the Hoe." *Schoolmaster* 1, no. 1 (March 1900): 22–4.

"Some Educators on Direct Legislation." *New Time* 3, no. 1 (July 1898): 7–10.

"Some Thoughts of a Wise Dog: Taken from the Original Barks." *Homo* 1, no. 6 (November 1901): 176.

"Some Words of Goodness That Have Brought Joy." Supplement. *Erudite* 2, no. 1 (October 1900): no pag.

Sorfleet, John Robert. "Transcendentalist, Mystic, Evolutionary Idealist: Bliss Carman, 1886–1894." In *Colony and Confederation: Early Canadian Poets and Their Background*, edited by George Woodcock, 189–210. Vancouver: University of British Columbia Press, 1974.

Sorrentino, Paul. *Stephen Crane: A Life of Fire*. Cambridge, MA: Belknap Press, 2014.

Soundview. Advertisement. *Ghourki* 3, nos. 2–3 (September–October 1903): no pag.

Spencer, Truman J. *The History of Amateur Journalism*. New York: The Fossils, 1957.

"The Spider." *M'lle New York* 1, no. 1 (August 1895): no pag.

Stanton, Frank L. "The Old Flag Forever." *New Time* 3, no. 1 (July 1898): 52.

Starr, Kevin. *Inventing the Dream: California Through the Progressive Era*. Oxford: Oxford University Press, 1985.

Steffens, Lincoln. *The Autobiography of Lincoln Steffens*. Vol. 1. Berkeley: Heyday Books, 2005.

– Schloma: The Daughter of Schmuhl." *Chap-Book* 5, no. 3 (15 June 1895): 128–32.

– "Yalan Mohamadac." *Chap-Book* 8, no. 1 (15 November 1897): 17–18.

"Stephen Crane." *Ishmaelite* 1, no. 2 (January 1897): back cover.

Stetz, Margaret Diane. "Life's 'Half-Profits': Writers and their Readers in Fiction of the 1890s." In *Nineteenth-Century Lives: Essays Presented to Jerome Hamilton Buckley*, edited by Laurence S. Lockridge, John Maynard, and Donald D. Stone, 169–87. Cambridge: Cambridge University Press, 1989.

– and Mark Samuels Lasner. *The Yellow Book: A Centenary Exhibition*. Exhibition Catalogue. Cambridge, MA: Houghton Library, 1994.

Stevens, G.W. "An Hour with Caesar Augustus." *Philistine* 2, no. 6 (May 1896): 187–93.

Stevens, Thomas Wood. “On Some American Bookmakers.” *Yearbook of the Bibliographical Society of Chicago 1900–1901*. 1901. New York: Kraus Reprint Corporation, 1963. 25–31.
– “The Story of a Book.” *Blue Sky* 4, no. 3 (January 1902): 111–19.
– “Stray Clouds.” *Blue Sky* 1, no. 1 (August 1899): 29–32.
– “Stray Clouds.” *Blue Sky* 1, no. 5 (December 1899): 147–9.
– “Stray Clouds.” *Blue Sky* 3, no. 5 (Summer 1901): 260–3.
– “Stray Clouds.” *Blue Sky* 5, no. 1 (April 1902): 72–4.
Stidger, William L. *Edwin Markham*. New York: Abingdon Press, 1933.
Stimson, J.W. “Bring on the Swab.” *Comrade* 2, no. 1 (October 1902): 18.
Stone, Wilbur Fiske. *History of Colorado*. Vol. 3. Chicago: J.S. Clarke Publishing Company, 1918.
Storey, Robert F. *Pierrot: A Critical History of a Mask*. Princeton: Princeton University Press, 1978.
Strouse, Norman. *The Passionate Pirate*. North Hills, PA: Bird and Bull Press, 1964.
Stuckey-French, Ned. *The American Essay in the American Century*. Columbia: University of Missouri Press, 2011.
Susman, Warren I. *Culture as History: The Transformation of American Society in the Twentieth Century*. New York: Pantheon, 1984.
Swift, Ivan. “Repair.” *Blue Sky* 1, no. 5 (December 1899): 139–40.
Swinburne, A.T. “Heart Stress.” *Lotus* 1, no. 12 (May 15, 1896): 328–30.
[Swisher, Howard Llewellyn]. “Harangues to the Ghourki by the Chief of the Tribe.” *Ghourki* 1, no. 5 (December 1901): 159–67.
– “Harangues to the Ghourki by the Chief of the Tribe.” *Ghourki* 2, no. 5 (December 1902): 443–9.
– “Harangues to the Ghourki by the Chief of the Tribe.” *Ghourki* 2, no. 11 (June 1903): 1–4.
– “Harangues to the Ghourki by the Chief of the Tribe.” *Ghourki* 2, no. 12–13, no. 1 (July–August 1903): 1–8.
– “Harangues to the Ghourki by the Chief of the Tribe.” *Ghourki* 3, nos. 2–3 (September–October 1903): 7–8.
Szefel, Lisa. *The Gospel of Beauty in the Progressive Era: Reforming American Verse and Values*. Basingstoke: Palgrave, 2011.
Taber, Harry P. “Side Talks with the Philistines.” *Philistine* 1, no. 2 (July 1895): 60–71.
Tassin, Algernon. *The Magazine in America*. New York: Dodd, Mead, and Co., 1916.
Tebbel, John. *The American Magazine: A Compact History*. New York: Hawthorn, 1969.

"The *Thistle* Advertiser." *Thistle* 1, no. 1 (March 1902): i–iv.

Thomas, Helen Sterling. "The Heart's Desire." *Blue Sky* 2, no. 4 (May 1900): 91–7.

"Thompson, [Charles] Vance." *National Cyclopædia of American Biography*, vol. 20, 241–2. New York: J.T. White, 1929.

Thompson, Ernest. "The Pack-Rat." *Quartier Latin* 1, no. 1 (July 1896): 25.

Thompson, Maurice. "The Conquering Provincial." *Clack Book* 1, no. 4 (July 1896): 93–9.

– "From the Critic's Point of View." *Chap-Book* 6, no. 7 (15 February 1897): 280–2.

– "Is the New Woman New?" *Chap-Book* 3, no. 10 (1 October 1895): 380–9.

– "Literary Greens." *Chap-Book* 6, no. 12 (1 May 1897): 495–7.

– "Nuts from Perigord." *Chap-Book* 2, no. 12 (1 May 1895): 473–8.

– "Poe and His Art." *Ishmaelite* 2, no. 2 (July 1897): 41–51.

– "The Return of the Girl." *Chap-Book* 4, no. 9 (15 March 1896): 401–10.

– "The Rustic Muse." *Chap-Book* 6, no. 4 (1 January 1897): 145–51.

– "Walt Whitman and the Critics." *Chap-Book* 7, no. 7 (1 August 1897): 194–5.

Thompson, Susan Otis. *American Book Design and William Morris*. London: British Library and Oak Knoll Press, 1996.

Thompson, Vance. "The Art and Artists of New York: Being a Story of Babies and Boiled Beef." *M'lle New York* 1, no. 5 (First fortnight, October 1895): no pag.

[–] "Foreword." *M'lle New York* 1, no. 1 (August 1895): no pag.

– "Newspaper Illustrators – Thomas Fleming." *Inland Printer* 18 (February 1897): 546.

[–] "Polite Letters." *M'lle New York*, 1, no. 2 (23 August 1895): no pag.

[–] "Scalpel or Branding Iron?" *M'lle New York* 1, no. 2 (23 August 1895): no pag.

– "The Technique of the Symbolists." *M'lle New York* 1, no. 7 (First fortnight in November 1895): no pag.

Thomson, Ellen Mazur. "Early Graphic Design Periodicals in America." *Journal of Design History* 7, no. 2 (1994): 113–26.

– *Origins of Graphic Design in America, 1870–1920*. New Haven: Yale University Press, 1997.

Thrift, Timothy Burr. "Heart Communion Talks." *Lucky Dog* 3, no. 1 (December 1901): 10–32.

[Tilden, J.H.]. "The Mob." *Stuffed Club for Everybody* 1, no. 3 (July 1900): 101–15.

Tolstoy, Leo. “Modern Slavery.” *Wilshire’s* 45 (April 1902): 49–51.

Torpedo 6, no. 3 (February 1907).

Towne, Charles Hanson. *Adventures in Editing*. New York: Appleton, 1926.

Townsend, Edward W. “By Whom the Offence Cometh.” *M’lle New York* 1, no. 1 (August 1895): no pag.

Trachtenberg, Alan. *The Incorporation of America: Culture and Society in the Gilded Age*. New York: Hill and Wang, 1982.

“Trolleyman, Joy.” “Little Delirics of Bliss.” *Philistine* 1, no. 1 (June 1895): 22.

“Tucheta” [Ora V. Eddleman] to “My Dear Chief” [Howard Llewellyn Swisher]. *Ghourki* 2, no. 1 (August 1902): 368.

Tucker, Susan, Katherine Ott, and Patricia P. Buckler. “An Introduction to the History of Scrapbooks.” In *The Scrapbook in American Life*, edited by Susan Tucker, Katharine Ott, and Patricia P. Buckler, 1–26. Philadelphia: Temple University Press, 2006.

“Two Minor Poets.” *Shadow* 1, no. 2 (1896): 41–2.

Ulrich, Carolyn to Frederick John Hoffman. 7 April 1943. Box 1, folder 14. Frederick John Hoffman Papers, University of Wisconsin-Milwaukee Libraries, Archives Department.

– 1 December 1943. Box 1, folder 14. Frederick John Hoffman Papers, University of Wisconsin-Milwaukee Libraries, Archives Department.

– 25 January 1943. Box 1, folder 14. Frederick John Hoffman Papers, University of Wisconsin-Milwaukee Libraries, Archives Department.

– Thursday night. Box 1, folder 14. Frederick John Hoffman Papers, University of Wisconsin-Milwaukee Libraries, Archives Department.

US Census Office. *Twelfth Census of the United States*. Vol. 13, *Occupations*, compiled by William Chamberlin Hunt. Washington DC: Government Printing Office, 1904.

Vallotton, Félix. “Arthur Rimbaud.” *Chap-Book* 5, no. 1 (15 May 1896): 9.

– “Le Bain.” *Chap-Book* 2, no. 3 (15 December 1894): 123.

– “Portrait of Emile Zola.” *Chap-Book* 3, no. 1 (15 May 1895): 14.

– “Portrait of Stéphane Mallarmé.” *Chap-Book* 3, no. 7 (15 August 1895): 253.

Via, Marie, and Marjorie B. Searle. *Head, Heart and Hand: Elbert Hubbard and the Roycrofters*. Exhibition Catalogue. Rochester: University of Rochester Press with University of Rochester Memorial Art Gallery, 2007.

Vilain, Jean-François. “*The Bibelot*.” In Vilain and Bishop, *Thomas Bird Mosher*, 48–51.

– “Mosher’s Concept of Series.” In Vilain and Bishop, *Thomas Bird Mosher*, 8–10.

Vilain, Jean-François, and Philip R. Bishop. *Thomas Bird Mosher and the Art of the Book*. Exhibition Catalogue. Philadelphia: Temple University, with F.A. Davis Company, 1992.

Vincent, John H. *The Chautauqua Movement*. Boston: Chautauqua Press, 1886.

Von Whalen, Joseph. "Sputterings of a Seething Cauldron." *Whims* 1, no. 4 (May 1896): 131–4.

Wall, S.W. "Napthaly Herz Imber: National Poet of Israel." *San Francisco Call*, 12 April 1896, 17.

Waller-Zuckerman, Mary Ellen. "'Old Homes in a City of Perpetual Change:' Women's Magazines, 1890–1916." *Business History Review* 63 (1989): 715–56.

W.D. [Warren Dean]. "Guests – and Guests." *Cypher* 1, no. 2 (22 February 1896): 1.

Weyman, Stanley J. "Flore." *Pocket Magazine* 2, no. 1 (May 1896): 1–68.

Wallin, Florence. *Mrs Van and the Philosopher Press*. Asheville, NC: Pine Tree Press, 2006.

Warner, Charles Dudley. "Editor's Study." *Harper's New Monthly Magazine* 93 (August 1896): 476–80.

Weinberg, Arthur, and Lila Weinberg. Introduction to *The Muckrakers*, edited by Arthur Weinberg and Lila Weinberg, xvii–xxviii. Bloomington, IL: University of Illinois Press, 2001.

Weir, David. *Decadent Culture in the United States: Art and Literature Against the American Grain 1890–1926*. Albany: SUNY Press, 2007.

Wells, Carolyn. "The Latest Thing in Poets." *Critic* 26. n. s. (14 November 1896): 302.

– *The Rest of My Life*. Philadelphia: Lippincott, 1937.

– "What a Lark." *Colophon*, Part 8 (1931): no pag.

"What Is Science?" *Higher Law* 5, no. 2 (March 1902): 39–44.

[Wheeler, La Verne F.]. "The Banditti." *Jester* 1 (1901): 16–18.

– Untitled poem about Boxer Rebellion. *Jester* 1 (1901): 5–6.

Wheeler, Otis B. *The Literary Career of Maurice Thompson*. Baton Rouge, LA: Louisiana State University Press, 1965.

W.H.H. Review of *Back Country Poems*, by Sam Walter Foss. *Writer* 7, no. 11 (November 1894): 170.

White, Bruce A. *Elbert Hubbard's The Philistine: A Periodical of Protest (1895–1915): A Major American "Little Magazine."* Lanham, MD: University Press of America, 1989.

White, Melvin R. "Thomas Wood Stevens, Creative Pioneer." *Educational Theatre Journal* 3, no. 4 (1951): 280–93.

Whitman, Walt. "To a Pupil." *Leaves of Grass.* Philadelphia: D. McKay, 1883: 302.
Wilcox, Ella Wheeler. "Attainment." *Papyrus* 6, no. 3 (April 1906): 32.
– "The Awakening." *Chap-Book* 5, no. 7 (15 August 1896): 289.
– "Goddess of Liberty, Answer." *Chap-Book* 9, no. 4 (1 July 1898): 112.
– "Illusion." *Chap-Book* 5, no. 2 (1 June 1896): 49.
– "My Belief." *Papyrus* 5, no. 1 (August 1905): 31.
– *Poems of Passion.* Chicago: W.B. Conkey, 1893.
– "What Love Is." *Papyrus* 3, no. 6 (December 1904): 24–5.
– *The Worlds and I.* New York: Doran, 1918.
Wilde, Oscar. "The Critic as Artist." In *The Complete Works of Oscar Wilde*, vol. 4, *Historical Criticism*, edited by Josephine M. Guy, 123–206. Oxford: Oxford University Press, 2007.
Williams, Raymond. *Marxism and Literature.* Oxford: Oxford University Press, 1977.
Wilshire, Gaylord. "Columbia's Race for Liberty." *Wilshire's* 45 (April 1902): 7–13.
– "Why a Workingman Should Be a Socialist." *Wilshire's* 45 (April 1902): 61–4.
Wilson, J. Stitt. "A Developing Fellowship." *Social Crusader* 3, no. 1 (January 1901): 13–17.
Wilson, Marjorie. "The Man Who Went Back to Boyhood Dreams." Pamphlet (reprinted from the *Sunday News Leader Magazine* [Cleveland], 12 September 1920).
Winship, Michael. "Manufacturing and Book Production." In Casper et al., *History of the Book in America*, 40–69.
W.J.K. "Some of New York's Rising Printers." *Inland Printer* 17, no. 4 (July 1896): 415–16.
Wolosky, Shira. "Poetry and Public Discourse, 1820–1910." In *Cambridge History of American Literature*, vol. 4, *Nineteenth Century Poetry, 1800–1910*, edited by Sacvan Berkovitch, 147–480. New York: Cambridge University Press, 2004.
Wong, Roberta. "Will Bradley and the Poster." *Metropolitan Museum of Art Bulletin* 30, no. 6 (June–July 1972): 294–9.
"Work." *Socialist Spirit* 1, no. 10 (June 1902): 8–9.
Yarrow, Edmund. "Merely an Experiment." *John-a-Dreams* 1, no. 1 (July 1896): 3–12.
"Yelps." *Kiote* 3, no. 3 (March 1900): 68–70.
"Yelps." *Kiote* 3, no. 6 (June 1900): 133–5.
Zanque, Handel. "The Junklet of Thoughts and Things." *Junk* 2, no. 1 (October 1901): 5–16.

Zarobila, Charles. "Bruce Rogers." *American National Biography Online*. February 2000. Accessed 15 August 2015. https://anb.org

Zboray, Ronald J., and Mary Saracino Zboray. *Literary Dollars and Social Sense: A People's History of the Mass Market Book*. New York: Routledge, 2005.

– "Nineteenth Century Print Culture." In *Oxford Handbook of Transcendentalism*, edited by Joel Myerson, Sandra Harbert Petrulionis, and Laura Dassow Walls, 102–14. Oxford: Oxford University Press, 2010.

"Zoe A. Norris." *Kentucky in America Letters*, by John Wilson Townsend (Cedar Rapids, IA: Torch Press, 1919), 135–7.

Zwerdling, Alex. *Improvised Europeans: American Literary Expatriates and the Siege of London*. New York: Basic Books, 1998.

Index

An italic *f* following a page reference indicates an illustration. An italicized page reference (for example, *312*) indicates an entry for the publication in the updated bibliography provided in the Appendix. An italic number preceded by *pl* refers to a plate (for example, *pl 9*).

Studies in Book and Print Culture

General Editor: Leslie Howsam

Hazel Bell, *Indexers and Indexes in Fact and Fiction*

Heather Murray, *Come, bright Improvement! The Literary Societies of Nineteenth-Century Ontario*

Joseph A. Dane, *The Myth of Print Culture: Essays on Evidence, Textuality, and Bibliographical Method*

Christopher J. Knight, *Uncommon Readers: Denis Donoghue, Frank Kermode, George Steiner, and the Tradition of the Common Reader*

Eva Hemmungs Wirtén, *No Trespassing: Authorship, Intellectual Property Rights, and the Boundaries of Globalization*

William A. Johnson, *Bookrolls and Scribes in Oxyrhynchus*

Siân Echard and Stephen Partridge, eds, *The Book Unbound: Editing and Reading Medieval Manuscripts and Texts*

Bronwen Wilson, *The World in Venice: Print, the City, and Early Modern Identity*

Peter Stoicheff and Andrew Taylor, eds, *The Future of the Page*

Jennifer Phegley and Janet Badia, eds, *Reading Women: Literary Figures and Cultural Icons from the Victorian Age to the Present*

Elizabeth Sauer, *"Paper-contestations" and Textual Communities in England, 1640–1675*

Nick Mount, *When Canadian Literature Moved to New York*

Jonathan Earl Carlyon, *Andrés González de Barcia and the Creation of the Colonial Spanish American Library*

Leslie Howsam, *Old Books and New Histories: An Orientation to Studies in Book and Print Culture*

Deborah McGrady, *Controlling Readers: Guillaume de Machaut and His Late Medieval Audience*

David Finkelstein, ed., *Print Culture and the Blackwood Tradition*

Bart Beaty, *Unpopular Culture: Transforming the European Comic Book in the 1990s*

Elizabeth Driver, *Culinary Landmarks: A Bibliography of Canadian Cookbooks, 1825–1949*

Benjamin C. Withers, *The Illustrated Old English Hexateuch, Cotton Ms. Claudius B.iv: The Frontier of Seeing and Reading in Anglo-Saxon England*

Mary Ann Gillies, *The Professional Literary Agent in Britain, 1880–1920*

Willa Z. Silverman, *The New Bibliopolis: French Book-Collectors and the Culture of Print, 1880–1914*

Lisa Surwillo, *The Stages of Property: Copyrighting Theatre in Spain*

Dean Irvine, *Editing Modernity: Women and Little-Magazine Cultures in Canada, 1916–1956*

Janet Friskney, *New Canadian Library: The Ross-McClelland Years, 1952–1978*

Janice Cavell, *Tracing the Connected Narrative: Arctic Exploration in British Print Culture, 1818–1860*

Elspeth Jajdelska, *Silent Reading and the Birth of the Narrator*

Martyn Lyons, *Reading Culture and Writing Practices in Nineteenth-Century France*

Robert A. Davidson, *Jazz Age Barcelona*

Gail Edwards and Judith Saltman, *Picturing Canada: A History of Canadian Children's Illustrated Books and Publishing*

Miranda Remnek, ed., *The Space of the Book: Print Culture in the Russian Social Imagination*

Adam Reed, *Literature and Agency in English Fiction Reading: A Study of the Henry Williamson Society*

Bonnie Mak, *How the Page Matters*

Eli MacLaren, *Dominion and Agency: Copyright and the Structuring of the Canadian Book Trade, 1867–1918*

Ruth Panofsky, *The Literary Legacy of the Macmillan Company of Canada: Making Books and Mapping Culture*

Archie L. Dick, *The Hidden History of South Africa's Book and Reading Cultures*

Darcy Cullen, ed., *Editors, Scholars, and the Social Text*

James J. Connolly, Patrick Collier, Frank Felsenstein, Kenneth R. Hall, and Robert Hall, eds, *Print Culture Histories beyond the Metropolis*

Kristine Kowalchuk, *Preserving on Paper: Seventeenth-Century Englishwomen's Receipt Books*

Ian Hesketh, *Victorian Jesus: J.R. Seeley, Religion, and the Cultural Significance of Anonymity*

Kirsten MacLeod, *American Little Magazines of the Fin de Siècle: Art, Protest, and Cultural Transformation*

www.ingramcontent.com/pod-product-compliance
Lightning Source LLC
LaVergne TN
LVHW010446080826
844660LV00027B/1225